FEDERAL ADMINISTRATIVE AGENCIES
Essays on Power and Politics

Howard Ball
University of Utah

Prentice-Hall, Inc., Englewood Cliffs, New Jersey 07032

Library of Congress Cataloging in Publication Data
Main entry under title:

Federal administrative agencies.

  Includes bibliographical references and index.
  1. Administrative agencies—United States.
  2. Administrative procedure—United States.   I. Ball,
Howard, (date).
KF5407.F42   1984   342.73'0664   83-13680
ISBN 0-13-308445-0   347.302664

**This book is dedicated to the memory of my father,
ABE BALL**

Cover design: 20/20 Services, Inc./Mark W. Beglash
Manufacturing buyer: Ron Chapman

© 1984 by Prentice-Hall, Inc., Englewood Cliffs, New Jersey 07632

All rights reserved. No part of this book may be
reproduced, in any form or by any means,
without permission in writing from the publisher.

Printed in the United States of America

10 9 8 7 6 5 4 3 2 1

ISBN 0-13-308445-0

Prentice-Hall International, Inc., *London*
Prentice-Hall of Australia Pty. Limited, *Sydney*
Editora Prentice-Hall do Brasil, Ltda., *Rio de Janeiro*
Prentice-Hall Canada Inc., *Toronto*
Prentice-Hall of India Private Limited, *New Delhi*
Prentice-Hall of Japan, Inc., *Tokyo*
Prentice-Hall of Southeast Asia Pte. Ltd., *Singapore*
Whitehall Books Limited, *Wellington, New Zealand*

CONTENTS

Acknowlegments vi
Introduction 1

PART I FEDERAL ADMINISTRATIVE AGENCIES: GROWTH AND POWERS 5

CHAPTER ONE
Growth of Federal Agencies 5

1. *The Emerging Concept of Administrative Procedure* 9
   Paul A. Verkuil

2. *Two Views on the Structure of Regulatory Commissions: Point* 19
   Stuart M. Statler

3. *Two Views on the Structure of Regulatory Commissions: Counterpoint* 25
   R. David Pittle

4. *The Reformation of American Administrative Law* 30
   Richard B. Stewart

5. *The Changing Face of Government Regulation* 38
   A. Lee Fritschler

6. *A Strong Beginning on Reform* 52
   Christopher C. DeMuth

CHAPTER TWO
Agency Powers 57

7. *Administrative Procedure* 60
   Paul A. Verkuil

8. *The Procedures by Which Informal Action Is Taken* 66
   Warner W. Gardner

9. *Like Big Joe's Forklift, Bureau Director Persevered* 73
   Michael Pertschuk

10. *A Unified Corps of ALJs: A Proposal to Test the Idea at the Federal Level* 79
   Jeffrey S. Lubbers

11. *"Toward Toughness"* 88
   Eugene Bardach/Robert Kagan

12. *Administrative Implementation: Organizational Structure and Bureaucratic Routines* 107
   Howard Ball/Dale Krane/Thomas Lauth

CHAPTER THREE
The Politics of Regulation 121

13. *The Origins of Regulation* 124
   James Q. Wilson

14. *Regulatory Delay as Political Strategy* 144
   Richard P. Barke

15. *Pills and the Process of Government* 157
   Robert Reinhold

PART II HOLDING ADMINISTRATORS ACCOUNTABLE: CONTROLS ON AGENCY POWERS   163

CHAPTER FOUR
Congressional Oversight 163

16. *Congress and the "Details" of Administration* 165
   Allen Schick

17. *Congressional Control of Administrative Regulation: A Study of Legislative Vetoes* 180
   Harold H. Bruff/Ernest Gellhorn

18. *Letter on Constitutionality of Legislative Veto* 197
   Benjamin Civiletti

CHAPTER FIVE
Executive Control of the Federal Bureaucracy 203

19. *The President as Manager* 205
   Dwight A. Ink

20. *Presidential Control of the Federal Bureaucracy* 216
   Howard Ball

CHAPTER SIX
Judicial Review of Agency Acts **227**

21. *Judicial Law Making and Administration* **231**
    Roger C. Cramton

22. *The Courts and the Rule Making Process: The Limits of Judicial Review* **238**
    J. Skelly Wright

23. *The Courts as Guardians of the Public Interest* **250**
    Donald L. Horowitz

CHAPTER SEVEN
Tort Liability of Public Officials **259**

24. *Public Administrators' Official Immunity and the Supreme Court: Developments during the 1970s* **262**
    David H. Rosenbloom

25. *Suing Federal Executives for Damages* **272**
    Jack Rabin/Gerald J. Miller/W. Bartley Hildreth

26. *The Mandate, the Mayor, and the Menace of Liability* **277**
    Cynthia Cates Colella

CHAPTER EIGHT
Opening Federal Agencies up to the Public **289**

27. *Let the Sun Shine In* **292**
    Allen Schick

28. *The Freedom of Information Act Revisited* **298**
    Samuel J. Archibald

29. *Whistleblowing and the Character of Public Employment* **303**
    Robert G. Vaughn

30. *Whistleblowing and Full Disclosure* **307**
    Richard F. Kaufman

31. *The Effect of an Ombudsman* **311**
    Paul R. Meyer

Appendix: Administrative Procedure Act **319**

ACKNOWLEDGMENTS

So-called "individual" accomplishments often reflect the efforts of more than one person, and such is the case here. The contribution of those colleagues who graciously allowed me to reprint their words is self-evident: This book would be poorer for their absence, and I would like to take this opportunity to thank each and every one of them.

I would also like to acknowledge the many reviewers—William J. Gore, of the University of Washington; Daniel M. Barber, of California State University; Marguerite A. Guinta, of Long Island University; James Anderson, of the University of Houston; Norman C. Thomas, of the University of Cincinnati; Robert D. Lee, Jr., of Penn State University; and Edward R. Padgett, of the University of Cincinnati. In reviewing an early draft of the manuscript, each brought a much-appreciated measure of scholarship to the task. The final shape of this book owes much to their comments, suggestions, and criticisms; and for that I am in their debt.

Students in my Administrative Law classes, at Mississippi State University, as well as faculty colleagues at Mississippi State and at the University of Utah have offered additional insights into the operations of federal regulatory processes, and I thank them for these comments and observations.

Finally, I wish to thank my lovely children, Susan, Sheryl, and Melissa and my wife Carol for their continuing care and affection during this process of developing a text in such a dynamic area of politics.

INTRODUCTION

There is a basic ambivalence in American attitudes about the public manager, the bureaucrat; it is almost a love-hate relationship that has developed in the past half century. We need the technocrat in government, yet we tend to feel that the bureaucrat has too much discretion and power, and that there is too little control over the discretionary actions of these government agents. There is the corollary belief that, while the administrative process is the best way to get governmental tasks done, administration is incompetent, inefficient, ineffective, wasteful, and possibly dishonest.[1] As we have moved into the age of high technology and complexity, into the age of the administrative state, Americans grow more uneasy and concerned about the behavior of these professional managers of governmental policy. There is a growing separateness or gap between the public and its political representatives and the personnel who administer the public policies formulated by the legislators. Rosenbloom has commented, in this regard, that the administrative state is "a shift in power from the elective to administrative (actors) which results in a loss of citizens' influence over government."[2]

"The growth of governmental control is characteristic of industrial societies. In this country, regulation was the logical instrument."[3] How does government get its job done? "From a strictly practical standpoint," wrote Davis, the job "can best be performed

[1] Dwight Waldo, *The Enterprise of Public Administration* (Novato, CA: Chandler and Sharp, 1980), p. 33.
[2] David H. Rosenbloom, "Public Administrators' Official Immunity and the Supreme Court: Developments During the 1970's," *Public Administration Review* 40 (March/April, 1980), p. 167.
[3] The White House, *Regulatory Reform: President Carter's Program* (Washington, D.C., 1980), p. 1.

through the administrative process."[4] Without the ability and time and expertise to deal with the problems of a technological, industrial, highly complex society, Congress created regulatory agencies and delegated powers and responsibilities to these legislative surrogates. Many federal agencies were created, in the words of the late House Speaker, Sam Rayburn, "to do what we don't have time to do."[5] By 1980, there were many dozens of administrative agencies, including 18 independent regulatory commissions, (annually) issuing 7,000 rules and policy statements, "including roughly 2,000 legally binding rules with significant impact on government or the private sector and over 150 with major economic effects."[6]

This recent explosion of governmental activity and control in the life of the person living in a highly industrialized society has heightened this sense of unease felt by the public. This enlargement of agency activity has highlighted a basic problem that confronts a democratic society: the scope of governmental (administrative agency) authority in light of private rights of persons guaranteed by the fundamental law—the Constitution. In our technological age, the problem is compounded by the basic fact that it is non-elected anonymous agency staff personnel and their managers who, through the implementation of broadly-written public policy, remodel and remake public policy and who then implement this policy. Bureaucrats, not directly accountable to sovereign citizens, are daily going about the policymaking task of reconciling and elaborating "lofty values into operational guidelines for the daily conduct of society's business."[7]

This relative shift in public power from elective to administrative actors is a recent development. In *Federalist* 68, Alexander Hamilton stated that the "true test of good government is its aptitude and tendency to produce a good administration." Government must produce, Hamilton concluded, an "energetic executive" who could secure "good administration." Good government is good administration; in our day this means that Chief Executives and other "external examiners"[8] of the federal bureaucracy must be able to exert control over the bureaucracy in order to achieve the ends of government: the good life for its constituents.

Today some claim that there is little or no control over the bureaucracy. Informal, discretionary activity, i.e, activities of agencies "without any effective means of independent review or reversal" accounts for between 90-99% of federal administrative agency work.[9] Both politicians and scholars alike are concerned about the enlargement of agency discretionary policymaking power and the concomitant inability of the elected agents of government to control and direct the federal bureaucracy. Two contemporary observers of the condition of bureaucracy in America have written that:

> Modern bureaucracy represents a challenge to good government because elected officials either are unable to direct and control the administrative process or they refrain from doing so. The resulting lack of administrative accountability has been promoted due to a continuing emphasis upon bureaucratic management techniques without a concomitant emphasis upon political leadership. While today's bureaucrats might be better prepared than ever before to deliver professional administration, today's citizens long for responsible government. One does not necessarily lead to the other. Professional bureaucracy, while contributing to expertise in administration, sacrifices responsibility in a republic. Managerial expertise is not

---

[4]Kenneth C. Davis, *Administrative Law and Government* (St. Paul, MN: West Publishing Company, 1975), p. 25.

[5]*Regulatory Reform*, p. 1.

[6]*Ibid*.

[7]Colin S. Diver, "Policymaking Paradigms in Administrative Law," *Harvard Law Review* 95 (December, 1981), p. 393.

[8]Ernest Gellhorn, *When Americans Complain* (Cambridge, MA: Harvard University Press, 1966).

[9]Gary J. Edles and Jerome Nelson, *Federal Regulatory Process: Agency Practices and Procedures* (New York: Harcourt, Brace, Jovanovich, 1981); p. 140.

enough because bureaucrats are engaged in something more than managing: they are involved in governing. . . . There is nothing wrong with politics in administration when it is properly understood. But there is great harm in an administrative machinery detached from political leadership.[10]

The contention is that government leaders, the elected politicians, especially the President of the United States (but also including the Congress, courts, pressure groups, and the bureaucrats themselves) all have a constitutional and ethical responsibility to ensure that public policies are administered and implemented in a fashion that reflects administrative responsiveness to the public interest as defined by the political leadership. "Political leadership of the bureaucracy is necessary to ensure administrative responsibility."[11]

Part One of this book on federal administrative agency activities focuses on the growth of the federal administrative agencies, on the powers of the federal agencies—rulemaking, adjudication, discretionary and informal actions—and, in Chapter Three, on the politics of regulation. From the beginning of the modern period of agency development—the creation in 1887 of the Interstate Commerce Commission—there has been a dramatic increase in the number of federal agencies and in the scope of federal regulatory activity. From the initial limited control over materials that moved in interstate commerce, federal regulatory agencies are now involved in rules and regulations affecting all types of social and economic activity: Clean air and water demands (and statutes), automobile safety, workshop safety, consumer protection, and equal employment opportunities are just a few of the substantive areas in which government has acted. The impact of these regulations on business and industry is dramatic: Estimates of costs for complying with the various federal regulations go as high as 5% of the Gross National Product. There is no doubt, as the readings in *Part One* will indicate, that the entire society feels the impact of increased federal administrative agency activity.

Agencies are "creatures of Congress. . . . The determinative question is not what an agency thinks it should do but what Congress has said it can do."[12] Whether agency activity achieves the goals established for it (and society) by Congress, and whether in its various activities the agency is following the guidelines established by the policymakers in Congress, is a question that will be addressed in *Part Two*. It is clear, however, that federal regulatory activity in this period of our history has raised some very fundamental questions—policy, political, and constitutional—about the role and scope of bureaucratic policymaking.

Part Two of the book examines the various devices that are in place that can be used to control and bring the administrative machinery under the direct control of the political leadership. Legislative, presidential, and judicial remedies are discussed, as is the notion of citizen awareness.

The legislative and executive agendas regarding regulatory agency activities call for control of regulatory activity through legislative oversight, budgetary control, legislative vetoes, and other devices that act out the paradox and the concern about administrative power. (The White House attempts to control the bureaucrats through executive reorganization, cost-benefit analysis, political appointments, etc.) In addition to legislative controls and executive orders, Congress has passed legislation opening up government to citizen review and has essentially eradicated the sovereign immunity protection in order to enable persons to sue the government and its agents. The federal courts have traditionally been involved in the examination of agency activity in light of parameters enumerated in both the U.S. Constitution and in the 1946 Administrative Procedure Act.

[10]Eugene Hickok and Gary McDowell, "The Administrative Theory of the Constitution," Paper presented at the 1981 meeting of the Southern Political Science Association (Memphis, TN), p. 19.
[11]*Ibid*. p. 20.
[12]*CAB v. Delta Air Lines*, 365 *US* 316 (1961).

While given responsibility for developing and implementing public policy for the nation, through enabling statutes with discretionary authority for agencies to act, these same agencies have had to deal with the basic (undercurrent) attitude that suggests less than positive motivations and actions by them. The chapters in *Part Two* examine how agencies have been held accountable and controlled by legislators, executive branch personnel, courts, and persons claiming deprivation of fundamental rights through regulatory agency activity. More than revealing these efforts at control, these essays illustrate the practical and philosophical dilemmas the national public policy formulators face due to their inherent mistrust of the bureaucracy

SUMMARY

The basic question remains to be answered by experience: Can these remedies (discussed in *Part Two*) improve the quality of government in our society and ensure democratic accountability vis-à-vis the federal administrative agency's structure, power, and policy-making processes? Luther Gulick raised this question in a recent essay: If the ideal of self-government is not working well, is it because of a lack of "good management"? Gulick's answer was that the present crisis of government "is not primarily managerial; it is first of all ethical and political, and it is aimed at the core of our democratic faith."[13] He claims that the challenge to administrators is to "give equal attention to defining ethical standards and goals, developing programs, educating voters, *harnessing technologies to the decision process*, and helping officials and laymen to evaluate the results achieved."[14]

This "epochal challenge" that Gulick talks about is one that confronts all those in the political system—elected officials and the nonelected bureaucracy—today. Failure to deal with these issues, including the failure of political leadership in our society, will create dilemmas that the men who met in 1787 hoped the Constitution would confront and would resolve within a democratic environment.

---

[13]Luther Gulick, "Democracy and Administration Face the Future," *Public Administration Review* 37 (November/December 1977), p. 707.

[14]*Ibid*.

PART ONE
Federal Administrative Agencies: Growth and Powers

CHAPTER ONE
GROWTH OF FEDERAL AGENCIES

Federal administrative agencies have existed since 1789, when the first Congress passed statutes giving port collectors licensing and rate-making authority.[1] Federal agencies have always been the institutionalization of responses to problems perceived by Congress and the President; they are the formal "program oriented"[2] institutional response to a societal problem in need of resolution. The political actors, seeking to deal with the societal dilemma (economic and, in more recent times, consumer and health-related issues), establish a governmental unit and charge it, in the enabling statute, to act—within limits defined by the statute and Constitution— to implement the public policy. The agency is responsible for implementing the policy formulated by Congress and president: agency administrators, given the general substantive guidelines provided by the statute, must proceed to find and devise ways to implement these policies. These agencies have, as a basic task, the "responsibility for deciding individual cases in a broader policy context" developed by the politicians—and by the agencies themselves.[3]

The various federal agencies, both in the executive branch and the independent regulatory commissions, have different missions, as determined by the policy formulators. The agency staff then go about the task of implementing these policies in a way that amplifies and specifies the central thrust of the legislative mandate. Agencies, then, fine tune and implement, using their discretionary authority, the public policy agenda of the policymakers. As legislators and presidents focus on new societal problems, the scope of governmental activities broadens because there is the need to

---
[1] Stat 29 (1789); 1 Stat 55 (1789).
[2] Gary J. Edles and Jerome Nelson, *Federal Regulatory Process: Agency Practices and Procedures* (New York: Harcourt Brace Jovanovich, 1981), p. 257.
[3] Ibid.

develop the instrumentalities to act as practical surrogates in the carrying out of the new public policy.

The growth in numbers, size, variety, and scope, of federal agencies reflects the growth of governmental activities in the lives of the community. This growth is not "merely a product of the steady and relentless forces of logic and political and economic interests." Federal administrative agency growth is a product of

> intermittent events or "occasions" that fire the political imagination and overwhelm the normal defenses of anti-regulatory interests. Most prominent are physical catastrophes, scandals that expose presumptive laxity, corruption . . . dramatic scientific discoveries; flareups of racial violence, and changes in administration.[4]

Essentially, the growth of these federal agencies (see Table 1-1 for a listing of federal agencies) is a reflection of the growth of governmental power in the twentieth century.

Government in modern, twentieth-century America has grown dramatically. We are in the Age of the Administrative State, a phrase that reflects this dramatic increase in governmental involvement in the areas of economic and human resource regulation. Governmental policies involve constant interaction between the agents of the state and its publics. In this interaction between government agency and sovereign citizen (or person), certain ground rules are present due to the imperatives of democracy.

The primary controlling device is the U.S. Constitution itself with its parameters respecting powers and abuses of liberties.[5] The Constitution contains basic grants of powers to policymakers (Articles I and II in particular). It also enumerates restrictions on governmental use of power (Articles I, IV, VI, the Bill of Rights, that is, Amendments 1–10, as well as the 13–15 Amendments to the U.S. Constitution). Congressional actions are controlled, ultimately, by the fundamental law; so, too, are the actions of the legislative surrogates—the federal agencies. In addition, federal agencies as "creatures of Congress," are restricted by the enabling statute itself. The policy implementers should be guided by the policy formulators. The legislators and other policy formulators, as *Part Two* will illustrate, do make efforts to constrain arbitrary agency actions through legislative oversight, judicial review, executive oversight, and, more recently, legislative review (and possible veto) of agency actions. Furthermore, in 1946, the Congress passed the Administrative Procedure Act. This watershed legislation, since amended several times, contains basic ground rules for agency rule making and adjudication and provides persons with access to agency records. (*See* Appendix for the Administrative Procedure Act, 1946, as amended.)

The essays in this chapter explore the growth of federal regulatory agencies to a point where, in the Age of the Administrative State, agency action is a prime locus of the policymaking process and where, in the 1980 presidential election, this fact became a major political issue. The Verkuil, Stattler, Pittle, and Stewart selections focus on the growth of administrative agencies from the 1887 creation of the Interstate Commerce Commission (the first independent regulatory commission) to the present. They illustrate the extensive use of the administrative remedy for societal problems and the problems that have developed as a consequence of legislative initiatives, such as the creation of independent regulatory commissions, to regulate economic activities.

Verkuil presents the historical view of the growth of modern administrative process. The Stattler and Pittle essays, written by two commissioners of the Consumer Product Safety

---

[4]Eugene Bardach and Robert A. Kagan, *Going by the Book: The Problem of Regulatory Unreasonableness* (Philadelphia, PA: Temple University Press, 1982), p. 22.

[5]*See* generally Howard Ball, *Constitutional Powers* (St.Paul, MN: West Publishing Company, 1980).

TABLE 1-1 *EXECUTIVE DEPARTMENTS: EXECUTIVE AGENCIES, INDEPENDENT AGENCIES, GOVERNMENT CORPORATIONS, AND QUASI-OFFICIAL AGENCIES, 1981-1982**

EXECUTIVE AGENCIES DEPARTMENTS

Department of Agriculture
Department of Commerce
Department of Defense
   Department of the Air Force
   Department of the Army
   Department of the Navy
   Department of Defense Agencies and Joint Service Schools
Department of Education
Department of Energy
Department of Health and Human Services
Department of Housing and Urban Development
Department of the Interior
Department of Justice
Department of Labor
Department of State
Department of Transportation
Department of the Treasury

QUASI-OFFICIAL AGENCIES

Legal Services Corporation
National Consumer Cooperative Bank
National Railroad Passenger Corporation (Amtrak)
Smithsonian Institution
United States Railway Association
United States Synthetic Fuels Corporation

INDEPENDENT ESTABLISHMENTS AND GOVERNMENT CORPORATIONS

ACTION
Administrative Conference of the United States
American Battle Monuments Commission
Appalachian Regional Commission
Board for International Broadcasting
Central Intelligence Agency
Civil Aeronautics Board
Commission on Civil Rights
Commission of Fine Arts
Commodity Futures Trading Commission
Community Services Administration
Consumer Product Safety Commission
Environmental Protection Agency
Equal Employment Opportunity Commission
Export-Import Bank of the United States
Farm Credit Administration
Federal Communications Commission
Federal Deposit Insurance Corporation
Federal Election Commission
Federal Emergency Management Agency
Federal Home Loan Bank Board
Federal Labor Relations Authority
Federal Maritime Commission
Federal Mediation and Conciliation Service
Federal Reserve System
Federal Trade Commission
General Services Administration
Inter-American Foundation
International Communication Agency
Interstate Commerce Commission
Merit Systems Protection Board
National Aeronautics and Space Administration
National Capital Planning Commission
National Credit Union Administration
National Foundation on the Arts and the Humanities
National Labor Relations Board
National Mediation Board
National Science Foundation

Growth of Federal Agencies

TABLE 1-1 *Continued*

	INDEPENDENT ESTABLISHMENTS AND GOVERNMENT CORPORATIONS
	National Transportation Safety Board
	Nuclear Regulatory Commission
	Occupational Safety and Health Review Commission
	Office of Personnel Management
	Panama Canal Commission
	Pennsylvania Avenue Development Corporation
	Pension Benefit Guaranty Corporation
	Postal Rate Commission
	Railroad Retirement Board
	Securities and Exchange Commission
	Selective Services System
	Small Business Administration
	Tennesese Valley Authority
	United States Arms Control and Disarmament Agency
	United States International Development Cooperation Agency
	United States International Trade Commission
	United States Metric Board
	United States Postal Service
	Veterans Administration

*Source: *United States Government Manual,* 1981/1982, pp. v–vxi.

Commission, examine the growth of the independent regulatory commissions. Stattle and Pittle offer a point-counterpoint statement about the values and costs of independent agencies. Stewart's essay examines the traditional model of administrative activity. He maintains that the traditional view is a reflection of the common social value in legitimating, through controlling rules and procedures (such as the APA and judicial review), the exercise of power over private interests by officials not otherwise formally accountable for their actions. (Stewart's interesting conclusion is that the traditional model of agency activity is not viable due to the element of discretion that administrators possess and which is largely outside the control of formal rules and procedures. This question of discretion is further discussed in *Part Two* of the book.)

Finally, the Fritschler and DeMuth essays discuss the impact of administrative agency growth and activity in the 1970s. Fritschler focuses on the rapid growth of the new social and health-safety regulatory agencies of the 1960s and 1970s and suggests reasons for the cry for regulatory reform/control heard from both Republican and Democratic legislators and presidential administrations in the past decade. DeMuth's essay, "A Strong Beginning on Reform," is a brief commentary, by an official in the Reagan administration, on the status of regulatory agency change after the election of Ronald Reagan in 1980. (Reagan's election campaign emphasized the concern many Americans felt about the rapid growth of federal agencies.)

ONE
THE EMERGING CONCEPT OF ADMINISTRATIVE PROCEDURE

Paul A. Verkuil

I. A HISTORICAL ANALYSIS OF ADMINISTRATIVE PROCEDURE

While the administrative process has been part of American government since the founding of the Republic,[1] the concept of administrative law as an independent area of law did not take shape until early in the twentieth century, and the study of administrative procedure commenced in earnest only in the 1930s. The explanations for this slow emergence of administrative law and its "sub-specialty," administrative procedure, are both simple and complex. Understandably, administrative law could grow no faster than the subject to which it attached: government regulation of the economy. But administrative procedure was, ironically, both an adjunct to and a reaction against economic regulation. It developed as much from deeply felt objections to government interference with the marketplace as from the necessity to make that interference coherent and credible.

---

[1] In 1789, in the first year of government under the new Constitution, Congress provided for the administration of the customs laws, the regulation of ocean-going vessels and coastal trade, and the payment of veteran's pensions, all functions that have familiar analogues today. *See* W. Gellhorn, Federal Administrative Proceedings 4-7 (1941). *See also* E. Freund, The Growth of American Adminstrative Law 16-20 (1923). It is said that the phrase "administrative law of the United States" was first used by Attorney General Caleb Cushing in the *Case of Spratt's Hemp Contract*. 6 Op. Att'y Gen. 99 (1853). *See* O. Kraines, The World and Ideas of Ernst Freund 64 (1974).

This selection is taken from the *Columbia Law Review* 78 (November 1978), 258–279. Used by permission. Most footnotes have been deleted.

A. The Twin Tyrannies of Administrative Law

By the end of the nineteenth century, private enterprise became subject to what defenders of the status quo might have described as the "twin tyrannies" of government regulation, those substantive and those procedural. "Substantive tyranny" was reflected in the market control mechanisms established by state and federal legislation during the Populist and Progressive eras. Well-known examples are the rate and entry regulations imposed upon railroads, public utilities, banks, and insurance companies. The purpose of these regulations was to control corporate behavior. Thus it was during this period that the term *liberalism* itself underwent conversion, from identification with nineteenth-century values of laissez faire to twentieth-century notions of social control of the marketplace. For those subjected to this direct attack, the tyranny of government intervention was apparent. Some fought back politically, with the result that regulation during this period was as much negotiated by private enterprise as imposed upon it. Others fought back judicially, ushering in the legendary era of substantive due process that frustrated much social and economic regulation legislation until the mid-1930s.

There also existed during this period "procedural tyranny," which, while less well identified, nonetheless triggered an equivalent range of due process objections. This perceived tyranny provides a means for tracing the development of administrative procedure. Procedural tyranny was reflected in the shift in decision control from the judiciary to administrative boards and commissions. Thus, early attacks on market control mechanisms challenged the form of government regulations as well as the substance. The Supreme Court distinguished substantive control of private behavior imposed by the legislature directly from that imposed by the legislature indirectly through administrative bodies. In the latter situation, the administrative structure itself was attacked because it deprived those subject to it of a procedural right to a judicial tribunal. Procedural tyranny, in this view, had a per se effect; it resulted merely from the removal of decision functions from the common-law courts. The public pressures to acknowledge the viability of administrative tribunals were enormous, however, and, despite continued objection here and abroad, the Court soon accepted the idea that administrative tribunals were not per se tyrannous. Indeed, over time the priority and even the exclusivity of administrative tribunals was established.

Justice Holmes laid the per se procedural tyranny argument to rest in *Chicago, B & Q. Ry.* v. *Babcock*, in which the Court rejected a challenge by railroad plaintiffs to property tax assessments by the Nebraska Board of Equalization. The railroads had managed below to cross-examine the board members as to their mental decision-making processes, which predictably made the board members, as well as the administrative process, appear confused and inept. Holmes' opinion for the Court found this cross-examination an inappropriate exercise of judicial power and granted the assessors the same decisional deference accorded the judiciary. This aspect of his opinion is well known, but the opinion also produced a corollary principle no less important: The choice of allocating business to an agency or the courts was solely for the state to make. Holmes reasoned:

> The Board was created for the purpose of using its judgment and its knowledge. . . . Within its jurisdiction, except, as we have said, in the case of fraud or a clearly shown adoption of wrong principles, it is the ultimate guardian of certain rights. The State has confided those rights to its protection and has trusted to its honor and capacity as it confides the protection of other social relations to the courts of law. Somewhere there must be an end.

While some limits on the legislature's power to convert common-law claims into administrative matters remain, this decision dissolved the per se notion of administrative inadequacy.

The focus then shifted from the choice of forum to what happened once the forum was selected, and what happened after the decision was made. In *Londoner* v. *Denver*, a state board of equalization case decided the next term, the Court set aside a street assessment order because the plaintiffs had been offered only the opportunity to file written comments and complaints concerning the assessment. The Court held that "a hearing in its very essence demands that he who is entitled to it shall have the right to support his allegations by argument however brief, and, if need be, by proof, however informal."

In effect, *Babcock, Londoner,* and subsequent decisions introduced the modern era of administrative law. First acknowledging the legitimacy of the administrative tribunal, they then addressed the question of what procedures the tribunal must follow. This inquiry was to create a profound clash over the role of the adversary system in determining administrative procedure.

B. The Adversary System and Administrative Procedure

The substantive values of the nineteenth-century liberal, noninterventionist state and the procedural values of the common-law, adversary model of decision making have a common core and are mutually supportive. Both sets of values reflected a common philosophical premise that the correct result would be achieved by the free clash of competing forces in the marketplace, or courtroom. As Jerome Frank noted, the "fight [or adversary] theory of justice is a sort of legal laissez-faire." If this connection is accepted, then the consequence of undermining one would be naturally to jeopardize the other; and, conversely, to support one would be to reinforce the other. Substantive tyranny thus possessed an exact procedural counterpart. The administrative tribunal did in effect double injury to traditional values. It undermined laissez-faire by enforcing the substantive mandates of regulation, and it compromised the adversary system by resorting to nonadversary administrative procedures.

The lawyers of the time fought hard, therefore, to keep decision making in the courts for two reasons. First, the adversary system with its opportunity for jury trials and other procedural protections meant less control by the decision maker over the process. Second, the judiciary's antipathy to government programs provided a favorable environment for decision. Thus, the adversary system held its place as an important value of classical liberalism even as the definition of liberalism was changing.

This connection between adversary procedures and laissez-faire had much to do with the bar's initial resistance to administrative solutions. The events surrounding Roscoe Pound's controversial address to the ABA in 1906 emphasize this phenomenon. Pound shocked the lawyers of that time by speaking derisively of the cherished adversary system as the "sporting theory of justice" and documenting its inefficiencies and intricacies. He also advocated a removal of certain matters from the courts to administrative tribunals where they could be subjected to disposition in more efficient, inquisitorial fashion. This attack upon the "scientific" adversary system was vigorously rejected by the bar, and Pound's ideas did not receive the unqualified endorsement of the ABA until 1976, when the chief justice of the United States adopted them as his own.

This opposition from the bar led administrative law instinctively down the judicial path. From the early 1900s, the bar (and through it, the public) remained confused and apprehensive about the role and purpose of administrative agencies. Adolph Berle described the mood of the time: "Already there has arisen the fear that public bodies, set to solve given problems, may develop into tyrannous institutions, amenable to no law and subject only to the doubtful safeguards of political action." Berle tried to provide a method of making administrative law a respectable field of study. He sought to liberate administrative law from the confines of constitutional law by refocusing concerns away from the study of separation of powers and checks and balances and toward the study of the law surrounding individual boards and commissions. In this way, a "systematic body of law" was to be created that would overcome "the dangerous and weakening period of floundering while business men, the administrative (sic) itself, and the courts solve what the sphere of the new organism is to be."

It would be easy to discount these sentiments as those of a budding social reformer who, seeing no substantive tyranny, was simply insensitive to the bar's fear of procedural tyranny. But Berle's call for systematic study of administrative law echoed views that had already been stated by some members of the legal profession who did not share his reforming instincts. Elihu Root's 1916 presidential address to the ABA sounded the same theme:

> There is one special field of law development which has manifestly become inevitable. We are entering upon the creation of a body of administrative law quite different in its machinery, its remedies, and its necessary safeguards from the old methods of regulation by specific statutes enforced by courts. . . . There will be no withdrawal from these experiments. We shall go on; we shall expand them, whether we approve theoretically or not, because such agencies furnish protection to rights and obstacles to wrong doing which under our new social and industrial conditions cannot be practically accomplished by the old and simple procedure of legislatures and courts as in the last generation. Yet the powers that are committed to these regulating agencies, and which they must have to do their work, carry with them great and dangerous opportunities of oppression and wrong. If we are to continue a government of limited powers, these agencies of regulation must themselves be regulated. The limits of their power over the citizen must be fixed and determined. The rights of the citizen against them must be made plain. A system of administrative law must be developed, and that with us is still in its infancy, crude and imperfect.

In retrospect, Root's call for a systematic approach to administrative law was of fundamental importance. This invitation served to implicate the law schools centrally in the process of developing administrative procedure and thus drew attention to scholarly work that otherwise might have remained in the background. In the 1920s, the academics responded to the challenge.

Since 1911, Ernst Freund's casebook on administrative law had been available as a unifying device. But with the subject then still in a crude state, much of the impetus for reform had been lacking. By 1928 Freund had dispensed with some of the constitutional materials, but he still saw the subject as largely concerned with judicial review rather than administrative procedure: "Administrative Law continues to be treated as law controlling the administration, and not as law produced by the administration." Nevertheless administrative procedure was placed on the reform agenda and others were to give it shape. Felix Frankfurter, writing in 1927, saw the "task" of administrative law as the creation of institutional safeguards through internal processes and machinery:

> These safeguards largely depend on a highly professionalized civil service, an adequate

technique of administrative application of legal standards, a flexible, appropriate and economical procedure (always remembering that "in the development of our liberty insistence upon procedural regularity has been a large factor"), easy access to public scrutiny, and a constant play of criticism by an informed and spirited bar.

These views of Frankfurter suggest that a workable system of administrative procedure was within reach during the 1920s. But the hopeful consensus of bar and academe that surrounded the calls for systematic study and design of administrative procedure disintegrated with the election of Franklin D. Roosevelt in 1932 and the pressures on administrative law produced by the New Deal's tidal wave of regulation.

C. The New Deal and Administrative Procedure

The sense of tyranny that permeated American administrative law in the beginning of the twentieth century revived and grew to dominate discussion about the subject in the 1930s. The Agricultural Adjustment Act (AAA) and the National Industrial Recovery Act (NIRA) were regulations of a new order of magnitude. They sought broadly to stabilize competition in many basic industries. The Supreme Court actively vindicated interests premised upon allegations of substantive and procedural tyranny through use of substantive due process, the nondelegation doctrine, and the expanded scope of judicial review of constitutional and jurisdictional facts. It was not uncharacteristic of the period for the Court to discuss charges of procedural tyranny by New Deal agencies by referring to "Star Chamber" proceedings.

1. The New Deal and Roscoe Pound. Anti-New Deal sentiment predictably revived the adversary system as a solution to the procedural tyranny of administrative agencies. In 1933, in response to the alarm about the AAA and NIRA, the Committee on Administrative Law was created by the Executive Committee of the ABA. The committee's declared function was "to be of service in a study of the practical operation of the various types of administrative machinery (particularly on the quasi-judicial side). . . ." The committee's first report in 1934 sought to secure the judicial function in administrative procedure by the limited device of a federal administrative court. By 1938, the commission had begun to propose legislation designed broadly to judicialize the administrative process. The proposal sought to establish intradepartmental review tribunals; to require all agencies and departments to issue, within one year, rules and regulations implementing "every statute affecting persons or property"; and to provide for judicial review of all orders under an expanded "clearly erroneous" scope of review. In a masterful disguise of its content, the ABA proposal was entitled: "[A Bill] To Provide for the More Expeditious Settlement of Disputes with the United States and for Other Purposes."

Roscoe Pound chaired the committee that issued the final ABA report in 1939. Rather than creating workable principles of administrative procedure, Pound focused his attention on what he labeled "administrative absolutism." In particular he was angered by statements of New Dealers that seemed to legitimate nonadversary decision making. He singled out James Landis, who had observed that "[i]nterpretation of sociological and economic data flourishes less happily in the overheated atmosphere of litigation than in the calm of scientific inquiry." To Pound these and comparable sentiments were no less than "Marxist ideas" and he so labeled them in the 1939 ABA report. Much of the report was cast in heated language including a list of ten "tendencies" of the administrative process that read like an indictment of administrative procedure. The report's operating premise, Professor Jaffe concluded, was a commitment to regard the judiciary with "unseeing awe."

This reaction against administrative procedure was in effect a reversion to the earlier view of the substantive and procedural tyrannies of administrative law. The reaction to the substantive programs formulated during the New Deal encouraged a return to procedural alternatives that had been largely rejected a decade earlier. Apparently, it was not a time for reasoned arguments about the strengths and weaknesses of administrative procedure. Even Roscoe Pound, once a major source of procedural innovation, succumbed to the mood of the time. Pound's advocacy of inquisitorial models for mass administrative cases gave way to his apotheosis of the judiciary. It is difficult to explain this rejection of earlier views. One hypothesis, consistent with the twin tyranny thesis, is that Pound belatedly realized that his procedural solutions could be used to facilitate a degree of substantive control to which he was fundamentally opposed. Without trying to sum up a man's career in a paragraph, it might be said that Pound was a substantive conservative and a procedural liberal. When one's views are so conflicting, reasoned discussion of administrative procedure is impossible. Yet the New Deal, by forcing such conflicts out in the open, facilitated deeper thinking about the meaning of procedure in the administrative state.

It would be a mistake to assume that the New Deal period was characterized by administrative arbitrariness, as the 1939 ABA report incident might lead skeptics to contend. But the procedural innovations explored then were in some ways as dramatic as the substantive. For one thing, the New Deal introduced the concept of the administrator as benign inquisitor. The Social Security Act of 1935 established what would become the most extensive and enduring social program of the entire New Deal. In addition to its substantive mandate, the act created the Social Security Board, which undertook to define new forms of administrative procedure. As guidelines for the legion of social security decision makers who had to adjudicate eligibility and entitlement to the old-age and survivors insurance program (and, as time went on, the disability program), the Social Security Board offered a new rationale for the role of the decision maker in the hearing process. In a 1940 statement, the board discussed the values to be achieved in an administrative hearing in terms of "simplicity and informality" as well as "accuracy and fairness." It referred to the social security decision maker as a "referee" or "social agent." This concept of the administrator as an agent for the public (working to ensure that the program goals are fulfilled) is different from the role assigned to the common-law judge. The social security "referee" thus emerges with a role that is independent of the judicial one.

In some respects, this role resembles more that of the judge in continental Europe, where the inquisitorial rather than the adversary model prevails. Critics of the New Deal programs might be quick to assert a connection between substantive coercion (through the redistributive aspects of the Social Security program) and the procedural coercion of the so-called inquisitorial model. One tyranny, the argument might go, begets another. But this fear, while by no means ungrounded, is of limited relevance to the administrative process. The decision model proposed by the Social Security Board was designed to make an enormously complex program work at low cost and with substantial public satisfaction. The scope of the inquisitorial solution was not intended to be carried over to the civil or criminal process. But it did signal the kind of innovative thinking about administrative procedure that would ultimately lead to the emergence of an independent procedural model for administrative law. But there was much that still stood in the way.

2. The Walter-Logan Bill: The high water mark of judicialization.

The bill proposed in the 1939 ABA report was promptly introduced in Congress and named after its sponsors, Representative Walter and Senator Logan. The bill spoke *ex cathedra* about adjudication, rule making, and judicial review. As to adjudication, it first created a procrustean dichotomy between single- and multiheaded government agencies and then provided for trial-type hearings to be conducted by a three-member hearing board in the single-headed category and by a single trial examiner in the multiheaded category. Any person "aggrieved" by a decision of any officer or employee of any agency could demand such a hearing. The rule-making section provided that all rules "affecting the rights of persons or peoperty" should be issued "only after publication of notice and public hearings." Rules under future statutes were to be issued within one year of the statute's enactment, and rules in existence for less than three years were to be reconsidered within one year after the bill became law if "[a]ny person substantially interested in the effects" of the rule so requested. The bill provided for judicial review that was particularly intrusive into the administrative process. Any person "substantially interested in the effects of any administrative rule" could ask the Court of Appeals for the District of Columbia to determine whether such rule was in conflict with the Constitution or the statute under which it was promulgated. To make this system work, the bill exempted certain agencies from its coverage.

It is hard to imagine a more controversial congressional proposal on administrative law reform. The report that spawned the bill was strongly criticized by Robert Jackson in the ABA House of Delegates, and the bill itself was emphatically denounced by the Association of the Bar of the City of New York: "[W]e think that the present bill, under the guise of reform, would force administrative and departmental agencies having a wide variety of functions into a single mold which is so rigid, so needlessly interfering, as to bring about a widespread crippling of the administrative process." Academic criticism also was intense; the best of it was directed at the bill's attempt, without empirical analysis, to impose a rigid, uniform procedural format upon the diverse functions of the administrative process.

It is not hard to picture the reaction this bill created in the Roosevelt administration. In a letter to FDR, Robert Jackson, by then Attorney General, renewed his objections on grounds that are substantially, but not entirely, justified today. Nonetheless, the administration was unable to keep the bill from passing Congress, and Roosevelt had to exercise his veto power to prevent it from becoming law. His veto message hammered at the necessity for separating the reform of administrative procedure from the reform of judicial procedure, which was also receiving attention at the time. FDR ultimately denounced the legal profession in language reminiscent of Roscoe Pound's 1906 address:

> [A] large part of the legal profession has never reconciled itself to the existence of the administrative tribunal. Many of them prefer the stately ritual of the courts, in which lawyers play all the speaking parts, to the simple procedure of administrative hearings which a client can understand and even participate in. Many of the lawyers prefer that decision be influenced by a shrewd play upon technical rules of evidence in which the lawyers are the only experts, although they always disagree. Many of the lawyers still prefer to distinguish precedent and to juggle leading cases rather than to get down to the merits of the efforts in which their clients are engaged. For years, such lawyers have led a persistent fight against the administrative tribunal.

When the House failed to override, Roosevelt noted with satisfaction that the "great propaganda drive" behind the Walter-Logan bill had failed.

The forces in favor of the bill were undoubtedly led by those who were substantively opposed to (or tyrannized by) the New Deal programs. Having lost on the substance, these forces sought to prevail by recasting their objections in procedural terms. They must have believed that if they could reassert the procedural analogue to nineteenth-century liberalism—the adversary model—they might succeed in frustrating the substantive solutions proposed by the welfare programs of twentieth-century liberalism. Roosevelt focused on these substantive conservatives in his veto message:

> In addition to the lawyers who see the administrative tribunal encroaching upon their exclusive prerogatives there are powerful interests which are opposed to reforms that can only be made effective through the use of the administrative tribunal. Wherever a continuing series of controversies exist between a powerful and concentrated interest on one side and a diversified mass of individuals, each of whose separate interests may be small, on the other side, the only means of obtaining equality before the law has been to place the controversy in an administrative tribunal. . . . Great interests, therefore, which desire to escape regulation rightly see that if they can strike at the heart of modern reform by sterilizing the administrative tribunal which administers them, they will have effectively destroyed the reform itself.

This analysis, however, only partially explains the collective motivation that allowed Walter-Logan to pass Congress. What makes this episode relevant today is an understanding of the motivations of members of Congress and the bar who did not hold substantive objections to the New Deal programs, but nonetheless shared procedural objections. There must have existed a group who felt this way or else the vast body of New Deal legislation would not have become law in the first place. These legislators saw not the twin tyrannies, but only the procedural tyranny. In effect they suffered the reverse of Roscoe Pound's dilemma and must have been no less frustrated. They were supportive of substantive intervention into the economy, but not supportive, if the analogy holds, of procedural intervention into the judicial system through development of a nonadversary system of administrative procedure. How large this body of procedural conservatives was then or might be in the future is virtually unknowable. What can be shown, however, is that they exist today and their presence helps explain some of the dramatic procedural due process decisions of the last ten years.

3. The 1941 attorney general's report: Administrative procedure comes of age.

It is unlikely that any report on administrative law has been more eagerly awaited by the administration that commissioned it than the 1941 report of the Attorney General's Committee on Administrative Procedure. FDR based his justification of his veto of the controversial Walter-Logan bill partially on the imminence of this report. Moreover, it was anticipated that the substance of the report would be persuasive and supportive of the administration; something an earlier presidential report had turned out not to be. When Roosevelt received the report on January 24, 1941, he was overjoyed, if one is to judge by the note added after his Walter-Logan veto message. This report, Roosevelt stated, "has confirmed my belief that the Walter-Logan bill was an abortive attempt to hamstring many progressive administrative agencies."

The report was, of course, much more than a vindication of New Deal procedural solutions (to the extent it was that at all). It was, and is, the best study of federal administrative procedure ever prepared. This is no historical hyperbole; academics and members of the bar recognized its excellence when it appeared and its value has scarcely diminished to this day. The importance of the report stems from its methodology and tone as well as its substance and conclusions. The committee and its research staff approached the administrative process without preconceptions and studied it empirically. What resulted was a series of highly useful statements about what agencies and departments do in fact and some predictably modest conclusions about how the process might be improved.

Procedures were seen as means to the end of fair implementation of government programs and their efficacy was to be measured by their contribution to that end. This functional view of procedure argued for flexibility and informality along with a recognition of adversary hearings. Thus the report considered the "informal" method of adjudication first because it recognized that "informal procedures constitute the vast bulk of administrative adjudication and are truly the lifeblood of the administrative process." Informal procedures (including settlement conferences, use of stipulations, inspections, and tests) were seen as indispensable methods for achieving the efficient operation of government business. As for the formal process, the report recommended the use of hearing commissioners, with enhanced independence and status, to conduct formal adjudications. Concerning rule making, the report emphasized the importance of outside participation prior to the issuance of rules, but urged against rigidifying the rule-making process. Finally, the report proposed the creation of an Office of Federal Administrative Procedure to "study and coordinate administrative procedures" and "to achieve and stimulate practical improvements in a manner not possible through omnibus legislation."

The report's ultimate significance rests in its moving discussion about administrative law into its third and mature phase: concern with administrative procedure as an independent model. Automatic and unexamined reliance upon the judicial model would never again satisfactorily resolve debate.

D. The Administrative Procedure Act: Compromise Without Retrenchment

Problems of administrative law reform became of relatively little concern in the war years following the reception of the report. But by the conclusion of the war, a variety of legislative bills inspired by the majority and minority positions in the 1941 report were pending before Congress. Ultimately, bills reflecting the minority position on the creation of an administrative code passed both houses and became law.

On the face of it, it looked like a victory for the old Walter-Logan forces who had earlier sought unsuccessfully to judicialize administrative procedure. Certainly some of the members of Congress who voted for the bill thought they were striking a blow against the old nemesis, administrative tyranny. But there were significant differences in the atmosphere surrounding the enactment of the APA, as well as in the substance of the legislation. In the first place, the sides were not clearly drawn; both the president and the ABA supported the 1946 legislation. Thus the APA was passed in a period of reconciliation and relative agreement about its goals and techniques. Moreover, the substance of the bill owed relatively little to Walter-Logan. It did not impose a procrustean procedural system on administrative agencies; rather it provided that the formal hearing provisions would be triggered by organic agency legislation. The APA also offered some important procedural innovations, in particular the preferred category of "informal" rule making. Informal rule making, however, was the only attempt to define an informal process. That vast realm of informal adjudication, the "lifeblood" of the administrative process, in the words of the 1941 report, was ignored by the APA. In certain other respects, the APA incorporated recommendations of the 1941 majority report.

On balance, the APA probably disappointed both the friends and the critics of the administrative process. It was not, because of limitations in scope, "comparable in many respects to the Judiciary Act of 1789," as Senator McCarran later stated; neither was it Walter-Logan reincarnate. The APA became and remains an important juncture in the development of administrative procedure. It reflects much of the progressive thinking about administrative law that emerged from the 1940s and does little to hamper or rigidify the administrative process. It looks beyond reactions motivated by the twin tyrannies of administrative law that had dominated earlier discussion. The APA provided a sense of accomplishment; as the Supreme Court subsequently recognized, it amounted to something of a catharsis for long contending forces: "The Act thus represents a long period of study and strife; it settles long continued and hard fought contentions, and enacts a formula upon which opposing social and political forces have come to rest." Several decades were to pass before Congress's administrative procedure reform instincts would revive.

E. Historical Assessment

Administrative procedure has been struggling to find recognition and respectability since the beginning of the twentieth century. The obstacle was, and to some extent still is, a perception among judges, lawyers, and legislators that the adversary system is the only legitimate way to make decisions in our society. This point of view is held most strongly by those who oppose the substance of the government regulations to which administrative procedures attach. There is little that can be done to accommodate this viewpoint short of deregulating, an option that is normally not considered procedural. Some who accept the basis for regulation, however, instinctively fear that displacing adversary procedures will lead to procedures that are inherently arbitrary and oppressive. The difficulty with accommodating this view is that it would paralyze the implementation of government programs. Moreover, this fear should have been largely allayed by the enactment of the APA. The APA was premised on the notions that (1) what the agencies did procedurally was not inherently arbitrary and (2) general procedural guides in rulemaking and adjudication would be adequate to assure fairness.

TWO
TWO VIEWS ON THE STRUCTURE OF REGULATORY COMMISSONS
Point

Stuart M. Statler

Most of us bask comfortably in our knowledge gained over many years about the way the federal government works. We cite the typically American remedy of the ballot box: If you don't like the rascals, throw them out. We point to the three branches of government—executive, legislative, and judicial—and pay homage to a separation of powers.

But a strange hybrid on the political landscape has elements of all three branches. It has certain legislative powers of the Congress. It enforces laws like the executive branch. It exercises some of the adjudicative powers of the courts. Yet on a day-to-day basis, it works outside the control of any of those branches.

I refer to the dozen or so independent regulatory commissions. In a period of regulatory reform and streamlining of government, few other areas warrant closer scrutiny than this so-called fourth branch of government.

The concept of independent regulatory commissions needs rethinking: independence from whom and for what purpose? The theory underlying the independent commission was enlightened; but changing economic and political circumstances can make even the boldest ideas obsolete. Through historical evolution particularly in the last decade the vaunted independence of these agencies has already been diluted. Today, one must question the continued value of this independence when viewed against a growing public mandate for more efficient, coordinated, and less burdensome government.

Instead of relying on the theory of how independent regulatory commissions

This selection and Chapter 3 are companion pieces, and both are taken from *Legal Times* III (May 9, 1981), 9–17. Used by permission of the publisher and author.

should perform, we can now look to experience to judge how they *do* perform. These commissions have major economic impacts, and they function beyond the control of our national leadership.

HISTORY OF "INDEPENDENCE"

The first independent regulatory commission was the Interstate Commerce Commission. When it was established in 1887, the ICC was not strictly independent: it was part of the Department of the Interior. In fact, the term *independence* does not even appear in the legislative debate about the ICC. Most of that debate focused on the commission structure—a group of coequal commissioners using majority vote to determine policy. The states had originated this mode of regulation; prior to the ICC, railroad regulation was a cacophony of many separate state commissions, with no uniform national plan. Congress simply adopted the commission form found in many of the states.

The issue of independence did not arise until two years later, in 1889. The concern of a Representative Reagan (D-Texas) about the possible adverse effects of President Harrison's influence on the commission led to a bill conferring full independence on the ICC. A man by the name of Reagan distrusted a sitting president, and we ended up with a constitutional curiosity.

What does independence connote today? All independent agencies are run by commissions. The commissioners are appointed for a set term of office and can be removed only for cause. For example, the five commissioners of the Consumer Product Safety Commission serve for seven-year terms and may be removed only for "neglect of duty or malfeasance in office." The decision maker, once appointed, does not depend on any political event or individual politician, not even the president, for continuance in office (although, in almost every case, an incoming administration can name its own designee as chairman).

This applies to all of the independent regulatory commissions. All of their commissioners serve for definite terms, may be removed only for cause, and operate outside executive branch control. They were meant to be insulated from partisan considerations and not to necessarily reflect the views of any particular administration.

Of the more than 100 federal regulatory agencies, very few enjoy this measure of autonomy. The bulk, instead, are executive branch agencies contained within the various cabinet departments, and answer ultimately to the president. Some are highly visible and semiautonomous; others are buried in the bureaucracy. Almost all are headed by a single administrator who is accountable to the department secretary. All the administrators serve at the pleasure of the president and may be removed at any time for any reason.

The Environmental Protection Agency is sometimes wrongly termed an "independent" agency in the executive branch because it is not part of a cabinet department. But being "separate" is not the same as being "independent." The administrator of EPA has no job security—like the head of other executive branch agencies, he or she can be fired at the whim of the president. The Federal Energy Regulatory Commission is a true hybrid: its commissioners have set terms of office with removal only for cause, yet the commission is wholly contained within the Energy Department.

Given the confusion about "independence," discussing it is difficult—critics and proponents often are not even talking about the same thing. Here, I am talking about those dozen or so commissions whose members have set terms and job security. Theory tells us that commissioners in these agencies can discharge their duties without fear of being tossed out because of a politically unpopular decision.

HAVEN FOR EXPERTS

Independence has a number of advantages. First, it insulates decision makers from the more pernicious influences associated with politics. We have certain assurances that securities investigation will not be compromised because it involves a large campaign contributor; that a television license will not be awarded arbitrarily to the president's friend. And requirements for open deliberations "in the sunshine" allow all to review the decision and satisfy themselves of its fairness and completeness. In theory, we have built a haven for goodwilled experts to make objective decisions about difficult policy issues without favoritism or fear of personal repercussions.

But some critics view this structure as undemocratic. Commissioners get together and decide what people and companies can and cannot do in areas like transportation, trade, securities, communications, and banking. By granting or denying a license or rate or route, prohibiting certain commercial practices, or banning specific products, they can make or break a business. Some contend that independent commissioners are just not accountable to anyone—the White House, the Congress, regulated firms, or the American public. That overstates the case, but there is some merit to the point.

Moreover, experience has taught us much about the shortcomings of these commissions. The most immediate failing of independence stems from its rather arbitrary application. No theory guides us regarding *when* a particular area should be regulated by an independent body. Why do so few of more than 100 regulatory bodies merit independence? Why should some types of regulation be promulgated by independent commissions while others are subject to White House influence or control? Why, for example, is the CPSC independent, while virtually every other health and safety agency (except the Nuclear Regulatory Commission) is not?

Those who urge retaining CPSC's independence argue that the health and safety area should be guarded against all taint of political motivation. But the current government safety setup does not reflect that view: the president can coordinate auto safety rules (through the National Highway Traffic Safety Administration) or food and drug regulations (through the Food and Drug Administration), but not the regulation of consumer products. Ironically, the first two areas have a far greater impact on the economy as a whole; yet, the president is denied any direct role in consumer products, which tend to have the least effect on the national economy. But the president has no influence on the construction and siting of nuclear power plants, which does have an enormous impact on the national economy, because of the independent stature of the NCR. From the standpoint of good government and consistent policy, this simply does not make sense.

But independance does offer valuable benefits. For example, the independent commissions do not suffer from "instant rewrite" of regulations by a new administration, which executive agencies can encounter. If the president wanted to redirect the CPSC's path, he could do so only through congressional legislation or by persuading—but not ordering—the commission to rescind regulations. The agency cannot be directed to change a decision, nor can the commissioners be fired if they choose not to.

Of course, such a request, even if politically motivated, may be soundly based. Regardless of the merits of any particular regulation, the overall effect of many diverse regulations on a particular sector of the industry (for example, autos) or on the economy as a whole may have such a negative impact that redirection is appropriate.

ELECTION RESULTS

Another benefit of independence is policy consistency. Election results will not dictate dramatic shifts in policy within the independent regulatory commissions, although an incoming administration can appoint a new chairman and fill vacancies as they arise, especially at the start of a new regime. But sudden departures from previous policy are unlikely.

But paradoxically, the downside of internal consistency within an agency can be inconsistency governmentwide. You may have a government fraught with contradiction or disarray on the national economic scene. Not one of the independent agencies has a national perspective; no one adds up the sum of the individual actions to assess their total impact. The economic chaos that affects the nation as a whole hasn't resulted from any single blunder; to the extent regulation is at fault, it is the cumulative result of many seemingly independent actions that are outside the direct control of an elected president pledged to take strong corrective action.

Independence also seeks, through nonpolitical expert boards, to foster informed decisions on technical matters that can have broad policy implications. The experts should be chosen for their knowledge, credentials, and interest in the field. A president should carefully select—subject to considered Senate approval—the most qualified experts to render public service on these commissions.

However, experience has proven this ideal to be well-nigh impossible. Because these commissions are independent, their performance doesn't reflect directly on the president. And since they generally don't reflect negatively on the administration, presidents have been known to abuse the appointments process. Commission appointments in many cases have become political plums.

Aside from political patronage, the ability of the appointed commissioners to regulate effectively is affected by an even more fundamental problem: the commission structure itself. Decision making by groups of coequal commissioners is probably the single greatest impediment to effective agency performance.

Critics of leadership-by-commission point to a failure to plan and develop long-range goals, a reluctance to formulate coherent regulatory policies, neglect of program review, and a tendency toward procrastination and delay.

FORM AND FUNCTION

The problem lies in a mismatch between form and function. A regulatory commission is like a miniature legislature; the regulatory function is closer to an executive one. The appropriate commission model is in the executive, not the legislative, branch. Single administrators, able to respond with dispatch, can better provide the more fluid regulatory framework to meet today's pace of economic, technical, and social change.

A single executive is more free to use modern management techniques—delegating more and rewarding or dismissing staff based on their performance. The allure of running one's own show should also attract more capable executives. Together with a streamlined structure, talent at the top can have a ripple effect, inducing more qualified staff to assume key positions throughout the agency.

The chief benefit of group leadership—diverse opinion and input—could be achieved by an able administrator's balancing the competing views of senior advisers, thus gaining the opportunity for deliberation and compromise. Ironically, group decision making is meant to do that, but more commonly reflects consensus as a "least common denominator" result.

The ungainly commission structure not only leads to less effective decision making—it also costs more than a single administrator would. Commission budgets include the obvious added costs of multiple salaries, travel expenses, and office space for commissioners and their staffs. But large-scale hidden costs include skewed priorities, pursuit of pet projects, staff indirection, management inefficiencies, protracted proceedings, and persistent second-guessing.

At the CPSC, notwithstanding the agency's much-improved record in recent years, I estimate that group leadership renders the agency only 50 percent as effective as it could be in protecting the public against unreasonable product risks. A high-level staff member observes that the inefficiencies of our group decision making absorb as much as 25 percent of our budget—around $10 million of $40 million.

Maintaining independence requires the commission form, since no one would advocate an independent single administrator. Yet commissions obviously cost us dearly—in both dollars and doldrums.

PURSE STRINGS

Congress has given the Office of Management and Budget (OMB) vast discretion over the independent commissions' budgetary and personnel matters; as a result, the commissions are becoming much more susceptible to pressures from the administration—pressures subtle and not so subtle.

The administration has come to exercise the power of the purse by setting the "mark" that all agencies must support in going to the Congress for an appropriation. This gives it enormous influence with the independents. While Congress retains ultimate control over agency funding, OMB sets the stage and the terms of the debate.

For example, CPSC received a proposed budget cut of 30 percent from OMB in February. No reason was given then for such a drastic cutback; for two months, there was not even a written document reflecting the OMB directive. Hardly any guidance was given on how CPSC should absorb that reduction. Yet the OMB proposal has become the basis not only for congressional debate on our budget but also for the amounts to be authorized by our oversight committees in both houses. With that kind of power, the administration has the "independent" regulatory commission on a very tight rein.

White House authority extends to other areas. OMB can review and veto an independent agency's information requests to industry and thereby frustrate agency investigation. OMB also sets personnel ceilings—how much staff an agency can have, regardless of how much money Congress appropriates. And they can—at a moment's notice—freeze all hiring activities. Finally, although independent agencies are not subject to executive orders, the pressures are intense to comply "voluntarily" with those directives. Congress often questions agencies about whether and how they are responding to those orders. The independent regulatory commissions have little recourse but to conform.

Congress has been no less energetic than the president in asserting its influence over the independent regulatory commissions. Funds may be slashed, or the reauthorization period may be shortened to give added leverage. For example, the CPSC may receive a double whammy this time around: a 30 percent budget cut and a short lease on life that may have to be renewed under still less favorable circumstances. Nothing is more likely to make a bold agency timid—reluctant to fully use its statutory powers.

Congress also does a lot of tugging and pulling through its oversight committees. Congress can and does call agencies on the carpet to investigate or cease inquiring into specific issues or cases, and minces no words in expressing its opinion about how the agency should proceed.

Finally, all the recent hue and cry about legislative veto indicates Congress' changing attitude toward independence. Basically, the veto idea gives Congress a simple mechanism with which to summarily overrule an agency's decision. Congress can already accomplish the same end through legislation itself. The legislative veto simply injects the congressional influence earlier and more quickly. When Congress decides to pass on agency rules even before they have had a trial run, agencies will become gun-shy, and their coveted independence will become even less meaningful.

Independence involves trade-offs. For too long it has survived by tradition alone, and it is time to reevaluate the whole concept.

To prevent the president from tackling large sectors of the economy that are regulated by a host of independent regulatory commissions—established and preserved largely through historical accident—may well be self-defeating. Despite all his powers, the president cannot today direct all the major players in the federal government to follow the same tune. Unless some compelling reason dictates otherwise, the president should have sufficient authority to coordinate the activities of as many of the federal agencies as possible. We should reevaluate case-by-case the current need for the independent commission structure. The CPSC would be a prime candidate for pilot-testing the idea of a single agency head.

We may need to retain a strong, independent presence in especially sensitive areas, such as those involving the allocation of scarce resources, or where the underlying function tends to be more analogous to adjudicating individual cases rather than issuing broad-based rules affecting industry as a whole.

Independent commissions diminish the power of the president to formulate and direct policy. Still, these commissions represent a valuable means of relieving some of the political pressures in the decision making of a representative government.

But tradition and happenstance should not dictate that independence be maintained. Some agencies that needed to be independent at an earlier time may not now have that same need. The evolution of watchdog media and public-interest groups, widespread openness in government decision making, toughened conflict-of-interest laws, and increased judicial review may be more than enough to guard against favoritism or impropriety.

THREE
TWO VIEWS ON THE STRUCTURE OF REGULATORY COMMISSIONS
Counterpoint

R. David Pittle

Here's an intriguing idea: Let's take the Securities and Exchange Commission, the Federal Trade Commission, the Consumer Product Safety Commission, and perhaps even the Federal Reserve Board, and put them into a cabinet department—say, Commerce—where the president, through the secretary of commerce, can direct their activities as he sees fit. Sound interesting? It would be the logical extension of a proposal by my colleague at the CPSC, Stuart Statler, to reexamine the concept of independent agencies with an eye toward abolishing them except where a "compelling reason" dictates otherwise.

Statler's notion is that independence began as a "historical accident" at the Interstate Commerce Commission in 1889 and spread without real scrutiny into modern times. But that idea conveniently ignores a multitude of studies, including one by the Senate Committee on Governmental Affairs in 1977 (when Statler served as minority counsel to the committee), that have examined the issue of agency independence repeatedly over the years. And, for the most part, those studies have concluded that independence is a good thing. Last year, for example, Congress rejected a recommendation to abolish independence at the Nuclear Regulatory Commission. According to the Senate committee report on the NRC:

> That particular form of government has been used in various circumstances by Congress for more than 90 years. It is not, however, a musty historical concept. Within the past 10 years, in four different areas of regulation, Congress has seen fit to either estab-

This selection and Chapter 2 are companion pieces, and both are taken from *Legal Times* III (May 9, 1981), 9–17. Used by permission of the publisher and author.

lish or continue independent commissions. Thus, Congressional commitment to this form retains modern day vitality. . . .

My colleague's argument that congressional haphazardness in establishing independence constitutes its "most immediate failing" puzzles me. Independence undoubtedly has been applied inconsistently over the years. So what? Knowing that simply tells us, not unsurprisingly, that Congress' views sometimes change. However, it does not tell us whether independence is good or bad. Statler's logic could just as easily lead to the conclusion that nonindependent agencies like the Food and Drug Administration or the Occupational Safety and Health Administration should be made independent.

Perhaps the biggest problem with Commissioner Statler's proposal is that he bases it on fundamentally contradictory arguments. On the one hand, he claims that presidential controls and influences have recently so overwhelmed agency independence that these bodies often have little recourse but to conform to executive direction. On the other hand, he insists that independent agencies have so much insulation from presidential authority that they constitute a major obstacle to White House policies. He cannot have it both ways; either independence has vitality or it does not. He should decide which he believes.

PUBLIC POLICY

I disagree with the call for less independence. I believe, on balance, that sound public policy supports the existence of independence as practiced at agencies like the SEC, FTC, NRC, and CPSC. Independence is a relative concept. Compared to federal courts where judges gain lifetime appointments, regulatory agencies have little independence. Also, compared to federal courts, where a single judge can invalidate a major piece of legislation, these agencies have little capacity to prevent a president from implementing his overall policies. However, compared to agencies like OSHA or the Environmental Protection Agency, they do nevertheless have a meaningful measure of independence. Their regulatory decisions, once made—usually after years of study and development and often spanning different presidential administrations—cannot be instantly reversed by an official within the executive branch after an hour's acquaintance with the issue.

Having been a commissioner for more than seven years, through the Nixon, Ford, Carter, and now Reagan administrations, I support independence because I believe that regulatory decisions should be made on the merits, to as great an extent as possible, free from partisan, political considerations. Independence does not guarantee wisdom, competence, or careful deliberation. But it does create an atmosphere in which decision makers seek to establish policies that promote the broadest public interest rather than simply to satisfy political special interests.

From my experience, the worst decisions at the CPSC—harmful both to industry and consumers—have occurred when the atmosphere at the agency has been "politicized" for one reason or another. I believe that most careful observers of the CPSC would agree.

Agencies should be in harmony with the *overall* policies and goals of the president. The president has ample authority to ensure this in a variety of ways—appointments, budget, personnel ceilings, cajolery. However, this does not mean that the president, or more likely, an assistant secretary of commerce, should be able to dictate every decision of an agency. Industry and consumers want regulatory policy to be more stable and predictable than that.

What we need for independence to work properly are competent, responsive appointees, vigorous oversight, and carefully wrought legislative mandates. Simply changing agency structure will lead only to the state of affairs described by banker Alan Stults: "Our problems are mostly behind us—what we have to do now is fight the solutions."

SINGLE ADMINISTRATOR

Statler's argument for a single-administrator structure of regulatory agencies is equally unconvincing. Congress has repeatedly opted for independent collegial bodies for a variety of sound reasons:

Thoughtful decisions: A fundamental premise of a free society is that policy ideas should compete for approval. A collegial system where members with a variety of backgrounds and perspectives—but of equal policymaking stature—debate complex issues is far more likely to air all sides of matters and reach thoughtful decisions than a single decision maker.

Statler would argue that diverse opinion and input could be achieved by an able administrator who selects dynamic advisers. But what about the tyrannical administrator we have all experienced at one time or another? In a collegial setting, one must hear differing views; in a single-decision-maker setting, one may hear only "Yes, boss, whatever you want!"

Greater staff objectivity: When staff members slant reports or recommendations to comport with views of superiors, serious problems arise. Collegial bodies usually avoid "slanted" staff reports because documents favoring one commissioner's views are likely to be challenged by a commissioner with an opposing view. Under a single administrator, this may not be so—why explore an option, however promising, that the agency head won't buy?

Stability: A collegial body whose members serve staggered terms provides policy stability and predictability. In my experience, new members learn from old members (and vice versa).

Openness: The "Government in the Sunshine" Act requires that collegial bodies open decision-making meetings to the public. Single administrators are exempt.

However, ignoring the old maxim, "If it ain't broke, don't fix it," Statler has resurrected the following charges:

Group management: In 1971, the Ash Council insisted that "Commissions of five, seven, or eleven nearly coequal members cannot, on the whole, satisfactorily perform the management functions necessary for effective regulation." My colleague repeats that charge. I agree. How could any organization get work done if the top honchos spent their time voting on whether to buy white or pink toilet paper? However, *no* federal regulatory agency functions this way.

The prestigious Administrative Conference of the United States called the Ash Council conclusions "simplistic" and "unsupported by empirical data." Professor Kenneth Culp Davis, an expert on American administrative law, commented that the council adopted its views "without analysis of facts or experience."

The fundamental flaw in the council's reasoning, as well as in Statler's, is the assertion that collegial agencies operate by "group management." According to an empirical study by Professor David M. Welborn, recent legislation and management techniques have given agency chairmen the administrative authority they need to run their agencies efficiently:

> It appears . . . that regulatory agency structure has proved to be much more flexible and adaptive than was assumed by the [Ash] Council. The tendency has been for the chairmanship to develop in such a way as to be capable of meeting many, if not all, of the requirements associated with effective regulatory program management. . . .

For example, at the CPSC, the chairman, by statute, exercises "all of the executive and administrative functions of the Commission. . . ." Since the agency began, each CPSC chairman has made all the day-to-day operating decisions.

In short, Statler has denounced a nonexistent problem.

ACT PROMPTLY

Emergencies: Another criticism is that collegial health and safety agencies are unable to respond to emergencies. This charge, first raised by the Kemeny Commission against the NRC did not convince Congress or the president to abolish NRC collegiality. Of course, emergencies of the potentially catastrophic NRC type do not arise at most agencies.

Speaking as a regulator for seven years, I believe that collegial bodies act promptly. The key is thoughtful delegation of authority (something that single administrators should also do). When emergencies occur, the CPSC relies on its enforcement staff, operating within commission guidelines, to conduct negotiations and file lawsuits. Commissioners do not expect to manage most crises on a day-to-day basis.

Further, although I intend this as an observation and not a criticism. I doubt that single-administrator agencies have demonstrated noticeably shorter response times to emergencies than collegial agencies.

Cost: Statler alleges that government wastes several hundred million dollars on collegiality. He is wrong. Admittedly, the care and feeding of additional commissioners costs money. However, if the CPSC is any guide, these costs are minor—less than 2 percent of the agency's budget. Even counting "indirect" costs, such as extra briefings or meetings, the costs are small. And collegiality produces better decisions. Moreover, single administrators require briefings and meetings just as collegial bodies do.

Besides, who would replace commissioners if collegiality were killed? One could see a growth in the personal staff of the administrator, then the addition of deputies and assistants with their staffs. Thus the savings attributed to having a single administrator might prove negligible.

Quality of regulators: Critics also argue that talented persons will reject appointments to collegial bodies. The Administrative Conference strongly challenged for criticism:

> Prior experience suggests that the quality of personnel in federal regulatory agencies, whether headed by a single administrator or by a collegial body, is highly variable from

agency to agency and from time to time. Other factors appear to have greater influence than agency strucure on personnel quality.

DUMPING GROUNDS

Collegial agencies have many outstanding members just as single-administrator agencies have duds. The problem lies not with the willingness of outstanding people to serve, but with the regrettable tendency of some presidents to use agencies, both collegial and single-administrator, as "dumping grounds" for political cronies.

I am particularly distressed at the recent suggestion of some (not my colleague) that the CPSC be placed in the Department of Commerce—under an assistant secretary. A body that *regulates* commerce should not be directed by one that *promotes* commerce.

Given the staleness and weakness of the "anticollegiality" case, the only explanation for its reappearance lies with Washington Irving: "[t]here is a certain relief in change, even though it be from bad to worse. . . ." I don't see that collegiality is bad. I do see mere change for the sake of change being hyped as reform.

FOUR
THE REFORMATION OF AMERICAN ADMINISTRATIVE LAW

Richard B. Stewart

American administrative law is undergoing a fundamental transformation that calls into question its appropriate role in our legal system. This transformation is largely the handiwork of federal judges, and it is upon their efforts, and its implications, that this article will focus.

The traditional model of administrative law, developed out of judicial decisions and legislative enactment during the first six decades of this century, has sought to reconcile the competing claims of governmental authority and private autonomy by prohibiting official intrusions on private liberty or property unless authorized by legislative directives. To promote this end, the traditional model affords judicial review in order to cabin administrative discretion within statutory bounds, and requires agencies to follow decisional procedures designed to promote the accuracy, rationality, and reviewability of agency application of legislative directives.

Two fundamental criticisms have been levied against the traditional model. First, it has been asserted that the limitation of the traditional model's protections to recognized liberty and property interests is no longer appropriate in view of the seemingly inexorable expansion of governmental power over private welfare. Second, it has been argued that agencies have failed to discharge their respective mandates to protect the interests of the public in given fields of administration, and that the traditional model has been unable to remedy such failure.

This selection is taken from the *Harvard Law Review* 88 (June 1975), 1669–1687. Copyright ©1975 by The Harvard Law Review Association. Used by permission of the publisher and author. Footnotes omitted.

In response to these criticisms, judges have greatly extended the machinery of the traditional model to protect new classes of interests. In the space of a few years the Supreme Court has largely eliminated the doctrine of standing as a barrier to challenging agency action in court, and judges have accorded a wide variety of affected interests the right not only to participate in, but to force the initiation of, formal proceedings before the agency. Indeed, this process has gone beyond the mere extension of participation and standing rights, working a fundamental transformation of the traditional model. Increasingly, the function of administrative law is not the protection of private autonomy but the provision of a surrogate political process to ensure the fair representation of a wide range of affected interests in the process of administrative decision. Whether this is a coherent or workable aim is an open issue. But there is no denying the importance of the transformation.

I. THE TRADITIONAL MODEL AND THE PROBLEM OF DISCRETION

An appreciation of the logic and operation of the traditional model of administrative law is essential to the understanding of its current transformation. Thus an account of the traditional model's premises and development is a necessary prelude to the principal subject of this article.

A. The Traditional Model

Our inquiry into the traditional model of American administrative law begins with the developments generated by the regulation of private business conduct which commenced on a broad scale in the latter part of the nineteenth century. The direct control by state, and then federal, administrative officials of rates, services, and other practices, first of railroads and then of a wide variety of other enterprises, grew so pervasive and intrusive that it could not be justified by reference to past executive practices. Accordingly, a body of doctrines and techniques developed to reconcile the new assertions of governmental power with a long-standing solicitude for private liberties by means of controls that served both to limit and legitimate such power. During the period 1880–1960 a coherent set of principles emerged. Though not fully applicable to every exercise of administrative power, this body of doctrine has nonetheless enjoyed such widespread acceptance that it may be termed the traditional model of administrative law. Its essential elements are:

(1) The imposition of administratively determined sanctions on private individuals must be authorized by the legislature through rules which control agency action. With the possible exceptions of military and foreign-affairs functions and times of national emergency, the Constitution recognizes no inherent administrative powers over persons and property. Coercive controls on private conduct must be authorized by the legislature and, under the doctrine against delegation of legislative power, the legislature must promulgate rules, standards, goals, or some "intelligible principle" to guide the exercise of administrative power.

The doctrine against delegation appears ultimately to be bottomed on contractarian political theory running back to Hobbes and Locke, under which consent is the only legitimate basis for the exercise of the coercive power of government. Since the process of consent is institutionalized in the legislature, that body must authorize any new official imposition of sanctions on private persons; such persons in turn enjoy a correlative right to repel official instrusions not so authorized. These principles would, however, be deprived of all practical significance were the legislature permitted to delegate its lawmaking power in gross. Choices among competing social policies would be made by nonelected executive officials. Moreover, the absence of meaningful statutory controls on agencies would deprive citizens of effective protections against the abusive exercise of administrative power; the legislature could not exercise continuous supervision of all agency actions, and without a guiding statutory directive the courts would have no benchmark against which to measure assertions of agency power.

The requirement that agencies conform to specific legislative directives not only legitimates administrative action by reference to higher authority but also curbs officials' exploitation of the governmental apparatus to give vent to private prejudice or passion. At the same time, private autonomy is secured in two ways by such a requirement. First, it promotes formal justice by ensuring that the governmental sanctions faced by an individual are rule-governed, which facilitates private avoidance of sanctions and allows interaction with the government on terms most advantageous to the individual. Second, on contractarian premises, the requirement ensures that sanctions have been validated by a governmental authority to which the individual has consented and therefore the restraints imposed by the threat of sanctions may be viewed as self-imposed.

(2) The decisional procedures followed by the agency must be such as will tend to ensure the agency's compliance with requirement (1). If agencies may exercise delegated powers only in accordance with legislative directives, and if effective limitation on administrative power is not to be more theoretical than real, agency procedures must be designed to promote the accurate, impartial, and rational application of legislative directives to given cases or classes of cases. Thus where the facts that would justify governmental action are disputed and important liberty or property interests are at stake, a hearing is generally required in which the person whose interests are threatened has the opportunity to present evidence and challenge the factual and legal bases for the agency's action. Moreover, the agency must normally decide the matter on the basis of the record developed at the hearing through factfindings supported by substantial evidence and the reasoned application of legislative directives to the facts found.

(3) The decisional processes of the agency must facilitate judicial review to ensure agency compliance with requirements (1) and (2).

(4) Judicial review must be available to ensure compliance with requirements (1) and (2). To ensure that administrative sanctions are imposed only in accordance with general legislative rules, judicial review is not a logical necessity. The combination of legislative supervision, popular opinion, and bureaucratic tradition might conceivably be adequate to ensure a tolerable degree of agency compliance with legislative directives. But such a view would rest on assumptions that with us appear too optimistic. Judicial review is normally available as an additional assurance that agencies not exceed their authorized powers. As a further corollary, agency decisional processes and findings must be adequate to permit the judge to ascertain with reasonable assurance whether the legislative directive was correctly observed in each case.

The traditional model of administrative law thus conceives of the agency as a mere transmission belt for implementing legislative directives in particular cases. It legitimates intrusions into private liberties by agency officials not subject to electoral control by ensuring that such intrusions are commanded by a legitimate source of authority—the legislature. Requiring agencies to show that intrusions on private liberties have been directed by the legislature provides a rationale for judicial review and also serves to define the appropriate role of the courts vis-à-vis the agencies. The court's function is one of containment; review is directed toward keeping the agency within the directives which Congress has issued. On the other hand, this conception of the reviewing function implies that the court is to pass upon only those matters as to which the statute provides ascertainable direction; all other issues of choice, whether general or interstitial, are for the agency. By subjecting agency impositions of sanctions to judicial review in order to ensure compliance with legislative directives, the traditional model of administrative law also seeks to mediate the inconsistency between the doctrine of separation of government powers and the agencies' conspicuous combination of various lawmaking and law-enforcing functions. To the extent that the separation-of-powers doctrine is construed as demanding only that the exercise of power by one organ of government be subject to check by some other governmental body, the traditional model furnishes such a check through the judiciary.

B. The Problem of Discretion

Vague, general, or ambiguous statutes create discretion and threaten the legitimacy of agency action under the "transmission belt" theory of administrative law. Insofar as statutes do not effectively dictate agency actions, individual autonomy is vulnerable to the imposition of sanctions at the unruled will of executive officials, major questions of social and economic policy are determined by officials who are not formally accountable to the electorate, and both the checking and validating functions of the traditional model are impaired. However, rather than being the exception, federal legislation establishing agency charters has, over the past several decades, often been strikingly broad and nonspecific, and has accordingly generated the very conditions which the traditional model was designed to eliminate.

So long as administrative power was kept within relatively narrow bounds and did not intrude seriously on vested private interests, the problem of agency discretion could be papered over by applying plausible labels, such as "quasi-judicial" or "quasi-legislative," designed to assimilate agency powers to those exercised by traditional governmental organs. But after the delegation by New Deal Congresses of sweeping powers to a host of new agencies under legislative directives cast in the most general terms, the broad and novel character of agency discretion could no longer be concealed behind such labels.

Defenders flaunted the breadth of the discretion afforded the new agencies by Congress, maintaining that such discretion was necessary if the agencies were to discharge their planning and managerial functions successfully and restore health to the various sectors of the economy for which they were responsible. Given the assumption that the agencies' role was that of manager or planner with an ascertainable goal, "expertise" could plausibly be advocated as a solution to the problem of discretion if the agency's goal could be realized through the knowledge that comes from specialized experience. For in that case the discretion that the administrator enjoys is more apparent than real. The policy to be set is simply a function of the goal to be achieved and the state of the world. There may be a trial-and-error process in finding the best means of achieving the posited goal, but persons subject to the administrator's control are no more liable to his arbitrary will than are patients remitted to the care of a skilled doctor. This analysis underlay the notion that administrators were not political, but professional, and that public administration has an objective basis. It also supported arguments by New Deal defenders that it would be unwise for the Congress to lay down detailed prescriptions in advance, and intolerably inefficient to require administrators to follow rigid judicial procedures.

However, many lawyers remained unpersuaded, and attacked the delegation of broad discretion to administrators as violative of the principles of separation of powers and formal justice which the traditional model was designed to serve. In theory the traditional model might have been effectively used to curtail the discretionary exercise by agencies of broadly delegated powers through a rigorous application of the nondelegation doctrine to require greater specificity in legislative directives. This solution, however, proved unworkable because of difficulties in implementing the doctrine and because of the institutional hazards involved in persistent, wholesale invalidation by courts of broad legislative directives. Instead, the courts, reacting in part to the Administrative Procedure Act and its history, turned to a number of alternative (and more enduring) techniques to control the exercise of administrative discretion.

First, by undertaking a more searching scrutiny of the substantiality of the evidence supporting agency fact-finding and by insisting on a wider range of procedural safeguards, the courts have required agencies to adhere more scrupulously to the norms of the traditional model. This judicial stance has promoted more accurate application of legislative directives. Additionally, more rigorous enforcement of procedural requirements, such as hearings, may have influenced agencies' exercise of their discretion and may have served as a partial substitute for political safeguards by, for example, facilitating input from affected interests. These developments may also have reduced effective agency power by affording litigating tools to resistant private interests and by providing judges with an additional basis for setting aside decisions.

A second technique which was developed to control the broad discretion granted by New Deal legislation was the requirement of reasoned consistency in agency decision making. Under this doctrine, an agency might be required to articulate the reasons for reaching a choice in a given case even though the loose texture of its legislative directive allowed a range of possible choices. Courts might also impose the further requirement that choices over time be consistent, or at least that departures from established policies be persuasively justified, particularly where significant individual expectation interests were involved. Again, these requirements were not directly addressed to the substance of agency policy. Their aim was, and is, simply to ensure that the agency's action is rationally related to the achievement of some permissible societal goal, and to promote formal justice in order to protect private autonomy. Yet these requirements may also have an impact on the substance of agency policy. A requirement of reasoned consistency may hobble the agency in adapting to new contingencies or in dealing with an individual case of abuse whose basis is not easily susceptible to generalized statements, and such a requirement may provide additional tools for litigants resisting agency sanctions and for judges seeking procedural grounds for setting aside dubious decisions.

Third, courts began to demand a clear statement of legislative purpose as a means of restraining the range of agency choice when fundamental individual liberties were at risk. A paradigm example is *Kent* v. *Dulles,* where Congress had made an apparently unrestricted grant of discretion to the president and secretary of state to issue passports, and the secretary had denied passports to persons with alleged Communist associations or sympathies. Stressing that a constitutionally protected "liberty" of travel was involved, the Court held that broad delegations of power would be construed narrowly in such cases and that, since Congress had not specifically authorized a refusal to issue passports on the grounds here asserted, the refusal was invalid. The technique has since been utilized in a variety of contexts to protect important individual interests where the agency had followed questionable procedures or dubious substantive policies. The technique is more discriminating than the nondelegation doctrine; it substitutes tactical excision for wholesale invalidation.

These various techniques, which matured in the twenty years after the enactment of the APA, were well adapted to selective application, and could be utilized to trim agency powers without intruding upon the major bulk of delegated authority implicit in a statutory scheme. Through adroit application of these control techniques, an uneasy truce between administrators and judges developed into working accommodation.

C. The Problem of Discretion Renewed

Today it is obvious that this working compromise has come unstuck. Judicial review once again "gives a sense of battle." Criticism of agency policies is widespread and vociferous.

One strand of this criticism has focused on the assertedly unlawful and abusive exercise of administrative power in areas where the traditional model has seldom applied and the private interests most directly at stake had not enjoyed its protections. These areas include interests in the continuation of advantageous relations with the government (such as the receipt of welfare benefits and eligibility to bid on government contracts) that had not been regarded as within the realm of legally protected liberty or property, and interests in avoiding sanctions imposed by agencies (such as prison authorities and school officials) that had hitherto been accorded considerable immunity from judicial review. Critics have asserted that such interests represent an important aspect of private autonomy and that they are at least as deserving of protection against unauthorized official power as traditional liberty and property interests. The obvious solution is the extension of the traditional model to protect these additional classes of private interests.

A second theme of contemporary criticism of agency discretion has been the agencies' asserted failure affirmatively to carry out legislative mandates and to protect the collective interests that administrative regimes are designed to serve. The possibility of such failure was no concern of the traditional model, which was directed at protecting private autonomy by curbing agency power. It was simply assumed that agency zeal in advancing the "unalloyed, nonpolitical, long-run economic interest of the general public" would be assured by the professionalism of administrators or by political mechanisms through which the administrative branch would "eternally [refresh] its vigor from the stream of democratic desires."

Experience has withered this faith. To the extent that belief in an objective "public interest" remains, the agencies are accused of subverting it in favor of the private interests of regulated and client firms. Such a "devil" theory at least holds out the possibility of redemption. However, we have come not only to question the agencies' ability to protect the "public interest" but to doubt the very existence of an ascertainable "national welfare" as a meaningful guide to administrative decision. Exposure on the one hand to the complexities of a managed economy in a welfare state, and on the other to the corrosive seduction of welfare economics and pluralist political analysis, has sapped faith in the existence of an objective basis for social choice.

Today, the exercise of agency discretion is inevitably seen as the essentially legislative process of adjusting the competing claims of various private interests affected by agency policy. The unraveling of the notion of an objective goal for administration is reflected in statements by judges and legal commentators that the "public interest is a texture of multiple strands," that it "is not a monolith," and "involves a balance of many interests." Courts have asserted that agencies must consider all of the various interests affected by their decisions as an essential predicate to "balancing all elements essential to a just determination of the public interest."

Once the function of agencies is conceptualized as adjusting competing private interests in light of their configuration in a given factual situation and the policies reflected in relevant statutes, it is not possible to legitimate agency action by either the "transmission belt" theory of the traditional model, or the "expertise" model of the New Deal period. The "transmission belt" fails because broad legislative directives will rarely dispose of particular cases once the relevant facts have been accurately ascertained. More frequently, the application of legislative directives requires the agency to reweigh and reconcile the often nebulous or conflicting policies behind the directives in the context of a particular factual situation with a particular constellation of affected interests. The required balancing of policies is an inherently discretionary, ultimately political procedure. Similarly, the "economic manager" defense of administrative discretion—under which discretion was bound by an ascertainable goal, the state of the world, and an applicable technique—has been eroded by the relatively steady economic growth since World War II, which has allowed attention to be focused on the perplexing distributional questions of how the fruits of affluence are to be shared. Such choices clearly do not turn on technical issues that can safely be left to the experts.

The sense of uneasiness aroused by this resurgence of discretion is heightened by perceived biases in the results of the agency-balancing process as it is currently carried on. Critics have repeatedly asserted, with a dogmatic tone that reflects settled opinion, that in carrying out broad legislative directives, agencies unduly favor organized interests, especially the interests of regulated or client business firms and other organized groups at the expense of diffuse, comparatively unorganized interests such as consumers, environmentalists, and the poor. In the midst of a "growing sense of disillusion with the role which regulatory agencies play," many legislators, judges, and legal and economic commentators have accepted the thesis of persistent bias in agency policies. At its crudest, this thesis is based on the "capture" scenario, in which administrations are systematically controlled, sometimes corruptly, by the business firms within their orbit of responsibility, whether regulatory or promotional. But there are more subtle explanations of industry orientation, which include the following:

First. The division of responsibility between the regulated firms, which retain primary control over their own affairs, and the administrator, whose power is essentially negative and who is dependent on industry cooperation in order to achieve his objectives, places the administrator in an inherently weak position. The administrator will, nonetheless, be held responsible if the industry suffers serious economic dislocation. For both of these reasons, he may pursue conservative policies.

Second. The regulatory bureaucracy becomes "regulation minded." It seeks to elaborate and perfect the controls it exercises over the regulated industry. The effect of this tendency, particularly in a regime of limited entry, is to eliminate actual and potential competition and buttress the position of the established firms.

Third. The resources—in terms of money, personnel, and political influence—of the regulatory agency are limited in comparison to those of regulated firms. Unremitting maintenance of an adversary posture would quickly dissipate agency resources. Hence, the agency must compromise with the regulated industry if it is to accomplish anything of significance.

Fourth. Limited agency resources imply that agencies must depend on outside sources of information, policy development, and political support. This outside input comes primarily from organized interests, such as regulated firms, that have a substantial stake in the substance of agency policy and the resources to provide such input. By contrast, the personal stake in agency policy of an individual member of an unorganized interest, such as a consumer, is normally too small to justify such representation. Effective representation of unorganized interests might be possible if a means of pooling resources to share the costs of underwriting collective representation were available. But this seems unlikely since the transaction costs of creating an organization of interest group members increase disproportionately as the size of the group increases. Moreover, if membership in such an organization is voluntary, individuals will not have a strong incentive to join, since if others represent the interests involved, the benefits will accrue not only to those participating in the representation, but to nonparticipants as well, who can, therefore, enjoy the benefits without incurring any of the costs (the free rider effect). As a somewhat disillusioned James Landis wrote in 1960, the result is industry dominance in representation, which has a "daily machine-gun-like impact on both [an] agency and its staff" that tends to create an industry bias in the agency's outlook.

These various theses of systematic bias in agency policy are not universally valid. Political pressures and judicial controls may force continuing agency adherence to policies demonstrably inimical to the interests of the regulated industry, as in the case of FPC regulation of natural gas producer prices. Moreover the fact that agency policies may tend to favor regulated interests does not in itself demonstrate that such policies are unfair or unjustified, since protection of regulated interests may be implicit in the regulatory scheme established by Congress. Nonetheless, the critique of agency discretion as unduly favorable to organized interests—particularly regulated or client firms—has sufficient power and verisimilitude to have achieved widespread contemporary acceptance.

The traditional model provides scant assistance in dealing with the problem of agencies' failure to exercise discretion under broad statutory directives so as to discharge their responsibilities equitably and effectively. The traditional model is an essentially negative instrument for checking governmental power; it does not touch "the affirmative side" of government "which has to do with the representation of individuals and interests" and the development of governmental policies on their behalf. Thus the protections of the traditional model have normally applied only to formal agency proceedings eventuating in sanctions on regulated firms. Those interests that have assertedly been disregarded by the agencies—notably beneficiaries of the administrative scheme—have not been subject to sanctions and thus have normally not been entitled to invoke the protections of the traditional model. Many of the policy decisions most strongly attacked by agency critics—the failure to prosecute vigorously, the working out of agency policy by negotiation with regulated firms, the quiet settlement of litigation once initiated—take place through informal procedures where the traditional controls have not normally applied.

FIVE
THE CHANGING FACE OF GOVERNMENT REGULATION

A. Lee Fritschler

The extent to which government should regulate private enterprise is today one of the most important political and economic issues facing the country. A few years ago, one heard little about deregulation or about regulatory reform. University courses were seldom offered on the subject; journal articles were seldom written; and attempts to do something—anything—about streamlining the regulatory process were greeted with wide yawns on Capitol Hill.

Not so today. Nearly 200 pieces of regulatory reform legislation were considered by the ninety-sixth Congress. They included measures to eliminate programs, extend the legislative veto, clip the jurisdiction of various regulatory agencies, and change administrative procedures. One would have gone so far as to reverse the fundamental delegation premise upon which most regulatory agencies operate.

This last proposal, the Bumpers Amendment, named after its sponsor, Senator Dale Bumpers of Arkansas, would forbid the courts that review administrative agencies' actions to defer to agency interpretation of the basic statute or to presume that agency action is valid. The amendment would abolish the deference currently given agencies in the interpretation of the statutes which they administer. It would require courts to consider any challenge to the agency's interpretation of its enabling statute as a fresh issue of law.

In so doing, it challenges one of the main reasons for the creation of regulatory agencies in the first place—delegation to them of a fragment of the legislative power.

This essay grew out of a 1981 speech which was given at and was later published by *The Maxwell School of Citizenship and Public Affairs* at Syracuse University. Used by permission of the publisher and author.

The Bumpers Amendment would seriously damage the historical development of the delegation doctrine and interrupt the continuity between Congress and the regulatory agencies it created. If it is recognized that when an agency sets rates or fixes air-quality standards it is exercising a subordinate part of the legislative power, what justification is there for requiring the agency to prove that its order is consistent with the statutory standard? We can, if we like, analogize the situation to a constitutional challenge to an act of Congress. No one would argue that the burden is on the government to prove that the law is consistent with the Constitution; the burden lies on the challenging party. To the extent that agency regulations are a continuation of the legislative process, the same reasoning should apply.

There is another less theoretical reason for rejecting the approach taken by Senator Bumpers. Interpretation and implementation of regulatory policy by the administrative agency designated by Congress to perform that task permits a nationally uniform scheme of regulation. The presumption of validity which presently attaches to agency action helps to preserve that uniformity. On the other hand, the federal court system is decentralized. Were the Bumpers Amendment adopted, the potential for conflicts among the federal courts would increase substantially. When applying the minutiae of regulatory statutes in highly technical areas, there is much room for reasonable people to differ—all the more reason to try to achieve uniformity by delegating a reasonable power of interpretation to a single body staffed by knowledgeable professionals. After all, not every choice made by agencies can be expressed as a legal issue, of the kind courts are best equipped to decide. On balance the Bumpers Amendment would detract from the regulatory process—overloading the courts, where delays are already anything but brief. It is unlikely to further the objectives Congress had in mind when it enacted the various regulatory statutes.

If Congress believes that regulatory agencies habitually exceed their mandates, the best remedy may be more specific and tightly drawn legislation. Neither courts nor agencies are likely to indulge in extensive "interpretation" if the statute itself if explicit enough. If Congress makes its wishes unmistakably clear, the courts should need no special powers in order to correct an errant agency.

The Carter administration is opposed to the amendment. In other areas it is taking an active role in refining the regulatory process and offering new initiatives. It is working closely with the Congress to develop comprehensive reform legislation. The administration has indicated, however, that it will not support legislative initiatives that paralyze those regulatory functions which are needed to serve the public. The administration's goals in regulatory reform are to let the market, rather than a government agency, secure the benefits of regulation when that is possible, and to make regulation itself a less expensive and time-consuming business. Senator Bumpers' proposal is not aimed at either of these goals; it would simply make it easier to nullify the results of the regulatory process by resort to the courts. There is an irony here. Court reversal of an agency decision almost always leads to yet more regulatory proceedings before the same agency. The Bumpers Amendment might help in those cases where an agency has simply exceeded or distorted its statutory mandate. Those cases are few; real improvements should be sought in improving the speed and flexibility of administration of regulatory statutes, and in allowing market competition to play its proper role whenever it can.

The Bumpers Amendment is radical and dramatic in its impact, reversing years of careful regulatory development. Even so, it has received widespread and strong support in the House of Representatives and passed in the Senate. The winds of regulatory reform blew up fast and developed gale force in the ninety-sixth Congress. The Bumpers Amendment is testimony to the ferocity of the storm.

What has given birth to the intense debate on regulatory reform epitomized by the Bumpers Amendment? Why is there such sudden and widespread interest in regulatory reform? What happened to put changes in our regulatory system near the top of the congressional agenda and on the front pages of newspapers across the country?

There are several factors at work. The first and most important is the change in what regulation is used for today as opposed to what it was used for in the quieter days of the past. The major purposes for which regulatory processes are used have shifted from economic and industrial matters to areas of social concern. When regulatory activities of government were focused on the traditional areas of economic regulation there was not much interest in reform. Shifting to social regulation has created a different regulatory environment—one which both business and government are having some difficulty adjusting to.

FROM ECONOMIC TO SOCIAL REGULATION

Businesses grew accustomed to economic regulation, and in many instances learned to profit by it. Regulation was the framework which assured the supply at reasonable terms and prices of the goods and services necessary for economic growth. In fields such as banking and securities, energy, communications and transportation, regulation permitted development while reducing the likelihood of system-wide collapses. During the period of expansion into the west, business was inclined to support big, centralized government, if only for the stability it provided—stability necessary for economic growth.

In the 1960s the picture changed somewhat as a number of social movements gained sufficient political strength to begin using regulatory agencies to achieve their goals. Also, the regulatory legislation passed by Congress in the 1960s and 1970s was significant both in terms of its quantity and shifting focus. Prior to that time, there was very little social regulation written by Congress. Since then, congressional efforts have been almost exclusively focused on social areas, while new initiatives in economic and industrial areas have been few. The listing of major regulatory programs in chronological order by the year they were established shows this shift in emphasis (see Table 5-1). It is a shift from a type of regulation which concentrates on the relations among seller, competitor, and customer—begun seriously in 1887 with the ICC regulation of railroads—to the regulation of a host of other relations focused on the health of the work force, the quality of the environment in the area impacted by the regulated firm, and so on.

One can argue that by the 1960s the nation had a lot of catching up to do in the social area. That might well be true. But what is undeniable is that the regulatory process to which the nation had grown accustomed over nearly 100 years of gradual development was suddenly being asked to solve problems far different from those it had been designed to solve.

Regulation now affects areas of management which had not been touched by regulation previously. Industrial and economic regulation generally had a fairly well-defined and narrow focus. Regulatory agencies were mandated to address questions of which kinds of business structures were permissible and which were not, what accounting and financial disclosures were allowed and mandated, prices, and to some extent what might be produced and what might not be. Social regulation, on the other hand, focuses less on the formal means and output of production and more on the side effects of production or externalities in economic parlance. Environmental concerns and the age, sex, and race of the work force are now consid-

TABLE 5-1　Major Regulatory Programs by Year of Birth 1863–1975

DATE	ECONOMIC & INDUSTRIAL REGULATION (AGENCY RESPONSIBLE)	SOCIAL REGULATION (AGENCY RESPONSIBLE)
1863	Chartering and supervision of national banks (Comptroller of the Currency, Department of the Treasury)	
1887	Railroad regulation (Interstate Commerce Commission)	
1906		Food and drug production regulation (Food and Drug Administration, Department of H.H.S.)
1913	Supervision of Federal Reserve Banks and Members Banks (Federal Reserve System)	
1914	Preventing restraints of trade, unfair competition, and false labeling and advertising (Federal Trade Commission)	
1916	Regulation of offshore waterborne commerce (Federal Maritime Commission)	
1916	Regulation of import trade (U.S. International Trade Commission)	
1920	Licensing hydroelectric projects on navigable waters (Federal Energy Regulatory Commission)	
1922	Regulating commodity futures trading (Commodity Futures Trading Commission)	
1932	Supervision and insurance of savings and loan institutions (Federal Home Loan Bank Board)	
1933	Supervision of nonmember state banks; deposit insurance (Federal Deposit Insurance Corporation)	
1933	Prevention of fraud in securities issuance (Securities and Exchange Commission)	
1934	Radio/TV broadcast licensing (Federal Communications Commission)	
1934	Regulation of security exchanges (Securities and Exchange Commission)	
1935	Restructuring and regulation of public utility holding companies (Securities and Exchange Commission)	
1935	Regulation of interstate wholesale electric traffic (Federal Energy Regulation Commission)	
1935		Regulation of collective bargaining (National Labor Relations Board)

The Changing Face of Government Regulation

TABLE 5-1 Continued

DATE	ECONOMIC & INDUSTRIAL REGULATION (AGENCY RESPONSIBLE)	SOCIAL REGULATION (AGENCY RESPONSIBLE)
1935	Regulation of motor carriers (Interstate Commerce Commission)	
1938	Regulation of civil commercial aviation (Civil Aeronautics Board)	
1938	Regulation of interstate natural gas; gas traffic (Federal Energy Regulatory Commission)	
1946	Regulation of civilian uses of atomic energy (Nuclear Regulatory Commission)	
1948		Certification of aircraft types and aircrew (Federal Aviation Administration)
1962		Air-quality regulation (Environmental Protection Agency)
1963		Equal Pay Act (Equal Employment Opportunity Commission)
1964		Prevention of discrimination in employment (Equal Employment Opportunity Commission)
1965		Water quality regulation (Environmental Protection Agency)
1966	Safety regulation of motor carriers (Federal Highway Administration	
1966		Safety regulation of railroads (Federal Railroad Administration)
1966	Safety and efficiency regulation of motor vehicles (Federal Highway Traffic Safety Administration	
1967		Preventing age discrimination in employment (Equal Employment Opportunity Commission)
1968	Full disclosure of credit terms ("Truth in Lending") (Federal Reserve System and Federal Trade Commission)	
1968		Regulate interstate firearms trade (Bureau of Alcohol, Tobacco, and Firearms, Treasury Department)
1970	Promote uniformity of accounting among government contractors (Cost Accounting Standards Board)	

TABLE 5-1 Continued

DATE	ECONOMIC & INDUSTRIAL REGULATION (AGENCY RESPONSIBLE)	SOCIAL REGULATION (AGENCY RESPONSIBLE)
1970		Regulate occupational safety and health performance (Occupational Safety and Health Administration, Labor Department)
1970	Supervise Federal credit unions (National Credit Union Administration)	
1970	Regulate postal rates and classifications (Postal Rate Commission)	
1970		Securing of environmental impact review of federal projects (Environmental Protection Agency)
1972		Regulating safety of consumer products (Consumer Product Safety Commission)
1972		Control of noise pollution (Environmental Protection Agency)
1973		Regulating lawful trade in narcotic drugs (Drug Enforcement Administration, Justice Department)
1973	Oil pricing, allocation, and import regulation (Economic Regulatory Administration, Energy Department)	
1973		Regulation of mine safety (Mine Safety and Health Administration, Labor Department)
1973		Employment of handicapped persons (Employment Standards Administration, Labor Department)
1974		Supervision of pension plans (Pension Benefit Guaranty Corporation)
1975		Transportation accident investigation; regulation of accident reporting (National Transportation Safety Board)

ered legitimate areas for the application of enforcement tools by government regulators.

The change in regulatory focus runs deep. It has affected the old, well-established political coalitions which concern themselves with older, well-established regulatory matters. It has activated those coalitions and forced them to compete in unaccustomed ways with new coalitions involved in social areas. It also has placed heavy demands on the administrative process which has developed over the years to deal principally with economic and industrial issues. These political and procedural changes warrant exploration, for they explain in large part the turmoil underlying regulatory affairs today.

The Changing Face of Government Regulation

ECONOMIC AND SOCIAL REGULATORY PROCESSES COMPARED

Economic and industrial regulation had its beginning in public-utility regulation. This is the traditional form of regulation—primarily exercised at state and local levels—involving the prices and services of electric, gas, water, and transportation firms. Here one should stress the word traditional. The roots of this type of regulation run deep. Seventeenth-century jurisprudence contains references to the need for regulation when an enterprise is "affected with a public interest." Today it is a familiar proposition that where the owner of an enterprise enjoys a monopoly, and the public must use his facilities to satisfy some economic necessity, then the owner must be restrained from exacting monopoly profits.

The seventeenth century was, of course, an age of economic paternalism and control—an environment accommodating to regulation. Yet the government-regulation concept survived the rise of laissez-faire doctrines in later years.

> The tendency for competition to displace public authority in the control of industry was stopped, however, when the turn came to apply the prevalent notion of unrestrained competition to certain public callings. Here the laissez-faire period served, in general, as a test of the merits of the restrictive system. Thus, in the case of these public callings, the essential elements in the medieval framework of regulation survived its general collapse. They continued to be businesses "affected with the public interest." . . . The law continued to require that the prices charged be reasonable.[1]

Here we find elements of both the traditional rationale for the public-utility regulatory mechanism and the current debate over deregulation. When there is good reason to permit a monopoly to exist in a particular market—and this is one of the earmarks of the public-utility enterprise—then we adhere to the ancient idea that its services must be adequate, reasonably priced, and made available to all without discrimination. We provide for governmental compulsion to ensure that these goals are met. But when competition among enterprises is possible, we now look to competition to achieve these same objectives. In this respect, of course, we have come round 180 degrees from the static and hierarchical conceptions of the Middle Ages, when direct governmental control of virtually every form of economic activity was considered natural. A major difference is how we draw a distinction between those enterprises that can be controlled by the marketplace and those that cannot.

Our current debate about deregulation is, or should be, an unprejudiced examination of whether the market can do the job or whether governmental intervention is required.

While the same enterprises that are subject to the traditional public-utility regulation may also be subject to social regulation, the latter has quite different characteristics. An electric utility, for example, may have to answer to (1) the Federal Energy Regulatory Commission and the Public Service Commission of New York for its rates and the quality of its service; (2) the Occupational Safety and Health Administration for the safety of its work environment; and (3) the Environmental Protection Agency for the level of pollutants its plants discharge into the air. The last two examples of regulation, however, differ considerably from the first.

In the first place, the regulation of safety or air quality does not depend on the distribution of economic power as between the enterprise and its customers. The fact that the electric company has a local monopoly neither strengthens nor vitiates

---

[1]M. Glaeser *Public Utilities in American Capitalism* (New York: Macmillan, 1957), p. 205

the case for regulation in these areas. Nor is there any reason to suppose that the introduction of competition between sellers would, by the operation of market forces, automatically cause the enterprises engaged in competition to make their work places safer or their stack gases cleaner. Indeed, it might be argued that competition might have the opposite result, since it would increase the incentive to cut production costs and lower prices.

In the second place, social regulation looks at interests other than those of buyer and seller. In theory, at least, almost any identifiable group affected in almost any way by the operations of an enterprise or industry may have a plausible claim of entitlement to some form of social regulation. Employees at large are affected by the safety of the work place, and so many insist on rules governing railings and light fixtures. Black or female employees may be able to show that they have not been given an equal chance in the labor market, and so call for equal-employment regulations. Citizens who never do a dollar's worth of business with a power company, but who fish in the river downstream from its plant, may demand limits on the amount of hot water it discharges into that stream. In contrast to the context of traditional public-utility regulation, which is a small set of relatively easily defined economic relationships, social regulation has a potentially unlimited field of operation.

Third, social regulation pays far less attention to the individual enterprise than does the traditional public-utility model. As it has developed in this country, public utility rate regulation rests firmly on the individual company's cost-of-service There have been departures from this model—for instance, the regulation of natural-gas producers by the area-rate method—but they have by and large been re sorted to for practical reasons and have been challenged vigorously as departure from the ideal. In general, regulatory commissions have examined the investment and operating costs of a particular company in fixing rates for that one enterpris and in licensing facilities have concentrated on its particular system and the needs its customers. Social regulation, by contrast, focuses on an overall goal which m not even be specific to a particular industry—let alone a particular firm.

This last difference is worth dwelling on since it accounts, in my opinion, fo difference in technique as well as in objectives. The traditional public-utility regu tory model, with its strong focus on individual firms, has given rise to a procedu framework much resembling a lawsuit. The firm makes a proposal to increase rates or build a new generating station or offer a new type of service, and a judi fact-finding process ensures. Supporters and opponents of the proposal are g their "day in court," and well-understood rules of procedural fairness govern proceedings. The regulators themselves may be men or women with substantia dependent knowledge of industry conditions and strongly held opinions regar the correct policy to apply to the industry's problems. But in deciding the case y are required to restrict themselves to information that has been tested adversary. This proposition also holds true when the agency takes the initiative, as in the c of a rate investigation brought against a particular utility. The possibility for fing expeditions might not be limited—but the chances of netting something ce inly are.

Social regulation, on the other hand, proceeds by generalized rule making. The rules governing these procedures are much less rigorous. The whole structure of the federal administrative process, under the legislation that has governe it for over 30 years, depends to a great extent on the notion that many types of rue making (and especially those that affect a broad range of enterprises) follow the procedural model of legislation rather than that of litigation. The public official who imposes a rule in a social regulation context is conceived to be acting in a particularly immediate way as a surrogate for Congress, and the information and expertise on which he can draw are less limited in scope and less subject to challenge by interested parties than would be the case if he were deciding a rate case involving a single company.

It would be possible, especially in these days when the entire subject of bureaucracy and regulation is a favorite discussion topic, to spend many hours debating the fine degrees by which "pure" rule making shades into "pure" adjudication. I think most observers would agree, however, that when a government department issues a substantive rule requiring the installation of some safety device or setting some particular standard for sulfur dioxide emissions, it is legislating in a way that a regulatory commission prescribing new rates for a water company is not. Yet both activities are legislative, in the sense that—given enough time and resources—Congress or a state legislature could enact binding rules requiring a specific treatment of the matter.

POLITICAL DIFFERENCES BETWEEN REGULATORY TYPES

The differences between the two major types of regulation are also political and historical. Economic and industrial regulations have had, over the years, considerable support from business and industry. One hears some complaining about them but it is clear if one looks at the history of these regulations that they often were proposed by business and industry. The Federal Trade Commission, in the period between 1930 and 1955, did little which did not originate in the industrial sector or have political support from industry.

An issue before the FTC in 1968 is a good example of what was common practice during that period. The commission had been asked by the radio manufacturers in the United States to look into a marketing problem. The U.S. market was being flooded by cheap transistor radios. These radios were being advertised as having 10 to 15 transistors in them and they were being sold for $15 or $20. The U.S. radio manufacturers knew that the industry could not produce these radios and sell them at those prices. So, industry representatives purchased several samples and opened them up. They discovered that, in fact, the radios contained the number of advertised transistors but only one or two were part of the circuitry. The others were dummies wired to the chassis.

The FTC heard this complaint and in a short time decided that this was an unfair trade practice. Henceforth radio advertising could only include the number of transistors which were part of the radio circuit: More regulation, more rules, more red tape. Yet this was a regulation the industry wanted badly. It corrected a serious marketing situation.

For years, regulatory processes were used for business purposes. Although one particular industry might not have liked some particular regulation, there was little interest in deregulation because most regulations on government books had some industrial support somewhere. And when regulations have industrial support they are hard to remove. Initially the preponderance of opposition to airline deregulation came from the major airlines, just as the opposition to trucking deregulation came from the licensed carriers. There was little talk about deregulation because the business community knew it benefited generally from economic and industrial regulation. They wanted to continue to be the dominant influence on the regulatory agencies "regulating" them; and they were willing to let other industries enjoy special relationships with regulatory commissions in other areas. A kind of regulatory pork barrel system was at work.

GROWTH OF FEDERAL AGENCIES

One should not be left the impression that industry satisfaction with traditional public-utility regulation was evidence that the regulatory system had betrayed its purpose or had been distorted into a kind of conspiracy against the consumer. One of the purposes of that type of regulation has always been—and one trusts will continue to be—to insure that the regulated enterprise remains sufficiently healthy to render adequate service to all who need it. That makes good sense when we remember that this form of regulation classically applied only to monopoly enterprises. One who can scarcely be accused of pro-industry bias, the late Supreme Court Justice William O. Douglas, put it succinctly in the *Hope Natural Gas* case:

> The rate-making process under the Act, *i.e.*, the fixing of "just and reasonable" rates, involves a balancing of the investor and the consumer interests.[2]

If that balancing is carefully and fairly carried out, *both* the owners and the customers of the regulated firms should have every reason to be satisfied with traditional regulation.

The political characteristics of social regulations are quite different. Their genesis is different from economic and industrial regulation. They were supported initially by large public interest groups, by groups behind important social movements—environmentalists, civil rights advocates, the elderly, and so on.

These newer regulations alter the political support system for regulation. They provide an opportunity for business groups to unite in opposition to regulation, for it is possible to develop a position on social regulation which cuts across industry lines. The history of business interest groups in Washington demonstrates this point. Since 1887, when the Interstate Commerce Commission was established, down to about the mid-1970s, the major lobbying group for business was the U.S. Chamber of Commerce. The chamber was ineffective in developing a "business position" to present to government. It was ineffective because its membership was overly broad. It represented all business and industry—small and large firms, manufacturing, service firms, and so on. For example, when a deregulation argument came up, the chamber did not know which side to take. The Chamber of Commerce took no position at all on airline deregulation because it represented both the major trunk carriers which benefited from regulation and the smaller airlines which would benefit from deregulation. There was a standoff in industry which was mirrored in the chamber.

In 1972, a new group was founded called the Business Roundtable. It is made up of 180 chief executive officers of 180 large corporations. It emerged from the idea that there were new issues being explored in Washington upon which businesses could unite—either for or against. The Roundtable was based on the premise that the expression of a general "business" position could be an effective tool for influencing consideration of these issues.

Things have not quite worked the way that the Roundtable founders thought they would, in part because it has become apparent that even in the area of social regulation there are benefits to some sectors of industry. The environmental-protection programs were started 10 years ago with no industrial support, indeed much opposition. Political support came from social activists not connected with business. By the mid-1970s the environmental pollution control equipment manufacturing sector was growing rapidly. In fact, between the years 1975 and 1977 it was the fastest growing industrial sector. For the first time, the Environmental Protection Agency found itself in the interesting position of having major industrial support for

---

[2]*FPC* v. *Hope Natural Gas Co.*, 320 U.S. 521 (1944).

the enforcement of its rules and regulations. Nevertheless, business, by and large, finds it easier to unite either for or against those programs than it did on economic and industrial regulations.

COST AND BENEFIT ARGUMENTS

The growing realization that regulation can add significantly to costs, while reducing productivity, has resulted in increased opposition to regulation, especially social regulation. While it is difficult—some would say impossible—to accurately assess regulatory costs, the Business Roundtable recently commissioned a study which examined the impact of government regulation on both the incremental costs to business as well as the secondary effects of these regulations. The incremental costs were considered the direct costs of those actions which businesses were forced to take solely to comply with a regulation—that is, they would not have taken it in the absence of a regulation. Secondary effects included losses in productivity of labor, equipment and capital costs, delays in construction of new plant equipment, misallocation of resources, and lost opportunity.

The Roundtable study identified some $2.6 billion in compliance costs considered wasteful and nonproductive, adding approximately 1 percent to the price level of their products, thereby exacerbating inflation.

It often appears to critics of regulation that government imposition of socially desirable requirements on business is an expensive way of achieving national objectives. They claim that compliance with the regulation can be a hidden tax, shifted from the taxpayer through the enterprise to the consumer. This tax may be more regressive than the federal income tax because the costs of government regulation can be expected to be passed on to all consumers who purchase affected products, without distinction as to income.

Although regulatory agencies account for only 1 percent of the federal budget, their rules have a major impact on large public-sector resources. The Regulatory Council estimates that in 1979 federal environmental rules imposed direct costs of about $25 billion. And, state and local environmental rules cost another $25 billion.

The effect of regulation is not only in compliance costs but also in the impact on business competition. Because of their size small businesses might bear a heavier proportionate share of the costs incurred as a result of regulation, and their ability to increase productivity and to innovate may be adversely affected.

On the other side of the argument, the benefit side, there is much disagreement among experts and nonexperts. There quite obviously are some benefits, but do they justify the costs associated with them? A recent study conducted by the MIT Center for Policy Alternatives lists several specific examples of benefits attributed to regulation. Regulation of air pollution from major sources has produced benefits estimating from $5 billion to $58 billion a year. Water pollution control, according to MIT, has produced a reduction in waterborne disease saving medical costs valued at $100 million to $1 billion a year, providing recreational potential valued at up to $9.5 billion, and substantially increased property values. Inspections by the Occupational Safety and Health Administration are estimated, on a yearly basis, to have prevented between 40,000 and 60,000 accidents in which hundreds of workdays and up to 350 lives would have been lost. And, motor vehicle occupant protection standards promulgated between 1966 and 1970 saved an estimated 28,000 lives from 1966 to 1974.

This list of regulatory benefits has much in common with other matters in political life—it is controversial. The figures are on the soft side and do not mean a great deal to executives focused on the harder statistical realities of profit and loss. There are reasons to expect that data on the benefits of regulation will improve, and support of social regulation will grow in the business community. But, there will continue to be disagreement in this area. The quiet days of presocial regulation will not return soon, if only because social regulation has opened a broad, new field, one fraught with controversy—the field of social cost-benefit analysis.

AGENCY OVERLAP AND DUPLICATION

There is another reason the spotlight has been turned on government regulation in recent years. The growing incidence of social regulation has focused attention on a very old problem in the governmental policymaking process. The problem is one of coordination between federal agencies in Washington on the one hand, and state and local government on the other. In most large governments, certainly in the federal government, most policymaking is done through small, semiautonomous decision-making systems. The important institutions and individuals in the federal system include subcommittees of Congress, bureaus of departments and agencies of the executive branch, including White House staff agencies such as the Office of Management and Budget and the Domestic Policy Staff, and special interest groups.

These decision-making systems tend not only to be semiautonomous but also very highly specialized. As they developed policy over the years, the incidence of overlapping and duplication was bound to grow. As business and industry have become more alert to the problems of regulation, the difficulties caused by duplication have been raised to higher political levels.

Some of the problems of duplication and absence coordination are almost laughable—but they point out the need for coordination to avoid confusion and duplication. There is the story about a meat-packing plant that was told by one federal agency to wash floors several times daily for cleanliness; another federal agency told it to keep its floors dry so that employees wouldn't slip and fall down. Some problems are far more serious like those discussed in the Business Roundtable study. In several instances regulations were found to be in conflict with basic national policies. For example, certain EPA regulations were found to result in an increased use of oil. Moreover, U.S. demand for foreign oil was particularly affected, thus straining this country's balance of payments and adversely impacting upon our drive toward energy independence.

CARTER ADMINISTRATION REFORMS

The Carter administration has been developing reforms designed to deal directly with the identified problems of regulations themselves and the processes through which regulatory programs are managed. The administration has focused primarily on two goals: (1) eliminating unneeded regulations and (2) avoiding the imposition of unnecessary burdens, brought about by duplication and overlap by those regulations that are needed,

This approach to regulatory reform is in one respect similar to the approach which Hippocrates set out in his admonition to new physicians. He told them, "Do thy patients no harm." Today federal regulators are enjoined to do competitive markets no harm and to restore competition whenever possible. The operating theory is to supplant, correct, or interfere with competitive markets only when intervention is absolutely necessary; only when government knows what it is doing and when it knows what the effects will be.

President Carter has had some successes in implementing his goal of returning to competitive markets. One area in which the administration is currently working with the Congress is telecommunications deregulation. The administration also has led in the introduction of legislation and support for deregulation of airlines, crude oil and natural gas pricing, financial institutions, trucking and railroads.

The other major thrust of President Carter's regulatory reform program is to improve regulatory management. The president's Executive Order 12044, issued in March 1978, established the Regulatory Analysis Review Group, a high-level White House organization which is to review selected new rules by regulatory agencies.

RARG focuses on proposed rules with an especially large impact—examining their rationale, projected benefits relative to costs, and the likelihood that they will be effective in achieving stated objectives. RARG's findings have helped to reduce the anticipated costs of new rules by billions of dollars. Such reviews, along with additional reviews performed by the Council on Wage and Price Stability, serve as an important decision-making tool.

The administration has in E.O. 12044 encouraged agencies to (1) devote more attention to planning the regulatory process; (2) facilitate greater public participation in that process; (3) analyze the cost-effectiveness of a proposed rule—selecting the least costly alternative to achieve a given objective; (4) reduce the burden of regulation upon small businesses; (5) review regulations regularly and prepare analyses of rules with major economic consequences; (6) establish agency-head accountability; (7) set expiration dates to assure that obsolete rules do not remain on the books; (8) reduce paperwork and write rules in plain English; and (9) develop an improved state-and-local coordination process.

In addition, in October 1978, the president established the Regulatory Council, composed of the heads of 36 executive departments and independent regulatory agencies. In its first two years the council has served as the coordinating agency for regulatory reform at the national level. Twice yearly the council publishes a *Calendar of Federal Regulations* which facilitates the process of public participation in rule making. The *Calendar*, which contains listings of proposed rules have an economic impact of $100 million or more, serves as an early-warning system for both regulators and regulated. The system is designed to minimize agency duplication and overlap.

A major thrust of the council's activities has been the investigation of alternative approaches to traditional regulation. In its recently published report, "An Inventory of Innovative Techniques, 1978-1980," the Regulatory Council summarizes some of the major innovative alternative techniques to traditional regulation. The report focuses upon 18 management-reform categories. Some of those cited as innovative management techniques include: (1) remove barriers to competition, (2) allow rights traditionally conferred by government, like certain licenses, to be sold in the marketplace, (3) create incentives for private-sector achievement of regulatory goals, (4) generalize performance standards, allowing a company to decide how it achieves overall standards, and (5) setting less demanding standards for smaller businesses.

Implementation of some of these regulatory improvements requires congressional action; some of it can be done by the agencies themselves. The Senate recently passed a bill to reduce all major regulatory requirements on small business. And, the recent Computer Inquiry II decision[3] demonstrates the FCC's attempt to

---

[3] FCC Second Computer Inquiry, Docket No. 20828 (1980).

utilize competition to control the marketplace for enhanced communications services, eliminating burdensome restrictions which previously had limited market entry. That agency has also moved to abolish requirements that cable television systems receive a certificate of compliance before beginning operations. The SEC has provided an exemption from registration—under very specific conditions—to help ease the burdens on small firms seeking to raise capital on public markets, and the ICC has tiered its financial and accounting reports based on earnings, significantly reducing the paperwork requirement imposed on 700 small firms.

EPA regulations lowering water-pollution controls on hundreds of industries will save $200 million in administrative costs without harming the quality of water. That agency has also accelerated the issuance of rural-water-treatment permits by more than a year—saving local governments several hundred million dollars annually. OSHA has cut out a thousand unnecessary and overlapping standards that did not contribute to worker safety; the coal-industry standard of this administration saves a capital cost of $2.1 billion. The public-education programs which in the past required an extensive amount of reporting of often unnecessary data have been reduced through the consolidation of forms and the elimination of nonessential information, thus saving an estimated 264,000 man-hours a year at the school-district level.

Since the implementation of E.O. 12044, federal agencies have made significant progress in regulatory reform. Essential regulatory programs are being better managed and innovative techniques are being applied to take advantage of market forces. Unneeded programs, regulations, and even agencies are being eliminated. And yet, as reform is implemented regulatory goals and objectives are not being compromised.

We are in the midst of a significant new movement in regulatory reform. Yet in our zeal to cut back on the deleterious aspects of regulation we must remember that the purpose of governmental regulation has always been the protection of the interests of the public. Proper regulation can be effective. It can encourage excellence and work to minimize delay. It can also encourage competition. If regulators have the necessary flexibility to review alternative approaches to public policy problems and offer innovative regulatory techniques designed to benefit the public, then regulation is capable of achieving its economic and social objectives.

The challenge is to streamline the process, reduce the imposition of unnecessary costs, and take advantage of market forces without compromising the underlying objectives or impeding progress toward them. Realizing that this nation has in recent years changed what it expects from regulation and that we are asking things of regulatory processes which we did not ask before is important. The realization will help us modify existing systems and develop new ones which will respond well to the demands certain to be placed on them in the future.

SIX
A STRONG BEGINNING ON REFORM

Christopher C. DeMuth

The Reagan administration's record on deregulation during its first year in office has not been perfect. Any close reader of *Regulation* magazine will be able to cite shortcomings and missed opportunities. On the other hand, the administration's record has been far better than that of any other administration, even allowing for the fact that it has had more to deregulate than any other. And, as the regulatory economists tell us, it is idle to talk of imperfection except in reference to a well-specified alternative.

Administration officials have done many good, specific things to rid the economy of harmful restraints that were nevertheless much in favor in Washington. Some were easy—unisex dress codes in schools, subway elevators in midtown Manhattan. Others were harder, especially where health or safety was involved and the administration would be accused of having blood on its hands. The most important of these was the rescission of the automatic seat-belt requirement, which would have added over $100 to the price of every new automobile for devices that are disconnected even by most people who buy them voluntarily.

My own favorite rescission was the quick *coup de grace* delivered to the petroleum price controls, which was greeted so confidently with charges that prices would skyrocket without much effect on supplies. As a result of this action, retail gasoline and heating oil prices declined in 1981—gasoline even in nominal terms in some areas—and successful new oil drillings hit record levels. Gas lines were replaced by gas

This selection is taken from *Regulation* 6 (January/February 1982), 15–18. Copyright © American Enterprise Institute for Public Policy Research. Used by permission of the publisher.

price wars, the first outbreak of this venerable American tradition in the experience of drivers under twenty-five. This winter is one of the coldest in memory and the first in years without heating oil shortages—an achievement hardly anyone noticed in the absence of government planners to take the credit.

The administration has also made improvements in policy and program management. The Department of Agriculture's recent guidelines on fruit and vegetable marketing orders are the first serious attempt to reform this program since it was enacted in the waning days of the New Deal. (*See* "Dispatch from the Nut Wars," page 8.) The Food and Drug Administration approved more wholly new drugs than in any other year since the 1962 Drug Amendments, doubling the number approved in the last year of the Carter administration. In approving a new application for an existing drug, timolol, the FDA reversed two of its sacred precedents in a single stroke—the requirement that proof of efficacy rest on two independent studies and the requirement that one of these studies take place in the United States. At the level of inspection and enforcement, businessmen today are much less likely to mistake a visit from EPA or OSHA for a visit from the FBI.

There have been, inevitably, some disappointments as well, especially in environmental regulation. Officials of the Environmental Protection Agency have been distracted by congressional and budgetary disputes. They have just begun to face scores of hard regulatory decisions that have been overhanging major markets and capital investment projects for years, and whose economic impact is vastly greater than EPA's entire budget. The costs of continued regulatory uncertainty would have been well invested if their result had been a wholly reformulated Clean Air Act. Sadly, the politics of environmental control have become so dominated by interregional and intraindustry economic interests that the prospects for fundamental improvement remain dim. For the near term we will have to be content with adjustments to the act's most unrealistic provisions.

But above the fray of battles won and lost, the administration's greatest achievement has been President Reagan's Executive Order 12291, requiring that all new regulations be supported by solid evidence demonstrating their economic benefits, and establishing a central review procedure to enforce the requirement. Looking back on the decade of the 1970s—on the growth of regulatory programs, on the dawning realization of the large costs of these programs, and on the nascent efforts to control regulatory costs in the Ford and Carter administrations—one might suppose that President Reagan's order was the easy last step in a natural evolution. But this was not the case. Making economic analysis a line function in the regulatory agencies and the Office of Management and Budget was a qualitative departure from all that had come before, and a decision that was and remains controversial. There is as much worry among conservative as liberal activists about "paralysis by analysis," especially when conservatives are coming to power. In the euphoria of a new administration, it would have been easy to assume that Reagan's regulators would do the right thing by instinct. It was an act of some insight to recognize that the regulatory juggernaut had grown so powerful, and the pressures for it to move forward so intense, that it needed a strong and formal restraint even in a conservative government.

Central oversight of the wide variety of rules laid down in the *Federal Register* is not without its problems. Critics of "cost-benefit analysis" are fond of describing it as a narrow, easily manipulated technique. This is nearly the opposite of the truth. The greatest practical difficulties in applying economic reasoning to political decisions arise from its qualities of breadth, rigor, and disinterestedness. Under relaxed economic assumptions, one needs no cost-benefit calculations at all to decide whether society will benefit from mandatory uniform quality standards for products such as automobile bumpers and fresh fruits that are easily judged by consumers; nor does the economist pause for long over most proposals to establish uniform prices or restrictions on entry or output. Yet these are the everyday stuff of regulatory policy, where the issues are so discrete and are pressed with such unabashed parochialism that the free marketeer—arguing from the inside rather than observing from the outside—is always prone to appear a little impractical, if not ridiculous. Thomas C. Schelling of Harvard University observes that we do not expect people to argue about leash laws the way they argue about the space shuttle; dog lovers are expected to oppose leash laws without appeal to any interest broader than their own. Economic analysis of regulatory issues, as embodied in President Reagan's executive order on regulation, is an attempt to get people to consider leash laws disinterestedly—and this in a town where people are used to debating the space shuttle the way New Yorkers debate leash laws.

A separate problem is that imposing controls from within is politically thankless. It is very difficult for an administration to get much credit for failing to issue unwise regulations; that it came close to issuing them anyway is hardly something to beat its chest over. Everyone understands that the Office of Management and Budget favors lower agency budgets than the agencies themselves. It is a different matter when OMB disagrees with an agency's regulatory proposal: assuming OMB's view prevails, the administration has no good deed to advertise and OMB must enjoy its good deed in silence. I believe the executive order review process has substantially deterred the publication of ill-considered new regulations, and for the present I can point to statistics showing dramatically fewer new regulations in President Reagan's first year than President Carter's last year. But as the administration grows older the Carter record will lose its relevance, and there will be no other points of reference to demonstrate the benefits of the review process.

Here again, however, one must judge the executive review procedure against the alternatives—and these, aside from a vast contraction in the regulatory statutes themselves, are constitutionally limited to two. The Congress is presently considering a variety of procedural reforms to restrain the regulatory process, and everyone can be categorized as either an executive, judicial, or congressional restraint. Congressional restraint through one form or another of "legislative veto" has recently been dealt a blow—I predict mortal—by Judge Wilkey's masterful opinion in *Consumer Energy Council* v. *Federal Energy Regulatory Commission*. But legislative vetoes are ineffective even if they are unconstitutional. There are already hundreds on the books and they are almost never exercised outside of the fields of foreign aid and arms sales. Given the enormous costs of organizing legislative majorities, vetoes of regulations championed by the executive branch can be expected only in the rarest of circumstances. Even the threat of such vetoes cannot provide a restraint comparable to routinized executive oversight.

Greater judicial restraint, in the form of the various "Bumpers Amendment" proposals for stricter judicial review of regulatory decisions, is equally problematic. One can imagine a good judge straightening out a bad regulatory decision, but one can also imagine a bad judge spoiling a good regulatory decision. There are, of course, good reasons for expecting judges to be freer of narrow political pressures than regulators, but the price they pay for their insular position is to be limited to issues of statutory consistency in the controversies brought before them. So long as the statutes themselves leave great discretion to the regulators, and so long as we are unwilling to permit judges to be policymakers outright, the role of the courts will remain limited under *any* standard of judicial review.

There is a practical solution to this dilemma, and it leads us back to the policies articulated in President Reagan's executive order. Few of us, including Senator

Dale Bumpers himself, are willing to abide more explicit policy making by courts than already exists. This leaves the alternative of narrowing the statutory discretion of regulators, which can be accomplished either by statute-by-statute revisions or by a general requirement that discretion be exercised according to an overriding criterion. But the statute-by-statute approach is much less promising than the general approach, and the general approach is most compelling when its overriding criterion is that of economic efficiency (or cost-benefit analysis). Where specific issues are involved, such as worker safety or carcinogenic food additives, legislators are less likely to acknowledge the two-sidedness of problems and more likely to insist on absolute-sounding legal standards; the current posturing over the Clean Air Act revisions is a good case in point. When policy is set at a more general level, however, legislators are more likely to acknowledge the common sense of requiring regulations to take due account of costs as well as benefits. This is why proposals to revise the Delaney Amendment along economic lines are currently bogged down, while the regulatory reform bills, which would require that all new regulations be economically justified, stand a good chance of passage.

The cost-benefit criterion strengthens judicial oversight more surely than any of the Bumpers proposals because it obliges regulatory agencies to include in the record evidence of the economic consequences of their decisions—evidence they must take some account of even under lenient standards of judicial review. We have already seen this effect in the Supreme Court's recent decisions in the *Benzene* and *Cotton Dust* cases. But the criterion is even more powerful as an instrument of executive oversight. The presidency, of all the offices in our system of government, is the one most suited to advancing a consistent program against narrow political pressures. Whatever the political philosophy of a given president, he is far more likely than Congress or the courts to take a broad view of the economic interest of the society, and far more able to impress this view on the federal bureaucracy. The economic principles set forth so unequivocally in President Reagan's executive order are a product of his own strong mind on federal regulation. I expect that, in spite of the difficulties mentioned earlier, the application of these principles will result in more carefully reasoned and empirically solid regulatory decisions, which will narrow the opposition to these decisions in Congress and the courts and strengthen the president's command over the course of regulatory policy. If so, the principles will endure—in statute, judicial doctrine, or executive conduct—as a lasting achievement of his administration.

With the economic assessment program in place, the administration is in a good position to press its regulatory reform efforts on two additional fronts. The first is revising the mass of uneconomic regulations already on the books. The Presidential Task Force on Regulatory Relief, chaired by Vice-President Bush, has already designated for reconsideration 111 existing regulations spanning the entire range of federal policies. Several important decisions have already been made (such as the automatic seat-belt rescission) but many more remain; we currently expect that about half of that entire group will be completed by mid-1982 and most will be completed by the end of the year. In this area, more than in the internal control of new regulatory proposals, the administration will be able to point to specific "relief" from its efforts. Revision of existing regulations will also provide market evidence of the economic effects of the administration's regulatory policies—such as the past year's evidence on petroleum decontrol—which should serve to mollify some who are currently skeptical of our intentions.

The second and more ambitious step is broad statutory reform. The administration has been criticized for not mounting a full-court press for statutory change already—a shallow criticism, considering that the cost of such an effort would have been reduced chances of victory on our initial tax and budget proposals. In any event, the history of deregulation is that major administrative reform is a necessary prerequisite to statutory reform. Before Congress itself will act, external changes are required to dislodge accumulated interests in the status quo and to assure the doubtful of the economy's ability to continue functioning in the absence of federal controls. How far one can go unilaterally is as much a question of politics and timing as of statutory language: while I have expressed some skepticism about the possibilities for fundamental improvement in the regulatory statutes, it should be obvious that the administration cannot continue indefinitely making hard choices, especially on matters of health and safety, without the active collaboration of the Congress. If we are to achieve major statutory reform in the last two years of President Reagan's first term, we must first build a solid foundation of administrative deregulation in 1982.

CHAPTER TWO
AGENCY POWERS

The federal agency, executive branch or independent, is the implementer of federal policies: it is program-oriented and decides individual cases with the broader policy in view. Administrators are charged with the responsibility for implementing the public policy formulated by the political policymakers. In the implementation of the public policy, agencies and administrators have a wide range of options available, as determined by Congress (in the enabling statute and the APA), to ensure citizen compliance with the public policy as redefined and implemented by the public-policy managers. Whether the public policy is regulatory, benefit distribution, or public management, the government agents have a great deal of power over their customers.

Agencies and bureaucrats, in the course of implementing the policy through orders and regulations (that operationalize broad public policies announced by the policymakers), may be authorized to:

1. conduct investigations
2. impose sanctions
3. determine rates
4. develop standards
5. seize property
6. issue fines and penalties
7. award benefits, contracts, subsidies
8. make on-site inspections
9. audit
10. approve or reject plans and programs
11. prosecute offenders
12. issue licenses

These activities, conducted by federal administrators, are the means and instruments used to implement public policy developed by Congress and president. These activities are also the characteristic properties of the bureaucrats as *policymakers*, that is, as implementors of policy formulations of the more "political" agencies—Congress, courts, and president, or as *policy initiators*, that is, development of specific policy based on a general grant of authority from Congress. Fundamentally, when agencies employ these devices in the course of policy implementation, there develops the occasional classic confrontation between (the scope of) governmental authority (to act on behalf of the "general welfare") and the private rights of individuals and corporations. The essays in chapter 1 illuminated the fundamental philosophical and practical problems that have arisen with the growth of the Administrative State. This chapter seeks to illustrate the various mechanisms employed by the federal agencies that brought the question of control and freedom to the fore in the early decades of the twentieth century and again in the past decade.

Agencies have some essential formal and informal policymaking procedures for developing rules and regulations that implement the public policy. The primary formal policy processes for determining how the agency will administer a general policy are informal rule making, adjudication, and discretionary actions. The heart of the administrative policy process is the millions of informal and discretionary actions taken by the many thousands of bureaucrats every day. These actions are the core of the regulatory process and have been the major concern of critics of administrative action who charge that there are no really effective controls over discretionary and informal administrative decisions.

Given the broad, general, statutory directives created by the Congress in the past, the dilemma of discretion is a very real one. Agencies and administrators can be overzealous in their efforts to operationalize a public policy written in very general terms. On the other hand, agencies and bureaucrats can defeat the goals of the policy formulators by not aggressively moving to implement, through the development of appropriate rules, regulations, and other informal actions, the public policy. (The Ball, Krane, and Lauth selection, "Compromised Compliance," illustrates the dilemma confronted by Department of Justice bureaucrats as they tried to implement the 1965 Voting Rights Act.)

Elsewhere, William Mayton has argued that Congress "intended its delegated lawmaking function (to agencies) to remain subject to public participation and scrutiny"[1] *exclusively* through the rule-making process. Rule making is a prospective activity of a general nature, that is, an agency will use the rule-making process to develop regulations of a substantive nature that become general statements of rule-making authority of the agency. Typically, until the Reagan administration, agency staff would develop a preliminary policy, go through the notice and comment stage, review comments, revise and then publish the final regulation that would take effect in the future and which would affect the lives of millions of persons subject to the agency's jurisdiction. (The Reagan Executive Order, 12291, February 1981, dramatically changed this review process. It will be examined in a subsequent chapter.)

Adjudication is a quasi-judicial process that is used by the agency to deal with, through the issuance of an agency order, individual persons or citizens or corporations who have, for one reason or another, run afoul of the agency policy and the problem has not been resolved informally. The adjudicatory process is an effort to rectify a past wrong committed by a person. As a consequence of the adjudicatory process, where an independent administrative law judge (appointed by the Office of Personnel Management) presides and renders a judgment (reviewable by the agency staff and

---

[1] William T. Mayton, "The Legislative Resolution of the Rulemaking versus Adjudication Problem in Agency Lawmaking," *Duke Law Journal* (November 1980).

administrators), a judgment is reached on the instant case before the ALJ. However, a consequence of this type of formal process is a set of decisions that, over the years, form the nucleus of a policy. Courts have been wary of the consequences of this type of backdoor rule making in the guise of adjudicatory hearings, and have invalidated some adjudicatory decisions because the agency was developing rules without notice and comment, but generally have accepted an incremental rule making of sorts through the adjudicatory process. (*See* Appendix, Administrative Procedure Act, Sections 554, 556, and 557.)

Verkuil's essay highlights six major types of administrative activity that are employed to implement broad public policies. The Gardner essay examines the character of informal activities of agencies and offers suggestions as to how these informal actions, the lifeblood of agency decision making, can be constrained so as to insure proper administrative behavior. (The Administrative Procedure Act of 1946 does not focus on this very important question of curbing informal and discretionary actions that infringe upon personal freedoms in an arbitrary manner.)

The Pertschuk and Lubbers essays afford the reader a close examination of major administrative actors in the policy-implementation phase: the key agency staffer and the administrative law judge. Institutional decision making "is now a way of life in federal agencies. Numbers of people have inputs in the process and there is a clear delegation of responsibility to staff personnel."[2] Pertschuk, a member of the Federal Trade Commission (formerly the chairman of the commission from 1976–1980), focuses on the value in this policymaking process of highly competent and motivated agency staff; his essay illustrates the tensions and dynamics that fill the life of the agency staff.

Lubbers, senior staff attorney in the office of the chairman of the Administrative Conference of the United States, carefully examines the role and functions of the administrative law judge and presents suggestions for streamlining this facet of administrative policymaking.

Given the fundamental assumptions surrounding agency actions: (1) broad frameworks for action given to agencies by Congress; (2) individual cases with particular facts and circumstances are the essence of agency activities; (3) some problems confronting government "cannot be governed by rules or even by meaningful standards because no one knows how to write the rules or standards"; (4) government "has always been a government of laws *and of men*," rules *must* be supplemented with discretion.[3] The discretionary power of agencies will continue to grow because (1) government cannot prepare "advance rules" and (2) "individualized justice" requires individualized judgments rather than the "mechanical application of a rule."[4]

The last two essays focus on this question of sound agency discretion, that is, agency actions that are nonreviewable. The Bardach and Kagan selection explores the growth of agency discretion in recent years and accounts for legislative responses to this development. Ball, Krane, and Lauth focus on the Department of Justice's Voting Section (in the department's Civil Rights Division) in an effort to illuminate the role of discretion in the department's efforts to implement the 1965 Voting Rights Act.

---

[2]Gary J. Edles and Jerome Nelson, *Federal Regulatory Process: Agency Practices and Procedures* (New York: Harcourt Brace Jovanovich, 1981), p.34.

[3]Kenneth C. Davis, *Administrative Law and Government* (St. Paul, MN: West Publishing Company, 1975), p. 33–34.

[4]Ibid., p. 34.

SEVEN
ADMINISTRATIVE PROCEDURE

Paul A. Verkuil

A. CATEGORIES OF ADMINISTRATIVE DECISIONS

For purposes of analysis, administrative decisions can be divided into functional categories which reflect differing decision-making roles and levels of impact upon individuals and the public at large. While other categories could be conceived, six categories would seem to encompass most administrative decision making. Those categories are:

1. Imposition of sanctions.
2. Rate making, licensing, and other regulatory decisions.
3. Environmental and safety decisions.
4. Awards of benefits, loans, grants, and subsidies.
5. Inspections, audits, and approvals.
6. Planning and policymaking.

These categories describe familiar activities. They do, however, differ from each other, and the relative importance of the procedural values of fairness, efficiency, and satisfaction may vary considerably among them. For example, it may be important in the first category—imposition of sanctions—to maximize fairness and satis-

This selection is taken from the *Columbia Law Review* 78 (November 1978), 294–303. Used by permission. Footnotes omitted.

faction, since individual and state interests are in direct opposition. In this situation, efficiency may be a less important value. On the other hand, in the last category—policymaking and planning—the values of fairness and satisfaction may be of lesser concern, and the public interest in efficient policymaking is of greater importance. In between, the four categories generate a variety of individual and public concerns and a shifting mix of procedural values.

1. Imposition of sanctions In imposing sanctions, agencies are concerned with punishment of past conduct and with curtailment of future activity because of prior conduct. Classic examples are unfair labor practice cases, broker-dealer disciplinary proceedings, and unfair trade practice cases. In these situations, the questions usually involve the facts surrounding an individual's conduct and the application of a standard of conduct previously established to those facts. As a result, the adjudicatory model predominates, much as it does in the civil or criminal process. If an erroneous decision is made, the procedures should ensure that it usually goes against the government, not the individual.

A good recent example of this category is provided by the Occupational Safety and Health Act of 1970, which imposes civil penalties upon employers who maintain unsafe working conditions. If employers object to the penalty imposed by an inspector of the Department of Labor, they may obtain an evidentiary hearing before an ALJ and discretionary review of that order by the Occupational Safety and Health Review Commission. The Supreme Court has made it clear that committing "public rights" determinations like these to administrative agencies does not deprive parties of a constitutional right to a jury trial; but short of that important distinction, the administrative model looks much like the civil or criminal models. Ultimately, the right to an evidentiary hearing, and perhaps judicial review of the penalty imposed, is grounded in the fairness values of procedural due process. Where sanctions are imposed, few would argue with the proposition that if the values of fairness and satisfaction should conflict with the value of efficiency, fairness, and satisfaction should predominate. Unfortunately, agreement about the procedures that should be utilized before sanctions are imposed only introduces a second debate over the definition of *sanction*. If the meaning of sanction is equated with imposition of penalties or fines, there is little dispute. Does the issuance of an SEC report that "unfairly" stigmatizes New York banks or its political leaders, or a presidential press release that maligns the oil companies, amount to a "sanction" because it injures reputations and even business position? FTC and SEC press releases often have a clear and calculable effect on business advantage that comes even closer to the sanction line. Even with this effect, however, one would be reluctant to elevate the issuance of press releases to the full hearing level accorded sanctions, if only because the deterrent value of such practices (properly employed) would be eliminated from the agency's policy arsenal. From the government's point of view, these activities seem more like planning and policymaking than sanctions; as such they should receive different procedural treatment (that is, that provided in category six). The APA does not solve the problem of identifying sanctions since its formula is overly inclusive. To be used as a minimal description of situations where fairness requires adjudicatory procedures, the APA definition would have to be narrowed considerably. In particular, the licensing function should be excluded, since that function forms the core of category two and rests on a balancing of procedural values significantly different from that of the imposition of sanctions.

2. Regulatory decisions This category encompasses the procedural heart of direct economic regulation by administrative agencies. It involves licensing, maximum and minimum rate regulation, and entry and exit control by agencies like the ICC, CAB, FCC, FMC, and FPC. There exists a tradition, sparked by early concerns with administrative arbitrariness, to subject these activities to formal hearing processes much like those provided for category one. In terms of procedural values, however, decisions in this category differ substantially from those in category one. Fairness and satisfaction remain important, but the inquiry necessarily expands to give efficiency equal weight. In the first place, fairness, seen as the maximizing of accurate decision making, is difficult to measure in this situation. In rate setting, the goal is to find a "zone of reasonableness"; and, in licensing, the "better" applicant. It is often difficult to know with precision whether the single best choice has been made. Thus, while procedures that enhance accuracy are important, the resulting decisions reflect policy choices much more than specific fact findings. This indeterminacy would be more troubling were it not for a second factor that characterizes regulatory decisions. The relationship of the private entity to the agency is a continuing one, and positions taken become well known and errors occurring in one year may often be corrected in another. In this situation, the need to decide these matters expeditiously and efficiently takes on great importance.

The agencies have recognized the interplay of these values in rate-making decisions. Conceptually, the breakthrough came with the characterization of rate making as an informal rule-making process. Following the lead of the FPC and its area rate proceedings, the CAB undertook to determine industry rates of return in its Domestic Passenger Fare Investigation, and the ICC has experimented in rate cases with all-written procedures that emulate summary judgment procedures available in the courts. While there remains a long list of rate decisions that could benefit from rule-making procedures, the trend toward rule making reduces the time and expense of the rate-making process; it maximizes the efficiency value at little apparent cost to fairness and satisfaction. Moreover, there is some indication that this trend toward rate making by rule making will also enhance the satisfaction value. The satisfaction value should extend to interested members of the public as well as to the parties themselves, since the concern is with perceptions of fairness by society at large. Indications are that public intervenors prefer rule making since they can better utilize their limited decision resources in that context.

3. Environmental and safety decisions   With the advent, in 1970, of the National Environmental Policy Act (NEPA), a new era of procedural responsibility befell those agencies (even traditional regulatory ones) whose decisions significantly affect the environment. It is fascinating to note that NEPA, which is primarily a procedural statute, provided no procedural format for producing its primary document, the environmental impact statement. Therefore, the courts, on judicial review, have become immersed in procedural questions. Since most of the issues at stake are scientific, variations on the usual trial-type procedures can be permitted; this fact offers an enormous opportunity for the creation of a truly administrative procedure.

Category three is the most difficult category in which to reach a balance of procedural values. All three values demand recognition. Fairness (to ensure accuracy) is crucial where scientific decisions are made that are often irreversible and can affect the lives of everyone. Satisfaction is equally important where the lack of public acceptability can frustrate program objectives. But efficiency is no less fundamental, because timely and inexpensive decisions are indispensible to a growing economy.

With all three values having strong claims for legitimacy, it is not surprising that procedural responses have been confused or contradictory. In an attempt to ensure accuracy, lengthy and unmanageable trial-type procedures have appeared, with the result that efficiency is frustrated. Satisfaction of the public is difficult to achieve when different members of the public have strikingly opposed views of the "public interest." Indeed, to some extent, the "proenvironment" forces have caused inefficient procedures to develop. There appears to be an ironic replay by these forces of the twin-tyranny theory of opposition to government economic regulation. Just as those seeking to avoid substantive economic regulation masked their defense behind opposition to the procedural tyranny of nonadversary procedures, some proenvironment forces seem to oppose substantive programs (such as the development and use of nuclear power) by arguing for procedural solutions that will delay the plant siting process. To deal with the problems in a rational way, administrative procedure must overcome resistance from modern procedural conservatives. Substantive debates should be resolved in their own terms and not recast as procedural ones.

With procedural values in conflict and with substantive opposition taking procedural form, it would be understandable if the procedures employed were in total disarray. But in the midst of considerable confusion, a growing procedural coherence has emerged. In particular, the procedures of the Environmental Protection Agency (EPA) seem to be regularizing around a modified version of the informal rule-making model, even where the matter under consideration does not fit the strict definition of rulemaking. Thus, limited cross-examination on important issues of disputed fact and carefully designed comment and rebuttal procedures have become typical solutions. While EPA's major decisions will continue to be the subject of careful judicial scrutiny, its procedural format has benefitted from experience and is proving workable. Other agencies have built upon the EPA experience. Thus, the Occupational Safety and Health Administration (OSHA), which has responsibility for the health and safety conditions of employees, has adopted by regulation a modified informal rule-making procedure that recognizes that "fairness may require an opportunity for cross-examination on crucial issues." The agency's experience with this approach seems generally satisfactory, although, as suggested below, procedural problems may loom on the horizon.

Nuclear power plant licensing by the Nuclear Regulatory Commission (NRC) presents several procedural problems. Because siting decisions involve the licensing function, the formal adjudicative procedures of the APA apply. This formalization assures careful fact-finding, but in some respects it is less satisfactory than the broader procedures utilized by EPA and OSHA. Decisions that precede the nuclear licensing application are outside the scope of the licensing hearing, but cast a shadow on the outcome. Projections of need and demand, allocation of capacity, and even purchase of the site are decided prior to the licensing hearing without the opportunity to assess public impact. Because the licensing hearing does not permit a public role in these important preliminaries, the resulting inquiry is both too intense and too narrow. In the process, the fairness and satisfaction values suffer. And, because there are so many other state and federal stops along the way, the efficiency value is frustrated as well.

4. Awards of benefits, loans, grants, and subsidies Traditionally, this category of decision-making (and the two that follow) has largely been governed by informal processes. This category effectively separates the formal process from the informal process. It includes the vast preponderance of government decisions, with the Social Security Administration (SSA) alone accounting annually for more decisions after hearing than the entire federal court system. The Veterans Administration (VA) and Department of Agriculture (USDA) also hear thousands of cases annually for benefits and subsidies. With this kind of decision burden, it is not surprising that the informal process has long been resorted to. As a result, the efficiency value must play a primary role if the benefactory arm of government is to function at all. Fairness and satisfaction provide some constraints, but the overriding public interest lies in effective implementation of the programs.

Despite the need for efficient decision making, the procedures employed within this category vary greatly, from informal, mostly written, decisions, to decisions after formal adjudicatory hearings. In the former category are the decisions of the SSA and VA that are based on the use of written medical and other reports in disability hearings along with brief oral presentations to ALJs and three-person non-ALJ hearing boards, respectively. The Farmers Home Administration administered some 2,000,000 loans totalling more than $6 billion during 1947–1974 by utilizing informal procedures that were mostly written, and the Economic Development Administration (EDA) administered public works grants, business development loans, and technical assistance grants with similar procedures. On the other hand, some benefactory decisions involve procedures that emulate formal adjudication. As a result of the decision in *Goldberg* v. *Kelly*, AFDC termination procedures fall into this classification, as do USDA food stamp termination procedures that were inspired by the *Goldberg* decision.

Because of their basis in due process, *Goldberg* procedures reflect the Supreme Court's willingness, in certain limited situations, to place virtually exclusive emphasis on the fairness value. In other situations, however, Congress and the agencies have resorted to formal adjudication without examining the competing claims of fairness and efficiency. A striking example is the Maritime Administration of the Department of Commerce, which uses formal ALJ adjudications to decide whether American flag vessels are entitled to subsidies. This function is similar to the FHA and EDA subsidy decisions described above, yet it is encrusted with procedures usually reserved for the imposition of sanctions or *Goldberg* "brutal need" situations. The social cost of procedural formalism in the Maritime Administration is staggering. An analysis of Maritime Subsidy Board cases over the last two decades reveals that they take an average of three years to complete. This delay in determining subsidy requests frustrates the attempts by the American merchant marine to gain relief under the statute. It appears to be a situation where the efficiency and satisfaction values have been ignored in an unexamined reliance upon the adversary process.

5. Inspections, audits, and approvals To some extent, this category is outside the realm of hearing procedures altogether. As the 1941 Attorney General's report pointed out, the best way to ensure the accuracy of an inspection or test is not to hold a hearing about it, but to perform another inspection or test to confirm or reject the first one. Whether the matter involves meat and poultry inspections by USDA, audits of money grants by the Department of the Interior, or tests for admission to the bar, the process has long been deemed procedurally sound if it provided for an opportunity to check accuracy by repetition, instead of hearing or appeal. Properly employed, this approach seemingly maximizes all three procedural values: fairness and satisfaction result from accurate and participant-oriented decision-making, and efficiency from low-cost resolutions.

The only real procedural concerns are the qualifications of the inspectors or testers (are they competent? are they impartial?) and the issue of notice of the inspection or test. In some situations, such as bar examinations, notice is obviously a crucial procedural requirement; without time to prepare, one cannot be expected to meet the test's demands. For some inspections, the notice requirement rises to fourth amendment or due process levels. Use of an administrative warrant, for example, is an important protection against administrative arbitrariness by the agent in the field. In exceptional situations, however, notice might frustrate the public purpose surrounding the program. If potential violators are alerted to the presence of government inspectors, notice becomes a totally inefficient procedure. Nevertheless, procedures in the fifth category can be important even though full adjudicatory hearings are not contemplated. The issue is whether the minimum procedural ingredients of notice and a statement of reasons should be displaced in order to satisfy program enforcement goals.

6. Planning and policymaking This last category is probably thought to be largely procedureless, since it involves agency implementation of its statutory mandate. From a procedural value perspective, the individual interest in fairness and satisfaction is frequently not implicated, since no particular decision context has been developed. The efficiency value would similarly support maximum procedural freedom. The public interest in responsible program development, however, may suggest certain minimum procedures. For one thing, the openness requirement imposed on agency policymakers by the Sunshine Act contemplates public scrutiny as an enforceable procedural right. Moreover, reasons requirements have been imposed on policymakers in a growing number of situations. The most dramatic development has come in the requirement of reasons for informal action.

In *Dunlop* v. *Bachowski*, the Supreme Court required the secretary of labor to give reasons for his refusal to bring a civil action to set aside a union election. The secretary's decision to commence litigation, like prosecutorial discretion, is normally considered policymaking of a discretionary nature. Nonetheless, the Court engrafted a reasons requirement upon a statute that was silent on the subject, emphasizing that "a reasons requirement promotes thought by the secretary and compels him to cover points and eschew irrelevancies." The language is broad enough to reflect a new approach to policymaking and some have so viewed it. The FCC seems to have accepted this approach to policymaking by subjecting its major policy statements to an informal process not unlike rule making. In the area of children's television programming, for example, the FCC issued a "policy statement," rather than a rule, after receiving public comment and meeting with industry members and public interest groups.

EIGHT
THE PROCEDURES BY WHICH INFORMAL ACTION IS TAKEN

Warner W. Gardner

These are troubled times, and it is pleasant for me to realize that there is one sizable area of governmental activity as to which I do not have major complaint. That is the administrative process as governed by the Administrative Procedure Act. Except only for the problem of delay in disposing of business, the act and the agency practices under it seem in the large to be working rather well. Much more often than not, we have meaningful administrative litigation, independent examiners, adequate opportunity to know the issues and to develop a case, absence of *ex parte* interference, reasoned decisions, and the availability of an appropriate degree of judicial review of law and procedure. On the rule-making side, a rather happy balance has been struck between public consultation and effective government action.

We have not by any means achieved perfection. In particular, we must find some way to expedite administrative adjudication without losing its typical fairness of procedure. But as human affairs and governmental activities go, the administrative process under the APA seems to me to be in pretty good shape.

A defensible generalization about organized activity of any form would be that if it looks good, you haven't seen it all. This may be the case with administrative procedure broadly defined. The formal procedures of adjudication and rule making embrace only a very small fraction of the government's activities which affect its citizens. My own guess is that perhaps 90 percent of the government's work is conducted outside the boundaries of the Administrative Procedure Act.

The formal processes of administrative adjudication and rule making have not

This selection is taken from the *Administrative Law Review* 24 (1972), 155–66. Used by permission. Footnotes omitted.

reached their generally satisfactory condition simply by accident. To the contrary they have for a half-century been the focus of an enormous amount of scholarly and professional effort. The bar associations and the committees of the Congress have for decades given regular attention to the formal administrative procedures and the literature has been enriched by thousands of articles and a score of treatises.

In dramatic contrast, the procedures which govern informal action by the government have until the last few years received almost no attention. The Attorney General's Committee on Administrative Procedure, to be sure, in its final report of 1941, recognized that "informal procedures constitute the vast bulk of administrative adjudication and are truly the lifeblood of the administrative process," and followed with a perceptive discussion of a score or so of representative informal functions. A number of particular recommendations related to the informal process, but it wisely avoided any legislative recommendation. The Landis Report to the President-Elect on Regulatory Agencies in 1960 gave some attention to policymaking, but otherwise confined itself to formal proceedings. None of the 30 recommendations of the 1960 Administrative Conference of the United States dealt with informal action. The professional literature, judging by a casual browsing through the index, has dealt with the informal administrative process only as a part of the substantive work of one agency or another, and not as a field lending itself to procedural study. In general terms, the procedure relating to the informal activities of government has gone unnoticed.

That comfortable state of inattention has in the last few years begun to disappear. Walter Gellhorn's formidable surveys of the ombudsman function have necessarily caused him, a quarter century after the attorney general's report, to revisit the vast territory outside of the APA. Kenneth Davis brought his growing concern to a focus in his 1966 Tulane lectures which in due course grew into his seminal *Discretionary Justice* (1969). The Administrative Conference of the United States, finally established in 1968 under the act of August 30, 1964, set up a Committee on Informal Action and is conducting an increasing number of ad hoc studies in that unexplored territory.

The work of the committee, if I may indulge in the self-criticism appropriate to its chairman, has not to date been impressive in its extent. This, I hope, is inevitable. The United States government carries out by informal means many thousands of functions. Each is different from all others. No generalization can be true, and no proposal can be practicable, if it reflects the circumstances of one informal activity and is applied without reexamination to another. The annual volume of business may vary from 4 construction-differential subsidy contracts for ship construction to the processing of 113.1 million income tax returns or the issuance of 309.6 million payments to social security beneficiaries. The dollar amounts will range from the few cents involved in a claim for overdue postage to several billions of dollars in the development of a new aircraft. One function will be discharged by a scandalously underemployed staff, another by a staff too desperately overburdened to give thoughtful attention to any part of its business. One function has by long tradition been discharged with meticulous care for the rights of those affected, another by equally long tradition with substantial indifference to the individual consequences. Delay in decisions may be viewed within one agency as the normal perogative of government, or within another as unforgivable inefficiency. We have, in short, an almost infinite diversity among the agency functions and practices. Only one generalization may safely be made, and that is that there *can* be no sound generalization about informal procedures.

I hope that in a decade the Administrative Conference, or the bar, or even the bureaucracy might show substantial movement toward adoption of procedural rules, or at least guidelines, for the conduct of informal activities by the government. There should by then, between the Administrative Conference and the profession, have been enough empirical studies to try to put them together into a generalized pattern. Professor Davis and other scholars will have carried forward the work he has begun. The courts will have built a much more elaborate body of law on the foundations which they are already beginning to lay. In perhaps two decades another commentator, of similarly tolerant spirit, may be able to say of informal action what I have said today of the APA—on the whole it is working pretty well.

So, too, Icarus, as he paused on the walls of the labyrinth, must have thought that someday men would fly with ease. I want today to yield to his temptation and, with certain knowledge that my wings will not survive the sunlight, to sketch the principles which would animate the Informal Procedure Act of 1980, *if*—God forbid—the draftsman then knew no more than I now do of the complex and diverse activities which he was seeking to reduce to a procrustean system.

1. Coverage The procedures should govern action within the executive branch of the government which affects a member of the public and which is not carried out by means of formal hearing or rule making. To this broad coverage there probably should be excepted military and foreign affairs functions, internal matters of personnel, the management of public property, and investigation and prosecution of offenses under the Criminal Code. The exceptions are for the most part unsound in principle but reflect, in varying degrees, tradition, prudence, and a simple lack of adequate knowledge.

2. Disclosure of agency law and policy Possibly the outstanding defect of contemporary governmental procedures is the prevalent failure to make publicly available the rules and the policies which govern agency action. This deficiency is already under broad attack, but legislative prescription will surely be needed. It might take this form:

(a) Within two years after enactment of any statute (or in respect of previously enacted law within two years after enactment of this act) the agency which administers that statute shall incorporate in rules and regulations all interpretations of the statute, all supplementary standards under which it is applied, and all criteria or guidelines, under which the agency makes decisions or exercises discretion in discharge of its functions under such statute. As additional or new interpretations standards, criteria, or guidelines are subsequently developed, they shall periodically (at least every two years) be incorporated in the rules and regulations.

(b) The rules and regulations shall include all matters found in instructions and manuals for the agency staff which affect members of the public except for material which would prejudice enforcement activities.

(c) The agency shall promulgate rules or regulations under this action even though it cannot do so with respect to the complete topic or area within which they fall and shall in that event make appropriate note that interpretations, standards, criteria, or guidelines have not yet been developed in respect of other aspects or applications of the statute.

(d) Rules and regulations promulgated under this section may in the discretion of the agency contain a provision declaring in substance that the agency may in unanticipated and exceptional circumstances apply a different rule, interpretation, standard, or criterion than that indicated by the words of the rule or regulation.

(e) Each agency which issues rules or regulations which directly affect more than ten thousand persons shall prepare a simplified condensation which shall be appropriately distributed to the public in pamphlet or other convenient form.

(f) These rules or regulations shall be promulgated under the procedures of 5 USC § 553(b)-(e).

(g) No sanction shall be imposed, nor any right or benefit denied, because of agency action pursuant to an interpretation, standard, criterion, or guideline which under this section should have been but was not incorporated into rules or regulations, unless there should be pending a request for an exemption or modification under the general exception provision made below.

3. Agency precedents The Administrative Procedure Act requires that all final opinions and orders made as the result of adjudication be indexed and made available to the public. 5 U.S.C. § 552(a)(2). The requirement reaches in its terms to all decisions whether or not they are otherwise subject to the APA. The requirement I should guess is honored much more frequently in the breach than in the observance. It is, in truth, overcomprehensive by far. Many final orders—as, for example, those of the customs or immigration inspector—are oral. Others, even if written, would offer no conceivable guidance to the public if someone of great diligence and great respect for the letter of the law were to compile and to index them; examples are IRS audits or affirmative actions on social security applications. The need is to find language which is discriminating enough to make sense in most of its applications; none can make sense in all of its applications. That modest objective might be achieved along these lines.

(a) Every final opinion or order which is of a type and issued in circumstances such that it might reasonably be used as a precedent shall be made available to the public.

(b) The opinions and orders made publicly available under paragraph (a) above shall be indexed to the extent and in a manner sufficient to make them readily available upon reasonable search by an interested and normally competent member of the public.

(c) No opinion or order which has not been made publicly available and indexed, as required by this Section 3, shall be used to impose any sanction or detriment in favor of the agency in any subsequent proceeding.

(d) In making its opinions and orders publicly available the agency may delete or mask identifying details, or may delay making them publicly available, in order to prevent a clearly unwarranted invasion of personal privacy on business confidentiality.

4. Informal advice to the public It is probable that, apart from the force of statutes and regulations in themselves, the majority of governmental controls are implemented by informal advice to the public. There are surely a thousand telephone and letter advices for every formal adjudication. The process of informal advice should obviously be given every encouragement. It presents, however, the basic dilemma: is it better to have immediate advice from whoever answers the telephone or dictates an answer to the letter, with all the risks of error and inconsistency, or to have a carefully considered and possibly long-delayed advice of the agency itself? Along with this choice goes the presumption, under the careful analysis of *National Automatic Laundry and Cleaning Council* v. *Schultz*,__F.2d__(CADC, March 31, 1971), 28 P. & F., AD. L.2D 532 (1971), that the advice of the agency itself will be subject to judicial review while that of the staff will not. The general exception provision offered below seems sufficient safeguard to permit either the agency or the private inquirer to elect the sort of advice to be given. A possible statutory framework would be:

(a) Each agency shall within one year from the enactment of this act publish regulations defining the procedures by which it may in its discretion issue declaratory orders defining the interpretation or application of its governing statute or regulations. These procedures may, as prescribed in the regulations or as determined by the agency in particular cases, consist of evidentiary hearing and adjudication or submission upon affidavit or written statement, and with or without briefs or oral argument.

(b) Each agency shall provide by regulation an informal procedure by which any affected member of the public may make oral or written inquiry of and receive advice from the agency or its staff as to the interpretation or application of its governing statute or regulations. Such regulations—

> (i) shall provide a procedure by which the inquirer may present adverse staff advice for agency review and determination; and
>
> (ii) may provide a procedure by which the agency on its own motion, and with due advice to the inquirer, may within a reasonable period take under review for its own determination any advice given an inquirer by its staff.

(c) The agency shall not impose penalty or detriment or deny benefits contrary to any order or advice given under this section.

(d) Orders and advice given under this section which have precedential value as defined in Section 3(a) shall be made publicly available as provided in that Section 3.

(e) All advice which is either adverse to the inquirer or has precedential value as defined in Section 3(a) shall indicate the reasons for the advised conclusion.

5. Agency action An attentive concern for full individual protection in the course of informal action could immobilize the government. The decision as to notice of contemplated action, or the opportunity to supply or to contest facts and reasons at the initial or the final level of decision, must in good sense vary according to the particular agency function in question. Yet a statute which preserved this necessary flexibility could be no more than hortatory. I have sought to escape this dilemma by making mandatory a minimum opportunity to participate in the agency action, and by encouraging a broader participation where feasible.

(a) Each agency which by its action might impose a penalty or detriment or deny a benefit should to the extent practicable in its function provide by regulation some or all of the following procedures to govern such action. Such regulations shall in any case include provisions designed to accomplish the requirements of paragraph (d) below, and shall include provisions designed to accomplish either paragraphs (c) or (e) below.

(b) Where the agency initiates such action upon its own motion, it shall advise the person or persons affected, or their appropriate representatives, that such action is under consideration, and shall give them a reasonable opportunity to supply relevant facts and the reasons why such agency action should or should not be taken. Similar notice and opportunity shall be given of any application or of any action by the agency on its own motion to third parties who would be affected by such action, either by way of precedent or by way of indirect consequences. The notice shall be given as is most practicable in the circumstances by publication in the *Federal Register* or by individual communication.

(c) When the agency staff has prepared a draft of agency action which imposes a penalty or detriment or denies a benefit, or has made a recommendation for such action, a copy of such draft or recommendation shall be made available to the person or persons affected and a reasonable opportunity afforded, before final agency action is taken, to contest the facts or reasons upon which the proposed action is based. That opportunity, as is appropriate in the circumstances, shall include one or more of the following procedures—

(i) a written statement, brief, or affidavit;

(ii) personal conference or oral argument; or

(iii) an evidentiary hearing, confined to the particular issues of fact in dispute.

(d) Any agency decision which imposes a penalty or detriment or denies a benefit shall set forth or indicate the facts and reasons upon which such decision is based. Checklists or other forms may be used where individually composed statements are not practicable.

(e) The agency shall by regulation provide a reasonable opportunity for any person who would suffer a penalty or detriment or be denied a benefit by its action to apply for reconsideration upon a showing that its action was based upon an erroneous understanding of the facts or upon invalid reasons.

6. Appeal Quite obviously the fairness of governmental action is improved by the possibility of appeal to higher and independent authority. Equally obviously, provision for such an appeal slows the process of government and exacts costs, in terms of delay and of drain on the time of superior officers, which might exceed the gains in a greater fairness of procedure.

The issue is narrowly balanced, but on the whole it seems wiser to avoid provision for appeal, even bearing in mind the general excepting provision made below. My reasons are: (a) In general, the appellate authority is going to be predisposed to sustain the agency action which is under appeal, and that predisposition would be strengthened in direct ratio to the number of appeals. (b) Adverse decision in matters of monetary or other consequence are likely in any case to be brought under judicial review, and the exhaustion doctrine would require the delay of appeal where one is provided, however slight the practical possibility of executive department reversal. (c) Expedition in governmental decision may often be better than a delayed wisdom, and this is especially the case if the delay is awaiting an appellate decision which is very likely to be affirmance.

7. Exceptions and exemptions I have I believe made adequately clear my belief that no man is wise enough to devise any rule, however narrow its scope and rich its obvious appeal, which can uniformly be applied to all informal functions. Most of the statutory provisions suggested above would be wildly imprudent if enacted as categorical imperatives. There must be some room for escape, to prevent grievous harm to the informal functions which the draftsman happened to overlook.

Administration of the escape clause cannot wisely be left to the agencies themselves, otherwise the act becomes purely hortatory. The most appropriate person to weigh the needs of fair procedure against the practical needs of the agency who finds the statute illy adapted to its function seems to be the chairman of the Administrative Conference. The act should accordingly provide: Any agency which concludes that any provision of this act cannot practicably be applied to any function performed by such agency may apply to the chairman of the Administrative Conference of the United States for exemption of such function from the provision which it believes to be impracticable in its application. The application shall be in a form prescribed by said chairman, and shall detail precisely the reasons compliance with the provision would be impracticable. Exception from the statutory provision shall be granted only upon a clear showing of impracticability, and may be for an indefinite or for a prescribed period of time. The chairman shall consult with the agency and investigate the function in question to the extent necessary and shall in his order specify the facts and reasons which lead him to grant or to deny the application. The agency need not comply with this act to the extent that it has filed and is awaiting decision upon such an application for exemption.

Such is the form which the Informal Procedure Act of 1980 would take if I were assigned the task of drafting it in 1971. By the time of actual drafting, and certainly by the time of enactment, many of the uncertainties which have troubled me today would be capable of resolution. But by that time there would have been uncovered many new and unsuspected problems to take their place. As experience and knowledge accumulate in this field it will, I believe, be found to be more rather than less difficult and complex. By the same token, I believe the need for statutory reform will be seen more clearly as the field of informal action is explored. At some point, enactment of an imperfect statutory code of procedure will almost surely be found to be preferable to inaction.

The result, like most procedural reform, will be only a modest change in the quality of government. The citizen will still be governed by ordinary men trying, with varying degrees of competence and energy, to do as good a job as they can under all the circumstances. Those circumstances may include inadequate manpower, conflicting statutory or administration policies, nagging wives, and simple tedium. No procedural reform can remove obstacles such as these to fair and efficient government. But they can, and should, remove much of the personal and unconfined discretion, much of the simple mistake of fact, and much of the unexplained and possibly indefensible decision making which is encouraged by the present absence in many informal functions of even the most rudimentary procedural requirements.

NINE
LIKE BIG JOE'S FORKLIFT, BUREAU DIRECTOR PERSEVERED

Michael Pertschuk

One day, the miniature forklift Big Joe Riddick piloted around the Federal Trade Commission garage, hauling and stacking the great mounds of paper that pour in and out of the FTC, broke loose at the top of a ramp and lumbered downward unmanned, gathering force before coming to a jarring rest in the backside of Al Kramer's scarred and bruised 1971 Plymouth. But the Kramermobile, survivor of countless chance encounters before this one, already bore so many scars of battle, no one could tell the new from the old. It took the beating from Big Joe's forklift without visible distress, and never missed a day in its honest performance.

And that's about the way it was with Al: Each day the fates conspired some new torment for the FTC's director of the Bureau of Consumer Protection. But he just shrugged off the day's disasters and bulled ahead.

The bureau director should be deep in talent and skill, but more to the point he must have a hide that weathers storm and outrage. Unaccountable bureaucrat? Hardly. The director is, in the first instance, accountable to the five-member commission (a management hierarchy that resembles a mushroom spreading eagerly at the top). He is accountable to them collectively for generating enough cases, rules, and reports to satisfy their demands—both studious and whimsical.

And he must do this while simultaneously responding to their insistence upon exhaustive groundwork, and bearing their incessant complaints of delay, which of course their sporadic pursuit of perfection invariably causes. All this, while the

This selection is taken from *Legal Times* III (December 21, 1981), 9–10. Used by permission of the publisher and author.

chairman and his fellow commissioners individually command adherence to a separate set of shifting and idiosyncratic goals, priorities, sensitivities, crotchets.

To Congress, the chairman and the commission are pleased to be held accountable—for those matters which receive universal acclaim! But when businessmen howl and their congressmen scowl, it is the bureau director who is served up by the commission for congressional accounting.

SOLICITOUS DUCKS

The commission is interlaced with supporting limbs and branches designed, in theory, to aid and succor the director in carrying out his mission. The reality is something else again. The director often feels as if he spends each day getting pecked to death by solicitous ducks.

The commission's general counsel, its institutional lawyer, removed from the responsibility for pursuing enforcement initiatives, invariably erects exquisite legal barriers to the bureau director's carefully laid plans, usually at the eleventh hour, always with Olympian disdain, normally objecting that "it cannot be done this way" and only rarely affirming "Here is how it can be done."

Over on the management side, the commission's executive director is charged with providing the material and human resources to support the bureaus, but he is the inevitable harbinger of nagging constraints. Before the bureau director can contract for the most crucial research, oil the creakiest chair, launch the most vital investigation, or paint the dreariest peagreen walls, he first must connive to get past the executive director. Then he must justify the budget before the commission, ready with cleaver in these austere times. And he must then persevere within that budget.

In the ivory tower recesses of the agency, the Office of Policy Planning veritably brims with fresh ideas—for the bureau director to carry out. Its visionary thinkers spin intriguing dreams for the future while depleting precious staff resources for the present, disdaining the slogging trench work of consumer protection projects that may have lost their glamour but not their worth.

There are the pressures of affirmative action, necessary but persistent, besieging him for demonstrable commitment to equal employment opportunity: the minority task force, the women's task force, the Hispanic task force, the older staff task force, the support staff task force, each demanding that more of each be hired and promoted, and given *meaningful* work in the agency's mission.

TROUBLE AT HOME

At "home," in the Bureau of Consumer Protection, the director must rely upon his corps of assistant directors, the commission's vital force of middle-managers, for support and results. As in many families, though, internal conflict can be the most unnerving. Division heads resist his authority, yet demand his uncritical advocacy of their pet projects before the commission and the world—often heedless of conflicting demands.

And then there are the staff lawyers in the commissions trenches, dedicated, committed—often caught up in enthusiasm and zeal for projects that in their eyes transcend all else. To them the director is the classic bureaucratic bottleneck, the insufferable naysayer, frustrating the manifest public interest in their projects. His incessant questioning borders on impudence, his streamlining of their proposals becomes a betrayal of the consumer cause.

The bureau director can also expect daily hounding from the director of public information: constantly alert for stories that trumpet the greater glory of the chairman and the commission, or transformed Hydelike into an avenging angel driven to ferret out embarrassing premature leaks.

In recent years, the bureau director has also been subjected to almost hourly badgering by the Office of Congressional Liaison. This unit, which in its newly elevated importance in the commission's hierarchy tends to take on some of Congress' own imperiousness, demands virtually overnight completion of those commission initiatives that have captured congressional whims, while praying (sometimes out loud) that the bureau director will temper or deep-six initiatives provoking congressional ire.

And of course there is the commission's Bureau of Economics—also newly elevated to heights of prominence in this era of cost-benefit regulation—elegantly demonstrating with the assistance of charts, graphs, numbers, and authoritative models that the Bureau of Consumer Protection's view of right and justice is a minus-sum game, or less nicely put, economic perversion.

So the director of the Bureau of Consumer Protection must accommodate this "help" from the sister branches of his agency, badgered by an imperial chairman who preaches harmony, trust, and cooperation among his top aides, while his own young assistants ply him, Iago-like, with rumor and gossip, bespeaking the unending perfidy of the others.

OUTSIDE DEMANDS

And from outside the commission, pounding on the director's door, come the demands of citizens organized and unorganized. The consumer advocates, grass-roots public-interest groups, parents and pediatricians, the elderly, women, blacks, Hispanics, nutritionalists, behavioralists, professions and quasiprofessions, organized labor; yes, and downtrodden individual consumers, battered and outraged in the marketplace, turning to the commission as a last resort, yet skeptical of ever receiving help from bureaucrats: all of them demanding, querulous, properly suspicious.

There are the small-business groups decrying over-regulation and big-business groups demanding no regulation; whole industries, like advertising, sensitive as an overbred racehorse rearing hysterically at the faintest signs of innovative moves to curb unfair or deceptive practices.

Then there is the press: the trade press, which flourishes on esoteric inside slivers of information (routine stories elevated by exclusive prematurity); and the national press, which must find global significance in each commission action—or nonaction. Each newly assigned national reporter pleading and wheedling for help and explanation, wanting first to know exactly what the FTC *does*, then soon enough feeling self-confidently expert and turning ferociously at the first hint of commission vulnerability.

Fueling this Washington madness are the centurions of the FTC bar, the lawyers, many of whom trace the roots of their expertise to fondly recalled days on the commission staff when the commission brilliantly but fairly took on only defined evildoers and not the innocent bystanders who now flood their stately offices seeking relief against the commission's "unfounded" inquisitions.

They are, most of them, honorable men and women who care deeply about the commission and would rally without hesitation were the commission faced with extinction. In return, however, they do expect to be treated with heightened familiarity and respect. Among other things, they expect the bureau director to be available to meet with them whenever junior staffers fail to appreciate the sweet reason of their arguments.

But pity the bureau director who understandably seeks to filter valid demands for meetings from the rest—he will find himself labeled as arrogant, hostile to business and the bar, unprofessional, close-minded, mean-spirited and, of course, a consumer zealot.

All in all, next to that of the Roman citizens who were served up to the imperial lions, it is hard to conceive of a position as thankless as that of the bureau director.

ACCEPTING CRITICISM, IGNORING PRAISE

And if you are Al Kramer, you are also assailed by a conscience that recognizes no limits of human capacity or physical endurance, and possesses an infinite capacity to absorb criticism and ignore praise.

What manner of human not only functions but thrives under such conditions? A secular saint; a stubborn and unyielding work machine ("it may be Thanksgiving to you, but it's only another Thursday to me"); an unremitting and unsentimental taskmaster; a disciplined legal scholar; a stubborn and profane proletarian; an elegant and disarming advocate.

There was no obstacle that deflected him from his course—but his single-mindedness could evoke a certain black humor. As, for example, the night the power failed in his sparsely furnished surburban home. He had worked until 2:00 A.M. and was dozing when he was suddenly awakened by a storm which in turn provoked a power failure. Realizing the meat in his freezer would spoil if unattended, he got up and spent the rest of the night cooking it. The following day, without sleep, he was early at work. Only a stifled midmorning yawn prompted a question. He responded without complaint, with only a wry, off-hand retelling.

A predisposition to martyrdom? Al heard criticism, accepted and absorbed blame, and never deflected responsibility for failure. Though each criticism and each embraced responsibility piled high the burdens he carried, he would never hear the balancing words of praise and true affection.

In the early days of our administration, the senior staff went on a "retreat" to review its working relationships. After two days in intensive, sometimes brutal analysis of each other's faults, we agreed to sit and receive at least one word of praise (no matter how modest) from everybody else. We went around the group in turn. The process, however contrived, took on a spontaneous warmth—coming in some cases from those who had earlier exuded hostility. Al spoke highly of each of his fellows, but when it came his turn to listen, he alone among us refused to be complimented. And, in accordance with the rules, his resistance was respected.

GLORIOUSLY PROLETARIAN

Not all saints, of course, are delicate in constitution or dainty in demeanor. In East Los Angeles, a tough part of town, his father eked out a living in the junk business. Al, one of nine children, was the only one to make it through college. All of five-foot-eight and a spare 100 pounds at full trim, he pulled himself through Berkeley on the back of a football scholarship. His coach at California, where he served as one of the smallest lineman in the school's history, told him one day, not without affection, "Though you're small, Kramer, you're not very fast." But he was bullheadedly determined.

He remained gloriously, profanely, and stubbornly proletarian in an environment otherwise suffused with middle-class liberal style, if not affection.

His sleeping habits are the stuff of legends. On an *ordinary* night he'd work until 2:00 or 3:00—then catnap, wake, and begin working again at 4:00 or 5:00 A.M. When the work demanded (or when he demanded the work) he would plow through the night, catnapping during the day (and nodding off when protocol, but not substance, required his presence at long, tedious commission meetings). He often ran the seven miles to work—in part to grind out the tension and stress. He trained and ran a marathon—but in sneakers, (bronzed for posterity as a farewell gift from his staff), no high-fashion running shoes for Al Kramer!

His clothes, like his speed, were functional no more. But even with greater wealth, one suspects Al's wardrobe would have remained the same. The same dogged resistance to liberal chic may also explain—to some extent—why this ascetic, dedicated consumer advocate was also a notorious, indiscriminate junk food junkie in an environment populated by health food devotees. If Al ever abused his authority in any way, it was in the rumored midmorning calls to staff members housed in one of the commission's outlying downtown offices—and known to be scheduled for a meeting in the Kramer office—asking if that person would mind stopping en route for an emergency supply of Hostess Twinkies.

NO GAME-PLAYING

When Al was first appointed and began reviewing work in progress, many of the senior attorneys who came under his scrutiny quickly began to complain that he was insensitive to their prerogatives as senior and experienced staff members. The truth is that they—as many of us—had rarely encountered anyone as direct and impolitic.

For the young FTC lawyer whose project was on his agenda, a work session was a mixed pleasure at best. There were no amenities, no acts of stroking, just a procession of hard, piercing questions and challenges laced with a string of expletives.

There was no game-playing, no easy camaraderie; he was demanding, earthy, grueling in his attention to detail and insistence on perfection. If work did not meet his standards, he sent it back. If a memorandum to the commission failed to spell out the weaknesses and risks in a proposed course of action, as well as the arguments in support of the staff position, he insisted that the paper provide the commission with a fair balance. He could be a forceful advocate for deeply felt staff convictions, but only when those convictions were built upon solid investigation of the facts and the law.

NATURAL TENSION

There is, of course, a constant and natural tension between managers and staff: between the freedom to innovate, take responsibility—and to *fail*—on the one hand, and the need and responsibility of the person in charge to make certain that policies and directives are carried out. At a time when every major commission action was subject to intense scrutiny, the bureau director had the added burden of making certain that no piece of work would be vulnerable to attack through inadvertence or inattention in staff preparation. While eventually he learned to ease up on the tightness of his reign, Al remained a hard and demanding taskmaster.

Toward the end of his time in office the rumor circulated that Al's management skills had been criticized by other members of the "management team." The staff, led by the assistant directors, caucused and spontaneously came to Al to tell him of their respect and support, and of their masochistic hope that he would stay and continue to make life miserable for them.

Kramer was perceived by the business and legal community as a fanatic consumer zealot. How could any man deeply trusted by Ralph Nader also be trusted by business? Among the "alumni" who make up the Brahmins of the FTC bar, this impression was reinforced by his correct but unaccommodating attitude toward them. Part of *their* stock in trade was their historic "access" to commissioners and bureau directors. But Al limited meetings with these lawyers to those necessary to resolve genuine issues or misunderstandings between outside counsel and the FTC staff.

Al was simultaneously disdained as a zealot by lobbyists and the FTC bar—and as a "conservative roadblock" by overeager commission staff. Of course, he was neither. He was a compassionate, hard-nosed manager—not an incompatible combination in one person, and a *necessary* one for a public servant of liberal convictions to be effective in a budget-slashing environment.

Perhaps the most telling paradox was that his most notable achievements lay not in innovative programs (though there were many true innovations and many accomplishments). His great success lay rather in taking hold of and taming the great mass of nearly formless regulations before the commission that ironically had been proposed by previous Republican administrations. These sat like unleavened dough on the public table, symbolizing the excessive sweep of regulatory appetite at a time when all forms of regulation were facing increased public odium. By sheer weight of determination and intellect, he stripped away the shoddy and excessive, the trivial and the marginal, the ornaments, and saved for the commission the *core* of the rules—what was effective and economically workable, and would involve only the necessary minimum of paperwork for industry and policing by the FTC.

Did the American voters really choose to get government officials like Al Kramer off their backs?

TEN
A UNIFIED CORPS OF ALJs
A Proposal to Test the Idea at the Federal Level

Jeffrey S. Lubbers

The administrative law judge (ALJ) is the central figure in formal administrative adjudication. This year 1,119 ALJs are employed by 29 federal agencies, and they decide more than 250,000 cases annually. In fact, they outnumber district judges two to one and they hear many more cases. Although almost all the decisions of ALJs are "initial decisions" subject to review by a board, commission, or agency head, in practice most of those initial decisions become the final agency ruling. Thus it is important to understand the role of ALJs and the operation of the ALJ program on the federal level in order to evaluate the fairness and efficiency of the administrative process, and the effectiveness of federal judicial administration generally.

The federal ALJ program, based on requirements of the 1946 Administrative Procedure Act (APA), is fairly easy to describe. The Office of Personnel Management (OPM)—formerly the Civil Service Commission—through its Office of Administrative Law Judges is exclusively responsible for the initial examination, certification for selection, and compensation of ALJs. OPM determines the minimum experience needed to be an ALJ, and OPM conducts interviews, administers a test of writing ability, evaluates the experience of applicants, and ranks eligible applicants on one or both of two registers maintained by OPM—one for those positions at the GS-15 level (primarily at the Social Security Administration) and one for GS-16 level positions.

When an agency needs to appoint an ALJ, it selects a name from the register of eligibles using procedures required by statute and OPM regulation. Generally

This selection came from *Judicature* 65 (November 1981), 266–76. Used by permission. Footnotes omitted.

speaking, most ALJs are recruited from within the government, often from within the appointing agency, largely because the salary ceiling for federal employees makes it difficult to attract experienced private practitioners.

A mere listing of some of the types of matters acted upon by ALJs shows how important they are to our daily lives and to the national economy: licensure and route certification of transportation by air, rail, motor vehicle, or ship; licensure of radio and television broadcasting; establishment of rates for gas, electrical, communication, and transportation services; compliance with federal standards relating to interstate trade, labor-management relations, advertising, communications, consumer products, food and drugs, corporate mergers, and antitrust; regulation of health and safety in mining, transportation and industry; regulation of trading in securities, commodities, and futures; adjudication of claims relating to Social Security benefits, workers' compensation, international trade, and mining; and many other matters.

The ALJ's role in such hearings is basically the same as that of any other trial judge—namely to administer oaths, issue subpoenas authorized by law, hold prehearing conferences, take or order the taking of depositions, question witnesses, vote on procedural motions, regulate the course of the hearing, and make findings of fact and conclusions of law.

In this article, I briefly document the changing nature of the role of administrative law judges in the federal administrative process, and I discuss, in light of this change, concerns about the independence of ALJs as reflected by the Administrative Procedure Act (APA) and other statutes. Finally, I address proposals that ALJs be made into a unified corps—to act as a separate and independent administrative judiciary—and I suggest that we partially restructure the current system to test the practicality of such proposals.

A REDUCED ROLE IN REGULATORY ADJUDICATION

When the APA was enacted in 1946, there were 196 ALJs, of whom 125 (64 percent) were engaged in conducting hearings for agencies generally considered to be economic regulatory agencies. This year the overall number of ALJs was 1,119, but only 109 (less than 10 percent) were employed by economic regulatory agencies. By contrast, 695 ALJs are employed by the Social Security Administration alone, and another 266 are employed by five labor-related agencies.

Table 10-1, which traces this development from 1947 to 1981, shows the almost uninterrupted growth of the Social Security ALJ corps, engendered largely by hearings under the Medicare and Medicaid programs established in the 1960s and the Supplemental Security Income program in 1972. Almost as striking is the growth in the labor-related agencies, which now employ nearly a quarter of all ALJs.

Table 10-1 suggests two trends in administrative law which impel renewed critical examination of the formal agency adjudicative process and the ALJ's role in it. One is the growing dissatisfaction with formal, so-called trial-type procedures as a means of resolving the kinds of "policy" issues that customarily arise in licensing, merger, and other cases involving economic regulation. Some of these issues are largely normative, involving a choice from among several reasonable alternatives. Others involve risk assessment and making extrapolations or other predictions from frequently imperfect data and scientific knowledge.

TABLE 10-1   Federal ALJs by Type of Agency (1947–1981)

	JUNE 1947[3]	JUNE 1954[4]	JULY 1962[5]	FEBRUARY 1974[6]	JANUARY 1979[7]	JANUARY 1980[8]	JUNE 1981[9]
Economic regulatory agencies[1]	125 (63.8%)	165 (59.4%)	221 (44.7%)	153 (19.3%)	157 (14.7%)	142 (12.4%)	109 (9.7%)
Labor-related agencies[2]	35 (17.9%)	49 (17.6%)	74 (15.0%)	143 (18.1%)	210 (19.6%)	257 (22.4%)	266 (23.8%)
Social Security Administration	13 (6.6%)	20 (7.2%)	164 (33.2%)	431 (54.4%)	660 (61.7%)	698 (60.9%)	695 (62.1%)
Other Agencies	23 (11.7%)	44 (15.8%)	35 (7.1%)	65 (8.2%)	43 (4.0%)	49 (4.3%)	49 (4.4%)
Totals	196	278	494	792	1070	1146	1119

[1]CAB, CFTC, CPSC, EPA, FCC, FDA, FERC, FTC, ICC, ITC, SEC, NRC, and predecessor agencies.
[2]NLRB, Labor, OSHRC, FMSHRC, FLRA.
[3]Mans, "Selecting the Hidden Judiciary," 63 *Judicature* 60, 64 (1979).
[4]Kintner, Doyle, Reynolds, and Winnings, "Appointments and Status of Federal Hearing Officers," *Report of Committee on Hearing Officers of the President's Conference on Administrative Procedure* (1954), Appendix D.
[5]Lester, "Report on Section II Hearing Examiner," Committee on Personnel, Administrative Conference of the U.S (1962), p. 25. (Indian Affairs judges not included.)
[6]Social Security Administration Subcommittee draft report to Civil Service Commission Study Committee for the Effective Utilization of Administrative Law Judges (La Macchia Report) (1974) Exhibit 2. (Does not include temporary ALJs.)
[7]Mans, "Selecting the hidden judiciary," 63 *Judicature* 60, 64, (1979).
[8]"Federal Administrative Law Judge Hearings—Statistical Report for 1976–1978," Administrative Conference of the U.S. (1980), p. 21.
[9]Table supplied by Office of Administrative Law Judges, U.S. Office of Personnel Management. See Table 10-2 of this article.

More and more, these questions tend to be taken out of the familiar formal adjudicative process and to be resolved by rule making or by procedural devices such as those instituted by the Food and Drug Administration and Civil Aeronautics Board to avoid or restrict the scope of evidentiary hearings. In 1977, the Senate Governmental Affairs Committee, after a comprehensive study of delay in the administrative process, approved of the movement away from formal adjudication in certain types of cases:

> Because formal adjudicatory procedures are not well-suited to certain kinds of cases now handled by such procedures and unnecessarily delay these cases, the [APA] should be amended to provide for a modified procedure to govern those cases. Specifically, the modified procedure should be made applicable to cases involving market entry and exit, rate regulation, approval of financial transactions and technical decisions.

The proposed modified procedure called for legislative-type hearings in which oral arguments and written testimony would be permitted but without cross-examination, followed, where necessary, by an adjudicative hearing in which cross-examination would be permitted to resolve particular factual disputes. This model likely would reduce (though not eliminate) the need for ALJs in licensing agencies, since they would presumably only be required in the adjudicative hearing stage.

Though they continue to receive serious consideration, those proposals to amend the APA have not been enacted, partly because agencies have been able to use the existing flexibility in the act to develop modified procedures tailored to their individual needs. And, of course, the increasing momentum of substantive deregulation has changed the rules in several key agencies—leading to an even more striking reduction in the need for trial-type decision making as market forces are substituted for regulation.

MORE BENEFITS AND ENFORCEMENT CASES

The second trend—the veritable explosion of benefits cases and of enforcement cases—is just as dramatic. The great majority of ALJs in the federal government preside over such cases; Social Security Administration (SSA) ALJs handle over 200,000 cases annually, and Department of Labor ALJs handle several thousand more benefits cases involving black-lung benefits claims and longshoremen's compensation. Though SSA procedural rules offer the opportunity for a hearing that has nearly all the elements of a formal APA hearing, these cases in practice generally involve short, informal hearings in which the government is not represented by counsel and the claimant is often unrepresented.

Some have concluded from this, and from the fact that other disability programs in the United States and other countries use non-ALJ panels, that SSA cases do not require the involvement of fully qualified ALJs. However, a recent comprehensive study of the system concluded that the costs of using ALJs are not prohibitive in view of the added perceptions of fairness and the actual informality of the process, as well as the costs involved in changing the system. There is little doubt then that the disability claims hearing process will continue to require a large number of ALJs.

The other major growth area is enforcement. Most of the agencies employing ALJs (including the five labor-related agencies) conduct proceedings to discipline license holders, revoke licenses, issue cease-and-desist orders, or impose civil money penalties. In the cases—which likely will increase in number as regulators concentrate less on developing new regulations and more on enforcing the rules already on the books—adjudicatory fact-finding and demeanor evidence are often at the center of the case, and policy issues absent or submerged.

Given the nature of the issues involved (and in some programs, the high volume of cases), the ALJ's decision is rarely reversed by the agency in such cases. Therefore, the ALJ's hearing and decision are governed by strict procedural safeguards, and the need for an independent fact-finder is quite apparent.

It is in these enforcement cases that questions are most often raised about agency ALJs deciding cases that another arm of their employing agency has initiated. Paradoxically, however, the high-volume nature of many of these benefits and enforcement programs also puts a premium on quantitative performance and even facilitates its evaluation, thus leading to an inevitable clash of independence values and productivity values.

Consider, for example, the recent brouhaha that developed between the Social Security ALJs and the management of the SSA's Office of Hearings and Appeals, resulting in an internecine lawsuit. Among the management initiatives most strenuously opposed by members of the SSA ALJ corps were a peer-review program, a monthly production goal/quota, and a quality-assurance program designed to identify ALJs whose decisions deviated significantly from the agency-wide trend. A federal appeals court has ruled that SSA ALJs can challenge the agency action, and returned the case to district court for further consideration.

PROTECTING ALJ INDEPENDENCE

The Administrative Procedure Act contains several provisions designed to preserve the independence and impartiality of the ALJ. It limits the role of the employing agency in the selection and appointment process, and it requires that the ALJ (and other agency decision makers) conduct business in an impartial manner. Moreover, if a party files a disqualification petition against an ALJ in any case, the agency must determine that issue on the record, as part of the decision in that case. The APA also prescribes that an ALJ may not be responsible to, or subject to supervision by, anyone performing investigative or prosecutorial functions for an agency. This "separation of functions" requirement is designed to prevent the investigative or prosecutorial arm of an agency from controlling a hearing or influencing the ALJ.

Finally, to ensure that the ALJ is insulated from improper agency pressure and controls, the APA contains two other provisions to make the ALJ more independent of the employing agency: ALJs are to be assigned to their cases in rotation so far as practicable, and they may not perform duties inconsistent with their role as ALJs. They also receive their pay as prescribed by the Office of Personnel Management, independently of agency recommendations or ratings, and they are removable only for good cause after a hearing before the Merit Systems Production Board.

Despite these safeguards, some observers suggest this quasi-independent status of ALJs should be transformed into complete independence. Indeed, Congress has, in several enforcement programs, provided specifically for increased separation of agency prosecuting and adjudicating functions. In 1947, shortly after the passage of the APA, Congress passed the Taft-Hartley Act, which created a strict separation between the NLRB general counsel and the board, its staff, and its ALJs. In other programs, Congress has gone even further.

Thus, in 1975 Congress established as an independent agency the National Transportation Safety Board (once part of the Department of Transportation) to hear challenges brought by pilots when the FAA issues license denials, suspensions, and revocation actions. It also established the wholly adjudicatory Occupational Safety and Health Review Commission in 1970 and Federal Mine Safety and Health Review Commission in 1977 to hear challenges to civil penalty impositions and abatement orders issued by the Department of Labor. The Safety Board and the two Review Commissions each have a separate corps of ALJs which makes initial decisions on such challenges, subject to review by the board or commission.

But even as Congress has created these adjudicatory agencies, which act somewhat like agencies and somewhat like courts (leading to some knotty procedural problems and turf battles), it has left unchanged the structure of older enforcement agencies like the FTC, SEC, and Postal Service. Meanwhile, it has also created new enforcement agencies like the Consumer Product Safety Commission and Commodity Futures Trading Commission, and added new enforcement programs in the departments of Agriculture, Commerce, Interior, and Labor that lack any elements of separation of prosecutory and adjudicatory functions beyond those specified in the APA.

A UNIFIED CORPS OF FEDERAL ALJs?

If the current administrative law judge system appears to be diverse, it is largely the result of the reactive nature of Congress. Despite this diversity, or perhaps because of it, there is renewed interest in the potential for increased efficiency and fairness in a unified administrative trial court, or at least a centralized corps of judges to be used by the agencies, but not formally employed or housed by them.

The suggestion that hearing officers be made a unified corps, appointed and employed by an authority other than the agencies, is not new. It was considered and rejected by the study group that originally proposed the APA in 1941; it was proposed by the Hoover Commission Report in 1955; it was espoused by the Federal Administrative Law Judges Conference in 1973; it was suggested for study by a federal advisory committee in 1974; and it was advocated by a former ABA president in 1976. Agencies have opposed the idea, fearing that they will lose the expertise of ALJs assigned to their agency, delaying and lessening the reliability of initial decisions.

Proponents of the corps concept point to the following benefits:

Operational efficiency would be enhanced by a corps made up of interchangeable judges, who could be assigned to agency cases as the need arises. Since agency case loads are not always predictable or within the agency's control, the number of ALJs employed under the present system by agencies may be too high or too low.

Centralized housekeeping and accounting would save money. Present redundancies in law libraries, docket clerks, case-tracking systems, administrative assistants, travel arrangements, and the reservation of hearing facilities would be eliminated. And unification would promote uniformity in the quality of office space, law clerks, and secretarial assistance.

Public confidence in the impartiality and independence of ALJs would be enhanced by a divorce from agency administration. Since many ALJs were also formerly lawyers for their agency, since some perquisites of the job (for example, office space, parking privileges, and travel to seminars) remain in agency control, and since long-term association with one agency's policies and personnel may subtly influence behavior, ALJs may be susceptible to a proagency bias that would be lessened if they were centralized in a separate corps.

If judges were not attached to agencies, they would require agencies to articulate their regulations in clearer language, much as federal judges often do.

Individual ALJs would acquire a diversified experience and not become stale from repeatedly hearing similar cases. This, apparently, has been a salutary by-product of the existing, but limited, loan program in which OPM allows understaffed agencies to temporarily borrow the services of willing ALJs from other agencies. This diversity of case load might also stimulate the recruitment of new ALJs.

Operation of a corps might facilitate performance evaluation of ALJs, both quantitatively and qualitatively. This is obviously a controversial issue since evaluation of judicial performance bears such a close relationship to independence values. But since the agencies would have a less direct interest in the evaluation of any particular judge, it could probably be done more objectively.

Operation of a corps might permit a return to a multilevel grade system whereby more routine cases could be handled by lower-level, less experienced ALJs. Professor Antonin Scalia has argued that a multilevel system would be more efficient and would also inject needed performance incentives into the corps.

OPPOSITION TO THE IDEA

Opponents think the problems and drawbacks would outweigh any of the advantages, however:

> A unified corps would reduce efficiency, since it would dilute the expertise that staff ALJs bring to their agency. Agency statutes, regulations, and precedent can be difficult to master in a short time, and practitioners would be forced to educate—and reeducate—ALJs unfamiliar with the particular field of regulation.
>
> A new bureaucracy would have to be created to train and rotate over 1,100 judges to 30 agencies for over 200,000 hearings all over the country. If evaluation or promotional responsibilities were also given to the new office, the director's independence and "clout" would become a critical concern. The wrong mix could lead to greater politicalization than critics find in the current program.
>
> An equitable system for allocating ALJs to agencies for hearings would have to be devised. Since judges are not "free goods," perhaps some sort of "user's fee" would have to be charged agencies. Otherwise agencies might draw too liberally upon ALJs for nonjudicial functions or reduce their own efforts to settle cases prior to the hearing stage.
>
> The agency's reviewing function might be altered in unforeseen ways. Some proponents argue that establishment of a corps should be linked to a restriction of the agency's ability to review initial decisions of ALJs. The wisdom in this is debatable, but without such a change agencies likely would feel the need to review more initial decisions more intensively (in light of their reduced rapport or familiarity with the judges), leading to an overall lengthening of the decisional process.

A PROPOSAL FOR AN EXPERIMENT

It is not easy to resolve this debate on a theoretical level. That is why the experience of the pioneering states like New Jersey and Minnesota should be valuable, especially after the state systems finish their shakedown period and survive the problems of leadership changes. Of course, it should be recognized that the lessons learned in these state "laboratories" many not be so readily transferred to the federal level. A platoon of 41 New Jersey judges may work well, but, 1,100 federal ALJs may make for an unmanageable corps. Furthermore, five federal agencies now employ nearly 1,000 ALJs and the other 24 employing agencies average fewer than seven judges each. Proponents of any reform must bear the burden of attending to the practical details of its proposed application to such a balkanized judiciary.

In my view there is no reason why administrative law judges, selected on the basis of a genuine, even if flawed, merit selection program, should not be able to preside over a mix of cases as varied as federal district or state court judges, many of whom are selected after less rigorous review. But the practical problems of instituting a centralized corps on the federal level cannot be ignored.

A pilot program would be the best way to test the idea, but it must be broader than the existing loan program, by which underworked judges are temporarily loaned on an ad hoc basis (with approval of the Office of Personnel Management) to understaffed agencies. OPM has recently taken this one step further by establishing a very small pool (or "minicorps") of three judges who reported to OPM and were assigned to understaffed agencies.

I would like to see a more ambitious experiment involving the creation of a larger pool, overseen by OPM, to serve most of the small-volume agencies. The largest agencies would be excluded from the experiment; thus, the Social Security Administration, National Labor Relations Board, and Labor Department could retain intact their highly structured systems. The two wholly adjudicatory agencies, Occupational Safety and Health Review Commission and Federal Mine Safety Health Review Commission, would be excluded because they are already functioning as separate trial courts. And the economic regulatory agencies (most of which are medium-volume) would not participate since they must first adjust to the effects of the deregulation movement, which is tending to reduce their caseloads while shifting their emphasis toward enforcement and away from initial licensing. These agencies would include the ICC, FERC, FCC, FTC, FMC, SEC, and CAB.

TESTING THE IDEA

That leaves 17 agencies (*see* Table 10-2) with 68 ALJs currently employed—all but three having seven or fewer ALJs. These 17 agencies conduct a wide variety of proceedings, and undoubtedly have fluctuating case loads. If these 68 ALJs (plus a chief

TABLE 10-2   Total Federal ALJs by Agency (June 1, 1981)

Social Security Administration	695
National Labor Relations Board	112
Labor, Department of	82
Occupational Safety and Health Review Commission	45
Interstate Commerce Commission	28
Federal Energy Regulatory Commission	23
Federal Mine Safety and Health Review Commission	16
Coast Guard	15
Federal Communications Commission	13
Interior, Department of the	11
Federal Labor Relations Authority	11
Federal Trade Commission	10
Environmental Protection Agency	7
Federal Maritime Commission	7
Securities and Exchange Commission	7
Civil Aeronautics Board	6
National Transportation Safety Board	6
Agriculture, Department of	5
Commodity Futures Trading Commission	4
Postal Service	3
National Oceanic and Atmospheric Administration	3
Merit Systems Protection Board	2
International Trade Commission	2
Bureau of Alcohol, Tobacco and Firearms	1
Drug Enforcement Administration	1
Food and Drug Administration	1
Housing and Urban Development, Department of	1
Maritime Administration	1
Nuclear Regulatory Commission	1
TOTAL	1,119

Source: Office of Administrative Law Judges, U.S. Office of Personnel Management. Data does not include loans or unoccupied slots.

judge, augmented by a few more judges who would also cover agencies that occasionally need an ALJ, but do not employ one full-time) were transferred into a corps under OPM control to service all but the specifically excluded agencies, the idea would be put to a good test.

Implementing the idea would require legislative authorization as well as budgetary resources for OPM (presumably to its Office of ALJs). The experimental program could be established in OPM for a five-year period, and it could require all 17 agencies to use ALJs from this corps (unless OPM granted a waiver because the agency had shown that the extremely technical nature of its case requires in-house judges). After five years, OPM (or perhaps the Administrative Conference) would be required to submit to Congress an evaluation of the program.

The administrative efficiencies that the agencies would achieve should mute any opposition from these small-volume agencies, especially since adjudication is not as central to the missions of most of these agencies as it is to the others. And any ALJ who balked could transfer to one of the excluded agencies; presumably an equivalent number would wish to transfer into the corps.

It is of course possible to develop scenarios for a corps encompassing all 1,119 ALJs. For example, four panels might be created: claims adjudication, labor relations, nonlabor enforcement cases, and initial licensing cases with, say, four grade levels corresponding to GS-14 through GS-17. Each panel could be staffed with judges at all four levels. Panel administrators (GS-18) would then assign cases to different level judges depending on their presumed difficulty—though all judges would have the same degree of independence and would be deemed legally and constitutionally qualified to render initial decisions in all cases.

But describing even the skeleton of such a totally revamped system mainly serves to suggest all the nagging loose ends. What is needed is some experience to assess. The states are beginning to provide it, the time has come to institute a pilot program on the federal level, too.

ELEVEN
"TOWARD TOUGHNESS"

Eugene Bardach/Robert Kagan

A regulatory inspector is a law enforcement official. When he tells the stern-visaged guard at the factory security gate that he wants to inspect the firm's maintenance records for air pollution control equipment, the inspector draws courage (or even a self-righteous officiousness) from the fact that he is empowered by law to do so. When he walks through a refinery, a nursing home, or a cannery and encounters a profusion of potentially hazardous procedures and machines, the inspector looks to his book of regulations for general guidance and for specific safety criteria. In conversation with the managers of the regulated enterprise, the information an inspector can confidently demand, the excuses he feels authorized to recognize, the sanctions he can credibly threaten to invoke are closely related to the specific provisions of "the regs."

Of course, there is room for varying interpretations of the rules in some cases. Different inspectors may see different things and evaluate the relative seriousness of a particular offense in different ways. But a major preoccupation of most enforcement agencies is to reduce the variations by developing common interpretations of the rules and a unified philosophy of enforcement. To regulatory officials, therefore, the law matters. They constantly refer to specific provisions in the statutes they administer, the legal powers the statutes grant, and the goals those statutes seek.

In a workshop that we convened in 1978, many enforcement officials referred to a shift in the nature of the laws they administered. Statutes and court decisions in

This selection comes from Chapter 2 of Eugene Bardach and Robert Kagan, *Going by the Book* (Philadelphia: Temple University Press, 1982), pp. 30–57. Reprinted by permission of the publisher and The Twentieth Century Fund.

the last decade, they said, enhanced their legal powers. At the same time, however, they lost discretion; now they must conduct inspections more with an eye toward what is legally proper. Much to the amusement of the industry representatives at the workshop, the regulators complained of being closely regulated, of being compelled to "go by the book."

The purpose of these changes has been to make regulatory enforcement tougher—more aggressive, more uniform, and more of a deterrent to undesirable conduct on the part of regulated enterprises.[1] But by constraining regulatory discretion, these legal changes also lay the premises for the problem of site-level unreasonableness.

THE TRADITIONAL LEGAL STRUCTURE OF ENFORCEMENT

In most law enforcement, the government investigator responds to a complaint about a past event—a burglary, a fraud, a discriminatory firing. He tries to resolve conflicting versions of what happened, gather evidence, or find a suspect who has disappeared. Enforcement of protective regulation by inspectors is different. Inspectors sometimes respond to complaints, but they usually come on their own initiative to enterprises that have not been accused of any wrongdoing. They search for *ongoing* violations, things that might go wrong in the future, and they check that certain precautions are being taken. Unlike policemen, who ordinarily patrol public places, inspectors regularly enter private buildings, pore over corporate records, and take product samples. To use the terminology of the Fourth Amendment, inspectors are regularly engaged in searches and seizures, often without "probable cause." In addition, inspectors in some agencies are granted summary powers to impose severe restrictions. Beginning in the nineteenth century, inspectors who discovered serious regulatory violations (or what they believed to be serious violations) could stop loaded ships from leaving port; order locomotives out of service; prevent occupancy of buildings; and quarantine or destroy diseased livestock, fruit trees, or food products. Today, inspectors can order a plane or pilot to stay on the ground, ban rail shipment of hazardous chemicals over poorly maintained sections of track, or "yellow tag" a dangerous machine on the spot, enjoining further operation.

These extensive powers of intrusion and control raise the possibility of misuse. A trigger-happy inspector could embargo food that is not in fact adulterated, generating adverse publicity about the firm in question. An overzealous enforcement officer might issue orders much broader than necessary, disrupting useful economic activity. A malicious inspector, annoyed at not being treated with the deference he feels he deserves, can deliberately harass an enterprise operating within the law. A venal inspector could steal trade secrets, extort bribes, engage in blackmail, or favor one firm while imposing heavier regulatory burdens on its competitors.

Under the theory of the state that has reigned since the founding of the repub-

---

[1]The changes in the legal structure of regulatory enforcement that we will describe have not been universal. There are literally hundreds of inspectorates, each concerned with a distinct array of processes and legal powers. Generalizations do not fall easily into place: legislatures enact regulatory programs one at a time and partially in response to specific political demands and technical enforcement problems. Some older agencies have remained largely immune to change, and all newer agencies are not created alike, so that it is easy to find examples that go against the trend toward the tougher enforcement that we describe. In addition, changes in the legal structure of regulatory agencies do not wholly determine how enforcement officials actually behave; they are only indicative

lic, the possibility of government abuse of coercive and intrusive powers must be checked. The inspectors themselves must be subjected to law. The enforcement process, in consequence, traditionally has been pervaded by a complex of legal rules and principles, which in turn have influenced actual enforcement practices.

The most salient legal rules are those that constrain coercive enforcement against allegedly serious violators—attempts by the agency to compel them to take certain remedial measures or to punish them for noncompliance. The basic legal model is the criminal justice system and its familiar principles of due process—the presumption of innocence, punishment only for proven and specific violations, separation of prosecutorial and adjudicatory powers, and adversarial hearings. Most agencies, accordingly, have been granted no formal remedial or sanctioning powers themselves, except for certain emergency situations. Inspectors can issue citations for violations of the law, but if the enterprise refuses to comply, the traditionally structured agency cannot levy fines or order the establishment to shut down; its only legal recourse is court action or the threat of such action. The agency petitions a *judge* to impose the penalty prescribed by law, be it an injunction, a fine, or a suspended license, and to "win," an agency must meet demanding standards of proof and legal certainty required by the judiciary. In other words, before an enterprise must accede to a regulatory order or penalty, it has a right to insist on a formal hearing before a judge—an official who is separate from the regulatory agency and therefore likely to be more committed to standards of formal legality and due process for the accused than to the particular agency's mission.

The legality of the agency's case, moreover, typically is examined a number of times before the case actually is presented in court. An agency seeking to punish a recalcitrant violator must persuade the public prosecutor assigned to do its trial work—the county district attorney, the state attorney general, or the U.S. attorney—to act. To convince the prosecutor that it has a valid legal case, the agency must have documented evidence of a violation of an applicable statute or regulation and a witness (usually an inspector) whose testimony will withstand cross-examination. This insistence on a case that will stand up in court usually extends back into the standard operating procedures of the agency. Inspection often is organizationally separated from prosecution. Even if an inspector is convinced that a violation exists and an enforcement action is necessary, *he* cannot initiate prosecution. He must first convince his superior or the district chief of enforcement, who must then turn the matter over to the agency's legal staff, who then determines whether or not the case is legally sound before forwarding it to the public prosecutor.

In certain emergency situations, as noted earlier, some statutes give regulatory officials authority to impose immediate penalties or orders on their own, without going to court and even without a prior administrative hearing. But what if the inspector mistakenly embargoes food that is not in fact adulterated or issues a "shut down" order much broader than seems reasonably necessary? The regulated enterprise can refuse to abide by the order and raise the defense when prosecuted in court for that refusal—but it is a rare enterprise that has the confidence to do so. Or the enterprise may later bring a civil action for damages against the inspector or the agency, although chances of recovery are very slim because of the judicial doctrines of sovereign and official immunity. Therefore, most agencies, pursuant to statutory requirements or their own regulations, provide internal safeguards. The front-line inspector must receive authorization from at least one tier of superiors before taking summary action. Often the regulated enterprise is given notice of the agency's intention to take immediate action and the opportunity to call and confer with agency officials. Thus even in an alleged emergency, the agency, in keeping with due process—and to maintain the confidence of the legislature, which grants (and retracts) enforcement powers[2]—generally provides its own internal checks and balances.

This array of due process mechanisms in both normal and emergency enforcement makes its weight felt at the front-line level—an inspector knows that his request for enforcement action will pass through legal reviews inside the agency, even before action is taken, and *might* involve review by a hearing officer or court. Few inspectors and enforcement officials take this possibility of review lightly; most treat legal rejection as embarrassing, a mark of their lack of professionalism.

THE DILEMMA OF RULES AND DISCRETION

While regulatory legal structures traditionally have been strongly committed to the procedural rules and multiple reviews of the due process ideal, they reflect a certain ambivalence about how closely enforcement practices should be "programmed" by substantive rules. From a legalistic perspective, all regulatory requirements and penalties should be prescribed in detail; all regulations and penalties should be applied uniformly. The contrasting view values official discretion. No system of detailed regulations, it would be argued, can adequately capture the diversity of experience; fixed rules and noncompliance penalties will sometimes be too lax, sometimes too strict. Thus enforcement officials must be given broadly worded grants of discretion that will allow them to order regulated enterprises to do whatever seems necessary and prudent under the particular circumstances, as well as discretion to relax the rules and tailor their enforcement procedures to the situation. From the legal viewpoint, however, such discretion invites chaos: without specific rules, regularly enforced, the deterrent effect of the law will erode, resulting in unpredictability, unequal treatment, a high risk of corruption, and ultimately serious harm to unprotected citizens; the rule of law, whatever its defects, is preferable to the discretionary rule of imperfect officials.

The dilemma of rule versus discretion is an ancient one, of course, pervading many areas of law and administration. In the area of regulation, lawmakers and agencies have tried to cope with the dilemma in different ways. Legislatures often have qualified strict-sounding statutory standards by adding such terms as *to the extent feasible*, or they have proscribed activities or substances "presenting an unreasonable risk of injury." The open-ended character of words like *feasible* and *unreasonable* permits enforcement officials a degree of flexibility.

However, regulatory programs involving continuous enforcement of health- and safety-oriented laws through field inspections are subject to especially strong pressures to substitute precisely worded technical regulations for "flexible" statutory terms. Builders and manufacturers want construction, sanitation, and product safety requirements to be carefully specified in advance so that they can be incorporated into blueprints. Precise rules, the businesses hope, will limit their exposure to unpredictable and expensive post hoc changes demanded by zealous individual inspectors. Specific rules, uniformly enforced, also provide businessmen some assurance that they will be regulated no more stringently than their competitors. Advocates of stringent regulation, too, demand more specific regulations. Precise rules close off "loop-

---

[2] At our 1978 workshop on regulatory enforcement, a nursing home regulator, referring to emergency powers, stated, "You've got to have some cool heads. All it takes is one bad move and you can lose that law."

holes," facilitate the advocate's ability to expose underenforcement by the agency, and make it easier for workers and consumers to assert their rights to protection.

For enforcement officials, rules that specify standards in objective, numerical terms facilitate proof of violations. It is easier to gather evidence and convince a judge that a nursing home has failed to maintain a specified numerical staff-patient ratio, for example, than it is to show that it has failed to provide "adequate staffing to maintain a decent standard of care." For the same reason, precise regulations make enforcement faster and more efficient: decisions can be made mechanically, more inspections can be performed each week, and the inspectorate can be staffed by relatively low-paid operatives rather than by highly trained engineers. Moreover, because direct supervision of a far-flung field inspectorate is inherently difficult, the more specific the rules and the more strictly inspectors are "programmed" to stick to the rules, the better the agency's chances of preventing piecemeal erosion of official policy by inspectors who are too easily influenced by the arguments of regulated enterprises. Rules also bolster the agency's reputation for fairness. Making decisions in accordance with specific rules, enforcement officials say, helps rebut charges that the agency is biased and helps repel attempts by politicians to reverse enforcement decisions on behalf of irate businessmen-constituents.

Inspectors themselves often call for more specific regulations. When a quality-control or safety engineer in a factory contends that a deviation from standard procedure "really isn't dangerous" under the circumstances, it is hard for the inspector to assess the true level of risk. It is comforting to have an authoritative rule, a determination by someone "higher up" in the system, to resolve the question. Finally, from the inspector's point of view, specific rules give an air of neutrality and legitimacy to his actions. When a housing inspector knows there is a housing-code provision that specifically requires landlords to keep all windows in working order (even if the tenant broke them), he can tell a landlord to repair a window and say, "This is not just *my* say-so. Moreover, I'm not just picking on *you*. It's the *law*." In this respect, inspectors *want* to be programmed.

Consequently, many inspection-type agencies do attempt to give ever greater precision to their regulations, continually elaborating and respecifying them to plug newly discovered loopholes and to adapt them to new production processes and emerging risks. The San Francisco Bay Area Air Pollution Control District's basic substantive regulations, three pages long scarcely more than a decade ago, now extend over 87 single-spaced pages. The Motor Carrier Safety regulations issued by the U.S. Department of Transportation, setting forth operating and maintenance (not design) standards for trucks, maximum hours of service for drivers, rules for transporting hazardous materials, and so on, fill a handbook of over 400 pages. U.S. Department of Agriculture (USDA) regulations specify the kinds of facilities, machines, and sanitation procedures that meat-packers must use, including such details as the composition of the salt solutions used to dress carcasses; a single section in the "Manual of Meat Inspection," governing routine postmortem inspection of beef carcasses, contains 15 single-spaced pages of instructions for the inspector.

But the drive for such detailed rules, of course, raises the specter of excessive rigidity. Concerning the meat-inspection regulations, Peter Schuck observes: "It is a commonplace in the industry, denied only by official USDA spokesmen, that if all meat-inspection regulations were enforced to the letter, no meat processor in America would be open for business." The needed flexibility, in such agencies, traditionally is attained by not enforcing the rules literally. In the USDA, says Schuck:

> The inspector is not expected to enforce strictly every rule, *but rather to decide which rules are worth enforcing at all.* In this process, USDA offers no official guidance, for it feels

obliged, like all public agencies, to maintain the myth that all rules are rigidly enforced. Unofficially, the inspector is admonished by his USDA superiors to "use common sense," to do his job in a "reasonable" way.

Many legal institutions, like the USDA, cope with the rule/discretion dilemma through a combination of specific official rules and unofficial selective enforcement. In the criminal process, for example, police officers are allowed, tacitly if not officially, to overlook some violations of the law and to let the offenders go with a warning. Federal prosecuting attorneys often do not prosecute violators brought to them by the FBI or administrative agencies, even when they have a strong legal case. Judges regularly suspend sentences and grant probation to proven lawbreakers. In sum, the criminal law on the books may be relatively clear and legally specific, but as a society, we willingly enable legal decision makers to suspend the rules (in the direction of leniency), to rely on warnings and informal adjustments, to distinguish between serious and nonserious violations, to consider extenuating circumstances, to use the rehabilitative potential of giving a second chance, and to strike a more discerning balance between social control and liberty than lawmakers, far removed from the particular case and the local culture, could envisage in advance.

A similar practice of prosecutorial discretion has characterized the traditional regulatory inspection program. Despite a structure of legal rules that seems to cast the inspector as a rule-applying bureaucrat, and despite the uniformity and control that might come from tightly programming inspectors to go by the book in every case, enforcement officials often have been allowed a good deal of leeway—to withhold prosecution even when they detect violations, to settle for partial rather than literal compliance, and to act more like a "persuader" or educator than a rule-bound bureaucrat. In some agencies, rather than issue a citation, inspectors simply call the violation to the attention of the regulated enterprise, provided it does not entail an imminent hazard. In other agencies, inspectors issue a citation that effectively is only a warning—that is, no further action is taken unless the inspector returns to the site and finds that remedial measures have not been instituted. Inspectors in some agencies negotiate informal, on-the-spot agreements about corrective action and the time period for completion, taking into account the costs and mechanical difficulties involved; only if the regulated enterprise breaks its agreement without good reason are formal charges made or "penalty actions" initiated. Indeed, many regulatory statutes implicitly authorize discretionary withholding of prosecution for first violations by stipulating that penalties are required only for "willful" or "knowing" violations.

Regulatory officials have justified their reluctance to prosecute all violations by asserting that most regulated enterprises in fact "do the right thing" once an inspector points out violations of the law. The California Industrial Accident Commission, charged with enforcing worker safety laws, stated in 1914:

> The attitude of the Safety Department toward employers and employees is not one of compulsion, but of cooperation. It is expected that compulsion will have to be resorted to in rare cases only. The letters on file show that the keenest interest is evinced by manufacturers who express in highest terms their appreciation of the practical suggestions offered by [our] safety engineers.

More recently, enforcement officials of the Motor Carrier Safety Unit of the California State Highway Patrol, in charge of enforcing truck safety and maintenance regulations, told us that they regard it as a failure when an inspector recommends formal prosecution of a trucking company; effective enforcement officials, they believe, should be able to win "voluntary compliance."

In keeping with this attitude, many agencies, even after an inspector or his supervisor loses patience and urges prosecution, inform the violator of the agency's intentions and call him in for an informal hearing; a top enforcement official or the agency's legal counsel presents the agency's case and attempts to extract a compliance agreement in return for suspending steps toward prosecution. Paul Downing and James Kimball, reviewing enforcement practices by certain state antipollution agencies, noted a decided preference for "telephone calls, site visits, warning letters, and conferences at the agency offices" over court action, and a willingness to forgive past violations if compliance is achieved or "in the offing."

In the few cases that resist settlement or are so serious that enforcement officials seek formal legal sanctions, the district attorney or U.S. attorney provides another discretionary screen. The prosecutor's office typically is dealing with a crowded docket of "real crimes"—rapes, burglaries, bank robberies, tax frauds. Agency officials, accordingly, must convince the public prosecutor not only that they have a strong legal case but also that the violation is sufficiently serious to warrant criminal prosecution and a portion of his scarce legal resources. Prosecutors do refuse to handle regulatory matters they regard as trivial. And they too are often quite happy to drop formal prosecution in return for a consent agreement. Finally, even after prosecution is initiated, judges often urge the parties to settle out of court rather than go to trial; even after conviction is obtained, judges often impose probationary arrangements rather than the full legally prescribed penalties.

THE TRADITIONAL LEGAL STRUCTURE AND REGULATORY INEFFECTIVENESS

Prosecutorial discretion allows the inspector (and the prosecutor and the judge) to distinguish between serious and nonserious violations, between the basically well-intentioned regulated enterprise that can be brought into line with a warning and the recalcitrant firm that clearly deserves punishment. At the same time, the constraints of legal rules and due process impose a check on regulatory overreaching: the regulated enterprise can, if it is genuinely outraged, insist on formal hearings and proof, or it can insist that the inspector's "suggested" remedial action go no further than is authorized by the facts and by a specific legal rule. But the legal rules, used in this way, constitute only maximum limits on what enforcement officials may demand; they do not establish fixed minima for what inspectors *must* demand (and hence for what citizens may expect in the way of uniform protective measures). Moreover, the multiple reviews made possible by due process protections impede the prompt application of the sanctions established by law. In a variety of ways, therefore, the traditional legal structure of enforcement may well diminish achievement of regulatory goals.

An inspector's discretion, for example, easily can lead to underenforcement. When he "writes up" a violation, an inspector's work is carefully reviewed by superiors; he may have to go back to the site to gather addditional, more formal evidence; he may incur the anger and hostility of personnel in the regulated enterprise who berate him for being unreasonable. Thus it is certainly *easier* for field inspectors to overlook violations or to rely on informal prodding than to initiate formal prosecution, even when prosecution is clearly warranted. In addition, when inspectors have discretion to overlook unimportant violations or to determine what is a reasonable time for remedial action, experts in regulated enterprises have an opportunity to do a "snow job" on the gullible inspector.

Even if the inspector is not deceived and seeks to impose legal sanctions on a violator, the multiple reviews and adversarial processes associated with the due process tradition provide the recalcitrant enterprise repeated opportunities to delay the day of judgment. A California Department of Health nursing home regulator told us, "I have never seen a license revocation legal proceeding go for less than 14 months if they fight it." An official of the California State Fire Marshal's office noted that "a legal contest" arising from an effort to prosecute fire code violators "takes from 9 months to a year. And once it goes to litigation we can't issue further recommendations or reinspect." An air pollution enforcement official in a southern state acknowledged that his agency was averse to formal enforcement actions because of the complicated—and slow—legal requirements.

> Nowadays you need to make repeated inspections and complete documentation to show that this condition is persisting over time and your sampling is entirely fair. You've got to give the company notice so they can take their own measurements at the same time as ours. Then the inspector, once he's put together his enforcement package, has got to take it to the Commission to request a complaint. Then you've got to set a hearing, giving the company a chance to respond, and that will generally take at least a month. Then, if the company fails to respond or the Commission decides to go ahead with enforcement, it's got to issue an order. There are the problems of formulating a precise and legally enforceable compliance order. Then, if there is still noncompliance, we've got to take the case to the state attorney general, and he's not always cooperative.

And if the case goes to court, additional problems and delays usually are encountered.

Aside from the delays resulting from legal formalities, multiple stages of review can gradually weaken the impulse to impose formal penalties. Decision makers farther removed from the front line may have the advantage (in terms of formal legal values) of detachment and objectivity, but they are less familiar with the details of the particular inspector-enterprise relationship, and less able to sense the urgency of the problem and to see through insincere or weak excuses. An air pollution inspector, driving near a refinery he frequently inspected, complained about lack of support from the lawyers at headquarters and their tendency not to trust his assessments and intuition when he recommends prosecution. "They figure the inspector is a dummy. . . . But I don't care how tall the headquarters building is over there. They can't see over here!" Officials in many agencies complain that public prosecutors and judges fail to treat violations and violators as seriously as the enforcers believe necessary.

Due process protections, moreover, sometimes mean that a regulated enterprise will be found legally innocent, when in fact it has acted irresponsibly. What was intuitively overwhelming proof to the inspector on the scene in the factory may appear to be unsupported speculation when the inspector is cross-examined on the witness stand. According to Keith Hawkins, British water pollution inspectors find the formal courtroom process an "alarming . . . ceremony, in which the available knowledge about [an act of] pollution . . . is submerged beneath the weight of procedural controls" and in which defense lawyers "can tear you to pieces."

In addition, judicial discretion in sentencing traditionally led to light regulatory penalties. Dr. Harold Wiley, the great force behind the pure Food and Drug Law, complained 20 years after its enactment:

> Last week a penniless thief was sentenced by one of the judges in Washington to ten years in the penitentiary for stealing twenty dollars. Those convicted under the food law often get by with a fine of five dollars.

Such results can be labeled a corrupt sellout to powerful business interests, but they usually represent a consistent application of general principles of penal law, one of which calls for a rough proportionality between the penalty and the relative seriousness of the offense. Seriousness generally is assessed in terms of the degree of harm caused by the offense; the criminal law, looking at results, punishes speeding less severely than vehicular homicide. Many regulatory rules, like those against speeding, are preventive; violations often involve failure to take some precaution that only *might* lead to harm. If no harm has actually resulted, the violation of a sanitation regulation in an otherwise respectable food-processing plant often does not seem very serious.

Another aspect of seriousness, and hence of proportionality, is culpability, which entails knowledge of wrongdoing, combined with some degree of malice, selfishness, or irresponsibility. Courts are thus notoriously hesitant to assign criminal responsibility to individual corporate employees: underlings directly knowledgeable about harmful activities often lack authority and responsibility, while high officials often lack specific knowledge. Moreover, regulatory offenses often are not clearly wrong, as are theft and assault. Unlike the burglar or the narcotics dealer, the regulatory offender often is a legitimate, socially useful enterprise whose officers believe sincerely, and sometimes justifiably, that their behavior was not really very bad.

Another basic penal principle is social utility, that is, that legal sanctions should provide a net social benefit. Thus the idea of rehabilitation, despite its frequent failure, pervades the penal process because it seems more efficient than incarceration. From this perspective, pushing a substandard nursing home to improve often is wiser than closing it down for having violated quality-of-care regulations. Just as courts prefer restitution to incarceration in many criminal cases, judges may prefer to extract an agreement from a factory to spend money on a sprinkler system rather than impose a "nonproductive" fine for violations of the fire code.

Because formal prosecution is characterized by delays and appeals, losses on technical legal grounds, and judicially "watered down" penalties, inspectors and higher enforcement officials tend to avoid the formal route even when it seems justified. When faced with a recalcitrant landlord, some housing code inspectors bargain for prompt repairs of certain violations in return for dropping citations against others. The compromise does provide some protection for the tenants, and more quickly and surely than court action.

More importantly, the agency may deliberately avoid bringing controversial charges or seeking innovative remedies when there is a good chance that the defendant will mount a strong legal defense; contested cases impose an enormous burden on the agency's understaffed legal section. It may seem more efficient for enforcement officials to concentrate on routine cases that are unlikely to be contested; although they contribute relatively little toward the achievement of regulatory goals, such routine cases guarantee the inspector and his agency a quick disposition and a numerically impressive enforcement record. This also means, however, that the most hardened and experienced violators, those that are ready to engage in protracted legal battles, are the regulated enterprises most likely to escape, or at least to delay, the burdens of compliance.

Finally, the practice of backing away from legal conflict can sometimes become a habit so that the inspectorate loses all thirst for aggressive enforcement, even when it is badly needed, and loses enforcement know-how. Testimony by inspectors in the pre-OSHA California Division of Industrial Safety indicated that formal legal sanctions—such as criminal prosecutions or orders shutting down jobs presenting imminent hazards—had been resorted to so infrequently that many inspectors were ignorant of the precise nature and applicability of the sanctions available. Others claimed that their superiors had berated them for taking formal action.

The traditional structure of inspection and enforcement is not necessarily a *major* source of ineffectiveness, and a tendency to bargain for compliance and cooperation may generally be wise policy, whatever its susceptibility to abuse or failure in particular areas. Railroads and processed foods have become safer, even though the ICC and the FDA infrequently resorted to formal prosecution of safety rule violators. In other fields, such as housing code and environmental law enforcement, some studies show that inspectors usually can obtain compliance merely by threatening prosecution or penalties, even if they have no intention of following through. They succeed because most businessmen and corporate engineers are not quite certain what the agency can or will do and because the threat of prosecution seems more fearsome and potent than it really is. Nevertheless, in the late 1960s, social reformers—or any concerned citizen or newspaper reporter—could readily point to serious injuries, injustices, and social harms that were not being prevented in fields already subject to regulation. There were numerous exposés of specific instances of lax enforcement: factories that violated state air or water pollution standards with seeming impunity, carcinogenic pesticides left on the market by the USDA and the FDA, fatal coal mine explosions not prevented by government inspectors, dangerous substances and occupational diseases ignored by state regulators and compensation systems, inhumane nursing homes that local licensing authorities allowed to stay in operation.

Partly for these reasons, the demand for more effective and comprehensive government regulation grew in the 1960s. These demands often took the form of an attack on the traditional enforcement style and the legal structure of regulatory agencies. Overall, the reformers called for a shift from the discretionary inspector-as-consultant style to the more aggressive prosecution-and-deterrence model of regulation. The inspectors and the agencies themselves were to be held to stricter account by outside critics.

CAPTURE AND ITS CURE

Reformers believed that enforcement had to be tougher and that the regulators had to be more closely regulated because business enterprises were fundamentally amoral profit-seekers, unwilling to abide by the law unless the prospect of legal punishment was swift, sure, and severe, and because regulatory agencies invariably were (or soon became) weak-willed, lethargic "captives" of the industries they regulated. The "capture theory," a tenet of academic political science, was popularized in the late 1960s and early 1970s by a steady stream of exposés of federal agencies by Ralph Nader's "Raiders." Regulatory officials were pictured as industry-oriented, as reluctant to jeopardize their postgovernment careers by being too tough, or as gradually co-opted by informal contact with representatives of regulated firms. In a passage reflecting the attitude of these books toward business as well as toward informal methods of enforcement, the author of Nader's study of food and drug regulation wrote:

> It became the practice of the FDA . . . to hold hundreds of meetings each year with representatives of industry to discuss . . . cooperative methods . . . to ensure that the provisions of the law were not violated. . . . If the Justice Department held regular meetings with the Mafia suggesting that it knew of gambling . . . which if not stopped

would lead to a raid of the premises, it would be following a procedure not unlike that used by the FDA to convince the food industry to obey the law.

By 1970, the capture theory was the conventional wisdom, repeated by Supreme Court judges and by intellectuals of the right. As for inspectors, everyone "knew" they could be "bought." Finally, many reformers and even congressional staff members believed that "American industry . . . could easily absorb all the costs imposed by [tougher] regulation out of its profit structure without significantly affecting the economy."

From this perspective, the reform agenda was clear: (1) install new regulators, preferably at the federal level (where proregulation public interest groups could concentrate their efforts), rather than at the even more discredited state or local level; (2) write more comprehensive and explicit regulations, without gaps and "balancing" language that would permit legalistic defenses; (3) curtail administrative discretion and leniency by more specific and stringent rules and by advocacy-group participation in rule making and enforcement; and (4) enhance deterrence by increasing the severity, speed, and consistency of sanctions.

This reform agenda was not adopted in toto; the legal structure of some existing agencies remained untouched, and new legislation often reflected compromises between the proponents and the opponents of tougher legislation. But to a considerable degree, the outpouring of regulatory legislation in the late 1960s and 1970s did reflect these enforcement goals. Congressmen showed themselves to be sensitive to the capture theory and to criticism in the media for enacting regulatory legislation with ostensibly weak enforcement provisions. Perhaps it is significant, too, that many major regulatory measures were enacted by a Democrat-controlled Congress that was deeply mistrustful of the Republican president, Richard Nixon, who was in a position to appoint the top regulatory officials. Hence, there was added reason to curtail regulatory discretion and to enhance legal controls over enforcement. The same political alignment prevailed in California during Ronald Reagan's tenure as governor. In any case, legislative willingness to change the traditional legal structure of regulatory enforcement can be readily outlined by referring to the major enactments of the 1960s and 1970s.

THE FEDERALIZATION OF REGULATION

In the late 1960s and early 1970s, Congress created the Environmental Protection Agency, the National Highway Traffic Safety Administration, the Consumer Product Safety Commission, OSHA, the Mining Enforcement and Safety Administration, and the Equal Employment Opportunity Commission. Moreover, the jurisdiction and enforcement powers of established federal agencies were expanded.[3] Although the newly created federal regulatory authority occasionally superseded state and local regulation, it more often supplemented and strengthened it. Sometimes the federal legislation established minimum protective standards for the entire country but permitted states to establish more stringent standards. Enforcement of some federal legislation was delegated to (or forced upon) state agencies under federal guidelines, federal agency oversight, and, in some cases, federal funding, which could be withheld for inadequate enforcement. For example, under the Occupa-

---

[3] For example, the FTC's jurisdiction was expanded from interstate commerce to intrastate transactions "affecting commerce," and hence to local deceptive or unfair sales practices.

tional Safety and Health Act, states could either leave enforcement to federal inspectors or maintain their own programs, provided their regulations and enforcement procedures were "at least as effective" as OSHA regulations and practices. The 1970 amendments to the Clean Air Act required states to prepare detailed State Implementation Plans for meeting federally set ambient air standards for various pollutants.

In some instances, regulatory functions were transferred from one federal agency to another to remove enforcement responsibilities from a group of officials that had long been committed to an education-and-cooperation regulatory style. In 1972, for example, federal regulation of blood and plasma products was extended to intrastate blood banks and plasma collection centers, and enforcement shifted from the National Institutes of Health to the new Bureau of Biologics in the FDA. That change, the head of the bureau wrote, "was more than a simple change in the organization chart. . . . [It] conveyed [enforcement] from a research-oriented organization, NIH, to the FDA, which was historically concerned with the compliance aspects of regulations."

MAKING STATUTES MORE STRINGENT

To reformers who were mistrustful of the regulators' integrity, traditional statutory terms, such as *reasonable* and *feasible* allowed for too much compromise. Reformers sought legislation that would articulate citizens' rights to protection in unambiguous terms, enabling citizen groups to take vacillating regulatory officials to court and compel them to achieve specific levels of safety or environmental protection. Most major environmental and protective legislation of the late 1960s and early 1970s followed this reform pattern. Statutes mandated ambitious levels of protection, set fixed deadlines for achieving them, and empowered citizen groups to take slow-moving agencies to court. And although most statutes indicated that economic costs and difficulties in achieving compliance could play some role in the formulation and enforcement of regulations, the weight accorded such considerations was diminished and carefully restricted.

Regulatory discretion in balancing competing values, for example, was more hedged in by explicit statutory provisions. Congress was not so apt to say, in effect, "Here's the problem. Do something about it!" The text of the 1970 Clean Air Act amendments, together with the extensive 1977 amendments, covers 135 pages. Primary ambient air quality standards, the law said, should be set at levels "requisite to protect the public health" with "an adequate margin of safety," rather clearly excluding concerns about the economic costs of compliance or cost-benefit analysis in establishing those standards. EPA administrators could consider economic costs in designating "best available control technologies" for new factories, but other provisions of the law forbade them to grant variances, because of economic costs or even technological infeasibility, from stringent enforcement plans designed to roll back pollution from existing sources.

The weight to be given economic considerations was also restricted by the statutory practice of stating basic regulatory goals in absolute, unqualified terms. The goal of the 1972 Water Pollution Control Act amendments was to eliminate *all* effluents by 1985; under the Clean Air Act carbon monoxide and hydrocarbon emissions from new cars were to be reduced 90 percent from 1970 levels by 1975. The Occupational Safety and Health Act articulated the employer's obligation to provide, and the worker's right to have, a job "free of known hazards" (although this is probably an impossibility for many jobs). The federal strip-mine legislation of 1977 prohibited *all* stream siltation and required the restoration of mined land to its "original contours," rejecting language calling for restoration "to the maximum extent feasible."

Buried in those statutes is language that gives the agency some flexibility in rule making, or that allows individual businesses to apply for exceptions or extensions on grounds of technological difficulties. But the congressional intent to achieve stringent controls was expressed so clearly that regulators often have been reluctant to give economic considerations substantial weight in rulemaking or in requests for variances. For example, the Occupational Safety and Health Act's emphasis on complete freedom from hazards is qualified by the concept of "maximum feasible protection." This provision, OSHA concluded, permitted it to consider whether proposed safety rules were beyond the economic (as well as the technological) capacity of employers. But OSHA had to fight lawsuits brought by labor unions that challenged that interpretation, and the agency has insisted that it is not legally obligated to balance cost against safety in rulemaking or to conduct cost-benefit analyses of proposed standards. Thus it has required employers to install expensive engineering controls to achieve the lowest detectible level of emissions shown to be hazardous in high concentrations, despite arguments that standards set at slightly less stringent levels (or the use of personal protective equipment) would probably provide adequate protection at much lower costs.

Statutes also restricted regulatory discretion in dealing with scientific controversy over possible hazards, compelling agency rulemakers to forbid products and practices that create a recognized *possibility* of harm, rather than making their own judgment about the *probability* of harm or the tolerable level of risk. For example, many public health professionals contend that it is impossible to establish with certainty "threshold values" (concentrations below which exposure is not carcinogenic) for substances shown to cause cancer in animals or humans exposed to high concentrations. Others reject the "no safe threshold" theory, arguing that carcinogens vary widely in degree of potency, that potency may drop off dramatically at lower exposures, and that extrapolations from animal studies to low-dose exposures to humans are quite problematic. Faced with this controversy, legislators (and regulators) sometimes—although not always—have acted on the no-threshold theory, forbidding any human exposure to the substance, despite the practical difficulties and high costs of moving from a standard calling for carefully controlled low exposures to one calling for zero exposure. The most famous example is the Delaney Amendment to the Food, Drug and Cosmetic Act, which absolutely forbids the sale of food products or additives shown to be even a very weak cause of cancerous tumors in laboratory tests of animals. The FDA, moreover, is not permitted to weigh the risk of cancer against the social benefits the product might provide or against the economic costs the ban might entail. Regulatory officials, in fact, often are grateful for the opportunity to escape responsibility for the intellectually difficult and politically touchy task of making such trade-off decisions. Donald Kennedy, commissioner of the FDA in 1977, stated, "Our law says to protect the public health, not the industry. Fortunately, our statute does not allow us to weigh adverse health conditions against dollars."

On the other hand, when regulators *have* been willing to consider the costs of enforcing an absolute prohibition or a rigid standard, other agencies, proregulation advocacy groups, or courts can invoke the statutory language as a barrier to any exceptions:

> The 1973 Endangered Species Act, read literally, protected all species: not only the furry mammals and attractive birds that probably were foremost in the legislators'

minds, but also obscure and unloved lizards and spiders. The Supreme Court reluctantly concluded that the statute required the courts to order a stop to the construction of the huge and costly Tellico River dam because opening the dam would destroy the habitat of the snail darter, a rare (but now famous) fish.

The San Francisco Bay Area Air Pollution Control District promulgated an "upset/breakdown" regulation in 1970, which allowed enforcement officials to excuse violations when excessive emissions resulted from mechanical failure or periodic maintenance of control equipment, or from temporary "upsets" in production processes. The firm had to report the situation immediately (or 24 hours in advance for scheduled maintenance of pollution equipment), and the exemption from penalties would only be granted if "the frequency or duration of upset conditions, breakdowns, or scheduled maintenance is . . . reasonable under all of the circumstances." The district was forced to repeal this exemption under federal pressure in 1978—the EPA claimed that the district had no legal authority under the Clean Air Act to grant such exemptions. District inspectors have since been directed to cite any violation of emission limitations regardless of cause.

SHIFTING THE BURDEN OF PROOF

In addition to stringent rules that enforcement agencies cannot easily water down, many new regulatory statutes attempted to bolster the enforcement process directly by making it easier to prove violations. One technique was to require regulated enterprises to maintain more detailed records of compliance-related activities and to make those records available to enforcement personnel. The enterprise, in effect, must constantly be able to demonstrate that it is in compliance. Enforcement leverage is further enhanced by making inadequate record keeping a separate, punishable—and easy to prove—violation. Trucking companies, for example, must keep detailed logs recording daily hours of service for each truck and each driver so that Department of Transportation inspectors can check compliance with maximum-hours rules designed to prevent accidents. Operators of chemical plants and refineries in the San Francisco Bay area must install continuous monitoring devices for all sources of sulfur dioxide emissions, calibrate and test monitors regularly as prescribed by agency regulations, and make the monitoring records available to inspectors on demand. The companies also must report to the agency within 96 hours pollution violations recorded by the monitors. Several statutes require firms to report incidents that merely suggest possible violations or danger to the public. Thus the Toxic Substances Control Act states that corporate personnel who obtain information indicating that a substance "presents a substantial risk of injury" to human health or the environment must immediately inform the EPA. Failure to do so is itself a serious violation.

In situations where enforcement agencies find it especially difficult to prove violations, regulated enterprises have been required to prove their innocence. A clear example involves not safety regulation but antidiscrimination law. It is difficult for agencies to prove that any individual who was not hired or promoted was in fact rejected because of sex or race, as opposed to merit. Certain affirmative action regulations, therefore, refer to "underrepresentation" or "underutilization" of women or minorities in the employer's work force, a much easier fact for the agency to establish. If underutilization is found, the employer then has the burden of proving that its criteria for hiring and promotion are not discriminatory. Construction contractors on federally- and on many state-funded projects who do not meet affirmative action guidelines for percentage of minority workers (and few of them do, in view of union practices), or who do not award subcontracts to minority-owned firms, must provide federal inspectors with detailed records showing "good faith efforts" to recruit or subcontract to minorities.

The ultimate method for shifting the burden of proof is to require the regulated enterprise to seek agency approval before undertaking an activity, such as marketing a product or operating an industrial process. In such prior clearance schemes, the enterprise must prove to agency officials that its methods are lawful and technically adequate. Compared with a post hoc inspection system, the recalcitrant enterprise's chances of evasion are diminished, and it gains no advantage from legal delay. The agency's refusal to grant a permit is a potent sanction. Prior approval laws have existed for many years for building code enforcement, for new prescription drugs, and for builders of new aircraft models. In the 1960s and 1970s, however, such requirements proliferated. In effect, agency clearance was required, for example, for companies that sought to market new pesticides, potentially harmful chemicals, and (to assure compliance with antipollution regulations) cars and gasoline additives. Meat-packers and drug manufacturers who wished to build plants were required to file detailed blueprints and to get clearance from the Department of Agriculture and the FDA, respectively, concerning compliance with detailed regulations governing the sanitary nature of facilities. Operators of both new and existing major sources of air and water pollution were required to obtain operating permits from state and federal agencies, conditional on a satisfactory plan to install legally required control equipment.

The burden of proof associated with prior clearance procedures is often quite substantial. In the San Francisco Bay area, for example, to obtain a permit for a new or expanded industrial process that will emit over 250 pounds of pollutants per year, the applicant must submit an extensive "Air Quality Impact Analysis" as well as detailed control plans. Enforcement officials point out, moreover, that the sanction of suspending a permit for violating specific pledges in the permit application is much easier to uphold in court than the postviolation fines or injunctions sought in traditional abatement actions.

INCREASING REMEDIAL AND SANCTIONING POWERS

Another striking characteristic of the regulatory legislation of the past decade is a major increase, by historical standards, in the severity of maximum penalties and in the range of legally available remedial orders.

Many new statutory penalties reflected the theory that only mammoth fines could deter violations by mammoth corporations. For example, the 1970 Clean Air Act and the 1969 Federal Mine Safety Act authorized the imposition of criminal fines against violators of $25,000 *per day* (thus reducing the incentive to delay the day of judgment), and $50,000 per day for repeat offenders. The 1977 Clean Air Act amendments and the 1976 Toxic Substances Control Act also authorized "civil penalties" of up to $25,000 per day; these differ from criminal fines primarily in that the agency does not have to prove guilt beyond a reasonable doubt, prove that the violation was intentional or "knowing," or jump other hurdles of criminal procedure. The proof standard in civil actions is usually "a preponderance of the evidence." The financial sanctions, however, are just as high, and judges may be more willing to impose them.

Following the lead of the 1938 pure Food and Drug Law amendments, many statutes in the 1960s and 1970s stated that criminal penalties could be imposed on individual officers for corporate regulatory violations. Moreover, some of these statutes have been construed by the courts to impose criminal sanctions against high officials who had no direct knowledge, criminal intent, or involvement in the violation, but who were "responsible" and "should have known." The 1977 Clean Air Act explicitly extends criminal liability to "any responsible corporate officer."

Regulatory agencies increasingly were granted the power to impose sanctions directly, without having to go to court and convince a judge that the penalty is warranted. OSHA, for example, was authorized to impose civil penalties on violators immediately, as were some state agencies, such as California's air pollution control districts and its agency that inspects nursing homes. Under the 1977 amendments to the Clean Air Act, the EPA was empowered to assess civil penalties equal to the financial "benefit" gained by not making the required abatement or by dragging out court proceedings. In these agencies, prosecution is assigned to an expanded legal staff, enabling the agency to avoid the delay (and the additional discretionary screen) of presenting enforcement cases through the public prosecutor. Most agency-assessed civil penalties, such as those imposed by OSHA, are not large, but they are swift and according to our interviews, are troubling even to very large corporations.

In addition, summary remedies—orders prior to any hearing—have been made available to enforcement officials in a broader range of situations and sometimes with looser definitions of "imminent hazard" than the older social regulation. The 1977 Clean Air Act, for example, empowers the administrator of the EPA to order an immediate shutdown of polluting operations in periods of dangerously deteriorating air quality. EPA officials also can order automobile manufacturers to close down their assembly plants and to recall cars to redesign and correct pollution-control gear that is not meeting regulatory standards. Federal mine inspectors are authorized by the 1969 Mine Safety Act to order immediate closure of mines not only when they think that miners are in imminent danger but also when prior abatement orders have not been complied with because of "unwarrantable failure." Perhaps the most drastic remedial power provided by the new regulation is the authority to order "recalls" of entire product lines. The National Highway Traffic Safety Administration regularly orders the recall of (or induces the company to recall) tens of thousands of automobiles for replacement of parts that may be causing problems. The expense is usually equivalent to a much larger fine than a court would ever impose, and the publicity attending such recalls often has an adverse effect on sales that far exceeds the direct recall costs. The Consumer Product Safety Commission has similar powers to recall hazardous toys. EPA can order manufacturers to recall industrial machinery that violates noise control regulations. The Department of Agriculture can suspend sales of pesticides and fungicides, without prior hearing.

As the federal government's purchasing and spending activities have penetrated more sectors of the economy and state and local government, another regulatory sanction has been created: the threat to bar violators of federal regulations from future contracts or to cut off existing grants. This sanction has been authorized, for example, for violations of federal antidiscrimination employment guidelines, federal criteria for local school programs funded by Congress (bilingual education, education for the handicapped, "special education") and federal regulations governing local water and waste treatment projects. The EPA recently cut off $301.5 million in aid to Colorado for highway construction and sewage-treatment plants because the state failed to establish a federally mandated inspection program for controlling automobile pollution. Although cutoffs are rarely used, they are threatening enough to get substantial results. Inspection of hospitals by Medicare officials to check compliance with quality-of-care regulations—which is a condition for continued Medicare payments—has had a greater effect on substandard hospitals, according to some observers, than years of local regulation and threats of license revocation.

REDUCING DISCRETION IN SANCTIONING AND ENFORCEMENT

More stringent rules, more record keeping by regulated firms, and more potent statutory sanctions might not add up to tougher regulation if inspectors and higher regulatory officials retained discretion to overlook or to decline to penalize violations. A major priority of regulatory reform, therefore, was to "program" the dispersed regulators more tightly, inducing them to adhere to the regulations that proregulation forces managed to get promulgated in Washington or state capitals.

One strategy for reducing discretion was to break up (or to restore balance to) informal relationships between regulators and regulated. In pursuit of this goal at the rule-making level, many statutes and judicial decisions expanded citizen-group rights to participate in the regulatory policymaking process; stipulated that agency decisions must be made in public session, after open public hearings; held that agency rule-making decisions must be based on a publicly disclosed evidentiary record; and made agency rules appealable to the courts by almost any "aggrieved citizen." As noted before, proregulation groups were empowered to sue agencies in court for failure to promulgate regulations in accordance with statutory deadlines or substantive statutory standards.

The parallel strategy was to make the *enforcement process* more visible, accountable, and subject to monitoring and influence by private advocacy groups and individual complainants. Here, too, one method was the lawsuit. Public interest law firms were authorized to seek judicial orders requiring agencies to enforce the law more literally or aggressively, and some statutes provided that successful public interest litigants could have their counsel fees paid by the government. In several instances, most prominently in the civil rights field, courts responded to suits by beneficiary groups alleging "systemic enforcement inadequacies" by ordering an agency to respond to complaints more rapidly, to adopt certain enforcement priorities, and, in one case, to petition the Office of Management and Budget for more enforcement funds. The precedents also seem applicable to health and safety regulations: a Denver public interest law firm sued the Department of Health, Education and Welfare, demanding a cutoff of Medicare funds or better enforcement of quality-of-care regulations for nursing homes; the federal district court ordered a thorough survey of enforcement inadequacies. A few courts have indicated inspection agencies might be liable for damages to persons injured as a result of negligent or weak enforcement; the leading precedents involve fire marshals' offices that failed to detect fire code violations or force repairs on buildings that subsequently caught fire. These precedents hardly eliminate the tradition of prosecutorial discretion and the doctrine of official immunity, but they represent steps in that direction, and they are well known to many enforcement officials, who regard them as significant messages to guard against charges of lax enforcement.

There are other techniques to make enforcement officials more responsive to complainants. The Freedom of Information Act expands the access of citizens, including investigative reporters, to agency inspection records. Agencies are explicitly commanded by some statutes to conduct an inspection within a specified number of days after receiving a citizen complaint and to report the results to the complainant. To encourage complaints, agencies are forbidden to reveal the complainant's name, and in many regulatory schemes, discrimination by the enterprise against complainants is a punishable offense. California's nursing home law also provides that any attempt to expel or deny privileges to a complainant or one on whose behalf a complaint is filed within 120 days of the complaint raises "a rebuttable presumption that such action was taken . . . in retaliation for the filing of the complaint." The Occupational Safety and Health Act contains similar provisions to protect worker-complainants. Employment discrimination laws, the Consumer Product Safety Act, and the Occupational Safety and Health Act authorize citizen lawsuits against the violator (and against the agency, too, in OSHA's case) if the agency fails to act against an alleged violator within a given period of time. To exert pressures against undue concessions in plea bargaining, a California statute requires the nursing home regulatory agency, if it modifies or dismisses a citation or proposed penalty in an informal conference, to "state with particularity in writing . . . the reasons for such action," and immediately to send a copy to any complainant. Citations involving serious violations must be posted in the view of patients and visitors. OSHA and the federal mine safety laws specifically empower employees to accompany inspectors on their tour of the workplace. Complaints are encouraged by such judicial rulings as the California Supreme Court decision allowing tenants to withhold rent when housing inspectors have found serious housing code violations on the premises.

Another important outside pressure on state agencies is federal review of their enforcement practices. Federal OSHA periodically reinspects establishments inspected by state occupational safety and health agencies. Federal health officials check dairy companies primarily inspected by state agencies. Federal Medicare inspectors resurvey nursing homes covered by state inspectors. The same occurs in truck safety regulation, meat processing, and blood banks. Reinspection is usually designed to encourage stricter enforcement and more complete reporting of violations by state enforcement officials.

Some legislation explicitly attempts to preclude inspectorial discretion, at least in the sense of overlooking minor violations or deciding to deal with violations merely by oral advice or warnings. One of the most extreme versions, perhaps, is OSHA, where inspectors are required to cite every violation of safety regulations they see and to assign a statutory fine for all "serious" violations. But the federal mine safety law prescribes the same approach, and some other agencies are close behind. FDA inspectors are told to report every violation of the immensely detailed "good manufacturing practice" regulations that they see in food and drug manufacturing firms. California nursing-home and air-pollution inspectors must cite all violations, and fines or "penalty actions" are prescribed for most of them. The Federal Water Pollution Control Act not only requires companies to report any discharge of oil into navigable waters but also mandates the automatic imposition of a "civil fine" on the reporting company (although the fine for not reporting would be higher).[4]

Many statutes now forbid inspectors to give any advance notice of inspections, thus curtailing their discretion to build a less suspicious and intrusive relationship with certain regulated enterprises. Discretion at the supervisor's level also came under review in some instances. The California legislature stipulated that, if an occupational safety inspector recommended criminal action and his supervisor disagreed, the decision to forgo prosecution first must be reviewed by top agency

---

[4]In June 1980, the Supreme Court rejected an oil driller's contention that the reporting plus fine requirement violated the Fifth Amendment's protection against self-incrimination. The court reasoned that the Fifth Amendment applies to criminal liability and that the fine in question is a civil, not a criminal, penalty. *U.S. v. Ward*, 65 L.Ed. 2d 742 (1980).

enforcement officials. Finally, discretion in the selection of inspection sites has sometimes been limited by statutes that prescribe specific priorities and frequencies for certain regulated enterprises. Thus the Federal Mine Health and Safety Act mandates four inspections per year for all underground mines and one each week for 200 mines with poor safety histories.

CONCLUSION

These legal changes have not characterized all regulatory programs. They represent a trend, not an invariant transformation. Many "traditional" enforcement programs remain, especially at the state and local levels. Even in the more "legalistic" programs, not every statutory standard is expressed in absolute terms. Applications for pollution discharge and building permits inevitably entail a good deal of negotiation. Statutory deadlines can be and have been bent when agencies or industry have had difficulty meeting them. Inspectorial and prosecutorial discretion is difficult to eliminate, no matter what the rules say. Determined enterprises can still delay compliance through legal challenges. The penalties authorized by law are still subject to administrative and judicial moderation in many instances. Courts have been reluctant to issue injunctions that would actually close down factories that are violating stringent pollution regulations because a shutdown creates unemployment. Moreover, as the 1980s began in an atmosphere of energy crisis, unprecedented inflation, and economic limitations, there were strong indications that the trend we have discussed may have peaked. Statutes and presidential orders required agencies to take economic and other costs of compliance into account in the rule-making process and to recognize more scope for private autonomy and responsibility.

Nevertheless, these statutory changes constitute a real and important trend. Strict legal provisions and rights to protection are difficult to remove, and enforcement styles, once structured by law, are slow to change. In the most significant regulatory areas, the law has been deliberately structured to prevent capture, to program inspectors to apply regulations strictly, to pressure enforcement officials to apply formal penalties to violations, and to adopt a more legalistic and deterrence-oriented stance vis-à-vis regulated enterprises.

TWELVE
ADMINISTRATIVE IMPLEMENTATION
Organizational Structure and Bureaucratic Routines

Howard Ball/Dale Krane/Thomas Lauth

INTRODUCTION

The passage of the Voting Rights Act of 1965 represented both an affirmation of principles and a statement of objectives regarding abhorrent practices of racial discrimination in voting in the United States. As is the case in most public policy situations, the policy formulators (Congress and the president) had delineated a policy objective, but it remained for the policy refiners (the Supreme Court and the bureaucracy) and the policy implementers (the bureaucracy) to develop the guidelines for compliance with the act. Before examining the bureaucratic routines of voting rights policy implementation, it is important to consider the events leading to the development of procedures for the administration of Section 5.

TOWARD THE DEVELOPMENT OF SECTION 5 PROCEDURES

Section 5 effectively froze all voting patterns in the covered jurisdictions as of November 1964, unless the U.S. Attorney General or the U.S. District Court was convinced that the proposed voting change would not dilute black voting strength. The

> This selection comes from Howard Ball, Dale Krane, and Thomas P. Lauth, *Compromised Compliance: Implementation of the 1965 Voting Rights Act,* pp. 64–68, 76–91. Used with the permission of the publisher, Greenwood Press, a division of Congressional Information Service, Inc. (Westport, Conn., 1982). Footnotes omitted.

section was to be employed to break the cycle of substitution of new discriminatory laws and practices when the old requirements were either suspended or declared unconstitutional. Procedurally, the Congress intended to have the U.S. District Court in Washington, D.C., examine all voting change proposals before they were implemented and to issue a declaratory judgment if the change was not discriminatory in purpose or effect. In the legislative process, however, the Department of Justice was added, almost as an afterthought, as a less expensive and less onerous method of obtaining federal approval of "simple" voting changes "susceptible" to ready and quick appraisal. In the haste to bring the legislation to the public as soon as possible after the events of Selma, the Congress kept both avenues to preclearance open but did not clearly delineate the responsibilities and differences between the kinds of submissions that ought to go to the District Court and those that should be submitted to the Attorney General.

Given the policy position of nonconfrontation, the small number of CRD attorneys assigned to voting rights, the CRD's commitment to Section 4 enforcement, very few Section 5 submissions were forthcoming from local jurisdictions. The DOJ had no attorney handling these submissions on a regular basis, and there were no guidelines for internal and external assistance. By 1969, however, events within DOJ and elsewhere led to the next generation of civil rights dilemmas: how to make sure that these newly enfranchised black voters would not lose their vote and how to prevent the dilution of this emergent political force. Because Section 5 was the legislative antidote to dilution, its enforcement now took center stage.

In 1966, the Supreme Court, in *South Carolina* v. *Katzenbach,* judged Section 5 to be constitutional. While admitting that the Voting Rights Act was an "uncommon exercise of congressional power," Chief Justice Earl Warren (reviewing the history of racial turbulence in the South) concluded that "exceptional conditions can justify legislative measures not otherwise appropriate." The test used to measure the constitutionality of Section 5 was the one Chief Justice Marshall had used in 1819: "Let the end be legitimate . . . then all means . . . consistent with the letter and spirit of the Constitution are constitutional." Three years later, in the opinion that combined three Mississippi cases with a Virginia case, the Supreme Court defined the scope of Section 5.

Private litigants in these two southern states had challenged the enforceability of state election laws and procedures. After dealing with a complex jurisdictional question (whether a private individual had the standing to invoke the jurisdiction of a three-judge district court in a Section 5 suit), the Supreme Court turned to the substantive question of whether the new laws in these states were subject to the approval requirements of Section 5 of the Voting Rights Act. The Virginia case involved a bulletin issued to local election judges to aid illiterate voters. This type of notice, the Court said, was subject to Section 5 approval. The three Mississippi cases involved 1966 amendments to Section 2870 of the Mississippi Code, 1942, which changed the method of voting for county supervisors from district to at-large, made the office of county superintendent of schools an appointive one in some counties, and increased the requirements of an independent candidate to gain a position on a general election ballot.

The Supreme Court, asked if these changes fell within the parameters of Section 5, concluded that "the Voting Rights Act was aimed to the subtle, as well as the obvious, state regulations which have the effect of denying citizens their right to vote because of their race." The Court concluded that Section 5 ought to be construed liberally and that lower courts would not be able to restrict the limit of the Section 5 protection.

In *Allen* v. *State Board of Elections*, the Court also addressed the issue of preclearance submission procedures. Appellees had contended that since no formal preclearance submissions were required by the Attorney General, their Section 5 obligations were fulfilled whenever the Attorney General became aware of state enactments. After taking notice of the absence of formal procedures, the Court stated that the Voting Rights Act "required that the State in some unambiguous and recordable manner submit any legislation or regulation . . . directly to the Attorney General with a request for his consideration. . . ."

Allen, along with *Perkins* v. *Matthews*, had a significant effect on the evolving implementation process. The Court outlined at least seven basic types of voting changes subject to Section 5 preclearance:

1. redistricting;
2. annexation;
3. polling places;
4. precinct changes;
5. reregistration procedures;
6. incorporations; and
7. changes in election laws such as filing fees, at-large elections, and so forth.

The Supreme Court's conclusion, that the scope of Section 5 was broad enough to encompass every action that affected the state or local electoral system in the covered jurisdictions, came at the time of great stress for the civil rights movement. While *Allen* was followed by an increase in the number of preclearances filed with the Department of Justice in 1969, the Department of Justice was under the direction of a new (Republican) president, Richard M. Nixon. Nixon had run on a platform that called for the withdrawal of even the smallest federal "presence" in the South in the area of civil rights.

The Nixon administration threatened "even the easygoing enforcement of the Voting Rights Act's key provisions because [the act gave] great discretionary power and authority to the Attorney General." This attack on the Voting Rights Act was a part of the "southern strategy," whereby the new administration would weaken or eviscerate various civil rights and social service measures that had been enacted under the leadership of Democratic presidents.

Nixon and his close friend and adviser (the new Attorney General of the United States), John N. Mitchell, believed that the Voting Rights Act had to be dramatically revised. Nixon was also very concerned about the personnel in the Department of Justice's Civil Rights Division. As he wrote years later, Nixon was "determined to ensure that the young liberal lawyers in the CRD would be prevented from running wild through the South enforcing compliance with extreme or punitive requirements they had formulated in Washington, D.C." The Nixon strategy was to try to kill the Voting Rights Act when it came up for renewal in 1970. Additionally, the Nixon Justice Department greatly weakened the Section 5 enforcement process by objecting to submitted voting changes only when the Civil Rights Division attorneys saw in the proposed change a clear case of racial discrimination. "The department's actual practices removed the burden on the submitting jurisdiction by requiring that either the department or interested private parties develop evidence that the proposed change would be iniquitous to blacks."

Despite the antipathy of the new administration (and, in part, because of it), there were a number of events that, collectively, led the CRD to construct a strategy and elaborate guidelines with respect to Section 5 implementation. These legal, administrative, and political forces had the cumulative effect of raising Section 5 to the "highest priority of the Voting Section of the Civil Rights Division."

These were (in addition to the 1969 *Allen* opinion):

1. reorganization of the Civil Rights Division during 1969, the first year of the Nixon administration;
2. the passage of the 1970 amendments to the Voting Rights Act and defeat of the Nixon proposals for eliminating Section 5;
3. the growing strength of civil rights groups in the South;
4. pressure for submission guidelines from conservative white leaders in the South; and
5. legislative oversight committee criticism.

The development of the regulations took place under trying circumstances. Section 5 had not been implemented at all by the Department of Justice during the Johnson years, 1965–1968, because of the policy judgment, made in 1965, that registration was the first priority of the Civil Rights Division in Justice. By the time Richard Nixon took office in 1969, there was a growing demand that Justice seriously work to implement Section 5 of the Voting Rights Act. Supreme Court opinions, especially *Allen*, led to increased filing by southern jurisdictions, but the submitters did not have any guidance. Within two years, however, the attorneys in the Civil Rights Division, confronted with hard, painful cross pressures (from an angry Nixon and Mitchell who wanted to see the Voting Rights Act die, from the Supreme Court, civil rights groups, and legislators in Congress who were extremely critical of the lack of formal rules to implement Section 5, and from southern whites who were under pressure from local civil rights organizations to submit voting changes), were forced to promulgate rules for the implementation of Section 5.

IMPLEMENTATION PRACTICES AND PROCEDURES

The organizational structure and the bureaucratic routines of an organization charged with responsibility for policy implementation can have a significant influence on the manner in which policy objectives are accomplished. Responsibility for Section 5 implementation rests with the lawyer-bureaucrats working in the Voting Section of the Civil Rights Division at the Department of Justice. The central concern of the remainder of this chapter is to examine how organizational arrangements and bureaucratic procedures have affected the manner in which the Voting Section has been able to achieve compliance with the requirements of the 1965 Voting Rights Act.

The Department Of Justice: Organization And Personnel

Although the Department of Justice was founded in 1870 and the office of Attorney General is as old as the Constitution itself, the Civil Rights Division was not established until 1957, and the Voting Section did not emerge until 1969. The Civil Rights Division was established in 1957 after the passage of the Civil Rights Act of that year. The CRD has primary responsibility for the enforcement of the Civil Rights Acts of 1957, 1960, 1964, and 1968, as well as the Voting Rights Act of 1965, and it reports to an Associate Attorney General who has responsibility for supervision and coordination of civil rights matters in the department. From 1957 until 1969, the CRD was organized into sections corresponding to geographic regions.

Each of the sections handled the full range of civil rights matters within a particular geographic area. In 1969, it was reorganized along function lines with Section 5 enforcement responsibility falling to the Voting Section.

However, voting rights enforcement is not, strictly speaking, the responsibility of the Voting Section; it is the task of a cadre of lawyers and paraprofessionals working in the section. At least two characteristics of those personnel are worth noting before turning to a consideration of the administrative processing of preclearance submissions.

During the 1960s, the Civil Rights Division devoted approximately 90 percent of its time to Section 4 (voter registration) enforcement. For division personnel, this often meant civil rights experience in the field as part of the Department of Justice's voter registration supervision activities. As one Voting Section official put it: "Right after the Act was passed, there was a large focus on trying to get blacks registered, and then through the voting process. That is where the manpower went in those sections; going into areas, finding out what the problems were, and determining whether or not they should be designated for Federal Examiners." In the early 1970s, some of the lawyer-bureaucrats who were handling preclearance submissions were, therefore, individuals with prior civil rights field experience and familiarity with local situations. In recent years, however, the Voting Section has been staffed with individuals who usually do not have direct knowledge of local situations. As a result, they have had to rely more heavily on whatever information local officials are willing to submit. This change in the nature of CRD personnel is one important factor shaping the interaction between Justice Department administrators and officials from covered jurisdictions.

A second important personnel characteristic is the training and background of Department of Justice personnel. As Richard Stillman has reminded us, Department of Justice staff members tend to be legal specialists rather than policy generalists. He has argued that "the narrow legal technical orientation gained from . . . case method training makes lawyers particularly unfit to address broad policy issues of large public agencies, particularly of the Department of Justice." Although the question of fitness to address broad policy issues is not our concern here, it does appear that the legal training of Justice Department lawyers has oriented them in the direction of preferring case-by-case solutions to problems. Compromise and bargaining are perceived to be normal and appropriate techniques for achieving acceptable issue resolutions. The lawyer's orientation to problem solving is, therefore, a second important factor structuring the interaction between Justice Department administrators and officials from covered jurisdictions. When Department of Justice lawyer-bureaucrats interact with lawyers representing the covered jurisdictions, the preclearance process becomes essentially a lawyer's game.

Administrative Processing of Preclearance Submissions

Although a few jurisdictions made preclearance submissions during the late 1960s (from 1965 to 1969, a total of 323 voting changes were submitted), Section 5 enforcement lay virtually dormant until the turn of the decade. The few early submissions to the Department of Justice were voluntary and done with very little understanding of exactly what Section 5 entailed. The Justice Department had not paid much attention to Section 5 enforcement, choosing instead to concentrate its efforts and manpower on achieving the voter registration objectives embodied in Section 4. Commenting on this lack of attention to Section 5, the head of the Voting Section noted:

> By the end of the decade that job [voter registration] had been largely accomplished, both by means of Federal registration and by the impetus that Federal registration had given to local registrars to go ahead and register people, then the focus turned to Section 5. This is an area of the Voting Rights Act we had not given much attention to up to this point.

After the events of 1969–1971 which led the Civil Rights Division to turn its attention to Section 5 enforcement, and the subsequent development and promulgation of administrative regulations in September of 1971, the number of voting changes submitted for preclearance increased dramatically (from 255 in 1970 to over 1,000 in 1971). In 1976, local jurisdictions submitted 7,470 voting "changes" to the Department of Justice. In each year since 1977, between 4,000 and 5,000 voting related changes have been submitted. A single submission from a covered jurisdiction often contains multiple changes like moving six polling places or 67 annexations. Each change has to be researched and analyzed as to the likelihood that it is discriminatory. Primary responsibility for processing the daily load of approximately 20 changes rests with the attorneys and paralegal staff of the Civil Rights Division's Voting Section.

The Voting Section is divided for operational purposes into the Submission Unit and the Litigative Staff, as illustrated in Table 12-1.

Before the 1975 amendments, Department of Justice attorneys reviewed voting changes with assistance from five paraprofessionals who were paired with attorneys to serve as "law clerks." With the anticipated growth in submissions resulting from the new minority language provisions, six more paraprofessionals were added as part of a February 1976, reorganization. After a period of training by Voting Section attorneys, the research analysts (the preferred title of the paraprofessionals) assumed principal responsibility for examination of voting changes. The position of paraprofessional was developed at the Civil Rights Division prior to the passage of the Voting Rights Act as the following description by the chief of the Voting Section indicates:

> . . . .John Boyd . . . came up with the idea of why should a lawyer have to sit down and go through all of those records? Why don't we use non-legal people with a good, practical, analytical mind [sic] to do that, and we did. It started out just using the secretaries to do that kind of thing and then we brought in people, college grads usually, right out of school and eager to get involved. We assigned them to doing that kind of

TABLE 12-1 Voting Section Professional and Paraprofessional Staffing as of July 1977

CHIEF

DEPUTY CHIEF[1]

SUBMISSION UNIT	LITIGATIVE STAFF
1 Senior Attorney Adviser[2]	1 Assistant for Litigation
1 Paraprofessional Director	13 Attorneys
11 Paraprofessionals	2 Paraprofessionals

[1]Responsible for administration of the Voting Section and election coverage activity.
[2]Also performs litigative activity.

Source: U.S. Comptroller General, General Accounting Office, *Voting Rights Act—Enforcement Needs Strengthening,* February 6, 1978, Appendix 6.

work and called them research analysts. That kind of took on and we spread it into other areas in the civil rights field after we got into the functional areas. After we created the Voting Section in 1969, I started pushing the idea that what we needed to do is get more research analysts into analyzing these submissions because most of it is factual—that is, gathering facts and making an analysis of a local factual-type situation.

The Section 5 unit's paraprofessionals and their director come from a diverse background. Presently, some are law students, others are simply college graduates who qualified for this GS 5-10 level job, and others have been clerical employees elsewhere in the department. In commenting on the prime talent he looks for in a candidate, the attorney responsible for the Submission Unit stated:

> Just the ability to speak to people in Mississippi or Alabama or Georgia, blacks and whites. Just an intelligent person who can learn just what we are looking for. Just willing to deal with people a bit resourcefully. . . . Writing ability is very important because they have a lot of letters to write.

No explicit training manual for the analysts exists; instead the training is essentially an on-the-job process.

Because the Voting Rights Act insists that submissions be acted upon within a 60-day time limit, the Submission Unit must gather, analyze, and verify the necessary evidence and then make a decision with speed uncharacteristic of adjudicatory proceedings. They cannot delay. Failure to review a submission in 60 days results in its preclearance, even if the proposed change is discriminatory.

In addition to the time factor, Voting Section personnel encounter another difficulty during the processing of preclearance submissions. The Voting Section is mandated to issue a federal imprimatur for all changes in electoral qualifications, practices, or procedures in all of the covered jurisdictions. Jurisdictions covering the original 1965 act include approximately 550 counties and several thousand cities, towns, villages, and other special districts. From the viewpoint of the Voting Section, the logistics of enforcement pose a nearly insurmountable task because the relatively small staff of the Submission Unit located in Washington, D.C., must monitor the actions of elected officials (in often isolated communities) throughout the Deep South without the aid of their own field personnel.

Given the volume of changes, the shortage of personnel, and the urgency of time, the preclearance process has not surprisingly evolved as a series of routinized tasks and discretionary judgments. Table 12-2 illustrates the process.

Designed to satisfy the record-keeping requirements of Section 51.26 of the act, the initial preclearance phase simply creates the necessary documentation for subsequent decisions. In contrast, the second phase of the preclearance process is pivotal because the paralegal research analysts make the initial (and normally upheld) determinations with respect to whether or not the proposed change has a discriminatory purpose or effect. Their casework includes not only gathering and analyzing sufficient information about the submission but also includes the critical decision on the action to be followed by the Voting Section.

A perusal of the steps comprising phase two discloses a rather ordinary and straightforward approach to processing submissions. Underlying these standard operating procedures are three points of decision, which entail substantial discretion. First, the preparation and analysis of the demographic and legal information about each change is in the hands of paraprofessionals who possess neither demographic/statistical skills nor legal training. Since Section 51.10 mandates that the covered jurisdictions transmit all relevant materials including census data, there is room for differences of opinion about the quality of the submitted data, as well as the distinct

TABLE 12-2 *VOTING CHANGE PRECLEARANCE PROCESS*

DAY 1

(60-day
time limit
begins here)

PHASE ONE: INITIAL PROCESSING

1. Letter from submitting authority passes through DOJ mail sort and arrives at Section 5 office.
2. Paraprofessional staff member logs submission in triplicate on an information card which serves as:
   (a) a label for the submission file to be maintained,
   (b) input data for computer listings,
   (c) a control card for compliance follow-up.
3. To complete the information card, the paraprofessional:
   (a) notes type of changes(s) in the submission,
   (b) assigns each change in the submission an identification number (change number),
   (c) dates receipt of submission by Section 5 office,
   (d) estimates review completion date,
   (e) describes submitting jurisdiction, and
   (f) lists name of the paraprofessional assigned to analyze the submission.
4. Paraprofessional director reads letter from submitting authority and assigns the submission to a paraprofessional, giving consideration to the geographic origin and complexity of the change and to the experience of the paraprofessional. (Some letters received by the Section 5 office are not submissions, but rather requests for information and receive appropriate response from the paraprofessional director at this point.)

PHASE TWO: CASE ANALYSIS BY PARAPROFESSIONAL

1. Previous record is checked for information, for example:
   (a) name(s) of city attorney,
   (b) form of government,
   (c) population characteristics.
2. If no previous file exists, new record is developed.
3. Demographic and legal information about the proposed voting change is obtained, for example:
   (a) nature of the area annexed.
   (b) location and number of new polling places,
   (c) existence of petitions to annex.
4. Contacts are made with minorities in affected area and officials of the submitting authority.
5. On the basis of this research, the paraprofessional recommends one of the following courses of action:
   (a) the submission cannot be reviewed under Section 5 at the time,
   (b) additional information should be requested from the submitting authority,
   (c) no objection should be interposed, or

TABLE 12-2 *Continued*

	(d) an objection should be interposed,
	PHASE THREE: FINAL DECISION
DAY 45	1. Paraprofessional director makes a procedural review of the case analysis.
DAYS 45 to 60	2. Legal review and decision are made by senior attorney, Section 5 office.
	3. If decision is either "no objection" or "change cannot be reviewed under Section 5 at the time," then a standard letter is returned to the submitting authority.
	END OF PRECLEARANCE PROCESS.
	4. If decision is to "object," then (a) Section 5 attorney prepares letter of objection, (b) chief, Voting Section, reviews letter of objection, (c) deputy assistant attorney general, Civil Rights Division, reviews letter of objection, (d) assistant attorney general, Civil Rights Division, reviews and signs letter of objection,
DAY 60	(e) Letter of objection mailed to submitting authority.
	END OF PRECLEARANCE PROCESS. **LITIGATION STAFF INVOLVED.**
	PHASE FOUR: FOLLOW-UP ON REQUEST FOR ADDITIONAL INFORMATION
	1. If submitting authority complies, then preclearance begins again at Day 1.
DAY 90	2. If 30 days elapse without receipt of additional information, Section 5 office initiates a memo requesting a FBI investigation.
	3. Memo is reviewed by chief, Observer Program.
	4. FBI visits submitting authority.
	5. Usually, submitting authority mails requested information.
	PRECLEARANCE PROCESS BEGINS AGAIN AT DAY 1.

possibility of data manipulation. In many cases, this issue does not pose a serious problem. In some of the more extreme situations, however, the absence of analytic abilities within the Submission Unit has led to the underestimation of the minority population.

The second major point of administrative discretion develops out of the standard procedure "to telephone minority persons in the locality to see if the voting change is going to bother them." The number of local minority contacts made per case depends, as one paraprofessional put it, "on the type of change—the more significant the change, the more contacts required." Research analysts in the Voting

Section select these "contacts" from an inhouse file of minority political leaders and other individuals considered knowledgeable about race relations in a given locality. Supplementing the documents from the submitting authority, contacts with local white officials are also normally made and received. From this brief description, it becomes obvious that the procedures used by paraprofessionals place them in an adjudicatory role.

This judgment takes tangible form in the recommendation about the case. While the paraprofessional can choose one of four options, it is the decision to object or not to object that is crucial to all parties. This choice, although ostensibly based on detailed information, confronts a fundamental substantive problem in the preclearance process: under what circumstances and given what characteristics will a voting change be objected to by the Department of Justice? Put another way, what is the "operational definition" of discriminatory purpose or effect as discussed in Section 5?

In essence, the determination of discrimination has become routinized through the adoption of some elementary decision rules. The research analysts are trained to spot "red flags" or "suspicious type changes." These include at-large elections, reductions in the number of polling places, changes in the location of polling places, and redistricting. Proposed changes such as these examples alert the paralegals to investigate the motive behind the change and the potential impact of the change. Investigating motivation and impact in often isolated localities throughout the South and Southwest without a field staff puts a premium on the telephone calls to on-site persons. Yet, even after a number of contacts and extensive documentation, the operationalization of discrimination ultimately becomes "situational." In the words of the director of the paraprofessional staff, "one looks at the circumstances of the change: the area, the people affected, what's going to hurt the people."

The final phase within the 60-day limit is the most hectic, with letters usually being mailed at the last possible moment. Casework on a proposed change must reach the paraprofessional director's desk no later than Day 45 for procedural review. Legal review and final recommendation by the Submission Unit attorney is the last step. Describing this process the Submission Unit staff attorney said:

> I want them [paraprofessionals] to do all the research on it and let the decision be made at a higher level than it is actually done. If they recommend objection and we are not objecting, we can just change it. If they recommend a no objection, and haven't done the homework on it, it's likely to go out that way . . . I might not catch it, or it just might not be visible to me while I'm checking. It's better that they make mistakes instead of doing too much.

Because of the review and signature steps in regard to interposing an "objection" will catch almost all errors, the chance of mistake is more likely in the finding of "no objection."

When the decision is to seek additional information from the submitting authority, a subsequent procedure is followed. If the local officials respond promptly, they merely go back to Day 1 and begin preclearance over again. However, if they delay more than 30 days, the Section 5 office initiates a memo, which brings the FBI to their community. The almost automatic nature of phase four comes out in this description by the Voting Section's chief:

> If they are out thirty days or more, we will send the FBI out to meet with the official and find out what the problem is. Usually that has the best result, when the FBI goes out and visits. We are getting a lot more of the submissions completed now than we once did.

Use of the FBI in this fashion is seen as a free resource by the Voting Section and serves as part of their surrogate field staff. Although Voting Section personnel believe that use of the FBI "is fairly effective in stimulating a response," the 1978 Government Accounting Office report on voting rights enforcement suggests that local officials do not necessarily tremble and quiver before the federal "muscle." Some jurisdictions have not responded in over two years after receipt of a request for additional information about a proposed voting change. Even more damaging, the proposed changes are often implemented and elections conducted without completion of the preclearance process.

THE CONSEQUENCES OF ADMINISTRATIVE PRACTICES AND PROCEDURES

What becomes clear from the previous discussion is that in operationalizing "discriminatory purpose or effect," Department of Justice officials have evolved some elementary decision rules which they call upon when confronted with a new submission. However, these are essentially cognitive decision rules that individual research analysts have come to learn from experience, rather than formal standards that delineate objectional kinds of voting changes. To be sure, 28 CFR 51 informs covered jurisdictions about the requirement to submit voting changes for preclearance; it tells them about the kinds of changes that must be submitted and about the types of supporting evidence required; but it does not (and probably cannot) provide much information about the criteria Department of Justice officials will be applying in making a decision as to whether or not to enter an objection (*see* Section 51.19). Two important consequences flow from this situation: (1) covered jurisdictions may be at least partially in the dark as to what counts as evidence on nondiscrimination, particularly when they have not had previous experience with the preclearance process; and (2) in the absence of standards that identify in advance the acceptability of certain kinds of voting changes, decisions regarding the acceptability of submitted changes are frequently a matter of negotiation between local officials and the Voting Section.

Since the burden of proof under Section 5 is on the submitting authority, it is important for covered jurisdictions to know what counts as evidence of nondiscrimination. Kenneth Culp Davis has argued that in addition to other safeguards (for example, judicial review), administrative actions should also be subject to predetermined or prospective rules which are known in advance to the affected parties. The Department of Justice has, of course, made some effort to inform covered jurisdictions about the requirements of Section 5. After 28 CFR 51 was published, Voting Section attorneys traveled to some jurisdictions to meet with local officials. By 1973, information packets (containing the amended 1965 act, the 1971 procedures for administration of the act, and a request to send all preclearances to either the Department of Justice or to submit them to the district court for a declaratory judgment) were sent to all covered jurisdictions.

It should also be noted that covered jurisdictions are not entirely without guidance as to the operational standard for determining "discriminatory purpose or effect." In its 1976 opinion in the New Orleans redistricting case, *Beer* v. *U.S.*, the Supreme Court articulated a standard that has come to be generally regarded as a bench mark. In the opinion written by Justice Stewart, the Court held that the purpose of Section 5 "has always been to insure that no voting procedure changes would be made that would lead to a retrogression in the position of racial minorities with respect to their effective exercise of the electoral franchise." This means that a change that results in an improvement of the position of minority voters is not likely to be objected to even if a better condition could have been achieved. As an attorney in the Submission Unit put it, "If a change makes something better, we're not supposed to object even if it is still not very good."

Attorneys in the Voting Section believe that over 90 percent of all voting changes are reported to the Attorney General, and that those that remain unreported are probably the least dangerous types of change with respect to diluting the black vote. Of those reported, approximately 95 percent are precleared. A major factor in the high preclearance rate is the process of informal discussion—advisement, assistance, and negotiation—between local government officials and Department of Justice officials. If there is a possibility of a Department of Justice objection, local officials often try to elicit from the Voting Section what they would minimally have to do to pass the preclearance test.

The Voting Section apparently does not want to interfere excessively in local policymaking processes and prefers to work with local officials in the covered jurisdictions (when asked) in a cooperative manner. This posture is illustrated by the following comment by the attorney in charge of preclearance submissions in the Voting Section:

> [Local jurisdictions] want guidelines, they want to know what we are going to look for. They're going to revise their city charter and the city attorney will call me up to ask . . . and this is a widespread type of request. . . . They have a job to do and they want to get our clearance . . . we'll do what we can for them . . . we try to make things go smoothly for them so they can hold elections.

There can be little doubt that the strategy of negotiating over the difficult parts of potentially objectionable preclearance submissions has facilitated the task of obtaining procedural compliance with Section 5 of the Voting Rights Act. That is a very positive accomplishment. However, this strategy—no matter what its virtues—is problematical in two important ways. First, it may produce substantive compliance at very marginal levels of acceptability. The negotiation process can produce "no objection" whenever the affected black population is not harmed by proposed voting changes, although their relative voting strength may not have been substantially improved. It may permit an unconstitutional scheme to be replaced with a less obnoxious, but possibly still somewhat discriminatory procedure. Second, a negotiation strategy is not very helpful in providing guidance as to what counts as evidence of nondiscrimination. As Lowi has noted, "there is an implicit rule in every bargained or adjudicated case, but it cannot be known to the bargainer until he knows the outcome, and its later application must be deciphered by lawyers representing potential cases." These are significant compliance problems that result from a policy implementation process that relies heavily on negotiated preclearances.

This individualized approach to obtaining compliance partially achieves the substantive objectives of the Voting Rights Act. Yet, the preclearance process transpires in the absence of specified decision criteria that are well known in advance to those who have the obligation to comply with Section 5. For Department of Justice decision makers, the problem is perhaps less severe since the experience of past decisions provides guides, or rules of thumb, for their future decisions. However, local jurisdictions, which are much less frequently involved and not themselves parties to past decisions involving other jurisdictions, are not much better off in terms of knowing "what counts" as the result of this implementation approach. It is doubtful that Department of Justice officials could ever formulate a complete set of decision criteria setting down exactly what counts as evidence of nondiscrimination—the nature of the subject militates against very precise standards. Perhaps, however, they can do better than they are now doing. If local jurisdictions are required to comply with federal regulations, they are entitled to have some guidance as to the decision criteria by which their preclearance submissions will be judged. (Hypothetical example cases drawn up with real situations in mind are a possible alternative to rules enunciating general principles.)

In perspective, however, the more serious of the two concerns may be that negotiation results in missed opportunities. Some voting changes are no doubt precleared that are free of all visible traces of racial discrimination—optimal preclearances. However, changes may also be precleared that only result in less discrimination than was present in the prior condition—suboptimal preclearances. Critics of the Department of Justice have argued that the all-too-frequent selection of suboptimal preclearances rather than optimal ones amounts to missed opportunities on the part of federal voting rights officials. In rebuttal, Department of Justice officials point out that to do otherwise may very well result in less Section 5 compliance than presently achieved.

Implicit in the foregoing discussion of administrative practices and procedures is the notion that voting rights policy implementation is an interactive process between those who interpret and apply the policy and those who are affected by it. Success in implementing voting rights policy has necessitated shared action across levels of government in a federal system where local responses to national government initiatives are not always automatic.

From the viewpoint of local governments upon which the burden of submission falls, the matter of compliance has seemed from the outset to reflect the agony Justice Black expressed in *South Carolina* v. *Katzenbach* about local officials having to entreat distant federal bureaucrats. In the face of continuing resistance both locally and in Washington to the act, the Civil Rights Division has had to devise a strategy of enforcement that would obtain compliance without turning the covered jurisdictions into "conquered provinces." From the viewpoint of civil rights leaders who are trying to consolidate their newly won electoral gains, anything less than vigorous enforcement by the Department of Justice is often perceived as a return to the "forgo" strategy.

The lawyer-bureaucrats at the Department of Justice have had to deal with the administrative dilemma of implementing national instructions in a constitutional system that permits subnational units a considerable degree of flexibility in determining the manner and the degree to which they will comply with those instructions. Nevertheless, the Voting Section claims that the vast majority of all voting changes are reported to the Attorney General. Given the original massive resistance to voting rights policy, the number of covered jurisdictions now submitting successfully precleared voting changes indeed seems remarkable.

CHAPTER THREE
THE POLITICS OF REGULATION

INTRODUCTION

For many observers of the political process, the federal bureaucracy "is the focal point of the political process in modern government."[1] But the federal bureaucrats and their agencies do not and cannot act alone as policy implementers. Agencies need the strong support of legislators and pressure groups. Consequently, in contrast to the formal governmental processes, there has developed the notion of a "shadow government" in Washington, D.C., consisting of informal "networks of high-level bureaucrats, private lobbyists, and congressional staff members, [who get] the work of government done."[2] (See Figure C3-1.)

These institutions—agency staff, congressional staff, pressure group leaders, executive branch staff, and, to a lesser extent, the federal courts—that work together to develop and implement public policy are constitutionally separated entities and, in the case of pressure groups, private power holders. The politics of regulation, in a fundamental theoretical sense, is (1) the overcoming of the concepts of checks and balances and separation of powers inherent in the U.S. Constitution in order to reach consensus on policy and (2) the process of imposing legal controls on private action in a fair, constitutional manner.[3] The politics of regulation is the bridging of gaps created by the

[1]A. Lee Fritschler, *Smoking and Politics* (Englewood Cliffs, N.J: Prentice-Hall Inc., 1969,) p. iv.
[2]Robert Reinhold, "Pills and the Process of Government," *New York Times Magazine*, November 9, 1980.
[3]James Q. Wilson, *The Politics of Regulation* (New York: Basic Books, 1980), p. vii.

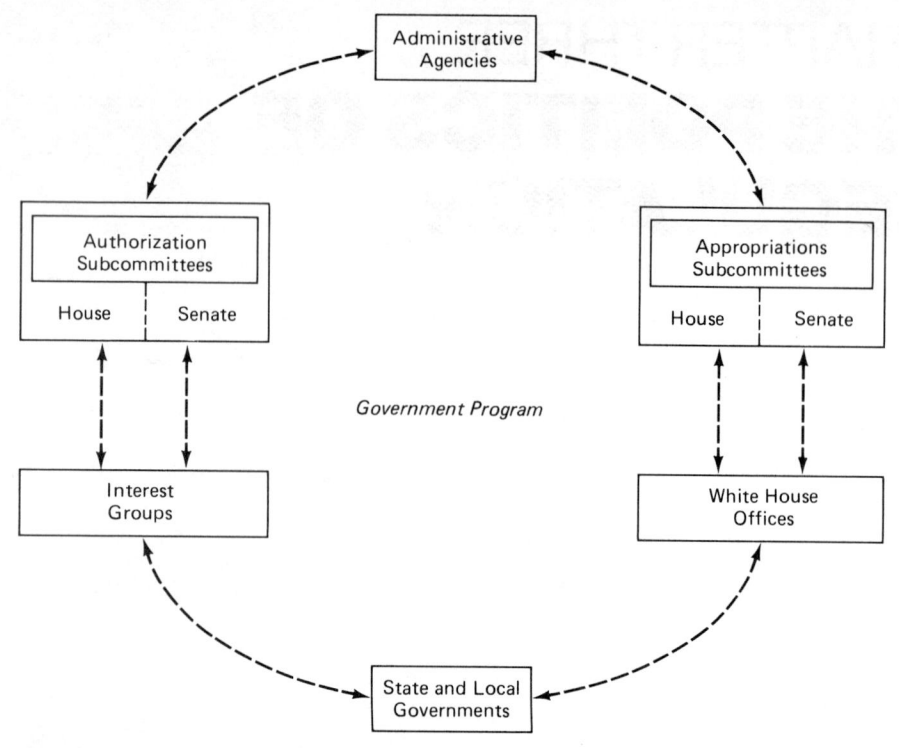

FIGURE C3-1 A Government Decision-Making System

From A. Lee Fritschler and Bernard H. Ross, *Executive's Guide to Government: How Washington Works.* Copyright © 1980 by Little, Brown and Company (Inc.). Reprinted with permission.

constitution's constraints on power through the process of building coalitions over those gaps.[4]

But, as the readings in this chapter clearly suggest, the bridge building is fraught with dangers. Alliances between the actors in the process are fragile and temporary for there is, in Fritschler's words, a "latent antagonism" present in any alliance forged by the necessity of the day.[5]

Agencies provide the legislature with the skill, the continuity, and the ideas necessary for the practical day-to-day implementations of public policy. As earlier chapters have illustrated, a "primary reason for the ascendency of agencies to power is the technical complexity of modern society and the resulting intricacies of administrative procedures."[6] But, while important agents for change in politics, the bureaucrats are vulnerable to political pressures and changes in the political and economic environment. "As government regulates more aspects of our lives, a greater variety of interests—occupations, professions, institutions, associations—acquire a stake in influencing the behavior of the regulatory agencies."[7]

[4]Fritschler, *Smoking*, p. 2. *See also*, generally, Howard Ball, *Constitutional Powers* (St. Paul, MN: West Publishing Company, 1980).
[5]Fritschler, *Smoking*, p. 9.
[6]Ibid., p. v.
[7]Wilson, *Politics*, p. ix.

A recent story in the *Chronicle of Higher Education* illustrates the political vulnerability of federal bureaucrats vis-à-vis outside pressures. The headline read: "No. 2 Man in Education Department Is Ousted, Cites Complaints From Conservatives." William C. Clohan, under secretary of education (second only to the secretary, Terrel H. Bell) was forced to resign, according to the report, because of his moderate Republican image and beliefs. "Forced to resign—abruptly by Bell—at the direction of the White House," Clohan stated that "there were indications that White House officials had sought his resignation under pressure from conservatives in and out of government who thought he was not a strong enough advocate of the president's policies." One observer of the firing stated that "it's a right-wing coup to eliminate a person who is moderate and well-respected on Capitol Hill and in the education community . . . Clohan is held in high regard by members of congressional education committees and has been an important link between the Department of Education and Capitol Hill."[8]

After Clohan's departure, Daniel Oliver took over as under secretary of education. Oliver is a former editor of a major news organ of modern conservativism, *National Review*. Clohan's final comment is illustrative of the political environment in which agency personnel work: "There was a general need to eliminate a moderate, and I was the handiest moderate around."[9] As a consequence, as a Republican staff member of the Senate education subcommittee states, Clohan's departure "would deal a serious blow to the ability of the administration to sell anything to the Senate."[10]

Agency leaders and staff have to work in this basically political environment; they are parts of a political process that reflects the pushing and pulling of a democratic, federal system of government that makes it difficult for policy to emerge and for new policy initiatives to replace older, more established programs. To understand the nature of agency activities and behavior is at once to understand the character of politics in America.

The politics of regulation, beyond the constitutional parameters, more practically involves goal determination, conflict resolution, setting of standards, and policy enforcement.[11] The readings in this chapter illustrate the character of the politics of this process.

James Q. Wilson's essay on the politics of regulation is a theoretical effort to explain why different types of broadly based coalitions, that is, congressional staff, pressure groups, agency heads, president, and so forth, join together, tenuously, to develop and implement public policies. His theory encompasses economic stakes and interests of participants, the belief systems of bureaucrats, and the general regulatory environment in the effort to make sense of regulatory activity in our political system.

The Barke paper examines a characteristic of agency activity—delay—and determines that it is frequently used as a political strategy by the agency. Delay, Barke points out, leads to a set of "serial adjustments, born out of political compromise, that provide the dynamics for both regulatory change and support."

The Reinhold piece illustrates the process by examining a particular agency's efforts to develop rules to provide information to persons using prescription medication. The Food and Drug Administration's problems in this quest to develop public policy to assist the larger community reflects upon and illustrates the shadow government, the iron triangle, of pressure groups, legislative personnel, and agency staffers at work and at odds.

---

[8]*Chronicle of Higher Education*, April 21, 1982, pp. 9, 10.
[9]Ibid.
[10]Ibid.
[11]Wilson, *Politics*, p. xi.

THIRTEEN
THE ORIGINS OF REGULATION

James Q. Wilson

What is striking about the origins of regulatory programs is that in almost every case, *the initial law was supported by a rather broadly based coalition.* Sometimes industry was eagerly and happily a part of that coalition (as with the CAB and the PUCs), sometimes it was a reluctant partner (as with the 1938 and 1962 drug amendments), and sometimes it was an outright opponent (as with much of the environmental and occupational safety legislation). The same pattern seems to be true for major regulatory laws studied by others. The act creating the Interstate Commerce Commission, for example, provided something for almost everybody: for railroaders, a ban on paying rebates to big shippers; for shippers, a ban on price discrimination against short-haul traffic. Even so, most railroad executives opposed the bill in its final form.

    Large coalitions are so often formed to support new governmental policies because in politics, unlike in the market, decisions must have justifications. Proponents who have a stake in the outcome must make an argument to convince people who do not have a stake, or have a different one. The argument may be good or bad and the symbols to which it appeals may change over time, but the argument must persuade. If probusiness values are widely shared, an argument to regulate business is hard to make. One must therefore either include provisions in the bill that will moderate business opposition (as with the 1906 drug laws) or hope for a crisis or

This selection comes from James Q. Wilson (ed.), *The Politics of Regulation*, pp. 364–394. Copyright © 1980 by Basic Books, Inc., New York. Reprinted by permission of the publisher. Footnotes omitted.

scandal that will evoke antibusiness sentiments (as with the 1938 and 1962 drug law amendments).

In recent decades, the perceived legitimacy of business enterprise has declined (corporations, especially oil companies, command scarcely more public confidence than does organized labor or Congress—that is, hardly any) and thus the concessions that must be made to business interests are fewer and the need for a crisis or scandal is diminished. But even in the heyday of Horatio Alger and popular sermons on the virtues of wealth, there was enough antibusiness opinion fomented by the Grangers and the muckrakers to make it difficult for any federal regulatory law to be purely business-serving. If business influence was to be truly successful, it would have to keep a regulatory proposal from being placed on the political agenda in the first place—something which no doubt occurred, but this meant that business thereby forfeited the opportunity to use regulation to maximize profits.

But though broad coalitions were formed in almost every instance of regulatory legislation, it would be foolish to claim that this is evidence of the public-serving quality of the regulation or to deny that in many cases business proponents of the regulations exercised decisive influence. To understand the origins of regulation, we must distinguish between cases in which business influence is likely to be strong and those in which it is likely to be weaker or more easily countered. In short, it is necessary to have a theory that helps us explain the kinds of coalitions likely to be formed and the arguments that will have to be made to create them.

Elsewhere I have suggested that policy proposals, especially those involving economic stakes, can be classified in terms of the perceived distribution of their costs and benefits. These costs and benefits may be monetary or nonmonetary, and the value assigned to them, as well as beliefs about the likelihood of their materializing, can change. Indeed, changes in the perceptions of these costs and benefits, at least among political elites, have become so common and have had such profound effects in recent years that special attention will be devoted to the phenomenon later in this chapter.

The political significance of costs and benefits arises out of their distribution as well as their magnitude. To simplify the analysis, I will emphasize the distributional effect. Magnitudes are certainly important (politics is replete with discussions of "windfall profits," "tax burdens," and "unmet needs"), but the incidence of these magnitudes is especially relevant to political action. As we shall see, the distribution of consequences affects the incentive to form political organizations and to engage in collective action. Moreover, perceptions of the fairness and unfairness of a policy profoundly affect the extent to which it is regarded as legitimate and thus the difficulty (or cost) of finding persuasive justifications for that policy.

A substantial body of psychological data supports the view that people are quite sensitive to the perceived equity of any allocation of rewards. They judge equity by comparing the ratio of burdens and benefits they must bear with the ratio of burdens and benefits others similarly situated must bear: what A gets in return for his efforts should be comparable to what B gets in return for his. People like legislators, whose consent is necessary for the adoption of a proposed regulatory policy, will feel uncomfortable or even angry if the policy seems inequitable. The supporters of such a policy must respond by either modifying its terms, changing the perception of its effects, justifying those effects, or inducing (perhaps corruptly) others to ignore those effects. In the private market, equity issues are resolved largely by changing prices. In the political process, there is either no "price" that can be altered (shall A or B receive the television license?) or the participants in the decision will refuse to allow the matter to be judged simply as a transaction that has no third-party effects.

Costs and benefits may be widely distributed or narrowly concentrated. Income and social security taxes are widely distributed; subsidies to a particular industry or regulations imposing costs on an industry that cannot be fully passed through to consumers are narrowly concentrated. Though there are many intermediate cases, four political situations can be distinguished by considering all combinations of the dichotomous cases.

When both costs and benefits are widely distributed, we expect to find *majoritarian politics*. All or most of society expects to gain; all or most of society expects to pay. Interest groups have little incentive to form around such issues because no small, definable segment of society (an industry, an occupation, a locality) can expect to capture a disproportionate share of the benefits or avoid a disproportionate share of the burdens. Not all measures that seem to offer a net gain to popular majorities are passed: proposals must first get onto the political agenda, people must agree that it is legitimate for the government to take action, and ideological objections to the propriety or feasibility of the measures must be overcome. All these issues had to be dealt with in the case of such conspicuously majoritarian policies as the Social Security Act of 1935 and the proposal to maintain a large standing army just before and just after World War II.

The passage of the Sherman Antitrust Act, and perhaps also of the Federal Trade Commission Act, arose out of circumstances that approximate those of majoritarian politics. No single industry was to be regulated; the nature and scope of the proposed regulations were left quite vague; any given firm could imagine ways in which these laws might help them (in dealing with an "unscrupulous" competitor, for example). But though there was no determined industry opposition, neither was there strong business support. The measures could not be passed until popular sentiment supported them (Grangers and muckrakers had first to persuade people that a problem existed and that there was a gain to be had) and elite opinion was convinced that it was legitimate for the federal government to pass such laws. (Prevailing Supreme Court decisions gave no assurance ahead of time that these measures would be constitutionally permissible and, as it turned out, the reach of the Sherman Act was sharply restricted by subsequent Court rulings).

When both costs and benefits are narrowly concentrated, conditions are ripe for *interest-group politics*. A subsidy or regulation will often benefit a relatively small group at the expense of another comparable small group. Each side has a strong incentive to organize and exercise political influence. The public does not believe it will be much affected one way or another; though it may sympathize more with one side than the other, its voice is likely to be heard in only weak or general terms. The passage of the Commerce Act in 1886 resulted from interest-group politics as each affected party—long-haul and short-haul railroads, farm groups, oil companies, and businessmen representing various port cities—contended over how, if at all, railroad rates should be regulated. Much labor legislation—the Wagner Act, the Taft-Hartley Act, the Landrum-Griffin Act, the proposed labor law reform act of 1978— is also a product of interest-group politics.

The Shipping Act of 1916 pitted those who shipped goods by sea against those who operated the ships; by and large, the former won. Steamship lines had been engaged in price fixing by means of cartels. The issue was whether the cartels should be put out of business as a violation of the antitrust act (as they almost surely were) or regulated in the interests of the shippers. Congress chose the latter course of action, allowing the rate-fixing cartels to remain, but not, it would seem, because the carriers demanded it. The shippers, in whose interests the rates would presumably be regulated, favored the continuation of the cartels because they feared that competition would drive all marginal carriers out of business until only a single monopoly carrier remained. The legalization of the cartels pleased the carriers even if they opposed the rate-fixing powers given to what later was called the Federal Maritime Commission. As with most examples of interest-group politics, there was something in the final legislation to please each affected party.

When the benefits of a prospective policy are concentrated but the costs widely distributed, *client politics* is likely to result. Some small, easily organized group will benefit and thus has a powerful incentive to organize and lobby; the costs of the benefit are distributed at a low per capita rate over a large number of people, and hence they have little incentive to organize in opposition—if, indeed, they even hear of the policy. As we shall see, however, an important organizational change has occurred that has altered the normal advantage enjoyed by the client group in these circumstances—the emergence of "watchdog" or "public interest" associations that have devised ways of maintaining themselves without having to recruit and organize the people who will be affected by a policy. Absent such watchdog organizations, however, client politics produces regulatory legislation that most nearly approximates the producer-dominance model. Countless industries and occupations have come to enjoy subsidies and regulations that, in effect, spare them the full rigors of economic competition.

The Civil Aeronautics Board arose from circumstances conducive to client politics and, after its formation, the CAB operated in a manner most solicitous of the health of the domestic aviation industry. Public utility commissions were created in part at the urging of electric utility executives; though one cannot be certain, the desires of these industry spokesmen may well have been the most important source of the PUC movement. But, as we have already seen, neither the CAB nor the PUCs conform exactly to the model of client politics. There was much public discussion of the matter, nonbusiness groups were important parts of the supportive coalition, and public-serving arguments were made and taken seriously. These circumstances are somewhat different from those normally associated with client politics: backstairs intrigue, quiet lobbying, and quick passage with a minimum of public discussion. (One thinks of the shadowy maneuvering by which various milk-producer organizations and their political allies have sometimes managed to get higher milk price supports.)

. . . We cannot say whether the political sources of the CAB and the PUCs were anomalous or are typical of policies having this pattern of costs and benefits. Perhaps more representative cases of client politics would be found in the origins of less conspicuous regulatory programs, such as state laws that license (and protect) occupations. Or perhaps the popular image of client politics is more commonly to be found where the government is supplying a cash subsidy to an industry or occupation. After all, in the case of the CAB and the PUCs, we are dealing with laws explicitly stating that an industry is to be regulated *in the public interest*. We may, in hindsight, dismiss such language as vague or even meaningless, but it was not meaningless at the time such laws were passed. If someone proposes, sincerely or hypocritically, to use the law to make behavior conform to general standards of rightness or justice, then one is obliged to devise more elaborate justifications—and thereby mobilize a more extensive coalition—than if one gives money away because somebody "needs" it.

Finally, a policy may be proposed that will confer general (though perhaps small) benefits at a cost to be borne chiefly by a small segment of society. When this is attempted, we are witnessing *entrepreneurial politics*. Antipollution and auto-safety bills were proposed to make air cleaner or cars safer for everyone at an expense that was imposed, at least initially, on particular segments of industry. Since the incentive to organize is strong for opponents of the policy but weak for the beneficiaries, and since the political system provides many points at which opposition is strong for opponents of the policy but weak for the beneficiaries, and since the political system provides many points at which opposition can be registered, it may seem astonishing that regulatory legislation of this sort is ever passed. It is, and with growing frequency in recent years—but it requires the efforts of a skilled entrepreneur who can mobilize latent public sentiment (by revealing a scandal or capitalizing on a crisis), put the opponents of the plan publicly on the defensive (by accusing them of deforming babies or killing motorists), and associate the legislation with widely shared values (clean air, pure water, health and safety). The entrepreneur serves as the vicarious representative of groups not directly part of the legislative process. Ralph Nader was such an entrepreneur, and the Auto Safety Act of 1966 was one result. Policy entrepreneurs are found not only in the politics of business regulation. Howard Jarvis was an entrepreneur who helped pass Proposition 13 in California; Joseph R. McCarthy was an entrepreneur when he galvanized large parts of the public into an anticommunism crusade.

Policy entrepreneurs and their allies inside the government were in large measure responsible for the laws enforced by the Environmental Protection Agency. Nader worked both with and against Senator Edmund Muskie to obtain a stringent clean-air act, just as he had earlier worked with Senator Abraham Ribicoff to obtain an auto-safety act. Dr. Harvey Wiley mobilized support for the 1906 Food and Drug Act and his cause was powerfully aided by the publication of Upton Sinclair's *The Jungle* in 1905. Thirty years later, the appearance of *American Chamber of Horrors* by Ruth Lamb and *100,000,000 Guinea Pigs* by F.J. Schlink and Arthur Kallet helped prepare the way for the 1938 drug laws. Senator Estes Kefauver and his staff skillfully laid the groundwork for the 1962 drug amendments by feeding to the press stories about the harmful effects of certain prescription drugs.

Occasionally, the work of a policy entrepreneur is made easier by scandal or crisis, such as that involving Elixir of Sulfanilamide in 1937 and thalidomide in 1961. We conjecture that such crises are most important when the regulated industry is associated in the popular mind with positive values, such as free enterprise, the accomplishments of technology, or the virtues of limited government. The need for a crisis declines as the value of these symbols—or the ability of business to attach itself to these symbols—declines. No crisis in auto fatalities preceded the Auto Safety Act; no grim industrial accident preceded the Occupational Safety and Health Act; no tragic deaths from air or water pollution preceded the various environmental protection laws.

Indeed, the passage of one regulatory law can prepare the way for another if the legislators believe the experience rewarding. The popularity of the Auto Safety Bill made it easier—that is, politically more attractive—to support the OSHAct, so much so that the policy entrepreneur in this case was only a little-known assistant secretary of labor who had become interested in the problems of uranium miners. (To be sure, his cause was powerfully aided by the support of organized labor; the OSHAct campaign has features of both interest group as well as entrepreneurial politics.)

Entrepreneurial politics depends heavily on the attitudes of third parties. The reaction of the regulated industry is predictably hostile (though in the case of the 1962 drug amendments, the more liberal spokesmen for the pharmaceutical companies were willing to accept the efficacy standard); the reaction of the public that is to benefit may be hard to discern or evident only in general terms ("do something about this problem"). Third parties are those members of various political elites—the media, influential writers, congressional committee staff members, the heads of voluntary associations, political activists—not affected by the policy whose political response to the entrepreneur's campaign is important. Reverend Martin Luther King, Jr. was such an entrepreneur when he led his small but dedicated band of civil rights followers into confrontations with the police in Selma and Birmingham. The vivid scenes of police violence that followed had a galvanic effect on key third parties, and, to a degree, on the public at large. The 1965 Civil Rights Act was the result.

In sum, the politics of regulation follows different patterns, mobilizes different actors, and has different consequences depending, among other things, on the perceived distribution of costs and benefits of the proposed policy. In some of these political patterns, the economic interests of the key actors are both plain and decisive—for example, in most forms of client and interest-group politics. In others, economic interests are either not apparent (at least among the proponents) or are not of decisive importance—for example, in many instances of entrepreneurial politics. In still other cases, such as certain examples of majoritarian politics, the material interests of affected parties may be plain but not decisive or too dependent on future events to be known at all. Any theory that fails to account for these and other variations in regulatory policies is defective.

A complete theory of regulatory politics—indeed, a complete theory of politics generally—requires that attention be paid to beliefs as well as interests. Only by the most extraordinary theoretical contortions can one explain the Auto Safety Act, the 1964 Civil Rights Act, the OSHAct, or most environmental protection laws by reference to the economic stakes involved. And even when these stakes are important, as they were in the case of electric utility regulation, the need for assembling a majority legislative coalition requires that arguments be made that appeal to the beliefs (as well as interests) of broader constituencies.

THE BEHAVIOR OF REGULATORY AGENCIES

Anyone who purports to explain the behavior of regulatory agencies must first make clear what behavior is worth explaining. By carefully selecting certain examples and ignoring others, the behavior of many of the regulatory agencies can be made to appear industry-serving in the narrow sense. Until recently, the CAB refused to allow any new airline to provide scheduled service on major routes, thereby shielding established trunk carriers from increased competition. The FMC routinely approved the rate schedules of the shipping companies. The FDA, at least during the 1950s, was lenient in approving new drug applications from pharmaceutical companies. For many years, the FTC devoted much of its effort to prosecuting minor violations of the Robinson-Patman Act, to the advantage of certain small business firms.

But a fuller list suggests that industry-serving behavior is only part of the story. The CAB may have helped the established major air carriers as a group, but its actions often penalized individual carriers by causing long delays or adverse decisions in specific route and tariff applications. And by the late-1970s the CAB was moving toward deregulation in a manner that, at least initially, caused great alarm among the carriers.

The FDA was energized in the mid-1960s by a series of new appointments and new laws that, by the 1970s, had moved the pharmaceutical industry and many physicians to complain bitterly of costly delays in the introduction of new drugs.

The FTC, after a major reorganization (under a Republican president) began to bring large "structural" cases against such firms as Exxon and the leading cereal manufacturers; at the same time, the Antitrust Division was attempting to expand the reach of the antitrust law by questioning the formation of conglomerates.

The California Public Utilities Commission adopted a "lifeline" electric rate over the objections of Pacific Gas & Electric, and the New York Public Service Commission adopted a modified form of peak-load pricing over the objections of many of that state's largest electric power users.

These particular instances might be dismissed as exceptions to the normal pattern of industry service by regulatory agencies, but a fair reading . . . suggests that they are a good deal more than that—they are the leading edge of either a broad shift in, or a previously undiscussed dimension of, bureaucratic behavior. To be sure, such examples cannot be found in every agency: the FMC continues to approve carrier rate requests without blinking an eye, except when the carrier types its requests on the wrong paper or with incorrect margins. But what might be exceptions in these "old" or "traditional" regulatory agencies is clearly the norm in the "new" agencies. EPA and OSHA have, in general, chosen stricter and more costly standards over more lenient, less expensive ones. And though the Office for Civil Rights (OCR) has not pleased civil rights organizations, neither has it endeared itself to schools and colleges. If it has been "captured" by anyone, it has been by a federal district court.

In short, the behavior to be explained is complex and changing; it cannot easily be summarized as serving the interests of either the regulated sector or the public at large. To account for this, I suggest we view these agencies as coalitions of diverse participants who have somewhat different motives. In some cases, the maintenance of the regulatory organization is only weakly affected by these differences (the members of the FMC are sufficiently like-minded to create few internal strains); in other cases, profound differences of opinion and interest make agency maintenance difficult. This coalition must be held together in a political environment that provides a changing pattern of rewards to each coalition member. In the remainder of this section, I will discuss the principal members of these coalitions and their motives; in the next section, I will take up the effect of the political and economic environment on how these motives are satisfied.

To simplify, government agencies have at least three kinds of employees who can be defined in terms of their motives. The first are the *careerists*: employees who identify their careers and rewards with the agency. They do not expect to move on to other jobs outside the agency or otherwise to receive significant rewards from external constituencies. The maintenance of the agency and of their position in it is of paramount concern.

The second are the *politicians*: employees who see themselves as having a future in elective or appointive office outside the agency. They hope to move on to better or more important undertakings. They may wish to run for Congress, become the vice-president for public relations of a large firm, enter the cabinet or subcabinet, or join the campaign staff of a promising presidential contender. The maintenance and enhancement of their careers outside the agency is of paramount importance.

The third are the *professionals*: employees who receive rewards (in status if not in money) from organized members of similar occupations elsewhere. They may hope to move on to better jobs elsewhere, but access to those jobs depends on their display of professionally approved behavior and technical competence. They may also be content to remain in the agency, but they value the continued approval of fellow professionals outside the agency, or the self-respect that comes from behaving in accordance with internalized professional norms. The maintenance of this professional esteem is of major importance to these employees.

These are obviously analytical distinctions; any given agency member may combine two or more motives. And no motive corresponds exactly to any given organizational position. However, we would expect to find politicians heavily represented among commissioners and agency executives, especially those whose appointment requires legislative confirmation; we would expect careerists to be found in all ranks, but perhaps especially in the ranks of middle-level managers; we would expect professionals, to the extent they exist in the agency at all, to be found among rank-and-file operators, especially if they have taken jobs in government to prepare themselves for more attractive careers elsewhere.

In virtually every agency . . . we find a coalition of differently motivated participants. (The FMC may be the conspicuous exception; it consists almost entirely of careerists). Tension and change in the agency involve competition among these variously motivated members.

Careerists

Careerists (and politicians facing a political environment that provides no rewards for making controversial changes in an agency) will develop, by experience and judgment, a view of what constitutes the essential maintenance problem of the agency. Every agency requires budgets, personnel, and political support, but in most agencies these things are available more or less routinely. Budgets and personnel are rarely cut; they usually grow incrementally (or, when the agency is new or in the spotlight, rapidly). Few officials need fear for their jobs and their salaries are determined by government-wide laws and regulations rather than by the size, rate of growth, or "success" (if such a quality can even be measured) of the organization. What *can* threaten the position, comfort, and prospects of a careerist is a crisis or scandal.

Many of the agencies here studied seem to have developed a shared view as to what constitutes a serious crisis. For the CAB and for the FMC, it was the possibility of a bankrupt major carrier. Agencies could explain away an unpopular rate or route decisions, they could ignore (up to a point) the anticompetitive results of these decisions, but they could not explain away the government allowing or forcing an airline or shipping company into economic collapse. The reason was clear: Congress said, implicitly if not explicitly, in the laws creating the CAB and the FMC, that they were to preserve, protect, and enhance the carriers.

For the EPA, FDA, and OSHA, a major scandal would be a dramatic loss of life or catastrophic injury among people nominally protected by the decisions of the agency. No arguments about the need to protect public health or to encourage pharmaceutical innovation have had a fraction of the impact on FDA as have the sulfanilamide and thalidomide scandals. In regulating pesticides, EPA is keenly aware that if a product it has registered is later shown to produce cancer on a large scale, the agency will be crucified and the careers of all concerned blighted, if not destroyed. The FDA is under a legal obligation to permit *no* carcinogenic additives in any food or drug (except tobacco). Indeed, fear of cancer (along, perhaps, with fear of deformed babies) has become the litmus test of any decision by these agencies. Whatever its incidence, whatever its harm compared to other illnesses or injuries, cancer has acquired a position in the public mind—and thus in political discourse—that subordinates almost every other consideration to its prevention. (The tolerance of cancer-inducing tobacco products is the conspicuous exception: here public opinion is divided—or, in an economist's language, people compare costs and benefits.)

Government agencies are more risk averse than imperialistic. They prefer security to rapid growth, autonomy to competition, stability to change. Exceptions exist, but they tend to be found among agencies with specially benign environments—strong public support and popular leadership. Much of what otherwise might seem puzzling about these agencies becomes clearer once we understand how they define the nature and source of potential threats to their security and support—in short, once they determine what constitutes a threatening crisis.

When the EPA was formed under the leadership of William Ruckelshaus, it gave almost no serious consideration to relying on effluent charges to reduce air and water pollution. Instead, Ruckelshaus immediately brought suit against several cities and large firms for violating antidischarge rules and activated machinery to ban discharges above some minimal amount. In the precarious early months of the EPA, when environmentalists were expressing skepticism about the Nixon administration's commitment to environmental programs, any sign that EPA was even considering effluent charges would have immediately been interpreted as an indication that the agency proposed to "sell licenses to pollute." Such a charge, however, misleading, would have dealt a serious blow to the EPA's need to find some political breathing room. Similarly, the maintenance needs of the FDA since the mid-1960s have been such that any public espousal of cost-benefit or cost-risk analysis of programs designed to protect health and safety would have provoked the damaging criticism that the agency was trying to "put a price on a human life."

Caught as it is between organized labor and organized business, OSHA has an especially difficult maintenance problem. The debate over the costs and effectiveness of its major regulatory policies—concerning vinyl chloride or coke-oven emissions, for example—is limited to a relatively small circle of activists. Nevertheless, each side in that debate knows that a much larger public, and thus many more congressmen, can be activated if OSHA can be shown to be doing something foolish, however unimportant. Hence OSHA finds itself constantly defending its decision to issue orders requiring the installment of split toilet seats to publish booklets in Basic English warning farmers to avoid slipping on manure. Ridicule is a powerful weapon, and OSHA has moved rather quickly to get rid of minor regulations that might stimulate such ridicule and to minimize the enforcement of those questionable ones that remain.

So also with OCR: the efforts it has made to constrain the hiring policies of private universities raise fundamental questions of public power and public purpose, but these questions are discussed only among a handful of specialists and in ways that elicit little, if any, congressional attention. But let it ban father-son banquets in high schools or all-girl basketball teams in Iowa, and the popular and congressional outrage is overpowering.

In short, agencies quickly learn what forces in their environment are capable of using catastrophe or absurdity as effective political weapons, and they work hard to minimize the changes that they will be vulnerable to such attacks.

That agencies are risk averse does not mean they are timid. Quite the contrary: their desire for autonomy, for a stable environment, and for freedom from blame gives these agencies a strong incentive to make rules and to exercise authority in all aspects of their mission. No agency wishes to be accused of "doing nothing" with respect to a real or imagined problem; hence every agency proliferates rules to cover all possible contingencies. The process is known familiarly in the bureaucracy as "covering your flanks." The more diverse the organized constituencies with which an agency must deal, the more flanks there are to be covered. Furthermore, regulations tend to multiply owing to the unanticipated consequences of any given regulation. James W. McKie has called this the "tar-baby effect." For example, a PUC may set the rate of return that an electric utility may earn only to discover that this rate diminishes the incentive the utility managers have to be efficient. As a result, the PUC must devise new rules to insure that levels of service to politically important consumers do not deteriorate. The more visible the agency, the greater the demands on it, and thus the more rules it must produce to assure its security and survival. The CAB became the inevitable locus of a variety of demands regarding air service, especially demands from small communities that feared they would be abandoned by the airlines if not for CAB-enforced service requirements. Finally, considerations of equity require that benefits given to one group be extended to others who can argue that they are similarly situated.

Critics of regulatory agencies notice this proliferation of rules and suppose that it is the result of the "imperialistic" or expansionist instincts of bureaucratic organizations. Though there are such examples, I am struck more by the defensive, threat-avoiding, scandal-minimizing instincts of these agencies.

Politicians

When appointment to a top position in a regulatory agency is seen as a political dead end—as a reward for an elderly defeated congressman or as a place in which to "bury" an untalented political hack with a powerful sponsor—the agency will be led by executives who act like careerists. They will have no incentive to make changes or play a visible role. Reappointment comes from avoiding enemies, not from winning friends. . . .

At one time, many if not all federal regulatory commissions may have followed this pattern. Perhaps it was because these commissions became, after their formative years had passed, dumping grounds for people who had to be "taken care of" that scholars such as Marver Bernstein began to formulate life-cycle theories of regulatory politics. It did not take a close student of Shakespeare's "Ages of Man" to recognize senescence when he saw it. Even today, many state public utility commissions still are of this character. When an agency's top posts are filled with old people on their way down and young people going nowhere—when, in short, there are neither political nor professional rewards available to incumbents—we are naturally tempted to speculate about the availability of economic rewards. In these circumstances, we might assume that politicians would cater to industry in exchange for lucrative positions after government service or material favors (or perhaps merely esteem) while still in that service. The examples uncovered in the occasional congressional inquiries into these matters are evidence that such speculation is not unfounded.

What is striking about the contemporary period is the extent to which service in regulatory agencies is now seen as providing future political rewards. William Ruckelshaus headed EPA at a time when he probably thought of himself as having a substantial political career ahead of him and, indeed, he later became deputy attorney general and acting director of the FBI. When Leonard Ross became a member of the California Public Utilities Commission, he was thinking of a larger, future political role and acting in ways designed to increase—not minimize—his public visibility. John Robson and later Alfred Kahn did not take up the chairmanship of the CAB out of a desire for pleasant obscurity or free trips to airline resorts. The selection of first Miles Kirkpatrick (by President Nixon) and then Michael Pertschuk (by President Carter) to be chairman of the FTC is hardly consistent with the view of that agency as a political graveyard: Kirkpatrick was a distinguished lawyer with an active career still ahead of him, Pertschuk an experienced congressional staff member with a good deal of energy.

As Douglas Anderson suggests, a "political market" has arisen in regulatory agencies that is as strong—or stronger—than the economic market. Why this political market should have emerged is a large question on which we shall touch in the next section, but it clearly has much to do with the arrival of a political elite that has absorbed the neopopulist outlook fostered by the 1960s: the suspicion of institutions, the criticism of business enterprise, the interest in speaking on behalf (or so they think) of unorganized consumers, and the conviction that such an outlook is not only morally correct but politically useful. They would appear to be right: President Carter evidently thought so when he appointed scores of environmentalists and consumer advocates to key administrative posts, much as Governor Jerry Brown in California and Governor Michael Dukakis in Massachusetts had done before him. That Carter, Brown, and Dukakis were viewed, by liberal activists, as "conservative" politicians reinforces my point: even officeholders criticized as illiberal believed that energetic advocates of regulation made desirable political appointees.

Professionals

Some regulatory agencies have tasks that only professionals—that is, people trained and certified by some external institution—can perform, or perform well. Lawyers are the most numerous of these professionals but economists, engineers, physicians, and public health specialists are increasingly common. The extent to which someone acts as a professional as opposed to a careerist depends on the extent to which he or she receives important rewards, intangible as well as tangible, from professional colleagues outside the government agency. Not all occupations conventionally called professions—and not all members of a given profession—are alike in this regard. Physicists may accept the standards and seek the esteem of fellow physicists more than lawyers crave the good opinion of fellow lawyers. But some lawyers, especially those seeking careers with the more prestigious law firms, will be highly sensitive to their reputation in the profession. And, in varying degrees, almost every member of a profession will have learned distinctive ways of thinking about policy problems.

The role of lawyers in the FTC and the Antitrust Division is crucial. They define their task as that of responding to complaints alleging violations of a statute, investigating the complaint, and initiating a prosecution if the law and facts warrant it. They are accustomed to thinking in terms of two-party adversary proceedings conducted by advocates who use all the evidence that supports their respective case and ignore or downplay evidence that weakens it. The benefits of a legal victory are measured in terms of the gain to the party whose rights were secured and to the law whose supremacy was vindicated. This leads lawyers, in both the FTC and the Antitrust Division, to favor a "reactive," answer-the-mail approach to the enforcement of the antitrust laws. Reinforcing this tendency is the ambition among younger attorneys—who are a majority of all the attorneys in these agencies—to find cases that can be investigated and prosecuted in a reasonably brief period of time with maximum display of legal acumen. The lawyers' opportunities to prove their legal talent in the courtroom or in consent-decree negotiations substantially enhance their market value to prospective private employers such as law firms and corporations.

This professional orientation has two policy consequences. First, antitrust lawyers have a strong incentive to investigate thoroughly and prosecute vigorously. The more lucrative the opportunities for postgovernment employment, the stronger the incentive. Private law firms and corporations hire the ablest antitrust lawyers; the ablest lawyers are the ones who have *defeated* the private law firms and corporations. . . .

Second, antitrust lawyers have an incentive to prefer simple cases in which one party alleges that the other party engaged in conduct explicitly prohibited by law.

These "conduct" cases are numerous; to the complaining party, they are important. To an economist, however, they may have only a small social benefit and may be less valuable than cases that prosecute firms, or combinations of firms, that by their size and structure dominate an industry. The lawyers disagree with this view: they claim that tackling complex "structural" cases is an exercise in futility—there is no guarantee the court will sustain the charges, the legal precedents are often shaky, the economic evidence is typically controversial, and, in any event, the cases drag on for years. Whoever is right about the social merits and demerits of these two kinds of cases, one fact is indisputable: no lawyer relishes the idea of burrowing through the files of an IBM for ten years or so, hoping eventually to get a chance to appear in court. As a result, lawyers tend to walk away from these cases.

The FTC has organized the competition between economists and lawyers into rival bureaus (the Bureau of Competition and the Bureau of Economics). When Donald Turner was the assistant attorney general in charge of the Antitrust Division, the division also tried to incorporate economic considerations into the case-selection process, but with only limited success. Even that success evaporated with the return of Turner to the Harvard Law School. The FTC case load has shifted toward structural cases and away from smaller conduct cases as a result of the influence of the Bureau of Economics and the support it has received from several recent FTC chairmen. It would be impossible to explain this shift by claiming changes in the "economic pressures" or "client demands" confronting the FTC.

The outlook and influence of lawyers also help explain the early strategy of the EPA. Alfred Marcus notes the extent to which lawyers came to dominate the EPA because they were skilled at issuing orders and filing lawsuits, methods the first administrator saw as important if the EPA was to gain visibility and public support. But these orders and suits were often based on incomplete or questionable evidence. Economists in the agency criticized some rules for being too costly or conferring too few benefits; scientists in the agency attacked them for being half-baked. As outside groups—other government agencies and private interests—hired economists and scientists to challenge EPA decisions, the power of economists and scientists within EPA grew. Which profession dominated EPA's decision making—lawyers, economists, or scientists—had an important effect on the kinds of decisions it made.

Physicians and medical scientists brought to the FDA a distinctive orientation. Paul Quirk notes that the key FDA professionals have had little interest in economic analyses and have favored an aggressive expansion of the agency's legal authority.

So also in OSHA. Businessmen and economists bitterly complain of that agency's preference for "engineering" rather than "personal equipment" solutions to such problems as noxious fumes or industrial noise. Rebuilding a foundry to reduce noise levels is exceptionally expensive; giving ear plugs to foundry workers is much cheaper. Still OSHA has maintained its commitment to engineering solutions. Part of the reason is that this attitude accords with the preferences of organized labor, which objects to personal equipment as inconvenient, easily misused, and inadequate.

But labor's demands alone do not explain OSHA's actions; after all, OSHA can choose between competing demands, each forcefully presented. OSHA's choice reflects in addition the preferences of the public health specialists who occupy the key decision posts in the agency. As Steven Kelman suggests, they have been trained to believe in engineering solutions; only such solutions, the textbooks argue, address the causes of the problem. Personal protective equipment deals only with "symptoms"; it is a "Band-Aid." Industrial hygienists are trained to "eliminate hazards," not to engage in cost-benefit analysis. To the extent that public health specialists dominate OSHA, they will come to play a larger role in corporations regulated by OSHA. As Harold L. Wilensky observed long ago, political rivals hire rival professional and intellectual specialists. But this may have unanticipated consequences, for the employer cannot easily limit the professional to being merely a rhetorical advocate; the professional is likely to start influencing the employer's own decisions as well.

So far we have seen instances of professional norms leading agencies to regulate more aggressively than they otherwise might. But such norms can have the opposite effect as well. Engineers dominate the staffs of public utility commissions, such as those in New York and California. Engineers define their job as achieving efficiency; as staff members of the California PUC, they took efficiency to mean setting electric rates to encourage the most efficient production of electricity. This, in turn, meant the engineers generally favored lower rates for large (usually industrial and commercial) users, either to encourage maximum sales (and thus achieve economies of scale) or to discourage large users from shifting to alternative energy sources (and thus avoid excess capacity). "Lifeline" rate proposals—giving free or below-cost electricity to small residential users—was contrary to this way of thinking and vigorously (though, in California, unsuccessfully) opposed by the engineers as "welfare" or a "free lunch."

In some cases, professional norms were decisive; in other instances, they were only a constraining factor. . . . Any such norm can be overcome, but the cost—in energy, persistence, conflict, and staff turnover—can be high, as Donald Turner discovered in the Antitrust Division and as Michael Pertschuk may yet discover at the FTC.

THE REGULATORY ENVIRONMENT

The political environment within which regulatory agencies operate affects their behavior. That unsurprising fact becomes more interesting—or more sinister—if only one feature of the environment is emphasized at the expense of others. Some critics draw attention to the activities of corporations, others to the rise of Ralph Nader. Both of these parties are important, but so are several others.

Technology and Economy

Some changes in regulatory practice can be explained simply by reference to important changes in the underlying technology of an industry or in its price structure. Electric rate regulation was not a political issue so long as the utility industry was able to reduce or maintain the price of electricity by taking advantage of economies of scale and installing new, more efficient generating equipment. State PUCs had scarcely anything to do: if rates were steady or falling, the most that would be expected of the PUCs would be to nod approvingly (perhaps after a suitable delay). It may have been this fact that led to the 1962 discovery by George Stigler and Claire Friedland that electric utility regulation had no discernible effect on rates. Though later studies modified this conclusion, no one suggested the PUC's had a dramatic effect on rates.

Sharp increases in oil prices, the absence of feasible new ideas in generating technology, and the exhaustion of available economies of scale put an end to this golden age. Rates began moving up inexorably, with the Arab oil embargo and the subsequent imposition of "fuel adjustment charges" on consumers' bills dramatizing the change. Now there was something to fight about. But even here, the economic changes *alone* did not alter the politics of regulation; electricity consumers, numerous and unorganized, rarely raised the issue spontaneously. As Anderson makes clear, liberal and environmental activists found the issue and exploited it.

The shift in medical practice toward increasing reliance on drugs created potential problems of safety and efficacy that had not existed before on quite the same scale or with quite the same degree of scientific uncertainty. It was easy to regulate useless patent medicine containing opium; it was something else again to decide how, if at all, to regulate the marketing and use of drugs that have beneficial effects for some patients, harmful effects for others, and unknown effects for still others. Even if the FDA had not been hit with scandals in the 1960s, it would have been on the firing line: as Paul Quirk notes, the agency has had to reconcile competing interests under conditions of risk and uncertainty.

Politics and Ideas

By far the largest number of regulatory issues arose not because of a fundamental shift in technology or prices, but because perceptions about what constituted a problem changed. As we have already seen, OSHA was created because the rate of industrial accidents became an issue even though that rate had been generally declining. EPA was born not because scores of people were dying from pollution, but because the *potential* (and possibly large) effects of pollution had become a matter of concern. The movement to deregulate domestic aviation and trucking arose not because the airlines or trucking companies had changed, but because the beliefs of key political participants had changed.

The effect of the political environment will depend in part on the configuration of forces confronting the agency. Earlier we saw how the creation of an agency was affected by the perceived distribution of costs and benefits of the regulatory policy. Where benefits remain concentrated and costs widely distributed, the pattern of client politics will persist. The FMC is in this position and thus receives unambiguous and consistent cues from its political environment, cues that provide little incentive for change. The merchant carriers benefit from its action; those who bear the costs of these benefits have little interest in organizing. This may seem strange, since presumably the shippers would want to keep costs down and thus would press the FMC to lower rates. But, as Mansfield indicates, for many firms the price of ocean shipping is a very small part of the cost of doing business. Moreover, the largest shippers can often negotiate, on an item-by-item basis, attractive rates with individual carriers and do not need FMC help. Indeed, since a negotiated low rate will benefit only themselves and not their competitors, they prefer to avoid appeals to the FMC. Small shippers that cannot obtain such favorable rates are too numerous to organize and in any event often deal with freight forwarders who charge a commission based on the rates paid that gives these middlemen no incentive to shop around for low rates. Similarly, for decades, the CAB dealt with a generally supportive client, encountering demands for change only during those periods when low-fare unscheduled air carriers were trying to initiate scheduled service on major routes.

Some regulatory agencies must deal with competing demands—that is, with interest-group politics—because their policies produce both concentrated costs and concentrated benefits. The National Labor Relations Board has always been in this situation; so has OSHA. But because the NLRB is a commission, the direction—prolabor or probusiness—in which it tilts can be altered rather easily by changing the political composition of the board. Changing the posture of OSHA, on the other hand, requires changing a single visible administrator and his key deputies, a move which has struck most presidents as politically too costly.

The Origins of Regulation

But the distribution of costs and benefits, and their effects on the distribution of political influence, do not alone account for the kinds of cues regulatory agencies receive from their environment. We have seen the CAB and the FDA change their policies over objections of their clients, the airlines and the pharmaceutical industry. HEW's Office for Civil Rights has continually expanded its regulations even though we would have expected schools and colleges, with their strong links to HEW and Congress, to be able to resist such encroachments. The National Highway Traffic Safety Administration has not become the pawn of the automobile manufacturers even though NHTSA closely regulates that highly concentrated industry. EPA has had to deal with as many complaints and lawsuits from environmentalists as from industry, despite the economic and political advantages industry presumably enjoys.

These apparent anomalies can all be explained: the cost of obtaining effective access to the political process has been lowered dramatically in the last decade or two. Once national interest groups could exist only if they had corporate sponsors or a mass membership; today "public interest" lobbies can be sustained by the availability of foundation grants and the use of computerized direct-mail fund drives. As Jeffrey M. Berry has found, many of these new lobbying groups have no "members" at all, but depend on the Ford Foundation or similar sponsors or on their ability to generate (as does Common Cause) a large income from mail solicitations of persons who are members in name only. Though such groups rarely have the legal staffs or war chests of a well-heeled business lobby, they have at least two offsetting advantages. First, they can enter the federal courts to challenge agency decisions rather easily because the rules governing standing have been liberalized and because in many cases (such as suits involving civil rights or the EPA) the plaintiffs may be reimbursed for their costs if they win. Second, the public-interest lobbies have many friends in the national media who are happy to cover their activities and publicize their complaints. Ralph Nader and his successors have been good copy for many reporters, especially for those who bring an antibusiness attitude to their jobs.

The cost of effective political access has also been lowered by the existence within government, especially in Congress, of people who are sympathetic to consumerist and environmental organizations. President Carter's appointments of these people to executive branch positions has already been mentioned; equally important is the rapid expansion of the size of congressional staffs and the recruitment to many of these staffs of persons who derive either satisfaction for themselves or political rewards for their superiors from their ability to mount investigations or draft legislation in the regulatory area.

It would be misleading, however, to label these young staffers, in many cases the product of the political turmoil at elite colleges and law schools in the 1960s, as "proregulation." No doubt many such activists share the general public distrust of corporations (and of institutions generally). But in addition they have views about specific political strategies and policy tools. In his study of the EPA, Marcus notes the extent to which congressional staffers and often younger congressmen have opinions about regulation quite different from those held by their predecessors. A student in college or law school in the 1930s and 1940s would probably have been taught that government regulation of entry into and the prices charged by an industry was desirable and that the commission form of regulation was optimal. James Landis's book on regulation was a root-and-branch defense of the desirability and feasibility of applying neutral administrative expertise to the management of economic enterprise.

By contrast, in the 1960s, college and law school students were exposed to books and articles written by people disillusioned with the regulatory commission, though not with the idea of regulation. Scarcely any student majoring in political science could have avoided hearing that regulatory agencies were "captured" by industry and that commissions went through a "life cycle" that led inevitably to senility or dependence. A bright student would also have heard economists say that regulation of entry and rates, as practiced by the ICC and the CAB, imposed costs on the consumer by keeping prices at above-market levels. At the same time, they would learn from each other, if not from their professors, that the environment was being degraded and the consumer "ripped off." These students would later enter government service carrying with them the political residue of these intellectual arguments: agencies should be reorganized to prevent their capture, regulation of entry and rates is of questionable value, and regulating the nature and quality of the product and the conditions of the work place will produce substantial benefits.

The executive order creating EPA and the laws that EPA was to administer were drafted with just such views in mind. The result was a series of new agencies headed by single administrators (rather than commissions), committed to regulating quality rather than price, and governed by standards and deadlines affording minimal opportunity for the exercise of discretion. One additional proposal that supposedly would have further reduced the presumed threat of capture was the consumer advocacy agency, but Congress was not persuaded. Finally, key congressional staff members, such as those serving Senator Edward M. Kennedy, began pressing for deregulation of rates and entry.

In short, the political environment of the regulatory agencies changed significantly in a short time. These changes had many sources, but one common characteristic: they reveal the extent to which intellectual descriptions (and criticisms) of institutional arrangements come to have practical consequences. Any generalization about how government works is vulnerable to the behavior of persons who have learned that generalization and wish to repeal it.

Institutions

The political changes I have described may strike some readers as rather fuzzy shifts in mood that are not likely to have the impact of dollars and votes. It would certainly be absurd to argue that politicians have no interest in reelection, bureaucrats no interest in advancement, and corporations no interest in profits. Nor do I argue this: there are clearly examples of these motives shaping the regulatory process. But the impact of these motives is constrained not only by the interests of professionals, the mobilization of opponents, and the intellectual baggage of public officials, but also by the uncertain connections between votes and dollars.

It is difficult to be certain about the relationship between campaign contributions, electoral success, and bureaucratic policy: these matters are not always open to scrutiny, and we cannot be certain whether the publicized cases of influence peddling are typical or exceptional. That there has been an incentive for regulated industries to supply campaign contributions, however, is beyond dispute. Long before the government began overtly subsidizing presidential campaigns, it had passed a number of de facto "campaign finance" bills—all those laws that made the profits of an industry or occupation dependent on the discretionary authority of government officials. The list of firms that made illegal (and legal) contributions to President Nixon's reelection effort in 1972 reads like a Who's Who of regulated industries—airlines, milk producers, truckers, bankers.

What is less clear is what these companies got for their money. The milk producers received higher government-fixed prices; beyond that, the facts are uncertain. The EPA remained aggressively committed to strict environmental standards, even though Maurice Stans, a Nixon fundraiser, used the example of EPA as a reason that corporations ought to give to the president's war chest. (We suspect that a vigorous EPA was more valuable to Nixon than a passive one. There is a fine line between bribery and extortion.) Marcus finds that the White House made an effort to curb EPA, but that it was largely unsuccessful. In 1974 conservative businessmen also gave (now in legal ways) to the Republican party, partly perhaps in response to President Gerald Ford's scathing criticism of OSHA, but if so it was to little avail—Kelman finds OSHA as tough-minded after the president's criticisms as before them. It is hard to imagine what feelings gripped the hearts of airline executives when, after giving lavishly to politicians of both parties, they saw first John Robson and then Alfred Kahn push them in the direction of price competition; however, we can safely assume that gratitude was not one of those emotions. . . .

By and large, the policies of regulatory commissions are not under the close scrutiny or careful control of either the White House or of Congress simply because what these agencies do has little or no political significance for either of these institutions. Votes are won or lost by grand issues (war and peace), by pocketbook issues (inflation, unemployment), or by personal style and party identification. There are scarcely any votes to be had from regulating or deregulating an industry (unless there has been a major scandal) or from intervening in specific regulatory issues. If an outraged constituent demands intervention, a politician can always promise to "look into" the matter and make a pro forma inquiry. If nothing happens as a result, it is, of course, because of "arrogant" or "unreasonable" bureaucrats. They could try to do more than this, and sometimes congressmen and other politicians have—but they run the risk of exposure (and possibly indictment) if they are caught taking money or selling influence. Even a small chance of such a penalty makes the likely benefit—a few votes, a few thousand dollars—seem rather unappealing to most legislators.

The appropriations committees of Congress, which have the greatest potential impact on regulatory agency policy, have largely ignored policy questions when marking up budget requests. Such interest as is shown in policy matters has been evinced by the legislative committees, and usually only a few of them. The House Merchant Marine and Fisheries Committee has watched the FMC with benign neglect, at best; the Senate Commerce Committee staunchly supported the CAB for years. Policy change comes when an "outsider" committee horns in on the act, as when Estes Kefauver's investigating committee looked at the drug industry or Edward Kennedy's Subcommittee on Administrative Practice and Procedure took an interest in airline and truck deregulation.

When it proposes appointments to the regulatory agencies, the White House would presumably take a considerable interest in the policy views of its nominees. Here, surely, the ruling party can affect, at little cost, the posture of the agencies. No doubt the White House is generally aware of whether a candidate is probusiness or a consumer activist, a liberal or a conservative. The Carter White House could not have been unaware of Michael Pertschuk's attitudes toward big business or Alfred Kahn's view of rate regulation. But we are equally struck by the shallowness of the White House assessment of the policy views of most nominees. No one seems to care what an FMC commissioner thinks; John Robson was appointed to the CAB because President Ford had confidence in him, but at the time neither Robson nor Ford has a well-worked-out view on airline regulation; when Mort Corn was selected to run OSHA, the White House seemed not to know that he was likely to persist in the very policies President Ford had been condemning; the various heads of the Antitrust Division have been lawyers whose general policies have been similar whatever the political coloration of the White House.

Organized groups no doubt affect the appointment process (though we gathered no information on that). Industry lobbies to have one of its number put on a particular commission; Ralph Nader makes clear to whom he will object; public-interest organizations and professional societies form a complex Washington network of information and candidacies. But, as with the selection of federal judges, the need to please a constituency, to satisfy the obligations of senatorial courtesy, and to take care of a political supporter combine to produce nominees who are, except in the unusual case, known by their general inclinations but not by their specific policy preferences.

In short, the relationship between electoral needs and policy outcomes is problematic because of the many diverse persons whose actions must be coordinated, the uneven but generally low political payoffs of any given policy, and the difficulty of predicting action from professed beliefs.

This very diffusion of political supervision of regulatory agencies has facilitated a striking growth in judicial supervision of them. The courts provide a ready and willing forum in which contending interests may struggle over the justification and interpretation of specific rules and practices, matters that ordinarily are of little interest to congressional committees or the White House except when dramatic events (or rivalry between two or more congressional committees) bring an issue to the fore. It is possible, of course, to devise a "maximizing" or "capture" model of judicial behavior, but thus far none seems especially useful or persuasive. Judges, like professors, have the occupational security that permits them to indulge, to an even greater degree than most political actors, in the explication and application of ideas. And though both industry and its critics grumble about the burdens of litigation, especially when a decision goes against them, one suspects that each finds court appeals of regulatory decisions an economical way to advance or protect its interests—lawyers may be expensive, but they are cheaper, and the outcome of their actions is more predictable, than is the case with efforts to change the ideological composition of Congress, or even of one of its committees.

Court supervision has its costs for the public at large as well as the participants. Decisions are made on a case-by-case basis, rather than by the development of policies. Uncertainty about the consequences of any action or rule is increased. All parties to a dispute have an incentive to stake out extreme positions so as to widen the area in which a final settlement may be reached. There is little sense of finality about an agency decision and this may weaken the agency's incentive to take seriously its responsibilities. Judges ordinarily have little expertise in the substance of an issue but may be nonetheless prepared to act as if they did. Not all persons affected by a decision will be represented in court; other than by further court appeals, there may be no feasible way of challenging judge-made policy.

CONCLUSION

Having set out to correct what we regard as an overly simple theory about regulatory politics, we may appear to have gone to the opposite extreme and left matters in such a complex—not to say confused—state as to preclude saying anything at all about the subject. If so, we should correct these appearances; continuities, if not cosmic generalizations, are evident to us.

One point involves the largely unsupervised nature of most regulatory activity. Whoever first wished to see regulation carried on by quasi-independent agencies and commissions has had his boldest dreams come true. . . .

The White House repeatedly tries to tidy up these relationships and bring the regulatory agencies under closer supervision, but the history of these attempts is one of dashed hopes and wasted energies. The Hoover Commission, the Ash Commission, President Carter's reorganization project—all have struggled in vain to produce more than cosmetic changes. As this is being written, the Regulatory Analysis Review Group (RARG) has been formed, made up primarily of members of the Council of Economic Advisers, the Office of Management and Budget, and the Council on Wage and Price Stability, and charged by Carter with getting regulatory agencies to pay more attention to the costs (as well as the benefits) of their rules, thereby implementing a presidential order to choose the least burdensome way of achieving regulatory goals. RARG is viewed with suspicion by the regulatory agencies, which have reacted by forming a Regulatory Council, made up of the heads of thirty-five such agencies, to compete with RARG. RARG has pressed the agencies to make some changes; the council has attempted to defend the agencies' turf; the outcome of these initiatives remains in doubt.

A second generalization is the absence of good evidence that there is a clear statutory solution to the problems that beset these agencies. A generation taught to fear the capture of agencies with broad administrative discretion has attempted to write into law strict standards, enforce tight deadlines, and guarantee frequent court review. The auto emission standards, the Delaney amendment banning carcinogens, the clean-water requirements, the administrative development of numerical-"goals" and "targets" for civil rights compliance—all are animated by a desire to minimize discretion.

But the effort to forestall one problem creates others. Agencies may no longer be captured (it is not clear they ever were), but costs and benefits are no longer compared, and competing values are no longer weighed. Or rather they are weighed, but by judges, rather than administrators. Friedrich Engels's hope that the government of persons would give way to the administration of things remains as chimerical in a welfare state as in a socialist one. Perhaps "juridical democracy," to use Lowi's phrase, is possible in a regime with a limited government and minimal public intervention in the market, but it is unrealistic to suppose that unambiguous legislative standards (or sunset laws, or bureaucratic accountability) can be achieved when the government plays a large role in human affairs. The larger the role of government, the more diverse the range of interests which it must reconcile and thus the greater the scope of administrative discretion—de facto if not de jure. This may be a good thing or a bad thing; but given an activist government, it is very nearly an inevitable one.

A third conclusion is that much of what appears to be the result of bureaucratic ineptitude, agency imperialism, or political meddling is the result of the sheer magnitude of many regulatory tasks. Improving the quality of our air and water, making the work place safer, guaranteeing that only efficacious drugs are used, regulating the price of natural gas, assuring that educational programs have no discriminatory effects—all these and many other laudatory goals impose simply staggering work loads on the responsible agencies.

Decades will pass before EPA can hope to have carefully reviewed all of the thousands of pesticides and other toxic chemicals and for it to have found, much less controlled, all effluent discharges. OSHA devotes 80 percent of its staff to inspecting work places, but manages, with the best efforts and intentions, to inspect only about 2 percent of all such places each year. The more careful the FDA is to protect users against dangerous drugs, the slower will be the rate at which new—and potentially useful—drugs reach persons they may benefit. OCR can make life miserable for college administrators by demanding vast amounts of paperwork on hiring practices, but in fact OCR would have to be many times its present size if it were realistically to hope to alter in a systematic manner the employment patterns of the thousands of (highly decentralized) colleges in this country. If the FMC really tried to set shipping rates on a case-by-case basis (instead of routinely approving everything that is filed on the proper form), it would drown in its own paperwork. This aspect of regulatory politics is not much appreciated by the supporters of regulation. As Peter H. Schuck, former Washington counsel for *Consumers Union*, has noted, the advocates of regulation tend to believe that motives and intentions are more important than results, and that implementation problems are matters of mere detail and goodwill.

Fourth, "regulatory politics" is not an especially useful category of analysis because it encompasses forms of political action that have little in common other than the fact that some agency issues or applies a rule. A single-explanation theory of regulatory politics is about as helpful as a single explanation of politics generally, or of disease. Distinctions must be made, differences examined. These differences are not endless or random. Here, an attempt has been made to bring them into a manageable compass by drawing attention to the distribution of costs and benefits (giving rise to entrepreneurial, client, majoritarian, and interest-group politics), the differing motives of bureaucratic actors, and the changing technology and economics of industries.

Last, we must be struck at every turn by the importance of ideas. Regulation itself is such an idea; deregulation is another. The targets of antitrust investigations are selected in large part because of the ideas of lawyers and economists; the value of regulation by command-and-control as opposed to regulation by the alteration of market incentives requires an assessment of two competing ideas. What Harold Demsetz said about the Antitrust Division and the FTC might be said as well about almost any agency that is not wholly under the control of external forces or its own weighty traditions: the "combination of unsatisfactory theory and the absence of 'captors' encourages [the agencies] to be overly influenced by the scribbling of academics." To the extent an agency can choose, its choices will be importantly shaped by what its executives learned in college a decade or two earlier.

FOURTEEN
REGULATORY DELAY AS POLITICAL STRATEGY

Richard P. Barke

Perhaps no word better summarizes the American public's frustration with bureaucracy than does *delay*. Criticisms of excessive government and all that it implies were central themes in the 1980 presidential campaign; many of the common pejorative symbols of the organizational quagmire—for example, "red tape," bureaucratic inertia," "regulatory lag"—refer to the apparent inability of government agencies to expeditiously execute the laws. According to the *Study on Federal Regulation of the Senate Committee on Governmental Affairs,*

> Delay is a fundamental impediment to effective functioning of regulatory agencies. Delay heightens frustration, impedes initiative, and postpones action on pressing problems. Its economic and human costs are staggering. . . . (U.S. Senate, 1977, p. 1)

The same flaw has been observed in other areas of the policy process: Eugene Bardach commented that "(i)f there is one attribute of the implementation process that everyone would agree was symptomatic of 'pathology' it would be delay.''

Considerable efforts have been made to identify, analyze, and ameliorate delays that result from the inefficient operation of governmental machinery. By focusing on "pathological" bureaucratic delay—by viewing it as an epiphenomenon or unintended by-product of the regulatory process, many academic studies of the problem have equated it with "irrationality." Regulatory procedures (such as case-

This selection was originally presented as a paper at the Southern Political Science Association meeting in Memphis, Tennessee (November 1981). Reprinted by permission of the author. Footnotes omitted.

by-case adjudication, or judicial review) are seen to obstruct decision making in a way that no one likes. Nevertheless, observers have recognized that in politics, not only does procedure often determine the outcome, but it sometimes *is* the outcome. Decisions not to decide are still decisions, and even America's lawmakers seem to respect the strategic value of delay through filibuster, as revealed by the rarity of successful cloture votes. Recent studies indicate that understanding the causes and functions of regulatory delay is important for our understanding of the regulatory process in general. In this paper I will examine delay as a sometimes deliberate device for affecting regulatory decisions. Several examples will be discussed, and I will conclude with some general comments about the politics of regulation.

PREVIOUS WORK

Bardach's discussion of delay in implementation is most useful for its distinction between purposive and nonpurposive delay.

> Often enough, delay is a synonym for perpetual procrastination, which is in turn a synonym for effective resistance or obstruction. In such cases delay is not pathological but purposive, in the sense that it serves interests or purposes in the games of at least certain parties.
> . . . Yet there are many delays that no one particularly wants or contrives. They just seem to happen.

His attention was focused on procedural obstacles to timely implementation, and the notion of deliberate obstructionism was not developed further in his work.

The argument was carried a little further in the *Study of Federal Regulation* (U.S. Senate, 1977). Here again, the emphasis was on the particular procedures that impede regulatory action. While acknowledging that the procedural/political distinction may be somewhat artificial ("procedures at certain agencies may provide perfect vehicles for parties who want to delay imposition of a penalty"), the report discussed flaws and possible remedies without recognizing that those flaws may have been created or tolerated because they somehow benefited one or more parties in regulatory disputes. The committee alluded to the incentives to create delays, but did not consider those forces when suggestions for procedural change were offered.

Perhaps the most complete statement so far about the compatibility of administrative procedure and politics was made by Owen and Braeutigam (1978). Their book, concerned with "how the game works," dealt explicitly with some of the ways that the regulatory process allows individuals and firms to pursue economic objectives—primarily to preserve the status quo by controlling entry, conferring legitimacy, and guaranteeing profits.

> "Delay is inherent in any decision-making procedure that is formalized. But the peculiar nature of the administrative process is to accentuate that delay and to make the period of delay responsive to the actions of the parties."

As economists, Owen and Braeutigam paid particular attention to the economic implications of such a regulatory system: the rationality of voters' and consumers' willingness to allow the market to be controlled, and the "efficiency and distributive consequences of replacing markets with courts." Their case studies were not analyses of the *political* struggles that retarded regulatory decision making, although they discussed some of the effects of the adversarial character of regulatory procedures.

Another economist (Lee) has presented a theory of "just regulation" that looked at regulation as an exchange process with regulators acting as arbiters. He used a game-theoretic model to assess pressures on agencies, and offered the argument that both "consumer groups" and "producer groups" can gain through regulations that involve no direct cash transfers. These involve an exchange of cartel enforcement for price arbitration (guided, said Lee, by "the social expectation of what is fair"). Lee stressed the role of procedures in allowing intervenors to affect outcomes by the strategic provision of information. While not concerned with delay, his approach clearly acknowledged the relationship between strategy, procedure, and outcomes.

What these economists' studies of regulatory strategy contribute to an understanding of the politics of regulation is that the procedures that engender delay can produce payoffs for contending groups or individuals that are more real than tokenism or symbolic sympathy. Of course, delays, like the adversary proceedings that often produce them, might sometimes be purely symbolic (Edelman, 1968), in that no actual transfers—direct or indirect—may occur as a result of waiting, but such costless delays are certain to be rare. A regulatory question is initiated because someone is losing something of value, and seeks a rule or finding that will protect his or her interests. Some citizens may receive some psychological gratification from being granted a hearing or from temporarily obstructing an unpleasant event; I will not be concerned with such nonsubstantive effects of regulatory delay. The topic is much more relevant, and more available for investigation, if we recognize that delay *costs* someone, either directly (by allowing or requiring the continuation of an undesired policy until a decision is obtained) or indirectly (by providing opportunities to *change* the outcome by providing new information, enlisting allies, or increasing the chances of error).

MECHANISMS FOR DELAY

(1) Rule Making versus Adjudication

The Administrative Procedure Act prescribed two primary methods by which agencies could make decisions. Today, *adjudicatory proceedings* are commonly cited as a principal cause of regulatory delay, and reformers advocate increased reliance on *informal rule making* for regulatory decision making. The problem with adjudication is that it often entails a trial-type hearing (officiated by an "Administrative Law Judge"), then an initial decision, then review by agency staff, then review by a subset of (or all) commissioners. In contrast, informal rule making involves only publication in the *Federal Register* of a "notice of a proposed rule making," opportunity for public comment, then publication of the final rule with responses to comments; trial-type hearings are discretionary options for the agency. This procedure has been becoming more common as courts and Congress have broadened its applicability—while simultaneously requiring agencies to offer *more* opportunities for oral hearings (albeit not trial-type hearings). Table 14-1 illustrates the effects of these procedures on delay.

(2) Modified Procedure

There have been suggestions that the Administrative Procedure Act be amended to allow a "modified procedure" involving, at most, legislative-type hearings (no cross-examination) followed by adjudicative hearings (with restrictions on cross-examination). The ICC has experimented with a similar system in regulating

TABLE 14-1 Elapsed Time in Rule Making and Adjudication

AGENCY	RULE MAKING (FY 1973)		ADJUDICATION (FY 1975)			
			ALL DECISIONS		APPEALED DECISIONS	
CAB	(N = 22)	170 days	(N = 54)	338	(N = 37)	475
FCC	(98)	357	(86)	359	(13)	1,057
ICC	(24)	429	(1,154)	489	(521)	693
NRC	(24)	282	(28)	675	(23)	676

Source: Adapted from (U.S. Senate, 1977, p. 27)

railroad abandonments: the results (before and after the reforms mandated by the 1976 Railroad Revitalization and Regulatory Reform Act) are shown in Table 14-2.

These past procedures and recent reforms imply that there has been a great deal of slack built into regulatory decision-making schedules, and attempts to expedite decisions have been only partially successful. In Table 14-2 we see that before the 4R Act the ICC disposed of modified-procedure cases about ten months faster than adjudicated cases, but still about six months slower than simple, unprotested cases. The 1976 reforms, which set deadlines for various stages of the procedures, cut the adjudicatory delay in half, but could not reduce the modified procedure delay proportionately. The difference between 323 days and 54 days suggests that Congress and the agency have left plenty of time for maneuvering, even in cases that do not require oral hearings for resolution of factual questions.

(3) Agency Review

The APA allows an Administrative Law Judge to make a decision that "becomes the decision of the agency" unless appealed. Then the agency may be required to review the entire record de novo—not only once, but several times. The statutes of individual agencies provide varying levels of flexibility in their power (or obligation) to review; for example, the Interstate Commerce Act requires at least two and as many as four levels of review at the ICC, while the NLRB may decline to review appeals of decisions made by regional directors. For most agencies, review is common—sometimes almost automatic—even if not explicitly required by law. All attempted reforms of agency review procedures have been ignored or effectively rescinded except for a procedural change at the CAB that only *temporarily* reduced review delays during the 1960s.

Other potential tools of regulatory delay are less susceptible to deliberate manipulation, and so are of little interest here. For example, the Senate Governmental Affairs Committee report cited poor management techniques resulting from unqualified agency leaders who fail to "instill an atmosphere of vigor" in an agency, the lack of incentives for managers to plan, and the lack of enthusiasm for removing bottlenecks. These and other organizational factors undoubtedly slow the regulatory

TABLE 14-2 Comparison of Elapsed Time in ICC Abandonment Decisions

PROCEDURE	PRE-4R ACT		POST-4R ACT	
Adjudication	(N = 59)	788 days	(N = 16)	360
Modified Procedure	(75)	494	(4)	323
Unprotested Cases	(126)	328	(86)	54

Source: U.S. Senate Committee on Commerce, Science, and Technology, "Implementation of the 4R Act," February 1979.

Regulatory Delay as a Political Strategy

process, but probably cannot be exploited or controlled by individual parties at interest. In the next section I will discuss examples of the strategic use of regulatory procedures for which there is good evidence of manipulation.

EXAMPLES

(1) ICC

In 1920 Congress gave the Interstate Commerce Commission a vague mandate to regulate the abandonment of rail lines according to "the public convenience and necessity. . . ."

The ICC can follow several procedures to produce decisions on abandonments. If there is little or no opposition to a railroad company's plan to discontinue rail service the case may be heard by an agency review board that eschews oral hearings and considers only written evidence; we would expect many of these cases to be granted. In the event of significant opposition to the carrier's application to abandon, an oral hearing may be scheduled before an ALJ—a process that takes quite a lot of time (*see* Table 14-2). Any of the resulting decisions by either process can be appealed to a "division" of the full set of commissioners, and then again to the entire commission. As expected, most appealed decisions are products of the procedures designed to handle controversy, namely, ALJ decisions; of the 141 dockets that I examined, 60 were appealed to the division level, with 45 originating from ALJ decisions and only 11 from review boards.

If we assume, as many others have, that the regulatory decision-making process is manipulable by organized interests, then we should expect that those ALJ-level cases (that is, those that were scheduled for hearings because of the existence of organized opposition) would be decided *less* on the basis of the facts of the cases (physical and economic characteristics) and more on the basis of political pressure. In other words, ALJ's should be *more* likely to deny a case than the review board, given the same objective characteristics of rehabilitation costs, operating expenses, and so forth.

Using a logit model to estimate the independent weights of ICC choice criteria, I found that those criteria were remarkably consistent across different levels of decision makers at the commission. Nearly all decisions could be predicted on the basis of a few variables. Only utility commissions and state agencies were able to tip the scales against the railroads, and only by presenting thorough and well-documented counteranalyses of the carriers' engineering and economic data. A dummy variable for procedure produced a surprise, however. The abandonment applications that went to oral hearings (presumably more questionable, if we assume that shippers were more likely to protest when the potential impact was greater) actually were more likely to be *granted*, ceteris paribus, than cases that involved no hearings at all, and were settled much faster.

A commissioner revealed that congressmen occasionally telephone the ICC to transmit constituent (shippers') messages that oppose abandonment. Congressmen rarely insist, or even suggest, that the ICC follow the demands of the complainants. Much more common is the suggestion that the commission "go out to the town and listen to them." The elected officials may have in mind only a symbolic act that will pacify their constituents and earn electoral gratitude, . . . but such hearings perform more valuable functions for the ICC.

The procedure delays the case and gives "the people" a chance to be heard. Then, having granted the delay, nearly always at some cost to the railroad, the Commission can go ahead and allow the abandonment. Everyone is moderately pleased with the outcome. The community has had an extra year or so of service, and time to find alternative means of transporting its goods. The Congresssman is seen as a useful man who knows how to deal with the Washington bureaucracy. The ICC has demonstrated its responsiveness and its concern with procedural fairness. And the carrier gets its abandonment.

The available evidence suggests that the delay engendered by the hearing process allows the ICC to decide in favor of the railroads. It is possible, of course, that the procedural decision (whether to hold a hearing) determines the final substantive decision (whether to grant or deny the abandonment); in that case we could indict the ICC for reaching decisions on the basis of pressure or controversy, rather than on the merits of cases. However, data analysis and subsequent interviews indicated that the ICC actually uses the earlier procedural decision to hold a hearing as a basis for later compromise. For example:

TABLE 14-3 Procedural Choices and ICC Abandonment Decisions

	FINAL DECISION	
PROCEDURE	GRANT	DENY
Hearing	N = 38	28
No Hearing	61	13

Table 14-3 shows that in a stratified random sample (with denials overrepresented) of 141 abandonment cases, a hearing did not guarantee a grant, since 28 of the 66 cases that were subject to delay actually were denied. Delay is treated by the ICC as an exogenous variable, and regulatory lag becomes a type of currency with both symbolic and economic value to the many interested parties.

I should emphasize that some of the congressional contacts with the ICC are ex parte, and strictly forbidden by the Administrative Procedure Act: the proper form of communication is by publicly available written messages. The content of the formal contacts is very similar to the ex parte telephone calls, however: most congressional mail regarding rail abandonments simply forward constituents' letters and suggest or request hearings. By either medium those congressional contacts can be seen as serving a legitimate function. If the major determinant in scheduling a hearing is the level of shipper protest, then the solicitation by those shippers of a congressman's services is one effective measure of that opposition.

Once again it is possible to interpret regulatory delay in a way that may not justify it on economic grounds, but at least may make its persistance more understandable. Some ICC officials appeared to be aware of the value of oral hearings in providing a basis for subsequent political (allocational) compromises. Such outcomes are preferred by the agency. The interim benefits accrue to a concentrated and vocal set of shippers, while the costs are temporarily borne by the railroad carrier who must cross-subsidize the rail line in question—an economic burden that finally settles on the scattered (and unaware) users of the carrier's other lines.

From the point of view of the ICC there is another benefit from such delays. Its legislative mandate was "to promote safe, adequate, economical, and efficient service" (Transportation Act of 1920), which was expanded by the Transportation Act of 1940 to include cross-modal considerations of adequacy and efficiency. By allowing shippers the extra time to find suitable motor carrier alternatives, the commission is, in one sense, fulfilling that mandate.

(2) OSHA

Mendeloff examined the Occupational Health and Safety Administration's approaches to implementing its legislative mandate to attain "the highest degree of health and safety protection for the employee," given the "feasibility" of the standards. The agency soon found that the two major techniques—engineering standards and personal protection (that is, respirators, earmuffs)—were the subject of a bitter dispute between the two major groups affected: business and labor.

Unions have been the primary source of political support for OSHA. Protection of workers is of paramount importance to organized labor, but they prefer that work place safety be provided at the expense of business rather than weigh the worker down with cumbersome and uncomfortable equipment. Business also has a large stake in OSHA's approach: engineering standards can directly cost companies large amounts of capital if existing plant has to be retrofitted, or can retard future growth by deflecting capital into nonproductive equipment. Some businesses foresaw bankruptcy as a likely result of OSHA engineering controls.

It is important to recognize that in this dispute there was no politically dominant group. OSHA was constrained on one side by its chief constituency—labor—who insisted that work-place safety was the responsibility of the employer. At the same time, OSHA knew that Congress (and eventually the courts) would come to the aid of businesses who could claim that engineering controls would not only be cost-inefficient but would drive many firms out of business. OSHA needed a solution that would minimize criticism of the agency; this required a regulation that allowed both labor and business to claim some measure of victory.

That solution was built upon delay. In Mendeloff's words:

> OSHA has found a middle road, chosen largely because of its administrative practicality. OSHA maintains the engineering requirement but grants *very lengthy abatement periods* during which personal protective equipment must be worn. The unions' concern with the ultimate use of engineering controls is preserved, but employers are essentially granted *as many extensions* as they ask for.

Mendeloff claims that this policy allowed OSHA to circumvent the dilemma of weighing costs and benefits of different implementation regulations, and therefore probably did not produce the most efficient solution.

However, it may be that weighing costs and benefits was *exactly* what OSHA was doing, in two senses. First, an agency's own calculations of costs and benefits will probably include itself as one of the potential winners or losers, unless constrained to purely (and publicly) economic criteria of cost. In effect, OSHA weighted its assessments of the two methods of abating hazards (each of which had some clear objective merits and drawbacks) by some measure of political costs and benefits. Through its use of delay, OSHA was able to choose both methods and thereby reduce its own political costs.

A second way of looking at this case might suggest that OSHA's solution was satisfactory, even in an economic sense. Once again, consider the dispute between the two groups. Any decision by OSHA that did not accede to some portion of both sides' demands would surely have been challenged. Labor could have claimed that, by requiring only personal protection equipment, OSHA was violating the standards of the Walsh-Healy Contracts Act: personal protection equipment was to be acceptable only if "feasible administrative or engineering controls" had been "determined and implemented in all cases." And if businesses had been required to bear the entire burden with engineering controls, horror stories of the certain doom of small businesses would have quickly surfaced. Either way, it is unlikely that

OSHA would have been able to weather such challenges and enforce its regulations without lengthy delays during which there would be *no* implemented work-place standards. In one sense, then, OSHA may have followed the proper course and expeditiously provided increased worker protection precisely by granting something to both sides of the dispute. It was able to do this by telling labor that it had won, but only in the long run, while at the same time telling business that it too had won, at least for a while—an interminably long while. The agency creatively used delay to provide a strategic compromise to what might have otherwise been an insoluble political dilemma.

The previous two examples might be taken as a suggestion that regulatory agencies sagely apply procedural delays to produce reasonable, if not optimal, outcomes. The effects of delay are not always so benign. Delay can act as a clot in the regulatory system, and its effects, not always undesired, may include the blockage of new technologies. . . . Such delays often result from lopsided battles; . . . new technologies can often be promoted only on the basis of conjectured benefits, while supporters of the status quo are likely to be better organized and more certain of the stakes.

(3) FCC

Direct broadcast satellites Communications satellites have been a part of the telecommunications industry since the mid-1960s, but now direct broadcast satellites (DBS) that can broadcast television signals directly to homes have reached the experimental stage and so have been the subject of fierce attempts by the television networks and the National Association of Broadcasters to delay DBS approval by the FCC. At present these efforts appear to be in vain, since the Commission's Office of Plans and Policy has recommended (and President Reagan's new chairman, Mark Fowler, has supported) nearly complete deregulation of DBS—liberating program content, licensing, and even frequency allocations within a general band. In April 1981 the FCC made a preliminary finding that approved efforts by Satellite Television Corporation, a subsidiary of COMSAT, to orbit a direct broadcast satellite by 1985 or 1986. (*Wall Street Journal*, April 22, 1981, p. 23)

However, the CBS network may have been trying to delay implementation of this competitive technology through its 1980 FCC filing of a suggestion that DBS be reserved for a still-to-be developed technology: high resolution television (HRTV). CBS proposed that the U.S. television industry develop a 1,100-1,500 line satellite complement (not a replacement) to the current television system that broadcasts 525 horizontal lines. While HRTV is technologically superior and therefore desirable, with finer detail, clearer color, and brighter images, the FCC would need to delay the deployment of the first DBS system until HRTV becomes "practical"—estimated to be at the end of the decade. (*Broadcasting*, October 13, 1980; March 2, 1981) Unless compatible with existing receivers, high-resolution television will be slow to find a large market, and until it does the demand for HRTV direct broadcast satellites will not exist; considering the high start-up costs for a DBS system (estimated at $250 million in 1981 dollars) the CBS plan could postpone its feasibility into the 1990s.

The broadcasters' strategy is not likely to succeed, given the deregulatory momentum of the FCC. In fact, the three major networks and RCA may all file for DBS authorizations before the end of 1981. And CBS is considering tests of transmitting HRTV to movie theaters; after the broadcasters and affiliates develop the hardware a transition period (25 years) to HRTV would begin, during which both conventional broadcasts and high resolution DBS would be available. (*Broadcasting*,

June 8, 1981) Recognizing the potential failure of its initial strategy of delay, CBS may be preparing to exploit its market position through the market—or with a little more help from the regulators.

Teletext/Videotext Besides facing new competition and reduced advertising revenues from the advent of video cassettes and disks, cable television, and DBS, the networks' markets have been threatened by still another new technology. "Teletext" is a new television service that allows viewers to examine textual material (such as news or shopping information) that is "embedded" into a standard broadcast signal; "videotext" is an interactive service that is carried over telephone or cable lines. The two systems would use the same engineering standards, but because teletext would directly affect television viewers' willingness to tolerate commercial messages (when they could be scanning the news or sports scores) that system in particular has been the subject of another attempt by an entrenched interest to have a competitive service delayed by regulators.

Once again it was CBS that led the battle. Several teletext systems have been developed (Antiope by the French, Ceefax by the British, and Telidon by the Canadians), and CBS has tried to exploit the confusion over which system the U.S. should adopt. The British Ceefax system has been actually operating since 1974, and is both simpler and less expensive than the French system. Antiope, at the time CBS promoted it as the U.S. standard, had never been used commercially and was not yet in production. In 1979, as the fight over the U.S. standard began to loom, the FCC asked the Electronics Industry Association to evaluate the systems and recommend one. By the summer of 1980 it became clear that the British system was favored by a plurality of the industry research committee (composed of broadcasters, manufacturers, and engineers), but before it could form a collective decision to recommend Ceefax, CBS petitioned the FCC to establish the French Antiope system as the standard technology for all U.S. teletext systems. Some other networks were confused by what appeared to be CBS' eagerness to develop a technology that threatened its revenues.

In fact, CBS seems to have been fighting for a delay in the commercial development of another inevitable competitor by asking the FCC to declare the more expensive system to be the American standard. According to Broad, when a CBS official was asked whether its promotion of Antiope technology to the FCC was intended to delay the development of the U.S. teletext market, "(he) started to answer, paused for a few seconds and said: 'Well, draw your own conclusions.'" CBS may have had the same interest the year before in opposing (unlike ABC, NBC, and PBS) closed-captioning, a similar service that also uses a decoder to produce textual graphics (subtitles for the deaf) from a broadcast network signal. (However, closed-captioning reduces the television signal's capacity for future teletext signals, so CBS' competitors may also have had some misgivings about teletext when they embraced the earlier service.)

The FCC indicated that it did not want to impose a standard for teletext. By March 1981 it still had not moved to decide and was suggesting that market forces should determine the outcome. During the same period CBS announced a test of the Antiope system in Los Angeles (with the help of $1 million of equipment provided by Telediffusion de France); a CBS vice-president proclaimed, "Teletext is the future and there is no way to avoid it. We want to be involved in shaping that future." (*Broadcasting*, November 11, 1980) Time, Inc. has decided to test a satellite-based system using the Canadian Telidon format, and NBC has asked the FCC for authorization to test Antiope on its owned-and-operated stations. (ABC is holding off: it will endorse teletext only if printers are provided so viewers need not miss their commercials.) Not to be left behind, the United Kingdom Teletext Industry Group has formally asked the FCC to quickly begin rule making to establish Ceefax as the U.S. standard.

The FCC's refusal to impose a regulatory standard and thereby delay teletext has apparently induced the interested industries to do exactly what the FCC wanted. AT&T (which had entered the fray with its Presentation Level Protocol videotext system), Antiope and its chief American ally (CBS), and the Canadian Department of Communication (Telidon) announced in May 1981 that the AT&T PLP was mutually compatible and agreeable to all parties.

> The catalyst for the consensus was apparently AT&T. . . . CBS learned early this year that AT&T had developed some kind of videotext system. After promising in writing to keep it secret . . . CBS received a copy of the AT&T specifications. The CBS and Antiope engineers were impressed by the way the AT&T PLP "diffused" the differences between Antiope and Telidon. They began working with Bell Labs on making their presentation level fully compatible with AT&T. . . . By the time CBS began its talks with AT&T, PLP was already compatible with Telidon, since the (Canadian) Department of Communication had been working closely with AT&T. (*Broadcasting*, May 25, 1981)

These proponents of the AT&T systems were soon joined by the National Association of Broadcasters and the Electronic Industries Association. However, ABC, PBS, and the National Cable Television Association have argued that it would be premature for the FCC to consider a rule-making proposal to adopt this teletext standard.

The final decision of the FCC is not certain, but considering the collective strength of the advocates of the AT&T system, and its ability to include most competing teletext technologies (perhaps even Ceefax), the commission will probably allow its development as the de facto or de jure U.S. standard. In retrospect it appears that the FCC's refusal to allow CBS to strategically exploit the government's standard-setting power was the most satisfactory decision since a generally acceptable system has emerged that not only serves more than one economic interest but may also serve the public best by accelerating the implementation of teletext services.

Why has the FCC been able to resist recent industry pressures to delay the new technologies of direct broadcast satellites and teletext? One obvious reason is the overall change in the role of the FCC in regulating telecommunications; in an age when it is considering or promoting new low-power television stations, more AM radio stations (by reducing frequency separations from 10 khz to 9 khz), and lottery systems for some broadcast license disputes, it would be inconsistent for the FCC to obstruct new telecommunications services simply because they threaten network revenues. Since the broadcasters' near monopoly of influence over the FCC had collapsed, the commission did not need to impose a delay as a means of pacifying a strong constituency.

In addition, the DBS and teletext cases differed from the OSHA and ICC examples in one crucial aspect: while the regulators *knew* who would gain and lose from their workplace safety or rail abandonment decisions (that is, unions or businesses, shippers or railroads) the FCC could not be certain who would pay if there was no delay. The parties that were beseeching the FCC to retard the development of new competitive technologies were also in a position to exploit those technologies themselves. Broadcasters had already shown their resiliency by entering the new markets of videocassettes, videodiscs, and cable television, so the FCC was in a position to disregard the claims of CBS that direct broadcast satellites and teletext would hurt their overall revenues. The rapidity with which CBS and other networks filed applications for DBS and teletext systems was an indication that the "losers" in this dispute might not actually lose, so there was no need for the FCC to accommodate their attempts to protect themselves through the regulatory process.

CONCLUSIONS

The four cases described above hardly constitute a random sample of regulatory decisions that were subjected to dilatory tactics, so any generalizations drawn from these examples must be carefully qualified. Nevertheless, it is possible to make a few comments about the efforts of agencies and outside parties to redirect the costs of regulating, or of *not* regulating, by way of slowing down the process of decision and implementation.

1. Not all delays are purposive. While the examples of OSHA work-place regulations and ICC rail abandonment decisions involve deliberate choices by agencies to use delay as an ameliorative device, other examples can be found that were not the result of manipulation, but had real economic effects. Linda Cohen . . . examined the process by which nuclear power plants are licensed, and reached conclusions that she found surprising:

> Delays in licensing are found to be mainly due to consideration by the NRC staff of important substantive issues. . . . Furthermore, delay does not result from public participants simply manipulating the process so as to hold up licensing, e.g., with procedural maneuvers or legalistic strategies. Such attempts are by and large unsuccessful. The study of licensing cases suggests that licensing delays are due primarily to NRC uncertainties about reactor safety.

We should therefore make a distinction between "nonpurposive" delays (those that "just seem to happen") and "pathological" delays (in the sense of being "unwholesome"). In an area like nuclear plant licensing delays are not deliberate strategems, nor do they accidentally occur: they are generic procedural devices designed to maximize the chances of uncovering critical information. Perhaps such time-consuming processes are not the most efficient or cost-effective means of reaching decisions, but they do suggest that regulators can impose caution on themselves by establishing formal insulation from demands for haste.

2. Delays are more likely when an agency has a vague mandate and when the costs to all disputants are nearly equal. This may not seem to be a very useful generalization, since most agencies have vague mandates; I point it out to emphasize that agencies with specific legislation behind their decisions need not try quite as hard to find compromises through delay. They can simply remind unhappy litigants of the law. (However, a little ambiguity goes a long way: OSHA's mandate includes one word—*feasibility*—that has provided much of the trouble over the last decade.)

The relative economic and political costs to the parties at interest are more significant. In the case of OSHA the contending forces had approximately equal stakes in the agency's work-place safety rules, so for the agency to have moved too obviously in either direction, toward personal protection equipment or toward engineering standards, would have produced unacceptable political or economic costs. And the ICC has found it politically expedient to provide a compromise to shippers and railroad carriers by arbitrating an exchange of long-term benefits (the carriers' abandonments) for short-term benefits (an extra year of service for shippers), since by offering a delay it can diffuse both the economic influence of the railroad and the political power of the protesting shippers. Finally, the FCC was able to avoid imposing a compromising delay on direct broadcast satellites and teletext largely because the potential economic costs to the opponents of the new technologies (that is, lost advertising revenues) were not comparable to the costs of restricting the development of new telecommunications markets.

3. Delays are more than ad hoc pacifications of public complaints. Hilton has written about "the basic behavior of regulatory commissions," stating that regulators "generate monopoly gain in one activity" and then require the industries to "dissipate it in uneconomic activity." Because of the potential political reaction to ignoring public complaints, regulators must respond through a "process of ad hoc pacification." Many regulatory responses are situational, but Cohen's examination of NRC procedures showed that delays can also be the result of deliberate general policies of agencies. And I have argued above that the effects of agency responses often go beyond "pacification" and can bring real economic benefits to contending groups. Railroad shippers may be calmed by a public hearing, but the extra service and time for finding alternate transportation is far more than a symbolic gratification.

4. The effects of delay are uncertain. The risk involved is of several types. First, any party who seeks to slow the regulatory process cannot be certain what effect the delay will have in the cast of participants. Noll suggested that agencies that develop complicated decision processes "will make participation in the process more expensive, which will reduce the number of groups entering the process." Delay may induce some groups to drop out for reasons of cost or exasperation, but it is also possible that *more* groups will become involved since there are more access points, and more time to exploit them, in a lengthy process. The roster of petitioners would not have been diminished if CBS had been successful in having the FCC consider a rule making on teletext, as subsequent events have demonstrated.

A complicated and drawn-out process may also increase the likelihood of procedural error by an agency. The Senate study on regulation proposed that, particularly in nuclear power plant licensing, groups may seek delays to increase the chance that a procedural stumble will provide an excuse to appeal an unfavorable decision. It is unfortunate for the strategies that such tactics may backfire: the review boards or courts that consider appeals on technicalities may show irritation with obvious obstructionism. Usually, however, delays should reduce the change of substantive error by decision makers. As Krasnow and Longley showed, the recent case of CBS and teletext standards is not unique. In the 1940s the FCC was rushed (by radio and television interests) into a decision to move the frequency of FM radio to 92–106 megacycles based on faulty technical data and a desire by entrenched economic interests who opposed competition from improved FM broadcasting. Even some erstwhile opponents of regulation have embraced the need for cautious delay. When asked about new OMB rules that *lengthen* the rule-making process, James C. Miller III replied that " . . . we think the time is necessary—and well worth it—to make sure that new rules do more good than harm . . . we think the requirements for thorough deliberation—even if it takes 210 days—are all to the good" (*Regulation*, March/April 1981, p. 17).

Finally, the environment of the potential obstructor is always imperfectly known and changing, so the decision to seek delay is inherently risky. For example, in the 1950s the FCC maintained the undersupply of television channels by mixing UHF and VHF stations (rather than shifting all television frequencies to the UHF range)—a policy that VHF broadcasters fully supported. For the last decade those broadcasters have faced the long-term consequences of their obstruction of UHF, namely, the growth of cable television. A firm's decision to seek delay depends on many factors, including their discount rates, their risk acceptance, the costs of participation, and the presence of competition. To accurately predict whether an interest will try to strategically retard regulatory decision making would require knowledge of its own decision criteria. Nevertheless, we can identify some of the factors that can aid our understanding, if not our predictions, of regulatory delay.

. . . I have tried to explain one much-criticized aspect of the regulatory process, not to justify it, but to put it in proper perspective. A blanket categorization of what seem to be undesirable features of regulation as "pathological" ignores one important function that regulation serves: it engenders a set of serial adjustments, born out of political compromise, that provide the dynamics for both regulatory change and support . . .

To characterize regulatory delay in purely economic terms would be to underrate the political significance of not only the electorate procedures for decision making, but also the responsiveness of the system—and the Congress that created it—to very real forces.

FIFTEEN
PILLS AND THE PROCESS OF GOVERNMENT

Robert Reinhold

It was the routine kind of event that passes with little more than perfunctory press notice every day in official Washington. On September 10, the federal government issued a new regulation: By order of the Food and Drug Administration, druggists would be compelled to provide leaflets giving basic information on the proper use, side effects and risks of 10 kinds of commonly used—and misused—prescription drugs.

On the surface, it seemed an innocuous, even sensible, regulation. But the story behind how this one ruling was hammered into being—after five years of bureaucratic maneuvering and intense industry resistance—tells the story of how government really works. It is not, so far as can be determined, a story of scandal, bribery, vote-buying, influence-peddling, or other misfeasance one hears so much about from Washington. Rather, it is the much less dramatic, but arguably far more important, saga of the political, economic, and legal realities that shape our lives. . . .

Repeated studies have shown that from 30 percent to 80 percent of patients fail to comply with their drug regimens, sometimes with unfavorable consequences. For example, a third or more of patients put on thiazides and other antihypertension drugs stop taking the drug before they should, endangering their health. Also, many patients are unaware of certain drug hazards. Clofibrate, for instance, is prescribed to prevent heart attacks, but it is now believed the drug may be dangerous for heart-disease patients with high cholesterol levels. Some medical experts also felt that ad-

This selection comes from *The New York Times Magazine* (November 9, 1980), pp. 32–35, 47–49. © 1980 by The New York Times Company. Reprinted by permission.

ditional information would help to cut down on the overprescribing of certain drugs, such as tranquilizers, and involve patients more actively in their own care.

In theory, drug information should be imparted by the doctor or the dispensing pharmacist, but studies have shown that doctors frequently do not provide it and may be ignorant of the latest findings about the drugs they prescribe. And customers at busy urban drugstores are not encouraged to consult the pharmacist, who usually works behind a barrier.

So, in March 1975, the Center for Law and Social Policy, a privately supported public-interest law firm, filed a petition with the FDA, also signed by the Consumers Union, the National Organization for Women, and other consumer and womens' groups, asking that patient package inserts be provided for certain drugs. The FDA agreed to look into the matter and did—very slowly. There were three years of hearings, symposiums, studies, discussions, written comments, and delay. The agency then spent a year drafting a 26-page proposal for a new rule, which, as it turned out, was even broader and covered more drugs than the petition had requested. In June 1979, the day before he left government, Dr. Donald Kennedy, then Commissioner of the Food and Drug Administration, signed the proposal and informed the industry that the FDA planned to require that inserts accompany 375 drugs, comprising nearly all prescription drugs, both when originally filled and when refilled. Each insert would contain specific information about the drug being dispensed.

The proposal contained what turned out to be a fatal flaw. It stressed the putative health benefits of the rule but did not examine whether the benefits warranted the added costs, which they estimated would amount to an additional 6.2 cents for the average prescription, raising its price from $6.44 to $6.50—about $90 million a year. Nor did the FDA explore whether there were cheaper ways to achieve the goal of providing patients with more information about drugs they were prescribed. With its flank thus exposed, the agency published its proposal in the Federal Register on July 6, 1979. It was not prepared for what took place during the ensuing 90-day review period.

While all parties said they favored more patient information, almost none of them were pleased with the way the FDA wanted it supplied. Doctors said the leaflets would interfere with the doctor-patient relationship, planting doubts about the physician's advice and possibly scaring patients into discarding needed drugs. Drug makers complained about the cost and logistics of distributing so many inserts. Druggists, who would bear the biggest burden of the rule, raised the loudest objections, saying they would have to redesign their stores to add storage space, hire extra help, and spend inordinate amounts of time answering customer questions. The American Pharmaceutical Association, representing 55,000 pharmacists, calculated the rules would cost $1.7 billion over five years—to be passed on, of course, to customers—and charged that the FDA had no conclusive proof that this expensive program would bring the desired results.

Critics also predicted that suggestible patients would begin to perceive and experience the side effects mentioned in the inserts and that millions of prescriptions would be returned by patients frightened by the warnings. Complex questions arose: How would a paranoid patient react to the warnings? What about the cancer patient, ignorant of the nature of his affliction, who read in the insert that the drug was meant to control the spread of cancer? Even consumer groups were not entirely happy; they felt the proposal should have gone further. One suggested that the inserts be translated into Braille and common foreign languages.

The FDA countered that studies had demonstrated consumers had found inserts useful and that hundreds of millions of dollars would be saved annually on medical care for those who failed to take drugs properly. It cited a study made by the Institute of Medicine, part of the National Academy of Sciences in Washington, which concluded that "virtually all studies" indicated patients considered P.P.I.'s a "useful source" of information, that inserts had been accepted and read, but that "little is known" about their long-term use.

The lobbying assault by an industry determined either to scuttle or emasculate the proposed rules was intense. More than 1,300 written comments were received by the FDA, not all of them unfavorable. Letters began to rain on the White House, the Office of Management and Budget, the Council on Wage and Price Stability, the office of Patricia Roberts Harris, President Carter's Secretary of Health and Human Services, and key congressional offices. Negative articles cropped up in the pharmaceutical trade press.

"The response was very emotional," recalls Louis A. Morris, the psychologist who heads the FDA's Prescription Drug Labeling Project. "They really got together. The lobbyists went to work on Congress and the White House. We took a lot of grief. But that's the way things are done. I learned a lot of politics."

The consumer groups that had petitioned the agency five years earlier were little help when the fireworks started. With limited resources, they had moved on to other issues. "No one in the consumer movement can devote sustained and regular attention to this issue," said Marsha Greenberger, a lawyer with the Center for Law and Social Policy. At any rate, the groups would have been little match for the lobbyists, lawyers, and public-relations people maintained in Washington by the drugmakers, the druggists, and the doctors.

Organizations such as the National Association of Chain Drug Stores, the National Association of Retail Druggists, the National Wholesale Druggists' Association, and the American Pharmaceutical Association knew where to aim their shots. The president of the chain-drugstore group, Robert J. Bolger, wrote to President Carter complaining of the "immense inflationary impact" of the proposal, which he said might raise drug prices by 8 percent to 16 percent at a time, he underscored, when other parts of the administration were trying to contain health-care costs. The letter made an impression on the president's health advisers. Mr. Bolger also wrote to Alfred E. Kahn, chairman of the Council on Wage and Price Stability, complaining of the "colossal paperwork jungle" the rules would create. Local druggist's groups around the country were urged to write their congressmen, and many did.

Their message, given Washington's antiregulatory mood, came through loud and clear. It stirred unease among the president's domestic policy staff and his science advisers in the Office of Science and Technology Policy. Even the Small Business Administration applied pressure against the FDA proposal. (In fact, the only high-level ally the agency found was Esther Peterson, the president's special assistant for Consumer Affairs.) The opponents' complains were summed up by Dena Cain, a lawyer and lobbyist for the pharmaceutical association: "The question is, do patients desire P.P.I.'s, and are they willing to pay the additional costs? The FDA is saying this information may be good for you, and therefore you should pay for it."

In November 1979, the P.P.I. proposal got "RARGed," as they say in Washington, meaning that the regulation was subjected to analysis by a new interagency panel, the Regulatory Analysis Review Group. The panel has no direct authority, but it exerts influence by reviewing a number of proposed regulations every year in an effort to make agencies more sensitive to the economic consequences of their actions. It cannot be assumed that the industry complaints triggered the review, but, staffed mostly by economists, the panel has generally been sympathetic to business interests.

"The FDA did not understand at first," said George C. Eads, a member of the Council of Economic Advisers, who chaired the review. "The analysis they did was primarily a cost analysis. We said they should be laying out the alternatives and their costs. We were not questioning their interest in developing the rules, but we were concerned that they had no way to find out if they were generating the claimed benefits." Even if the patient has the right to know, Mr. Eads said, "that in itself is insufficient grounds to make decisions. At least you should have some notion of what you are doing and that there are alternatives you are ignoring."

While not necessarily embracing the industry's view, the review group's report said further: "We are troubled that FDA has not stated how the knowledge gained in its initial implementation steps will be reflected in subsequent ones." It added, in what seemed to presage the agency's eventual decision, that the FDA should consider a limited, phased-in test of P.P.I.'s. "We call on FDA to publicly commit itself to testing and evaluation before proceeding to mandate patient labeling for all drugs."

The RARGing was painful for the FDA staff. "We failed to protect ourselves where we were most vulnerable—on the economic side," said Dr. Morris. "How naive of us! We put out the regulation and *then* did the cost-benefit analysis. It did not have the documentation it should have had."

In the meantime, Dr. Jere E. Goyan, himself a pharmacist and defender of patients' rights, became the new Commissioner of Food and Drugs. He soon let it be known that he planned to scale back the P.P.I. requirement to just 10 drugs. Dr. Goyan stated forthrightly in a recent interview that he was confronted by such mass "antipathy" from druggists, drugmakers, doctors, Congress, and other quarters that he felt his beleaguered agency could not enforce a broader patient-information program. A survey taken by the agency found that only 39 percent of druggists spontaneously gave out the inserts now required with estrogens. His was, he said, a "political" decision, in that he went as far as he felt he could at this time. He said he had also feared Congress might pass a law canceling the regulation if it was too broad, as it had when it thwarted the FDA's effort to ban saccharin.

Dr. Goyan had not yet officially scaled down the P.P.I. proposal from 375 to 10 prescription drugs, and when he appeared before the powerful Congressional appropriations subcommittees last March, he found himself subjected to hostile questioning on the P.P.I. issue, particularly by Representative Bill Alexander, an influential Arkansas Democrat. After Dr. Goyan testified that "I would not want to swallow a pill about which I knew nothing," Representative Alexander extracted a promise from him that the FDA's drug-information program would begin with no more than 10 drugs.

In its report, the appropriations committee ordered the agency to proceed "only in an orderly, step-by-step manner," keeping Congress "fully advised in advance" and to issue no more than 10 inserts over the next two years.

Thus the die was cast. Dr. Goyan announced the final regulations on September 10. After June 1981, P.P.I.'s would have to be included with 10 prescription drugs or drug categories, accounting for 16 percent of all prescriptions. Some of the categories included are ampicillins, a class of penicillin-type antibiotics; benzodiazepines, which include the tranquilizers Valium, Librium, and Tranxene; propoxyphene, a painkiller marketed as Darvon, and thiazides, diuretics used in the treatment of high blood pressure. Among other things, the new regulation dropped the requirement that every refill also contain a P.P.I., cutting costs by 40 percent. Enforcement of the program, which will have a three-year trial, will begin in mid-1981. The estimated cost of the inserts is 18 cents apiece, which is expected to be passed on to the consumer.

Dr. Goyan disputed suggestions that he had retreated from his oft-stated commitment to patient information. On the contrary, he said, the final decision was a strategy to achieve the same goal. "The way we were going about it looked too much like a bludgeon," he said. "This will make doctors and pharmacists much more at ease. We have to move in a different fashion to make it work out politically. If all we did was cut down a lot of trees and had no effect, it would have been worse. I believe we will be better off 10 years from now if we do this than if we had had a complete face-off with industry."

Oddly, the announcement was greeted warmly by the Pharmaceutical Manufacturers Association, whose president, Lewis A. Engman, promised to do "all we can to help make the project a success." Oddly, because his organization had pressed, and lost, a lawsuit challenging the FDA's legal authority to mandate P.P.I.'s.

But the drugmakers could afford to be generous and helpful. For, in a real sense, the new regulations represented a victory for them and for the nation's thousands of retail druggists and drugstore operators. They had successfully mustered their considerable political clout and lobbying skills to stave off the FDA. Consumer groups, however, expressed extreme disappointment.

But there is more to the story, for sometimes, simply by proposing a regulation, regulators can induce change. The long and disputatious history of the P.P.I. ruling has had the effect of forcing druggists, doctors, drugmakers, and other groups to think about providing more and better information to patients. They were not thinking this way a decade ago. Indeed, the Peoples Drug Store chain recently began using the issue as a promotional lure, providing its customers with a book of information on drugs to be kept at the counter. Also, several drugmakers have voluntarily decided to include inserts in some of their prescription products, perhaps seeing this voluntary approach as more palatable than the Drug Regulation Reform Bill. Passed by the Senate last year but facing tough going in the House, the Drug Regulation Reform Bill would give the FDA explicit authority to require P.P.I.'s for all prescription drugs.

Thus, Washington's shadow government, the informal network of high-level bureaucrats, private lobbyists, and congressional staff members, gets the work of government done. Dan Evans, the former governor of Washington, once called this triad the "iron triangle." It works with considerable independence of the president, his top appointees, and the elected members of Congress. It does respond to them, but with all the agility of a supertanker.

The network is powerful because it knows when and where to use its muscle. It quietly takes over when everyone else loses interest—*after* a law is passed. Its members know that the way a law is implemented is at least as important as what the law actually says. They work out the nitty-gritty, boring but consummately important details of shaping the regulations that implement the law long after congressmen have forgotten what they voted for. Indeed, regulation writers probably write more law than lawmakers. Once finally approved and published, a regulation has the full force of the law on which it is based.

For a variety of complex reasons, Congress often prefers to leave laws vague, delegating responsibility for filling in the crucial details to the bureaucracy. Thus, for example, Congress may decide that cancer-causing agents should be banned from foods, but it has neither the time nor the expertise to list them, to establish criteria for carcinogenicity, or to set penalties. This gives the agencies, and the lobbyists and congressional staffers to whom they respond, enormous power. Small differences in definitions can mean millions to an industry.

The bureaucracy can effectively subvert a law, or carry it further than Congress may have intended. Indeed, it often does not even wait for Congress to pass an explicit law to propose new regulations. In the case of the P.P.I.'s, the FDA moved merely by unilaterally enlarging its interpretation of the existing Food, Drug and Cosmetic Act of 1938, which gives it authority to require proper "labeling" of drugs and to prevent their "misbranding."

It may be, as Dr. Goyan argues, that the public interest will ultimately be served best by his go-slow, let's-see-how-it-works-first approach to the P.P.I.'s. But, for better or worse, it was not primarily the public interest that shaped the decision. It was shaped by influential special interests—the triangle of bureaucrats, lobbyists and congressional staff members—without whose cooperation the regulation would have been rendered ineffectual.

PART TWO
Holding Administrators Accountable: Controls on Agency Powers

CHAPTER FOUR
CONGRESSIONAL OVERSIGHT

INTRODUCTION

How do you hold the federal agencies created by the legislature accountable to the legislature when Congress delegated powers, including discretionary authority, to these surrogates because it felt powerless and unable to cope with the specifics of the public policy issue in the first place? This has become a major question for the Congress in recent years, given the expansion of the regulatory process. To an awesome extent, persons and industries are controlled by the actions of these federal administrative agencies—both executive branch agencies and independent commissions. The practical, daily administration of the program is power in government; agencies, to a large extent, have this power. It is a power that has been delegated to the administrative units by the legislature. The Congress, as Schick and Bruff and Gellhorn indicate, *episodically rears up* to attempt to assert control (and power) over the administrative agencies.

In this occasional reassertion of power and authority, Congress generally has at its disposal a number of oversight mechanisms which can be used in the effort to control the bureaucrats. These would include:

—creation and organization of agencies (authorization committees),
—control of agency budgets (appropriation committees),
—investigation of agency activities (government operation committees),
—general legislation controlling agency process (such as the Administrative Procedure Act and its amendments),
—legislative veto.

Essentially these basic elements, plus additional legislative innovations which include organizational reform, close legislative scrutiny of appointments to positions of importance on regulatory commissions, procedural changes in rule making, reflect the legislative arsenal in its efforts to constrain and hold accountable the regulatory agencies.[1] Whether the legislature can effectively and continuously scrutinize agency activity when the legislators are primarily concerned about constituent needs is a question addressed in the essays that follow. On its face, for example, "funding programs is a principal means through which the legislature is able to exercise control over administration."[2] (Whether the reality comes close to the hope is another matter insofar as budgetary control is concerned.) In sum, the Congress has a number of oversight powers that can, if effectively employed, constrain agency activity. Whether Congress uses these devices effectively is a question reviewed by the essays that follow.

The Schick essay examines the relationship between the legislature and the regulatory agencies. As agency powers and discretion grew over the years, so too did the concerns of legislators about this growth of agency power. Schick examines the legislative response to administrative government through the examination of oversight mechanisms, the legislative veto, and the authorizing legislation power of the legislature.

Both the Bruff and Gellhorn and the Civiletti essays examine the use of a legislative veto as a mechanism for controlling and holding accountable administrative agencies. The legislative veto is the power of the Congress to void administrative regulations which, in the estimate of the legislature, either exceed statutory authority or implement unsound public policy. Bruff and Gellhorn examine the legislative veto in light of the role the regulatory agency plays in the political process. The Civiletti piece, written by President Carter's Attorney General, examines the constitutionality of the legislative veto from a very practical point of view, that is, the U.S. secretary of education was confronted with the prospect of a congressional veto of DOE regulations and she turned to Civiletti, the U.S. Attorney General, for a legal judgment. (For both policy and constitutional reasons, both essays reject the viability of this legislative control mechanism.)

In June 1983, the U.S. Supreme Court invalidated the use by Congress of the legislative veto. In *Immigration and Naturalization Service v. Chadha*, __US__(1983), a seven person majority struck down the use of the legislative veto as written into Section 244 (c)(2) of the Immigration and Naturalization Act. By implication, the justices also invalidated over 200 other statutes passed by Congress since 1932 that contained legislative veto provisions. Chief Justice Warren Burger concluded that while the legislative veto may be a "convenient shortcut; an appealing compromise," the Founding Fathers "ranked other values higher than efficiency," i.e., the *Checks and Balances* and *Separation of Powers* concepts. Article I, concluded the Chief Justice, "erected enduring checks on each branch and to protect the people from the improvident exercise of power by mandating certain prescribed (Article I) steps," i.e., bicameralism, presentment to president, presidential veto, and legislative override of presidential veto. These "step-by-step" procedures were "considered so imperative that the draftsmen took special pains to assure that these requirements could not be circumvented." The Court held that because the legislative veto short-circuits these processes, it is an unconstitutional exercise of legislative power. The *Chadha* opinion will profoundly affect the manner in which the legislature will be able to constrain bureaucratic rulemaking.

---

[1]*See* generally Robert Gilmour, "Congressional Oversight: The Paradox of Fragmentation and Control," and Phillip J. Cooper, "Congress in the Administrative Process: The Dangers of 'Reform,'" both presented at the 1981 meeting of the Southeast Region ASPA, October 1981.

[2]Gary Peters, *The Politics of Bureaucracy* (New York: Longman, 1978) p. 214.

SIXTEEN
CONGRESS AND THE "DETAILS" OF ADMINISTRATION

Allen Schick

A former president once wrote of Congress: "it has entered more and more into the details of administration until it has virtually taken into its own all the substantial powers of government." This protest was not composed by a recent president railing against the renascent assertiveness of Congress in the post Vietnam-Watergate era. It was written by Woodrow Wilson in 1885, almost 30 years before he attained the presidency, and only two years before the publication of his influential essay "The Study of Administration," which demarked public administration of an activity and discipline separate from politics.

There is a certain ambivalence in Wilson's complaint, one which has persisted through 200 years of American government and which helps to account for disparities in legislative and executive views about control of administration. Wilson refers to the "details of administration" as if these everyday matters were unworthy of legislative attention. Congress, the phrase suggests, should not be distracted from the big and important affairs of state by the minutiae of public administration. But Wilson clearly recognizes that control of these very details of administration could give Congress "all the substantial powers of government." Administration, Wilson implies, is the source of power in modern governments; hence, control of administration means control of the government. This view of administration and statecraft dominated his 1887 essay.

Reprinted with permission from *Public Administration Review* 36 (September/October 1976), 516–526. © 1976 by The American Society for Public Administration, 1225 Connecticut Avenue, N.W., Washington, D.C. All rights reserved. Footnotes ommited.

Throughout American history, the executive branch has tended to advance the first interpretation while intending the second. (Nobody bothered to explain why, if administration is indeed merely a matter of details, executives should be concerned by legislative intrusions.) For its part, Congress has instinctively realized that loss of the details would diminish its political role. It is not that every small detail brings big power, but that the accumulated loss of control over administrative details unquestionably aggrandizes executive power at the expense of Congress. From the perspective of administrative reform, this has not been an unintended or unwanted outcome. There was no place for Congress in the new discipline of public administration, nor has Congress been given much attention in the subsequent development of the field. Hyneman's *Bureaucracy in a Democracy* is a distinguished (and still relevant) exception, but "if we simply assume that public administration is what students of public administration study, the executive is clearly the solid center of their special concern." For 100 years, American public administration has functioned in the service of executive power, an arrangement that has accommodated this discipline to the realities of American politics.

THE QUIESCENCE OF CONGRESS

The Wilsonian division of government labor (and power) has had its ups and downs in the course of American history. At the start, as Leonard White noted in his administrative history of the United States, the Federalists sought a national government "which left substantial freedom of action to high officials and kept Congress out of most administrative details." This preference for executive power was successfully challenged by the Jeffersonians who "were more energetic in their effort to control administration than had been their predecessors. . . . They emphasized the responsibility of the executive branch and the administrative system to Congress." The legislative branch generally was dominant through most of the nineteenth century (wartime was an exception), though the particular control exercised by Congress over administration varied with changes in the presidency. Congress fashioned a variety of controls over administration centered, as Wilson protested, in its increasingly specialized and powerful committee system.

The trend began to change, however, shortly after Wilson wrote, about the time that public administration was emerging as a distinct and important discipline. War, economic expansion, and a host of other influences (including public administration itself) bolstered the claim for administrative independence from detailed legislative control. But the dominant factor was the huge expansion of the national government and its administrative structure. During the half century between 1871 and 1921, civilian employment in the executive branch multiplied elevenfold, from 50,000 to 550,000; during the same period, federal expenditures soared from $292 million to more than $5 billion, although they dropped to about $3 billion later in that decade. Big government weakened the ability of Congress to govern by controlling the details and it vested administrators with more details over which to govern. In the face of bigness, Congress could master the small things only by losing sight of the important issues.

Nowhere has the congressional abandonment of administrative details been as visible as in the shift from line item to lump sum appropriations. The specificity of appropriations was one of the great issues over which Congress and the executive branch fought during the early years of nationhood, and it was the triumph of itemized appropriations which assured legislative supremacy during the nineteenth century. But as the federal government expanded, the lines were merged into bigger and bigger appropriation units in a process which still is going on. There are substantially fewer "lines" in the $375 billion budget for 1976 than there were in the $265 million of expenditures for 1876. A single appropriation act in 1876 for the Military Academy had about 40 lines (a number of which were subdivided into discrete items) for an appropriation totalling perhaps $200,000. There are only about 50 appropriation accounts in the 1976 budget for the Defense Department's nearly $100 billion of new budget authority. In fact, although the 1976 budget has about 1,000 accounts, fewer than 100 of these amount to more than $300 billion.

Why did Congress let control slip from its grasp? The details were too numerous to be comprehended; each detail was too small to be of consequence. Congress could not line itemize a $400 billion budget in the same manner as it had detailed the nineteenth-century appropriations. Moreover, Congress harbored the expectation that the president would function as its agent of control over the administrative agencies. In the same year that Wilson left the White House, the Budget and Accounting Act empowered the president to establish budget control over government agencies. Control by executive direction was substituted for control by legislative means.

This was exactly what the new discipline of public administration advocated. The persistent message that a legislature should not trespass on administrative matters inevitably registered on congressional thinking about its appropriate role, especially because the theme was so attractively laced with the promise of order and efficiency in the public service and carried the warning that legislative intervention would be injurious to good government. In the course of decades, Congress became a grudging subscriber to the notion that it should refrain from most administrative entanglements. Some of its retreats were comprehensive and truly significant, such as the establishment of the executive budget system. More commonly, however, congressional withdrawal was piecemeal, such as the extension of civil service coverage to additional federal employees. Inch by inch Congress gave ground until it no longer was a dominant participant in the conduct of administration.

However, the extent of congressional withdrawal from administration was clouded by its incompleteness. When it wanted, Congress (or its members or committees) continued to meddle in administrative particulars, intervening in behalf of interests, writing restrictions into legislation, using its investigatory powers to spotlight an administrative problem, holding on to old administrative prerogatives. At will, Congress could penetrate to the smallest administrative detail, but these usually were pinpricks, mere nuisances compared to the countless matters which escaped legislative control. Appropriation bills might still limit the number of cars that could be procured, but the constrained agency could function with little hindrance in everyday administrative matters. With the growth of big administration, the zone of indifference (or perhaps more accurately, of ignorance) came to encompass most of the business of administration.

But the congressional retreat never has been sufficiently complete to satisfy administrative reformers. Congress was always stepping over the line, intruding on matters beyond its legitimate sphere of action. This failure to achieve administrative purity has sustained the reformist ethic of public administration for several generations.

In addition to the sway of administrative doctrine and governmental necessity, two ideological factors influenced Congress to expand the scope of administrative discretion. One was the spell of nonpartisanship in international affairs; the other was the dominance of pluralism in domestic politics. Nonpartisanship conveyed the assurance that unchecked executive power would be applied benevolently in the national interest of the United States; pluralism suggested that administrative discretion would be used to the advantage of the salient interests. Nonpartisanship normally escalates during wartime (Vietnam was a notable exception), so that the protracted cold war extended the influence of this ideology over a considerable period of time. Whatever the virtues of nonpartisanship, it effectively diminished the ability and inclination of Congress to superintend executive actions. Pluralism, always a presence in American politics, came to be regarded as its democratic linchpin in the mid-twentieth century. With the blossoming of what Lowi has termed *interest group liberalism*, the use of government power to provide benefits to powerful interests, the great bureaucracies of the federal government functioned as dispensaries of the "who gets what" of American politics. But since this distributive politics depended on administrative performance, an overly obstructive Congress would have hindered the flow of public goods and services to the intended beneficiaries. Interest groups were the political link between a Congress that authorized and a bureaucracy that delivered benefits. Rather than viewing one another as adversaries, these two power centers forged a political symbiosis that enabled the interest group state to flourish. Congressmen might still rail against bureaucrats or intervene to influence the award of a grant or contract, but administrators were given, as Kenneth Culp Davis has shown, enormous discretion to run their own operations.

THE RESURGENCE OF CONGRESS

Congress is chronically ambivalent about the limited role into which it has been cast, and it episodically rears up to assert its control over administration. These spasms can be very discomfitting to the administrators who must cope with legislative intervention or harassment, but they cannot adequately assure that the overall conduct of administration is faithful to legislative interests. The spasms miss much more than they hit, leaving wide gaps in the coverage of administration by Congress. Nor have the regularized means of securing legislative control sufficed. Administrators have to supply more reports to Congress, are subject to more legislative investigations, and are monitored by more congressional staff, but, at least from the perspective of congressmen, these are not enough.

Nowadays Congress seems to expect more control over administration. Vietnam robbed nonpartisanship of its seductive hold on the loyalty of Congress; Watergate stripped much of the allure from executive dominance of domestic politics. Even before these shocks, revisionist scholars had begun to question the intellectual foundations of nonpartisanship and pluralism. Many other minishocks registered on congressional consciousness and contributed to dissatisfaction with a political arrangement which legitimized dominance by the executive branch. President Nixon overreached in the constitutional gray areas between the two branches such as executive privilege and the impoundment of funds. Disillusionment with the Great Society initiatives of the 1960s impacted on Congress, along with concern about the size and direction of the federal government. Regulations poured from executive offices in record quantities, as did complaints about the efficacy and fairness of regulatory policies. More and more of the budget was beyond effective congressional control, and deficit spending became a perennial practice. Congress underwent some destabilizations of its own as a result of unusually high turnovers in membership and an erosion of party and committee leaderships.

In the 1970s, the Congress has sought new methods for holding administrators to account and has applied old controls more extensively. While Congress has not perfected a comprehensive or consistent set of controls—most have been improvised or applied for particular problems—the cumulative effect of the congressional initiatives has been at least a temporary halt in the growth of administrative independence from the legislative branch. Examples of the recent congressional interventions in the "details" of administration include the following:

(1) The requirement of Senate confirmation has been extended to a number of presidential officials in recent years. The executive director of the Council on International Economic Policy was made subject to Senate confirmation in 1972 and the director and deputy director of the Office of Management and Budget were covered in 1973.

(2) Congress also has moved to obtain more direct influence over the appointment of government officials. The Congressional Budget Act of 1974 established one of the first legislative offices to be filled solely by determination of Congress— the director of the Congressional Budget Office. Older legislative branch positions such as the Comptroller General, the Librarian of Congress, and the Public Printer still are appointed by the president with the advice and consent of the Senate.

(3) Perhaps the most direct attempt to enlarge the role of Congress in the selection of government officials was the original composition of the Federal Elections Committee, established in 1974. Two members each were to be appointed by the president, the Speaker of the House, and the president pro tem of the Senate. All of the appointments were to be subject to confirmation by both houses of Congress. In addition, the Secretary of the Senate and Clerk of the House were to be ex officio members of the commission. This arrangement was ruled unconstitutional in a 1976 decision of the Supreme Court, which held that appointments of "officers of the United States" cannot be made by Congress.

(4) Congress has taken a number of steps to assure its and the public's access to administrative information and to open administrative proceedings to the public. The Freedom of Information Act has replaced the "need to know" test of the 1946 Administrative Procedure Act with a general presumption in favor of disclosure. Certain exemptions were permitted in the 1967 FOI Act, but these were tightened in 1974 Amendments. The Federal Advisory Committee Act of 1972 opened most of the meetings of these organizations to the public. "Sunshine" legislation moving toward possible enactment in the Ninety-fourth Congress would open up the meetings of most administrative agencies.

(5) The Budget and Accounting Act of 1921 barred federal agencies from submitting their budget estimates to Congress except at the request of the House or Senate. But a number of recently established agencies are required to furnish Congress with their estimates at the same time that they are submitted to the Office of Management and Budget. The Consumer Product Safety Commission, the Federal Elections Commission, and the Commodity Futures Trading Commission, among others, are required to make concurrent submissions of their budget estimates. Legislation to extend this requirement to all federal agencies has been considered in both the Ninety-third and the Ninety-fourth Congresses, and though none has passed, many agencies now supply their original budget estimates at the requests of congressional committees.

(6) The 1973 War Powers Resolution requires the president "in every possible instance" to consult with Congress before military forces are entered into hostilities and to "consult regularly" with Congress while such forces are engaged in hostile situations. The resolution intends that "the collective judgment" of both branches be applied before forces are committed to combat.

(7) The Congressional Budget Act of 1974 establishes a legislative process for

determining national programs and priorities. This new process begins with much less involvement by executive officials than has been customary in the authorization and appropriation processes.

(8) Finally, Congress has broken new ground in the legal representation of its interests. The Impoundment Control Act authorizes the Comptroller General to bring court action to enforce the new impoundment procedures. In 1975, the Comptroller General sued to secure the release of $264 million impounded by the Department of Housing and Urban Development. The Justice Department moved to dismiss the action, noting that "it is apparently the first suit ever brought in the judicial branch by the legislative branch in its official capacity against the executive branch in its official capacity." On a broader front, the Ninety-fourth Congress is considering a Watergate Reform Act which would establish an Office of Congressional Legal Counsel to represent Congress in certain legal matters.

The above list is necessarily incomplete, but it suggests the range of congressional efforts to control the executive branch. In the sections that follow, three additional types of control are considered in detail. Each affects a different stage of the administrative process. (1) Legislative oversight and evaluation occurs after the administrative action has been completed. (2) The congressional veto relates to pending administrative matters. (3) Congressional authorization of programs and agencies enables Congress to shape government policy before agencies act.

LEGISLATIVE OVERSIGHT AND EVALUATION

The dominant feature of legislative oversight is review after the fact. The main form of oversight is investigatory activity by congressional committees or other reviews (such as appropriations hearings) of past administrative actions.

Official policy with regard to legislative oversight is not in doubt; its practice is another matter. The Legislative Reorganization Act of 1946 charged each standing committee with responsibility "to exercise continuous watchfulness of the execution by the administrative agencies concerned of any laws, the subject matter of which is within the jurisdiction of such committee." The 1970 Reorganization Act restated the review functions of legislative committees and required most of them to submit biennial reports on their review activities. The legislative commitment to oversight was further elaborated by the House Committee Reform Amendments of 1974, which tasked each House committee "to establish an oversight committee, or require its subcommittees, if any, to conduct oversight in the area of their respective jurisdiction." To assure compliance with their oversight duties, House committees are to develop oversight plans at the start of each Congress.

This official commitment to legislative oversight thus goes back 30 years (although some oversight functions were established in the early 1800s); the theory on which it is based is much older, as we shall soon note. But despite increased investigations by congressional committees, such oversight still is not practiced in a regular or comprehensive fashion. At best, Congress gets oversight by exception in the sense that a small number of matters that provoke legislative attention are subjected to review. At worst, Congress persists in an arrangement in which most of what the administrative branch does is beyond legislative cognizance.

There appears to be general agreement that regular oversight ought to be conducted, but is not. Walter Oleszek has identified seven factors that inhibit legislative oversight of bureaucracy. In perhaps the first book-length examination of oversight, Morris Ogul draws a dismal conclusion:

> There seems to be consensus in the Congress on the principle that extensive and systematic oversight *ought* to be conducted.
>
> That expectation is simply not met. . . . The plain but seldom acknowledged fact is that this task, at least as defined above, is impossible to perform. No amount of congressional dedication and energy, no conceivable increase in the size of committee staffs, and no extraordinary boost in committee budgets will enable the Congress to carry out its oversight obligations in a comprehensive and systematic manner. The job is too large for any combination of members and staff to master completely.

Something even more fundamental is awry in the expectation that Congress will become an overseeing branch. This expectation is grounded on executive presumptions about how Congress ought to behave, not on the preferences manifested by Congress in its own actions and priorities. Even as it has embraced the theory of legislative oversight, Congress has refused to subscribe to the division of labor implicit in the theory. One of the earliest statements of that theory appears in *Congressional Government*, the book in which Woodrow Wilson castigated congressional intervention in administrative matters. "Quite as important as legislation," Wilson insisted, "is vigilant oversight of administration." Wilson conceived of oversight as a counter to the excesses of legislation. "There is no similar legislature in existence which is so shut up to the one business of lawmaking as is our Congress." Laws constrain administrative discretion in advance; oversight has the advantage of allowing full scope to administration, with legislative scrutiny occurring afterwards. The oversight role renders broad administrative discretion legitimate by making it accountable to legislative authority.

The contemporary significance of oversight derives entirely from the enormous growth of administrative discretion. As Arthur MacMahon noted in a 1943 article on the subject, "the need for such oversight increases with executive initiatives in policy and the delegation of discretion under the broad terms of statutes." The theory of legislative oversight, however, is more than a de facto accommodation to the enlargement of administrative power. It welcomes that development and seeks the recasting of Congress from a lawmaking to an overseeing body. As argued by Huntington,

> Explicit acceptance of the idea that legislation was not its primary function would, in large part, simply be recognition of the direction which change has already been taking. It would legitimize and expand the functions of constituent service and administrative oversight, which, in practice, already constitute the principal work of most congressmen.

Much of the literature on oversight views Congress from an executive perspective. Congress is told to oversee more and legislate less. But Ogul and others conclude that Congress cannot handle the comparatively modest oversight chores it now has. Congress is asked to trade away its historic role for one which it cannot perform the way the theory expects it to perform.

The deal simply won't wash. There is an important place for oversight in the spectrum of congressional functions, but not as the dominant activity, and certainly not one that is preemptive of lawmaking interests. Expectations about oversight must be scaled down to accord with Congress' own preferences about its place in the political system. Congress is incurably ambivalent about the amount of control and independence it is willing to invest the administrative branch with. But its 200-year history demonstrates that Congress prefers making laws to overseeing their execution. If oversight is to flourish on Capitol Hill, it will not be at the expense of more traditional legislative activities.

Much the same can be said of program evaluation, which is a specialized form of oversight. Evaluation focuses on the results rather than the processes of administration. Unlike legislative oversight, it does not scatter its attention to the details of administration, except to the extent that these affect the costs or effectiveness of programs.

Judging from recent developments, legislative interest in evaluation is on the upswing. The 1970 Legislative Reorganization Act directs the General Accounting Office to make cost-benefit studies of government programs on its own initiative or at the request of congressional committees. Title VII of the Congressional Budget Act of 1974 authorizes congressional committees to conduct evaluations on their own or by contract and it directs the GAO to assist committees, at their request, in formulating statements of legislative objectives. GAO also is authorized to develop program evaluation methods for Congress and to establish an Office of Program Review and Evaluation. In addition to these general mandates, Congress in recent years has prescribed, or earmarked funds for, the evaluation of particular programs.

Unlike oversight, which is clearly a legislative responsibility, evaluation does not operate with a differentiation of legislative and executive roles. Both branches can evaluate, and there is no *prima facie* expectation for a legislative evaluation to differ in form or content from one conducted under executive auspices. For both, evaluation is supposed to be an objective activity, meaning that it is to be divorced from the interests and constraints of the organization conducting it. Perhaps for this reason, the GAO has been assigned the lead role in evaluations of programs.

If there is no distinctively legislative type of evaluation, why consign this responsibility to Congress at all? An obvious but compelling answer is that administrative organizations cannot be trusted to evaluate themselves objectively. Self-evaluating organizations are administrative aberrations and they rarely rank among the more successful or durable executive agencies. From time to time organizations invest in stocktaking and retrospection, but not at the risk to their security and growth.

The exceptions shed some light on the normal impulse for self-promotion. During its sad and brief existence, the Office of Economic Opportunity excelled in its sponsorship and utilization of program evaluations, even to the extent of terminating some of its most promising initiatives (such as performance contracting for education) when they proved to be ineffective. In OEO, evaluation came to be a substitute for action, a manner of existence appropriate for a mendicant rather than an affluent organization. Well-supported agencies tend to move into action before they have evaluative confirmation of their program innovations, and they often continue what they are doing even if the results are unfavorable.

There are a number of reasons why agencies do not genuinely evaluate their own performance. One has to do with the annual budget process. Agencies are not neutrals in the recurring budgetary wars; they are budget maximizers. The language of budgeting is geared to advocacy and justification, not to an objective search for truth. A truly objective evaluation can damage an agency's budget position by arming outsiders (such as OMB or Congress) with reasons to reduce spending below previously authorized levels. For this reason, evaluators quickly become outsiders within their own organization, with their views and loyalties suspect. Organizations probably would be more receptive to evaluations if they consistently upheld the worthwhileness of programs. But in recent years it has appeared that for every evaluation highlighting program success there have been handfuls pronouncing failure or uncertain results. The market for evaluation dries up when evaluation becomes an anti-organization weapon.

The role of Congress, therefore, is to assure objectivity in the conduct of evaluation, sometimes by superintending the executive activity, sometimes by doing the job itself. But Congress has its own incentives for nonobjectivity, its own reasons for dragging its feet of evaluation. A keen participant in the legislative process for many years recently wrote of congressional committees: "Those who are program advocates in the beginning become program protectors along the way." The very factors which constrain executive commitment to evaluation also dampen congressional enthusiasm. Many committees are "captured" by the agencies they are charged to oversee, a predicament which is induced by the close and continuing contact between committee and agency staffs. Some authorizing committees consider it advantageous to inflate authorizations in order to protect their favored programs at the later appropriations stage. Like agencies, committees can behave as budget maximizers for the agencies under their jurisdiction.

Congress has no inherent advantage vis à vis the executive terms of objectivity, though there surely are instances in which legislative committees do a better job of program evaluation. Both branches are prey to the same tendencies to see things their way, to close off potentially threatening avenues of inquiry, and to seek evidence in support of positions already staked out. But evaluation by Congress assures that the biases are legislative rather than executive ones, that Congress is not "snowed" by the mass of data and findings thrust upon it by administrative agencies in the name of program evaluation. There is much to be said for this subjective use of evaluation. Tainted evaluation competes against tainted evaluation and though the truth might not emerge from this process, it is less likely to be suppressed than if only one side of the story were told. Evaluation thus serves as a means of increasing congressional independence from administrative influence.

Program evaluation still is the exception, but it has been applied much more extensively in recent years, particularly by GAO, than in the past. However, before rallying to this new banner, a few caveats ought to be admitted. First, Congress cannot possibly acquire sufficient staff or resources to evaluate more than a small fraction of the programs subject to its review. The bulk of evaluation efforts always will have to come from the executive side, and these can make Congress even more beholden to administrative persuasion. Second, Congress cannot effectively conduct evaluations as after-the-fact inquiries in the manner of its general oversight functions. Evaluations which lack some sense of legislative intent are open to interminable confusion and conflict over their meaning and validity. If Davis is right that much contemporary legislation implies that "We the Congress don't know what the problems are; find them and deal with them," then the evaluators can only respond, "And we don't know the solution." Finally, the quantity of evaluation should not be taken as a measure of legislative (or executive, for that matter) commitment to the cause. As difficult as it is to evaluate, it is even more difficult to apply the findings to government programs, especially when client support is established and benefits are flowing to advantaged interests. Few evaluations offer such compelling findings as to lead inexorably to legislative action. Almost all evaluations are vulnerable to challenge and conflicting interpretations. A decade later, for example, scholars and practitioners still are quarreling over the soundness and policy implications of the Coleman report.

As long as each evaluation is an "event," a special accomplishment that commands notice and applause, we can be sure that progress on Capitol Hill is inadequate. Only when it becomes a regular feature of the legislative process—with congressmen behaving as consumers of evaluations done by their own staffs and outsiders—will program evaluation impact on public choice. By this test, Congress still has a long way to go.

CONGRESSIONAL VETO OF ADMINISTRATIVE ACTIONS

Oversight and evaluation are forms of congressional activity after an administrative action has occurred. A second type of control is activated by Congress in the course of the administrative process. The leading control in this category is the congressional veto of proposed executive actions.

As used here, "congressional veto" covers a variety of statutory provisions which authorize either or both houses of Congress (or one or more committees) to review and overturn executive actions. The congressional veto is generally regarded to have made its debut in the Economy Act of 1932 which authorized the president to reorganize federal agencies by executive order. A proposed reorganization could not take effect for 60 days, during which period it could be disapproved by resolution of the House or Senate. This new device had a slow beginning, with another 23 laws containing 25 congressional veto provisions enacted between 1932 and 1950. The number of review requirements increased during the next two decades, with 34 laws (embodying 36 provisions) enacted during the 1950s and 49 laws (with 70 provisions) enacted during the 1960s. But there has been an astounding rise in the adoption of congressional review procedures during the first half of the 1970s. At least 89 laws and 163 provisions for the review of administrative actions were enacted between 1970 and the end of 1975. Approximately half of all the congressional veto requirements have been established in just half a dozen years. This expanded use undoubtedly has been provoked by congressional concern over recent excesses by the executive branch.

The congressional power to disapprove or defer a proposed executive action rests on the principle that the administrative authority derives from a delegation of power by Congress and that Congress, therefore, can set the terms and limitations under which administrative action is to be taken. The constitutionality of congressional review has been questioned from time to time, but the Supreme Court has never ruled on the issue.

There are many variations on the congressional veto concept. Almost all require the executive branch to notify Congress of the proposed action. Some merely authorize review by Congress without providing specifically for disapproval of the action. Others provide special procedures for committee and floor consideration of disapproval resolutions. Most establish a fixed period within which Congress must act if it is to disapprove or defer the executive action. The most popular waiting period is 30 days, but some are as brief as five days and one is as long as three years. Some provide for two-house review; others permit review by the House or the Senate; still others provide for review by the committee of jurisdiction.

The actual effects of these veto procedures on legislative-executive relations depend on how they are applied by the two branches. Delegations of power by Congress to the executive branch can vastly expand the authority of the president (or other executive officials) to act without advance legislative approval. But the veto process offers Congress an expeditious way to intervene and overrule executive actions. Both possibilities are latent in the impoundment controls enacted into law during the last month of the Nixon presidency. The Impoundment Control Act of

1974 establishes different review procedures for rescissions (repeal of appropriations) and deferrals (delays in the expenditure of funds). Proposed rescissions lapse, and the funds must be released, unless a rescission law is enacted within 45 days (as defined by the statute). Deferrals, however, can remain in effect until the end of a fiscal year unless they are disapproved by either the House or the Senate. This arrangement is generally more advantageous to the president in the case of deferrals than for rescissions. If Congress does nothing, proposed rescissions terminate while deferrals continue in force. The Impoundment Control Act concedes the de facto authority of the president to impound funds, but the act also establishes, for the first time, a legislative means of controlling and overturning executive impoundments.

The statistical evidence is that with the exception of impoundment control, the hundreds of congressional veto provisions have not induced wholesale interventions by Congress in the conduct of administration. Clark Norton of the Congressional Research Service has examined congressional veto activities during the 16 years between 1960 and 1975. For this period, Norton identified 351 House or Senate resolutions that were introduced pursuant to congressional review authority, and more than 100 of these were duplicates. Only 63 resolutions became effective through passage by one or both houses as required by law, and almost two-thirds of these adoptions occurred in 1975. During the 16-year period, most of the congressional veto provisions generated no legislative action whatsoever, not even the introduction of a resolution. Only one in six of the introduced resolutions was passed.

These statistics do not cover committee-level actions, nor do they address the possible effects of the congressional review process on executive branch behavior. But they show that congressional reviews have been selectively applied to particular concerns; they have not been across-the-board challenges to executive power.

When Congress is disturbed by the exercise of executive power, it can utilize the review process more forcefully. This has been the experience thus far with the new impoundment controls. Despite their potential for enlarging presidential power, the impoundment controls definitely have curbed administrative discretion. Although they have been in effect for less than two years, the controls account for almost two-thirds of the congressional vetoes since 1960. The congressional controls have been applied with varying effect to rescissions and deferrals.

During fiscal 1975, the president proposed 87 rescissions totalling $2,732,678,218. In addition, the Comptroller General notified Congress of two rescission actions not reported by the president and he reclassified seven reported deferrals as rescissions, raising the total during fiscal 1975 to $4,292,500,218. Congress enacted three rescission bills during the fiscal year, rescinding less than 15 per cent of the amount proposed by the president and only about 9 per cent of the adjusted amount reported by the Comptroller General.

During fiscal 1976, the president proposed 44 rescissions totalling $3,274,602,655. An additional $26.3 million in rescissions were reported by the Comptroller General. Three rescissions—totalling $138.3 million—were enacted, so that during fiscal 1976 the enactment rate dropped below 5 per cent.

In responding to rescission proposals, Congress appears to have drawn a fairly clear distinction between routine and policy impoundments. With few exceptions, Congress has approved routine rescissions involving no change in government policy, such as when funds no longer are needed to accomplish the purposes for which they were appropriated. In cases of policy rescissions, when the president has sought to eliminate funds appropriated in excess of his budget requests, Congress has not wanted to give the president a "second chance" to accomplish by means of the new impoundment process that which it has denied to him only weeks or months earlier

Congress and the "Details" of Administration

in the course of the appropriations process. The very high rejection rates indicate that the president was repeatedly rebuffed in his efforts to convert impoundment control into an opportunity to reorder the budget priorities established by Congress. However, most of the enacted rescissions did not involve substantial questions of policy. Most of these routine cases concerned comparatively small amounts of money, while the policy impoundment often dealt with very large amounts. The median amount proposed for rescission in the approved cases was less than $3 million; in the rejected rescissions the median was $14 million.

During fiscal 1975, President Ford submitted 161 deferral messages to Congress, seven of which were subsequently reclassified as rescissions by the Comptroller General. These deferrals totalled approximately $25.3 billion, with two-thirds of the funds concentrated in federal grants to states for the construction of highways and water pollution control facilities. During the fiscal year, 82 impoundment resolutions were introduced in Congress and 16 were adopted. The deferrals disapproved by the House or the Senate totalled $9.3 billion, and an additional $9 billion of water pollution funds were released by the Administration.

During the 1976 fiscal year, the president submitted 111 deferral messages totalling approximately $8.8 billion to Congress and the Comptroller General notified Congress of a failure to report the deferral of $10 million of youth conservation funds. During the year, 22 deferrals of 1976 funds were disapproved by the House or the Senate, compelling the president to release $388 million.

The distinction between routine and policy impoundments also applies to deferrals. In various reports to Congress, the Comptroller General identified approximately half of the deferrals as being routinely authorized by the anti-deficiency Act.

Congressional activity in the form of impoundment resolutions has been concentrated on policy deferrals. The 82 resolutions filed during fiscal 1975 related to only 30 impoundments, almost half of which attracted resolutions in both the House and the Senate. In virtually every instance that impoundment resolutions were introduced in both the House and Senate, the deferral was disapproved. The vast majority of deferrals permitted to continue in effect did not generate any congressional action because they were routine financial transactions involving no change in governmental policy.

The veto provisions of the Impoundment Control Act are coupled to new legislative enforcement procedures. The Comptroller General must inform Congress if the president has failed to report a proposed rescission or deferral or if an impoundment has been improperly classified. The congressional veto can then be applied "in the same manner and with the same effect" as if it were reported by the president. Congress can veto an executive action which has not been reported to it by the executive branch. Moreover, as was noted earlier, the Comptroller General is empowered to bring suit to secure compliance with the new impoundment controls.

When Congress feels that the delegation of power to the executive branch is not sufficiently constrained by the congressional veto, it can terminate the arrangement altogether. This has happened with regard to executive reorganization, the first area to which the veto device was applied. During the decades that the president was authorized to propose reorganizations, Congress disapproved about one out of every five plans that were submitted to it. Harvey Mansfield found that:

> the reorganization plan method has provided a compromise procedure for safeguarding congressional interests while permitting presidential initiatives on matters where considerable stakes of power and prestige are at issue and in situations where deadlock might otherwise prevail.

However, shortly after Mansfield drew this judicious conclusion, President Nixon used his reorganization authority in a way that aggrandized presidential power at the expense of Congress. Reorganization Plan No. 2 of 1970 transferred the functions and powers of the Bureau of the Budget to the president, who in turn delegated these by executive order to the new Office of Management and Budget and the Domestic Council. The effects of this two-step procedure were to enable the president to make future changes in the executive office without going through the reorganization process and to weaken the accountability of presidential subordinates to Congress. A resolution of disapproval was considered in the House, but it failed by a small margin. However, in 1973 Congress permitted the reorganization power of the president to expire, thereby foreclosing its future use to disadvantage the legislative branch.

AUTHORIZING LEGISLATION

Congressional oversight and vetoes are directed at past and current administrative actions. The authorization process gives Congress an opportunity to control future administrative behavior. The extent to which Congress avails itself of this opportunity depends on the use of annual or multi-year as opposed to permanent authorizations.

At one time, permanent authorizations—without limit of time and usually without limit of money as well—were the standard practice. At the end of World War II, as much as 95 per cent of the federal budget (exclusive of one-time projects) was under permanent authorization. The usual formula was, "There are hereby authorized to be appropriated such funds as may be necessary." In effect, Congress would set up an agency or program and authorize it to continue in operation until further notice. These permanent activities would be considered by the Appropriations Committees; there would be no routine review by the substantive committees of Congress.

During the past 25 years there has been a trend toward fixed authorization periods. In the case of annual authorizations, Congress usually is motivated by a desire to bolster its control over executive agencies or by a desire of its authorizing committees to expand their legislative influence over the programs within their jurisdiction. But regardless of the original motive, a shift to limited-term authorizations enhances the ability of Congress to intervene in administrative matters.

The list of agencies and programs now operating under annual authorization includes the National Science Foundation, the Maritime Administration, the National Aeronautics and Space Administration, and the Energy Research and Development Administration. In dollar terms, the largest annual authorizations apply to certain programs of the Defense Department. Section 412 of Public Law 86-149 (enacted in 1959) requires annual authorization for the procurement of aircraft, missiles, and naval vessels. In subsequent legislation annual authorizations were extended to virtually all of the procurement, construction, and research activities of the Defense Department.

An important recent addition to the list is the State Department which, together with the United States Information Agency, was placed under annual authorizations by the Foreign Assistance Act of 1971. The State Department thus became the first cabinet department to be subject to annual authorizations for its entire appropriation.

Multiyear authorizations range in most instances from two to five years and have been popular for many of the grant-in-aid programs established during the past two decades. In seeking a middle course between permanent and annual authorizations, Congress apparently has been unwilling to accord permanent status to new and untried programs, but it also has been sensitive to the needs of state and local governments for some advance indication as to the amounts of federal aid that may be forthcoming in future years.

In dollar amounts, permanent authorizations still dominate the federal scene. Most of the major entitlement programs such as social security, veterans benefits, public assistance, and medicare are permanently authorized. Less than one-quarter of the federal budget requires authorization in a particular year. Like the congressional veto, Congress has used its authorization process selectively, to bolster its intervention in those policy areas where it wishes to maintain closer control over the executive branch. When Congress no longer feels it necessary to give such close attention to a program, the reauthorization process becomes a *proforma* exercise. Such now is the case with regard to the annual authorization of the saline water program.

But when Congress wishes to exploit its authorization process to control executive activities, it can write specific conditions into authorizing legislation. This has been the case in recent years for the authorization bills dealing with foreign policy. The 1976 Foreign Relations Authorization Act, for example, bars the State Department from developing a machine-readable passport system; declares that political contributions should not be criteria for the award of ambassadorial positions; urges the reopening of a consulate at Gothenburg, Sweden; instructs the Arms Control and Disarmament Agency to study the effects of arms limitations on military expenditures; modifies statutory requirements with regard to security investigations for contractors; limits United States contributions to certain international organizations and activities; calls for the temporary assignment of foreign service officers to congressional, state and local, and other public organizations; establishes detailed grievance procedures for foreign service personnel; and authorizes certain government employees to carry firearms. This is just one law's list of congressional actions affecting the conduct of foreign policy. Each of these controls piggybacked the annual authorization process to enactment.

The foreign relations area is vastly different from the policy areas in which permanent authorizations prevail. In the latter cases, an agency can escape detailed review by its authorizing committee for many years and the legislation under which it operates often is cast in broad terms, with few specific controls or restraints. Even if considerable annual review comes through the appropriations process, it is likely to focus on financial rather than on other substantive issues and it is not likely to occasion as thorough an inquiry into the agency activities as can be provided by a dual authorizations-appropriations process.

In the Ninety-fourth Congress more than half of the senators have sponsored "sunset" legislation to require the periodic termination of all but a few federal programs and agencies. Substantive laws would not be directly affected; only authorization provisions would terminate. But Congress would be able to use its consideration of reauthorizing legislation to review all activities of a program and agency and to attach new conditions substantive laws. The sunset concept has attracted considerable support in a brief period of time, but if it were enacted, Congress probably would continue in its selective ways. Not every corner of federal activity can be reexamined every four or five years; sudden death will not become a Washington routine. The periodic sunset of government agencies will enable Congress to focus on particular programs and make changes as it deems desirable.

BACK TO THE DETAILS OF ADMINISTRATION?

Details are important and control over the details is important. Congressional control over the details means conflict and confrontation, for it clashes directly with the executive branch's preference for freedom of action. Control runs to the particulars of policy; to its manner of implementation, not just to its general shape. Moreover, the emphasis in Congress is on controlling current activities: telling the president "no" when he wants to act.

Shortly after Woodrow Wilson complained about congressional meddling in the details of administration, the executive branch embarked on a major expansion of its power and administrative discretion. Thirty years ago, Arthur MacMahon complained that "Congress seeks in sundry ways to claim what it gave; it asserts the right of continuous intervention." Once again the Executive Branch enlarged its power and discretion.

Congressional attempts to reassert its control have characterized legislative-executive relationships during the 1970s. Divided political leadership and pervasive mistrust of executive power have whetted the congressional appetite for control. But neither Congress nor the executive branch relishes perpetual collision. When the passions of recent times have cooled, we may look to a more balanced relationship which combines reasonable executive discretion with congressional involvement in the important details of American policy.

SEVENTEEN
CONGRESSIONAL CONTROL OF ADMINISTRATIVE REGULATION
A Study of Legislative Vetoes

Harold H. Bruff/Ernest Gellhorn

Complaints of a malaise in the administrative process and calls for regulatory reform are not new. Recently, however, these attacks on government regulation have been renewed with special fervor. Numerous cures have been proposed, ranging from general deregulation to sunset and sunshine bills. One idea receiving special attention in Congress has been a proposed amendment to the Administrative Procedure Act (APA) providing that substantive rules issued pursuant to the notice-and-comment procedures of 5 U.S.C. § 553 must be submitted to Congress for review before taking effect. Then, if either house of Congress (or both houses, under some proposals) should disapprove a proposed rule within a specified period, such as sixty days, it would not take effect. The purpose of this "legislative veto," which would not require the concurrence of the president, would be to give Congress an opportunity to void administrative regulations which, in its judgment, exceed statutory authority or implement unsound policy.

In recent years, Congress has added legislative veto provisions to an increasing number of laws governing agency action. Most of these statutes involve executive action other than rulemaking; they range in subject matter from the reorganization of the executive branch to the conduct of foreign affairs and the administration of public works programs. No legislative vetoes have been applied to adjudications,

This selection is taken from the *Harvard Law Review* 90, 7 (May 1977), 1369–1440. Copyright © 1977 by The Harvard Law Review Association. Used by permission of the publisher and authors. This Article is based on a report prepared for the Administrative Conference of the United States. The conference, however, has not approved the article, and the authors have sole responsibility for it. Footnotes have been omitted.

however, since they are constitutionally protected from direct congressional scrutiny.

Since 1972, Congress has extended the legislative veto to a series of agency programs involving rule making. Most of the current federal experience with legislative veto of rule making has occurred in five programs: the Office of Education's establishment of family contribution schedules for its program of basic grants for postsecondary education; the Department of Health, Education, and Welfare's rules issued under the General Education Provisions Act since 1974; the Federal Energy Administration's exemptions from price and allocation controls on petroleum products; the General Services Administration's regulations regarding public access to the papers and tapes of the Nixon presidency; and all of the Federal Election Commission's rules governing the conduct and financing of campaigns. The proposals currently before Congress would substitute a legislative veto having broad applicability to rulemaking for this ad hoc approach. . . .

I. THE BACKGROUND: CONSTITUTIONAL, STATUTORY, AND POLICY ISSUES SURROUNDING THE LEGISLATIVE VETO OF RULE MAKING

Any proposal to impose broadly applicable limits on agency authority to develop policy is intimately related to the long struggle of administrative agencies for legitimacy and independence. American attitudes toward the agencies have always demonstrated a fundamental ambivalence. On one hand, administrative agencies are viewed as necessary vehicles for the development of policy and are often created to resolve issues that Congress is unwilling or unable to decide. They are expected to develop experience and specialized knowledge and to provide efficient administration of complex and burdensome tasks. On the other hand, Americans are suspicious of delegation of lawmaking authority to agencies, which seems inconsistent with the Constitution's allocation of the responsibility for lawmaking to Congress. An assessment of the legislative veto of administrative regulations requires an understanding of its place within the statutory and constitutional scheme that has evolved to define the role of the agencies.

A. The Legislative Veto as a Substitute for the Delegation Doctrine

Over the course of time, constitutional doctrine has developed to support administrative lawmaking. The courts have come to recognize that it is impractical for the legislature to make the innumerable policy decisions necessary to the daily operation of a large and complex government. Therefore, modern courts applying the delegation doctrine, which theoretically limits congressional grants of power to the agencies, have rejected ancient and rigid dicta that the lawmaking power vested in Congress may not be delegated elsewhere. Today the courts purport to require only that statutory delegations of congressional authority contain basic policy standards for the administrator to follow. This "standards" requirement is designed to preserve the separation of powers by placing broad policy determinations in the hands of elected representatives rather than appointed bureaucrats and by facilitating judicial review. Yet even this minimal requirement has proved to be unworkable in practice. Almost without exception, the courts have refused to enforce constitutional constraints on congressional delegations of lawmaking authority to the agencies. The Supreme Court has been unwilling to require Congress to specify policy standards as clearly as possible, or to revise broad standards as experience permits. The result is that lawmaking power is now lodged in administrative hands without any constitutional assurance that the agencies are responsive to the people's will.

The legislative veto can be viewed as a mechanism to help fill the void left by the decline of the delegation doctrine. Its purpose is to limit agency rulemaking authority by lodging final control in Congress. But instead of controlling agency policy in advance by laying out a road map in the statute creating the agency, Congress now proposes to control policy as it develops in notice-and-comment rule making, after the agency's expert staff and interested members of the public have had an opportunity to assist in its formation. In this way Congress can be fully informed before primary policy is decided. Still, the legislative veto is only a negative check on policies proposed by the agencies, not a means for making policy directly.

B. Separation of Powers

Legislative veto provisions raise a series of constitutional questions involving the separation of powers. Chief among these is whether legislative vetoes constitute an impermissible evasion of the president's veto authority, or an impermissible intrusion into the powers vested in the executive or judicial branches of government (depending on whether the veto is meant for policy or legality review). Supporters of the legislative veto argue that since it is a control on administrative lawmaking similar to that which the delegation doctrine purports to impose, it is fully consistent with the separation of powers. They emphasize that the branches of government are not wholly separated but often have a limited role in one another's functions. For example, the president's veto gives him a role in legislation; the power of advice and consent gives the Senate a role in administration. If, then, the legislative veto device gives Congress an appropriately limited role in the executive function, it constitutes an appropriate counter-weight to broad delegation. By returning policymaking authority to Congress, it helps preserve the separation of powers. Opponents argue that legislative vetoes are functionally like legislation in that they foreclose otherwise permissible readings of statutes. To foreclose such interpretations similarly by legislation would require the approval of the president or the concurrence of two-thirds of both houses of Congress to override his veto. Thus legislative vetoes passed without presidential concurrence arguably abridge the president's role in the legislative process. Furthermore, for Congress to pass on the legality of administrative rules may usurp the judicial function.

If a single house may veto regulations, the fundamental principle of bicameralism may be violated. The Constitution lodges legislative authority in a bicameral Congress, in part as an internal check against the aggrandizement of congressional power. Proposals allowing one house to veto administrative regulations appear to circumvent that check. Since the legislative veto is designed as a negative constraint on policymaking, however, supporters argue that it gives each house no more power than the bicameral system, under which legislation may also be blocked by either house. They also emphasize that the statute authorizing the legislative veto must itself be passed by the normal legislative process involving concurrence of both houses and presidential approval or veto override. Nevertheless, Congress cannot by legislation alter the bicameral system engraved in the Constitution. Moreover, the substantive policy created by the agency's rule, if within the bounds of the statutory delegation, arguably had the approval of both houses and the president in the original delegation. To the extent that a legislative veto by a single house may redirect this policy, serious questions are raised about the veto's consistency with the Constitution's legislative scheme.

Whether the legislative veto will founder upon these constitutional objections is unclear. Although Mr. Justice White rejected them in his concurrence in *Buckley v. Valeo*, a majority of the Supreme Court specifically left the question for another day. The Court of Claims, however, recently has upheld the constitutionality of a one-house veto.

C. The Legislative Veto in Context: Developments in Rule Making

The Administrative Procedure Act provides generally applicable procedural constraints for the agencies' delegated policy-making. It thus defines the procedural context in which an increased congressional involvement in rule making functions. The basic assumption upon which the APA rests is that policy is developed and applied in one of two ways: by adjudication or by rule making. Most agencies have broad discretion to choose which approach is more suitable. However, this bipolar analysis reflects the formal structure more than the reality of the administrative process. Much agency action is neither adjudication nor rule making: the APA does not provide special procedures for executive actions such as consent settlements, policy statements, and contracts. Nevertheless, the APA's constraints are important. Adjudication must adhere to most of the common law safeguards of a trial, including notice of the charges, a hearing before an unbiased tribunal, and an opportunity to present evidence and to challenge or rebut contrary proof. The ultimate findings and decision must be supported by the record. Informal rule making, in contrast, has traditionally required only published notice of a proposed rule, an opportunity to comment on it, and a concise statement of the basis and purpose of the final rule.

During the past several decades, the procedures of formal adjudication have become increasingly elaborate and time-consuming. They have therefore seemed ill-suited to many new regulatory programs in such fields as environmental protection; Congress accordingly has set the agencies administering them on a course of rule making. Whether spurred by Congress or on their own initiative, agencies have relied increasingly on rule making or other informal executive action rather than on adjudication. Because the APA has few explicit procedural requirements for such activities and because no formal record is required, judicial review has been difficult. Courts have responded to this challenge by importing procedural requirements into various informal proceedings on both constitutional and statutory grounds. Illustrative of this broader trend is a series of cases imposing new procedural requirements for informal rule making. These judicial requirements have been summarized as follows:

> First, both the essential factual data on which the rule is based and the methodology used in reasoning from the data to the proposed standard must be disclosed for comment at the time a rule is proposed.... Second, the agency's discussion of the basis and purpose of its rule—generally contained in the "preambles" to the notices of proposed and final rulemaking and in the accompanying technical support documents—must detail the steps of the agency's reasoning and its factual basis. Third, significant comments received during the public comment period must be answered at the time of final promulgation.... Fourth, only objections to the regulations which were raised with some specificity during the public comment period, and to which the agency thus had an opportunity to respond, may be raised during judicial review.

Congress has also imposed special procedural requirements beyond those in the APA in several recent delegations of rule-making power, in order to assure that agencies have fully considered the issues and proposed solutions. For example, the Federal Trade Commission's new rule-making authority includes requirements for cross-examination and specific findings based on evidence in the record.

Several purposes are discernible in these new statutory and judicial requirements. One is to assure fair treatment of persons submitting comments by requiring actual agency consideration and response. A second is to foster reasoned agency decision-making by exposing thinking within the agency to public criticism and by requiring reasoned resolution of the issues. A third is to facilitate judicial review by providing a record to justify a final rule. Obviously, these purposes are closely intertwined.

Introducing legislative veto provisions into this scheme raises issues at the foundation of modern rule making. To what extent is rule making a normative or political process which is brought closer to the people's representatives by the legislative veto, and to what extent is it an expert or rational process that should not be subject to "political" influences? Recent commentators have attacked the "naive" view of rule making which characterizes it as a decision by experts divorced from political considerations. They emphasize that there is no ideal resolution of policy in service of some unitary public interest; there are only resolutions of greater or lesser acceptability to experts and to the various interest groups that make up the American public. Certainly the notice-and-comment portion of the rule-making process retains some "legislative" characteristics, in that anyone affected by a proposed rule may make his views known, although tinged by self-interest. Yet whatever the role of political conflict, the premises of democracy demand that it be in the open. There is ample justification for procedural constraints on rule making to exclude unseen political influences.

The new statutory and judicial requirements thus seek to exclude secret influences and to assure the openness of the rule-making process. Their premises are that a meaningful statutory standard, or at least rationality review by the courts, constrains the substance of the resulting rules, and that the agency staffs have a contribution to make in formulating rules even if they are not Solomonic. Any statutory provision for a legislative veto should be evaluated for consistency with these emerging aims of the rule-making process. Of particular importance to the courts is that there be some sort of agency record for review and that information in the record be the exclusive basis for decision. When a legislative veto system is implemented, informal contacts between the agency and the committees, staff personnel, and members of Congress may increase. By their very nature these contacts are likely to be secret, or at least undisclosed by the administrative record. If the result is to deny interested persons fair treatment, to deflect an agency from its statutory grounds for decision, or to impair the ability of the courts to review rules, a violation of due process or the governing statute may result. A careful examination of the actual interactions between Congress and the agencies that occur in the presence of a legislative veto provision is therefore necessary to a judgment of the desirability and constitutionality of the veto.

D. Policy Issues Surrounding Legislative Veto Provisions

So far, we have discussed only the theoretical consistency of the legislative veto technique with the statutory and constitutional schemes governing the agencies. There seems to be no clear a priori answer to the question of the constitutionality of the veto or its consistency with the statutory scheme of administration. Therefore, any decisions to apply it broadly to administrative rule making in general should rest partly on an informed judgment regarding its likely effects in practice on the agencies, the courts, and Congress. . . .

A question of central importance is whether the addition of congressional review to administrative rule making will diminish the effectiveness of the other procedural checks which Congress and the courts have imposed on the rule-making process. The problem is that the congressional review process may not be governed by rules as strict as those applicable to agency rule making. Present procedures might be replaced by a less visible or closed process of review by congressional committee members and staffs, as well as other interested congressmen. And if interest groups can lobby Congress during the review period, their influence might render currently required public procedures for rule making ineffective. In any case, a veto statute may reduce public participation before the agencies by shifting the focus of attention to congressional review procedures. This is not meant to suggest that Congress need adopt the same procedures it imposes upon the agencies, thereby producing a largely redundant review process. It does suggest, however, that the differences between the legislative and administrative process may make it difficult to reconcile congressional review with other aspects of rule making.

An overall appraisal of a legislative veto provision must examine whether it helps to assure the acceptability of agency regulations to Congress as a whole. If review authority is actually exercised by congressional committees, which are less broadly representative than the full membership of either house, the intent of Congress as a whole may not be realized. The same may be true if committee action is not visible to the other members, so that there is no attention and assent to what the committees do.

Another fundamental issue is whether the opportunity for subsequent review of agency regulations will lessen pressure in Congress for specificity in legislation delegating rule-making power. A purpose of legislative vetoes is to allow Congress to postpone deciding policy questions until a concrete resolution appears in the form of a proposed rule. Whether the effect of this approach is to increase or to decrease agency discretion will depend on the extent to which agency regulations receive actual review.

Delay is said to be a serious problem in rule making; Congress and the courts have often responded by imposing deadlines for promulgating rules. The legislative veto creates an additional source of delay because rules must lie before Congress for the statutory period whether or not there is serious consideration of a veto. It is difficult to estimate the costs of delay in promulgating rules that lie before Congress without awakening actual review. Such costs seem likely to vary in their visibility and their seriousness. And they would be without any corresponding benefit unless the very presence of review authority improves the drafting process by increasing agency attention to the acceptability of rules to Congress.

When review of a rule does occur, irreconcilable differences in policy between the agency and Congress may lead to long-term impasses. As a result, the implementation of administrative programs may be considerably delayed or entirely thwarted. Thus, it is important to appraise whether active congressional review will tend to produce the speedy resolution of policy. This will depend on the time between rules submissions and vetoes, and on the willingness of agencies to modify vetoed rules in accordance with the will of Congress. Agencies may respond to the possibility of program interruption through legislative vetoes by using adjudication rather than rule making to form policy. If so, delay problems may be exacerbated by the increased use of slow adjudicative processes.

In addition to increasing delay in the administrative process, legislative veto authority may also increase Congress' already considerable work load. Much of the work of screening regulations for review must be done by hired staff, rather than committee members; consequently, already burdened staffs would have to be enlarged to implement a generally applicable veto. Furthermore, especially where proposed rules deal with complex and technical subjects, the review process itself may be difficult and time-consuming for the members of Congress. Hearings must be held and committee reports written. If a veto resolution is reported to the floor, there must be study, debate, and a vote. Whether a significant number of rules would reach this stage remains to be seen, but there is the potential for an alarming increase in the volume of Congress' business.

A final concern is that of the legislative veto's effect on judicial review. The failure of Congress to veto a rule might be construed as its ratification, and a court might feel bound to defer to Congress' implied judgment that the rule is not ultra vires or irrational. But congressional review may turn either on these legality considerations or on a rule's soundness as a matter of policy—and the nature of judicial review may depend on the nature of congressional review. Courts may be more reluctant to question the judgment of Congress where review is based on considerations of policy than where it is purportedly limited to questions of statutory intent, which are within the traditional province of the courts. Moreover, the extent of a court's scrutiny may depend on whether the rule received careful examination in Congress, at least by a committee, or was not reviewed at all. If the judiciary defers to agency rule making on a theory of implied ratification by Congress, there may result a net loosening of constraints on agency discretion whenever rules have received little direct examination in Congress. All of these legal questions would complicate the process of judicial review, and their resolution might entail close judicial scrutiny of the internal workings of Congress.

IV. THE DESIRABILITY OF A GENERAL LEGISLATIVE VETO FOR RULE MAKING

An initial question in evaluating the desirability of a statute subjecting most informal rule making to legislative veto authority is the extent to which our case studies provide a valid model for analysis. At first glance, there seems to be one obvious distinguishing feature. In the case studies Congress selected a group of programs for which it had special concern, and subjected them to active review. Given the vast amount of rule making activity in the federal government, it seems clear that Congress has neither the time nor the inclination to extend active review under a general veto power to more than a few highly controversial rules. Even a substantial increase in congressional staff to canvass forth-coming agency rules would not necessarily lead to frequent review by congressmen, because their number is fixed and their time is limited. Meaningful review, whether by congressmen or their staff, seems likely to be episodic, because much agency rule making is routine, technical, or otherwise noncontroversial.

Reflection suggests, however, that a view which minimizes the practical impact of a general veto provision is oversimplified. It does not adequately account for the nature of rule making and the nature of the agencies' present relations with other branches of government. Under a general legislative veto provision, agencies may be inclined to abandon rule making in favor of other procedures less vulnerable to congressional scrutiny for the development of policy. Moreover, if in practice

Congress does not exercise the veto power assiduously, the broader delegations of authority which it fosters may result, contrary to expectations, in a net decrease in control over agency discretion. Partial duplication of the judicial function by Congress may create profound problems for the courts in their review of both congressional action and agency rules. Finally, in its use of the veto power Congress may in practice venture beyond mere supervision to improper interference in the administrative function.

A. Effects on Agency Behavior

The agencies have been repeatedly criticized for pursuing an ad hoc, "rudderless" course that emphasizes adjudication, rather than moving decisively to form policy by rule making. Rule making is frequently relegated to relatively technical or noncontroversial aspects of an agency's mission precisely because the agency does not choose to resort to it for resolution of hard policy issues. The reasons for this practice are instructive in evaluating a general veto provision.

Currently, strong incentives for agencies to avoid vigorous policymaking inhere in the relations of the agencies to Congress. Many of the policy issues that agencies do not currently resolve arise under broad delegations by a Congress which was unwilling or unable to resolve the issues itself. Political pressures or uncertainties that prevented a statutory resolution of policy in Congress also hamper resolution by the politically weaker agencies. A vigorous agency assertion of policy is likely to meet with countervailing pressure from interest groups lobbying congressional committees. Consequently, agencies may resort to adjudication—which is constitutionally protected from direct congressional supervision—for the making of policy.

The case studies suggest that a general veto provision will increase the power of interest groups to block or deflect agency policy initiatives through pressure on congressional committees. Such pressure would not always require the detailed and time-consuming negotiation process that occurred in the case studies. A committee not having the time or inclination to negotiate a given set of rules could simply report a veto resolution, which, if passed by the entire house, could lead to the kind of indefinite policy impasse found repeatedly in the case studies. Alternatively, it could attempt to deter agency submission of a rule altogether. Whenever an agency is not statutorily restricted to policymaking by rule, the threat of such pressure is likely to drive it toward greater use of adjudication. Unlike the agencies involved in the case studies, many federal agencies are free to choose adjudication. Thus, by increasing agency reliance on adjudication, a general legislative veto provision might have pervasive effects on the nature of policymaking in federal agencies.

To the extent that a general veto power would increase reliance on adjudication at the expense of rule making, it would have the reverse of the effect intended, for it would encourage the agencies to act in ways that are even less amenable to congressional oversight than rule making is now. Other disadvantages of excessive adjudication would also be increased, principally delay in forming overall policy. Congress could attempt to avoid excessive resort to adjudication by requiring the agencies to engage in rule making for the formulation of policy. But both Congress and the courts have traditionally recognized broad discretion in the agencies to proceed by adjudication or rule making as their judgment dictates. Any requirement to proceed exclusively by rule making could sensibly be imposed only after careful study of each program involved and might be overly rigid even then.

A general legislative veto might have a particularly disturbing effect on the independent regulatory agencies, since their freedom from presidential supervision may make them more susceptible to congressional control than the executive agencies dominating the case studies. They currently operate under broad delegations and have traditionally relied heavily upon adjudication. These agencies have recently shown encouraging signs of moving away from full adjudicative procedures toward rule making for the formulation of policy. It would be unfortunate if the indirect effects of a general veto provision were to reverse this trend. In addition to increasing their reliance on adjudication, a general veto provision might adversely affect the independent agencies in two ways. First, it might produce frequent policy impasse between these agencies and Congress due to vetoes, because most of their rules are of the kind that would be subject to review only once, and because the congressional committees overseeing them have demonstrated their capacity to stall rule making through informal pressure. Second, the presence of a veto provision would provide another opportunity, after public comment, for regulated interests to obtain changes in a rule or to block passage of a rule-making program. This opportunity would exacerbate current problems of the "capture" of the independent commissions by their regulated constituencies.

B. Effects on Congressional Delegations of Rule Making Authority

However ineffective the delegation doctrine has been in limiting broad grants of legislative power, its underlying purposes have not lost their force, and it still imposes some constraints upon statutory delegations. Nevertheless, the courts have realized that the requirement for policy standards in legislation can be overemphasized at the expense of other means of confining administrative discretion. Unwilling to require Congress to decide complex policy questions in advance under the delegation doctrine, the courts have emphasized various means of assuring that agency action is authorized and that agency procedures are accurate and fair. This is illustrated by *Amalgamated Meat Cutters* v. *Connally*, which upheld a grant of authority to the president to establish wage and price controls, even though the statute established no clear standard for the level or timing of their imposition. The court derived adequate limits on the president's discretion from several sources. From the historical context and other wage-price control statutes it was able to divine a congressional purpose of fair and equitable stabilization sufficient to guide the president. Further, it noted statutory limits on the president's power to single out an industry for special treatment and the limited time for which controls could be applied. Finally, the court incorporated the procedures of the Administrative Procedure Act and expanded the scope of judicial review. As Judge Leventhal emphasized in *Meat Cutters*, the delegation doctrine should be viewed as a requirement that Congress impose controls of any appropriate sort on the exercise of delegated power. Since legislative vetoes are designed to provide controls on agency power delegated by Congress, this approach suggests strongly that Congress has not only the right but a constitutional duty to oversee the exercise of its delegated powers through some technique such as the veto.

Further consideration, however, suggests that in practice the legislative veto may fail to define more exactly the limits of agency discretion. Existing veto provisions, particularly those in the energy statutes, often accompany broader grants of power than Congress would have made without having the veto power as a check upon their exercise. And Congress has forgone subsequent opportunities for legislative resolution of issues emerging in rule-making programs subject to veto, preferring instead to react to the agency's policy initiatives. These facts, coupled with Congress' frequent difficulty in resolving policy by statute, indicate that a general veto provision might encourage Congress to make broader delegations than it would otherwise. If this occurs, the veto will produce a net increase in congressional control of the agencies only to the extent that there actually is close review pursuant to it. Yet under a veto statute broadly applicable to rule making, limits on time and resources would make it impossible for Congress to exercise continuing, close review, even with a massive increase in staff. It therefore seems likely that only a few rules would receive the careful scrutiny necessary to fulfill the assumptions underlying broad original grants of power.

Thus, this proposed technique for increasing congressional controls on delegated powers may actually result in *decreasing* those controls in practice. As *Meat Cutters* emphasized, constraints on the agencies in statutes may be quite diverse, but they should work together, and not against one another, to satisfy the ultimate goals of the delegation doctrine. Offered as a means of implementing the requirements of the delegation doctrine, legislative veto schemes might ultimately be viewed as violating it.

Whatever the requirements of the delegation doctrine, the legislative veto may be ill-suited as an aid to the final resolution of policy for several reasons. First, it is negative in its impact. Unlike legislation, it does not promulgate a new rule, but merely leaves a void. Second, under a one-house veto, irreconcilable disagreement between the houses of Congress may prevent the formulation of any effective policy by the agency. Finally, as experience shows, some controversies between the agencies and Congress are long-standing, leaving a policy vacuum without any strong impetus toward a final resolution. Indeed, the legislative veto may contribute to a vicious circle now present in regulatory policymaking. Congress, beset by conflicting political pressures or uncertain of the best approach to a new problem, makes a broad delegation to an agency without resolving policy. The agency, subject to the same pressures or uncertainties, then proceeds to deal with issues in an ad hoc fashion, emphasizing adjudication, without forming any clear policy. This failure of the agency to resolve the original issues leaves Congress with nothing concrete to consider, thereby disadvantaging it in later attempts to meet the policymaking responsibility it did not discharge in the original delegation. To the extent that the legislative veto encourages Congress to make broad delegations in the first instance with the hope of resolving policy upon executive initiative, there is a danger that it will exacerbate current problems.

C. Effects on Judicial Review

The federal courts have yet to confront the question of how to review an agency's rules when they are subject to a legislative veto. The question is a complex one, involving the relationships between the three branches of government and in some cases the "fourth branch"—the independent regulatory agencies—in all their permutations. To what extent should courts defer to congressional judgments on the legality of a rule, especially if they seem mixed with policy considerations? Although congressional review is often ostensibly based on legality, consideration of policy in a legislative body is inevitable. To what extent should courts intervene if congressional review is explicitly based on policy? These are delicate questions freighted with separation of powers concerns.

It is fundamental that the courts, not Congress, have the ultimate responsibility to interpret the law. To the extent that congressional review of rules duplicates the function of the courts, it does not seem a wise use of congressional time. Moreover, Congress is ill-equipped, both by inclination and competence, to determine its own former intent with the care and restraint customary in judicial review. The members of Congress have less time and no better resources (briefs, memoranda of law) than the federal courts. One might suggest that Congress has better access to "real" legislative history than the courts or the agencies. But the subjective intent of committee members not recorded in publicly available committee hearings or reports and not reflected in floor debates seems better characterized as views on policy than as evidence of the intent of Congress. It is not a part of the formal legislative history that can legitimately be read into the statutory language as having been accepted by Congress as a whole. For this reason, when Congress is unclear initially in forming legislative history, it is unlikely to contribute more than the agencies or the courts in later attempts to reconstruct it. Furthermore, the validity of a legislative purpose that is purportedly part of the law but not reflected in ordinary sources of legislative history diminishes as time passes and a new Congress with new members convenes.

The more appropriate role for congressional review is policy review, because it is a natural part of the legislative process that is not engaged in by the courts. Even policy review, however, may not have the characteristics claimed for it in veto proposals. The level of congressional interest in a rule will depend on its political sensitivity, not the persuasiveness of the agency's justifications for it or even its consistency with other regulatory programs. This means that the process is not necessarily a coherent one. Although the same inattention to coherent and reasoned formulation of policy may be present in the legislative process, it is likely to be more pervasive in the context of oversight. This is true because oversight has had a lower priority in Congress than legislation and Congress has traditionally been weak in its exercise. Yet despite its shortcomings in the context of the legislative veto, policy review is clearly more appropriate than legality review for purposes of congressional oversight.

Hence, if Congress treads on judicial ground by declaring a rule ultra vires in a resolution, it seems appropriate for a court to disagree. That would restore the rule's effectiveness, subject to an authorized veto on policy grounds or to statutory change. On the other hand, if Congress voids a rule on policy grounds, the wisdom of its judgment should ordinarily be beyond judicial review.

Occasionally, the statute governing congressional review requires not only that a veto be for ultra vires action, but that Congress make findings. This latter requirement is not likely to prove enforceable in court. Consider the extent to which the findings should have to be adequate explanations in the typical administrative law sense. For example, the required findings in the veto resolution for HEW's title IX regulation would be considered unacceptably conclusory if they came from an agency. Yet it would be difficult for a court to ask for more detailed explanation without making an extraordinary intrusion on the legislative process. Thus, a court's reluctance to direct Congress to speak coherently in giving reasons for a veto would arise from sensitivities that have led to the demise of the standards requirement of the delegation doctrine. This suggests that when a veto occurs, the comparative persuasiveness of Congress' findings with those of the agency will not be reviewed.

If Congress does not veto an administrative rule, a court can review its legality in the normal way. But what inference is it to make if the rule has received attention but no veto from Congress? Some statutes provide that the failure of Congress to veto a rule shall not be construed as ratification; such provisions must be considered. Certainly rules that receive little or no attention from Congress should not be viewed as ratified by it. However, when a floor vote is held in both houses and the rule survives, it could be argued that Congress has ratified the rule. Nevertheless, if congressional review is based on legality, the courts should retain a duty to determine that question. Even on policy review, Congress' failure to veto a rule does not necessarily mean there has been attention to legality, or that Congress should be viewed as an authority regarding that determination. Thus, judicial review would be appropriate in either case. If the veto process has not reached the stage of producing committee reports or findings by one or both houses of Congress, there is no basis on which a court can identify even an implied judgment by Congress as a whole. In the end, the irony of a ratification doctrine is that it would give legitimacy to precisely those rules raising the greatest congressional displeasure short of veto. This too suggests its inappropriateness.

Congress may impose statutory limits on judicial review of rules subject to veto. For instance, the FEA's legislation contains a provision forbidding judicial invalidation of its rules for arbitrariness or for the absence of sufficient factual foundation. This provision was designed to make the substance of rules a matter for internal resolution between the executive and congress. Broad use of similar provisions limiting judicial review could insulate great numbers of rules from scrutiny by the judiciary without subjecting them to close scrutiny in Congress as a substitute. If increased accountability of administrative rules is the goal of veto provisions, restricting judicial review without ensuring congressional review is a backward step.

Recent developments affording closer judicial review of agency action, in rule making as well as other areas, are fundamentally inconsistent with the likely consequences in practice of a general legislative veto. We argued above that the courts should not regard congressional action short of a veto as the ratification of a rule. Perhaps, therefore, the courts will review rules not vetoed in the usual fashion. But to the extent that the presence of the veto causes the agencies to draft rules to meet political considerations unrelated to public procedures, as occurred frequently in the case studies, review by the courts will be made more difficult. Courts will be less sure that an agency rule is what it purports to be if unknown considerations may be the ground of decision. Courts have not prospered in their searches for motivation underlying official action; situations encouraging or necessitating that search are to be avoided. Perhaps legislative veto procedures could be altered to protect the courts' capacity to review agency rules. Existing procedures, however, do not seem to suffice.

One obvious but important practical effect of the combination of congressional and judicial review is the increased potential for impasse. As a separate branch of government, the courts have a duty to insure that agencies adhere to constitutional and statutory norms and that the actions of Congress remain within constitutional bounds. In the process of fulfilling this duty, the courts may create obstacles to policy accommodation between Congress and the agencies. For example, the Supreme Court's decision in *Buckley* v. *Valeo*, which invalidated the composition of the FEC on constitutional grounds, caused much of the prior accommodation between the FEC and Congress to be wasted. Such obstacles are not created solely by decisive constitutional rejection of the governing statute. As the GSA's response to *Nixon* v. *Administrator of General Services* demonstrates, mere dicta may provoke or exacerbate conflict between the agency and committees charged with the responsibility for congressional review. The possibilities are endless. Repeated remands are common in administrative law; their potential for disruption of emerging political accommodations between an agency and Congress is obvious. Finally, there is the possibility that a court will invalidate the only rules which can survive a congressional veto, creating a deadlock that the agency cannot break. It could be argued that this potential for disruption and wasted effort is the price of government by reasoned judgment. Certainly delay and disruption are common features of the political and judicial processes. Yet at present the interactions between the agencies, Congress, and the courts are primarily two-sided. Congress delegates, the agency executes, and the courts review. Legislative vetoes, by placing Congress and the courts in similar roles, make possible a three-sided interaction, with heightened potential for delay, disruption, and unforeseeable results.

D. Congressional Interference in Rule Making

The congressional procedures required to bring a legislative veto resolution to the floor of either house are cumbersome and time-consuming. It is therefore in the interest of both the agency and its congressional oversight committees to avoid resorting to these procedures by resolving policy issues informally. As the case studies show, informal negotiations with compromise on both sides is characteristic of the review process under a legislative veto provision. These negotiations are a highly efficient review technique in the sense that they resolve policy differences between the agency and the committees relatively quickly, and without destroying the coherence of the resulting rule as an item veto might. Indeed, it is when negotiations fail and the formal machinery is invoked that policy impasse threatens.

Yet however efficient review by negotiation and compromise may be, it has one critical feature: it involves congressional committees and staff deeply in the rulemaking process. In a series of decisions, the federal courts have subjected similar ex parte influences in agency decisionmaking to increasing scrutiny. The principles and reasoning of these decisions do not readily permit an exemption for congressional interference. The case law is still sparse, but developments indicate that judicial scrutiny once reserved for adjudication and informal executive actions may be extended to rule making.

Pillsbury Co. v. *Federal Trade Commission* is the leading case on judicial scrutiny of congressional interference in adjudication. In open hearings, congressmen importuned Commissioners and agency counsel to accept a certain interpretation of an antitrust law. Because the hearings focused on a case pending before the agency, the reviewing court felt that congressional influence was improper: "[W]hen . . . [a congressional] investigation focuses directly and substantially upon the mental decisional process of a Commission in a case which is pending before it, Congress is no longer intervening in the agency's *legislative* function, but rather in its *judicial* function." The court feared that adjudicative proceedings held under overt and heavy congressional pressure might not be impartial.

Until recently, any attempt to extend the reasoning of *Pillsbury* to the quasi-legislative rule-making functions of an agency would have encountered a nearly insuperable barrier. For legislative processes have traditionally been immune from the type of due process scrutiny to which adjudication is subject. Courts and commentators have lately begun to recognize, however, that a strict theoretical dichotomy between legislative and adjudicative functions is untenable. The line between the two categories is indistinct: there are many agency actions which do not fit neatly into either category. And the justifications for disapproval of secret ex parte contacts in the adjudicative context—fairness, openness, reasoned decision making based on a record, and ease and accuracy of judicial review—are now seen to apply in rule-making proceedings as well.

Two decisions by the District of Columbia Circuit well illustrate the imprecision of the strict dichotomy between adjudicative and legislative functions in administrative proceedings. One of these is *D.C. Federation of Civic Associations* v. *Volpe (Three Sisters Bridge)*, which involved informal executive action. A congressman had threatened to block appropriations for Washington's new subway system until the Secretary of Transportation approved the construction of Three Sisters Bridge cross the Potomac River. Because the congressman's pressure had introduced a factor not authorized by statute into the secretary's decision, the reviewing court invalidated his approval. The court noted that, if the secretary's action had been "purely legislative," it might have been allowed to stand despite a finding that "extraneous pressures" had been considered. The action was not purely legislative, however, because Congress had already established the boundaries of the secretary's discretion. Thus, the action "fell between [the] two conceptual extremes" and should have been based only on factors which Congress had intended to make relevant—a principle the court thought "elementary and beyond dispute."

A second case in which strict categorization of administrative actions was disapproved was *Sangamon Valley Television Corp. v. United States*. An order of the Federal Communications Commission changing the allocation of VHF and UHF television channels was set aside because of secret ex parte contacts and minor favors granted commissioners by interested parties. The commission insisted that the order had been based on a rule-making proceeding and that therefore the ex parte contacts should be ignored. The court responded that "whatever the proceeding may be called," if it involves "the resolution of conflicting private claims to a valuable privilege . . . basic fairness requires [that it] be carried on in the open." The court implied that it could scrutinize undisclosed ex parte contacts on constitutional grounds where the interests at stake in a rule-making proceeding resemble those normally dealt with in adjudication.

The trend toward careful scrutiny of influences surrounding nonadjudicative actions that began in *Sangamon* and *Three Sisters Bridge* has been continued and elaborated by the same court in the recent case of *Home Box Office, Inc. v. FCC*. In that case the FCC's rules for pay television were set aside, in part because members of the FCC had been party to repeated off-the-record contacts by both private interests and congressmen. The FCC admitted that ex parte activity was often present in its rule-making proceedings. Although the agency attempted to allocate time for oral argument fairly among competing interests, arguments often continued ex parte, with compromise positions and the "real facts" reserved for the private sessions. The court disapproved these off-the-record sessions on several grounds. First, it noted that if actual positions were not revealed in public comment but only in private discussions, the public procedures required by statute and the agency's own rules would be reduced to a sham. Second, the court observed that a complete administrative record is necessary for a reviewing court to test an agency's decision for arbitrariness or inconsistency with statutory authority. Since such tests are impossible when the agency's record does not contain "relevant information that has been presented to it," the agency is not entitled to the usual presumption that its action is proper. Third, the inability of opposing parties to respond to secret presentations deprives the agency of the benefit of the "adversarial discussion" which is a primary purpose of statutory notice-and-comment procedures. Finally, the court observed that secrecy in communications with the agency is inconsistent with "fundamental notions of fairness implicit in due process and with the ideal of reasoned decision making on the merits which undergirds all of our administrative law." Thus, although a constitutional ground was not necessary for the decision, the court asserted that one was available.

Nowhere in its opinion did the *Home Box Office* court attempt to distinguish between the ex parte contacts made by private interests and those made by congressmen. Even in prescribing ground rules for future presentations to the agency, the court made no exception for members of Congress. It would have been hard pressed to justify such an exception, for its opinion was based on the fact that the substance of unrecorded ex parte contacts is unavailable to both opposing parties and the reviewing court—and this is true regardless of the source of the contacts or the status of the parties making them. Moreover, both *Pillsbury* and *Three Sisters Bridge* make clear that congressmen have no special license to interfere with agency decision making. Thus, both the principles and the reasoning of *Home Box Office* seem to apply to ex parte contacts by members and subunits of Congress whenever those contacts are off the record.

Read together, these cases suggest growing judicial disapproval of informal congressional pressure on an agency during rule making. There is no reason why this disapproval should not extend to off-the-record negotiations between Congress and an agency over the substance of a proposed rule. Since most of the decisions condemning congressional interference rest primarily on statutory grounds, Congress might be able to remove the objections by making congressional displeasure relevant and authorized ground for an agency's decision. Indeed, statutes implementing legislative vetoes could authorize negotiation expressly. This, however, may only succeed in forcing courts to explicitly constitutional grounds in order to disapprove improper influence in the administrative decision-making process. In any case, the statutory basis for disapproval of informal contacts—ease of judicial review, fairness to interested parties, and reasoned decision making based exclusively on a record—is solidly grounded in policy. These policies, relied on by the court in *Home Box Office*, are central to the scheme of administrative law developed over decades. Even if Congress has the constitutional power, it should think twice before undermining them in order to implement a legislative veto.

E. Modifications and an Alternative

Traditional devices for congressional oversight of agency action have not furnished a means for systematic review of agency rule making. The legislative veto is designed to fill that need, and the case studies reveal that it has significant impact on agency rules, at least for programs in which Congress has an active interest. The case studies also reveal, however, serious problems in current practice under the veto procedure, principally in its fairness to interested parties, its consistency with effective judicial review, its furtherance of broad political accountability, and its overall impact on effective policymaking in Congress and the agencies. Despite lingering theoretical doubts that due process applies to rule making, the courts are likely to insist that any negotiations be carried on in the open, and they should do so. Policies central to the function of rule making in administrative law, which we have pointed out above, demand no less. Moreover, it seems a small intrusion on the flexibility and efficiency of negotiations to require them to be in open session and transcribed as part of the rule-making record.

Secrecy, however, is not the only problem with the legislative veto as it is currently used in practice. The congressional review process adds a second stage to rule making, one in which not all interested persons now participate, and in which not all interests receive equal attention. Thus there is a problem of substantive as well as procedural fairness to those affected by a rule, deriving from the narrow political accountability implicit in a committee-dominated review system. Opening the negotiations to public scrutiny and placing them on the record might lead to broader accountability than is present now, by attracting more attention in Congress and increasing pressure on the committees from a wider range of private interests. This alternative, however, would not eliminate the effects of pressure on the committees by those interested groups most affected by a rule and best organized—typically the regulated industries. The capture of agencies by their regulated constituency to the disadvantage of the general public is presently reinforced by pressure on the agen-ies through congressional committees having members sympathetic to that constituency. The informal negotiation process surrounding legislative veto provisions seems likely to exacerbate this problem, even if it is required to be open.

In essence, the problem of equal access to the agency is a political one. It exists under the present system of administration and may inhere in the quasi-legislative nature of administrative rule making. Nevertheless, the special advantages which financial resources or influence give certain private interests are discordant with the basic theme of democratic government—especially if those interests are the very ones to be regulated. One of the fundamental principles of American political democracy is the negation of faction. Congress' broad constituency, encompassing virtually all regional and special interest groups, is expected to average out the demands of the various factions to produce a fair result. To the extent that legislative veto authority allows special interests to achieve their ends by pressuring administrative agencies through congressional committees, such authority works to promote, rather than negate, faction.

Perhaps agency-committee negotiations should be opened not only to public scrutiny but to public participation as well. However, such a change would not remedy unequal financial ability to participate, and the efficiency of present negotiations would be lost as they became multilateral. Ultimately, open negotiaions in which the public participates would tend merely to duplicate notice-and-comment proceedings. In any case, it is unlikely that Congress would assent to such drastic changes in the ground rules of review.

An alternative response to these problems of substantive fairness would be to forbid negotiations between congressional committees and the agencies, while retaining veto authority. To keep a proper distance from the executive resolution of delegated policymaking, Congress could abjure bargaining over the substance of proposed rules, awaiting their arrival in final form. It would then rely on formal veto resolutions to void rules objectionable to either house as a whole. Since negotiations involve the members of Congress rather deeply in the essentially executive function of implementing statutes, such a restriction would have a constitutional underpinning in the separation of powers. Such an arrangement, however, could have serious disadvantages. By eliminating the chief current technique for reaching policy accommodation, it might increase the probability of impasse between agency and Congress. Moreover, it would fail to reduce the veto's present disincentive to affirmative resolution of policy in Congress by legislation. Finally, it would relegate the legislative veto to the cumbersome and inefficient congressional machinery which gave rise to negotiations in the first place.

Since the disadvantages of the legislative veto inhere in its very nature, no combination of ameliorating techniques can eliminate them all. Congress should abandon it as a device for the oversight of agency rule making. There are other means by which Congress can exercise its oversight responsibility effectively without exceeding the proper bounds of its authority. Informal consultation between agency staff and congressional committee members or staff is certainly appropriate to inform Congress of agency action and to initiate a dialogue on policy; the problem is one of limits. Existing procedures allow congressional participation in rule making to occur in a perfectly appropriate fashion. The notice-and-comment period preceeding formulation of a final rule provides an opportunity for any member of Congress, any staff member, or even a committee or a house as a whole to state its views on the legality or wisdom of a proposed agency rule. While such presentations by Congress before an agency may seem anomalous in light of the agency's ostensibly subordinate role, they have occurred in the past, and there is no reason that they ought not to continue. Congressional views can be made part of the rule-making record through the kind of written submission typical of notice-and-comment rule making, or by open congressional testimony at an agency's public hearing.

Perhaps Congress should alter some agency procedures to facilitate this kind of congressional activity. For example, new requirements for more elaborate explanations of rules proposed by the Federal Trade Commission may better alert congressional staff to issues of importance to the members. If Congress makes open submissions within established boundaries of fair procedures for agency rule making neither its expertise nor its political views will be lost. It seems unlikely that an agency would fail to respond in its reasons for a final rule to an explicit and reasoned congressional submission. The courts could then decide whether the agency's resolution of the problem is within existing parameters of agency discretion. This arrangement would have the prime virtue of encouraging policy dialogue between Congress and the agencies consistently with the fundamental responsibilities implicit in a scheme of separate but interdependent powers.

EIGHTEEN
LETTER ON CONSTITUTIONALITY OF LEGISLATIVE VETO

Benjamin Civiletti

Attorney General Benjamin R. Civiletti issued an opinion letter to Secretary of Education Shirley M. Hufstedler June 6, authorizing her to implement four regulations that have been disapproved by Congress under the legislative veto provision §432 of the General Education Provisions Act.

Civiletti's letter concluded that §432 was unconstitutional, and that it was severable from the basic grant of substantive power given to the Education Department in the Education Amendments of 1978.

Full text of the Civiletti letter follows. (Certain footnotes have been omitted.)

Honorable Shirley M. Hufstedler
The Secretary
Department of Education
Washington, D.C.

My Dear Madam Secretary:

I am responding to your request for my opinion regarding the constitutionality of section 431 of the General Education Provisions Act (GEPA), 20 U.S.C. §1232(d). That provision purports to authorize Congress, by concurrent resolutions that are not to be submitted to the president for his approval or veto, to disapprove final regulations promulgated by you for education programs administered by the Department of Education. Acting under this authority, Congress has recently disap-

This letter is a matter of public record. It originally appeared in *Legal Times* II (June 6, 1980), 9–12.

proved regulations concerning four programs of your department. For reasons set forth below, I believe that §431 is unconstitutional and that you are entitled to implement the regulations in question in spite of Congress' disapproval.

Under 20 U.S.C. §1232(d), your department is required, when it promulgates any final regulation for an "applicable program," to transmit that regulation to the Speaker of the House and to the President of the Senate. This section further provides:

"Such final regulation shall become effective not less than forty-five days after such transmission unless the Congress shall, by concurrent resolution, find that the final regulation is inconsistent with the Act from which it derives its authority, and disapprove such final regulation."

In short, the two houses of Congress can, without presidential participation, prevent the executive from executing substantive law previously enacted by the Congress with respect to education programs. Moreover, §1232(d), on its face, purports to delegate to the two houses of Congress the constitutional function historically reserved to the courts to ensure that the execution of the law by the executive is consistent with the statutory bounds established in the legislative process.

In designing a federal government of limited powers, the Framers of the Constitution were careful to assign the powers of government to three separate, but coordinate branches. They vested legislative power in the Congress, the power to execute the laws passed by the Congress in the executive, and the power finally to say what the law is in the judiciary. In ordering these relationships, the Framers were careful, in turn, to limit each branch in the exercise of its powers. The power of Congress to legislate was not left unrestrained, but was made subject to the president's veto. Neither was the president's power to execute the law left absolute, but Congress was empowered to constrain any executive action not committed by the Constitution exclusively to the executive by passing legislation on that subject. Should such legislation be vetoed by the president, Congress could use its ultimate authority to override the president's veto. Both of the political branches were, in turn, to be checked by the courts' power to take jurisdiction to determine the existence of legislative authority for executive actions, and to review the acts of both Congress and the executive for constitutionality. This, in simplest form, is our carefully balanced constitutional system.

The legislative veto mechanism in §1232(d) upsets the careful balance devised by the Framers. Viewed as "legislative" acts, legislative vetoes authorize congressional action that has the effect of legislation but deny to the president the opportunity to exercise his veto power under Art. I, §7 of the Constitution. Viewed as interpretive or executive acts, legislative vetoes give Congress an extra-legislative role in administering substantive statutory programs that impinges on the president's constitutional duty under Art. II, §3, of the Constitution faithfully to execute the laws. Viewed as acts of quasi-judicial interpretation of existing law, legislative vetoes arrogate to the Congress power reserved in our constitutional system for the nonpolitical judicial branch. Thus, however, they may be characterized, legislative vetoes are unconstitutional.

A. THE PRESENTATION CLAUSES

As illustrated by the four recent exercises of legislative veto power under §1232(d), legislative veto devices are functionally equivalent to legislation because they permit Congress, one of its houses, or even, on occasion, one or two of its committees, to block the execution of the law by the executive for any reason, or indeed, for no reason at all. Under §1232(d), the two houses of Congress could, by passing successive concurrent resolutions, bring to a halt substantive programs, the authority for which was enacted by prior Congresses with the participation of the president. Such legislative veto devices cannot stand in the face of the language and history of the Presentation Clauses, Art. I, §7, cls. 2 and 3.

Clause 2 provides that every bill that passes the House and the Senate shall, before it becomes law, be presented to the president for his approval or disapproval. If disapproved, a bill does not become law unless repassed by a two-thirds vote of each house.

At the Philadelphia Convention of 1787, the Framers considered and explicitly provided for the possibility that Congress, by passing "resolutions" rather than bills, might attempt to evade the requirement that proposed legislation be presented to the president. During the debate on Art I, §7, James Madison observed:

"If the negative of the President was confined to *bills*; it would be evaded by acts under the form and name of Resolutions, votes &c—[and he] proposed that "or resolve" should be added after "*bill*" . . . with an exception as to votes of adjournment &c." 2 M. Farrand, *Records of the Federal Convention of 1787* 301 (rev. ed. 1937).

Madison's notes indicate that "after a short and rather confused conversation on this subject," his proposal was at first rejected. However, at the commencement of the following day's session, Mr. Randolph, "having thrown into a new form" Madison's proposal, renewed it. It passed by vote of 9-1. *Id.*, 301-35. Thus, the Constitution today provides, in addition to Clause 2 of §7 dealing with the passage of "bills," an entirely separate clause, Art. I, §7, cl. 3, as follows:

"Every Order, Resolution, or Vote to which the Concurrence of the Senate and House of Representatives may be necessary (except on a question of Adjournment) shall be presented to the President of the United States; and before the Same shall take Effect, shall be approved by him, or being disapproved by him, shall be repassed by two-thirds of the Senate and House of Representatives, according to the Rules and Limitations prescribed in the Case of a Bill."

I believe it is manifest, from the wording of Clause 3 and the history of its inclusion in the Constitution as a separate clause apart from the clause dealing with "bills," that its purpose is to protect against *all* congressional attempts to evade the president's veto power. The function of the Congress in our constitutional system is to enact laws, and all final congressional action of public effect, whether or not it is formally referred to as a bill, resolution, order or vote, must follow the procedures prescribed in Art. I. §7, including presentation to the president for his approval or veto.

B. THE SEPARATION OF POWERS

(1) Executing the Law

The principle of separation of powers underlying the structure of our constitutional form of government generally provides for the separation of powers among the legislative, executive, and judicial Branches, and provides for "checks and balances" to maintain the integrity of each of the three branches' functions. Generally speaking, the separation of powers provides that each of the three branches must restrict itself to its allocated sphere of activity: legislating, executing the law, or interpreting the law with finality. This is not to say that every governmental function is inherently and of its very nature either legislative, executive, or judicial. Some activity might be performed by any of the three branches—and in that situation it is up to Congress to allocate the responsibility. *See*, for example, *Wayman* v. *Southard*, 10 Wheat. 1, 42-43, 46 (1825) (Chief Justice Marshall). Once Congress, by passing a law, has performed that function of allocating responsibility, however, the separation of powers requires that Congress cannot control the discharge of those functions assigned to the executive or the judiciary, except through the plenary legislative process of amendment and repeal.

The underlying reason, well stated by James Madison, is that otherwise the concentration of executive and legislative power in the hands of one branch might "justly be pronounced the very definition of tyranny." *The Federalist*, No. 47, at 324 (Cooke ed. 1961). The shifting of executive power to the legislative branch which would be occasioned by these legislative veto devices is, I believe, undeniable; the concentration of this blended power is precisely what the Framers feared and what they set about to prevent.

The Constitution's overall allocations of power may not be altered under the guise of an assertion by the Congress of its power to pass laws that are "necessary and proper for carrying into Execution . . . Powers vested by [the] Constitution in the Government of the United States, or in any Department or Officer thereof," Art. I, §8, cl. 18. As the Supreme Court made clear in *Buckley* v. *Valeo*, 424 U.S. 1 (1976), the exercise of power by Congress pursuant to the Necessary and Proper Clause is limited both by other express provisions of the Constitution and by the principles of separation of powers.

In *Buckley*, it was argued that officers of the Congress could, under the Necessary and Proper Clause, appoint commissioners of the Federal Election Commission, notwithstanding the fact that Art. II, §2, cl. 2 of the Constitution placed the appointment power in the president. With regard to the relationship between the exercise of power under the Necessary and Proper Clause and other provisions of the Constitution, the Court stated the rule as follows:

"Congress could not, merely because it concluded that such a measure was 'necessary and proper' to the discharge of its substantive legislative authority, pass a bill of attainder or *ex post facto* law contrary to the prohibitions contained in section 9 of Art. I. No more may it vest in itself, or in its officers, the authority to appoint officers of the United States when the Appointments Clause by clear implication prohibits it from doing so." 424 U.S. at 135.

The Constitution establishes the president's veto power as clearly as it establishes the appointment power or prohibits bills of attainder and ex post facto laws. Under *Buckley*, the only reasonable implication of the Framers' inclusion of Art. I, §7, cl. 3, in the Constitution is that the Necessary and Proper Clause is not a source of power for evasion of these specific limitations through the enactment of legislative veto devices. I would add that, in reaching its holding in *Buckley*, the Court considered and relied upon earlier cases that seem most relevant to the constitutionality of legislative veto devices. In quoting from *Myers* v. *United States*, 272 U.S. 52 (1926), the Court recognized the relationship between the grant of executive power to the president and the issue before it. 424 U.S. at 135-136. I believe that *Buckley* and the cases relied on by the *Buckley* Court foreclose arguments that the Necessary and Proper Clause grants Congress the power to provide for legislative veto devices.

Because to characterize the power exercised by the two houses under §1232(d) as "legislation" would necessarily require Congress to respect the president's veto power by presenting its resolutions for his approval, it is necessary for proponents of such power to deny that the power is "legislation" in the constitutional sense. They argue instead that the device is a means for Congress to oversee the execution of the law by the executive, in aid of its undoubted constitutional powers to pass legislation and appropriations. Such an argument, however, cannot withstand scrutiny. Without a legislative veto, the regulations of your department, unless invalidated by a court, would have the force of law. In depriving them of that force, the necessary effect of a legislative veto is to block further execution of a statutory program until the executive promulgates further regulations in compliance with the current views of a Congress that may well be different from the Congress that enacted the substantive law. The difference between this kind of congressional "oversight" and the legitimate oversight powers of Congress in their effect on the constitutional allocation of powers could not be more profound. By its nature, for example, the exercise of a legislative veto would be beyond judicial review because the exercise of such powers could be held to no enforceable standards. In exercising its veto, I believe it clear that Congress is dictating its interpretation of the permissible bounds for execution of an existing law; a result that can be accomplished only by legislation.

The foregoing discussion demonstrates the flaw in the argument, occasionally made, that the doctrine of separation of powers protects the executive branch only in areas that are inherently executive, and that Congress may reserve to itself control over activities entrusted to the executive which are not "truly" executive in nature. This reasoning overlooks the basic truth that there are few activities that are clearly executive, legislative, or judicial. The first two categories, in particular, overlap to an enormous extent. Much, if not indeed most, executive action can be the subject of legislative prescription. To contend, therefore, that Congress can control the executive whenever the executive is performing a function that Congress might have undertaken itself is to reduce the doctrine of separation of powers to a mere shadow.

The test is not whether an activity is inherently legislative or executive but whether the activity has been committed to the executive by the Constitution and applicable statutes. In other words, the Constitution provides for a broad sweep of possible congressional action; but once a function has been delegated to the executive branch, it must be performed there, and cannot be subjected to continuing congressional control except through the constitutional process of enacting new legislation.

2. Interpreting the Law

Section 1232(d) authorizes disapproval of a regulation by concurrent resolution if Congress "find[s] that the final regulation is inconsistent with the Act from which it derives its authority. . . ." That section, on its face, purports to vest in the two houses of Congress an extralegislative power to perform the function reserved by the Constitution to the courts of determining whether a particular executive act is within the limits of authority established by an existing statute. It is clear that the president constitutionally can be overruled in his interpretation of the law, by the courts and by Congress. But the Congress can do so only by passing new legislation, and passing it over the president's veto if necessary. That is the constitutional system.

Proponents of the legislative veto, however, argue that such devices actually fortify the separation of powers by providing Congress with a check on an agency's exercise of delegated power. No doubt congressional review provides a check on agency action, just as committee review or committee chairman review would provide a check. But such review involves the imposition on the executive of a particular interpretation of the law—the interpretation of the Congress, or one house, or one committee, or one chairman—without the check of the legislative process which case Congress is either usurping the power of the president to execute the law, or of the courts to construe it; or Congress is legislating. If it is legislating, the Constitution is explicit that the president must have the opportunity to participate in that process by vetoing the legislation.

Because it is my opinion that §1232(d) is unconstitutional, it is necessary for me to consider whether that provision is severable from the underlying grants of statutory authority upon which the regulations promulgated by you were based. Section 1232(d) was enacted in 1974. When the various authorities for the four regulations disapproved by Congress were enacted in the Education Amendments of 1978, Congress gave no indication that the substantive rule-making powers delegated to you were to be extinguished if the legislative veto device in §431 were to be found unconstitutional. Thus, I conclude that §431 is severable from this basic grant of substantive power. *See*, for example, *Champlin Refining Co.* v. *Corporation Commission of Oklahoma*, 286 U.S. 210, 234 (1932), quoted with approval in *Buckley* v. *Valeo, supra*, 424 U.S. at 108.

Within their respective spheres of action the three branches of government can and do exercise judgment with respect to constitutional questions, and the judicial branch is ordinarily in a position to protect both the government and the citizenry from unconstitutional action, legislative or executive; but only the executive branch can execute the statutes of the United States. For that reason alone, the Attorney General must scrutinize with caution any claim that he or any other executive officer may decline to defend or enforce a statute whose constitutionality is merely in doubt. Any claim by the executive to a power of nullification, even a qualified power, can jeopardize the equilibrium established by our constitutional system.

At the same time, the executive's duty faithfully to execute the law embraces a duty to enforce the fundamental law set forth in the Constitution as well as a duty to enforce the law founded in the acts of Congress, and cases arise in which the duty to the one precludes the duty to the other. In rendering this opinion on the constitutionality of §431, I have determined that the present case is such a case.

Section 431 intrudes upon the constitutional prerogatives of the executive. To regard these concurrent resolutions as legally binding would impair the executive's constitutional role.

More important, I believe that your recognition of these concurrent resolutions as legally binding would constitute an abdication of the responsibility of the executive branch, as an equal and coordinate branch of government with the legislative branch, to preserve the integrity of its functions against constitutional encroachment. I, therefore, conclude that you are authorized to implement these regulations.

CHAPTER FIVE
EXECUTIVE CONTROL OF THE FEDERAL BUREAUCRACY

INTRODUCTION

For the president who comes into the White House there is the basic ambivalency about the federal bureaucracy: it is "the hated enemy yet it is a potential source of power and influence."[1] As governmental operations have grown more complex, the need for managerial leadership increases. The president, as head of the federal executive agencies, *must* manage this vast leviathan. While presidents come into the White House with all kinds of plans for managing the federal bureaucracy, typically after some time in office the incumbent complains about the difficulty encountered in the effort: "I underestimated the inertia or the momentum of the federal bureaucracy," stated President Jimmy Carter in 1977. "It is difficult to change," he concluded.[2]

Carter did attempt to gain control over the federal bureaucracy through a series of regulatory reform measures (recall the Fritschler essay in chapter 1). Recent presidential initiatives to centralize management control of the federal agencies began, however, with the Nixon administration efforts in 1971. Frustrated by his inability to achieve basic policy goals through working with a Democratic Congress, Nixon was urged to move to a managerial strategy to achieve his programmatic objectives.

A basic assumption made by his staff was that there were sufficient management tools available to the president and his top managers in the White House for this important

[1]Malek Manual, White House Personnel Office, in Frank J. Thompson, *Classics in Public Personnel Management* (Chicago: Moore, 1979), pp. 84–85.
[2]Ronald Randall, "Presidential Power vs. Bureaucratic Intransigence," *American Political Science Review*, 75, no. 3 (September 1979), 795.

203

task. "When used adroitly," these tools would enable Nixon to dominate the federal bureaucracy—"free from the glare of publicity, congressional control, and the awareness of the public."[3] To achieve this domination of the key policymakers in the federal regulatory agencies, thereby enabling the president to effect social changes deemed desirable by the White House, ultimately means to control and to manipulate the federal bureaucrats. If the president can master the bureaucracy, if he can control it, then he effectively controls governmental operations. Fred Malek, one of Nixon's advisers, indicated to the president:

> You cannot achieve management, policy, or program control unless you have established political control. The record is replete with instances of the failure of program, policy, and management goals because of sabotage by employees of the executive branch . . . because of their political persuasion and their loyalty to others rather than the executive that supervises them.[4]

The tools available to the president are various powers such as: appointment and removal of executive personnel ("When a bureaucrat thumbs his nose, we're going to get him. . . . Demote him or send him to the Guam regional office. There's a way. Get him the hell out," exclaimed Nixon[5]); Office of Management and Budget (OMB) controls including preparation of regulatory budgets, program evaluations, program performance data, enforcement of various statutes[6] that have the effect of OMB control of agency activity, control of federal spending; reorganization of the federal executive branch to enhance the possibility of greater control.

The essays in this chapter focus on various efforts to use the powers of the White House to effect greater control over the federal executive agencies by the president and his staff. Dwight Ink's article suggests how a president, who must control the federal agencies, can go about the task of providing effective management. The Ball article is an examination of how President Reagan and his White House staff went about the multifaceted task of trying to control the federal regulatory agencies.

---

[3]Ibid., p. 808.
[4]Malek Manual, p. 87.
[5]Joel D. Aberbach and Bert A. Rockman, "Clashing Beliefs Within the Executive Branch," *American Political Science Review*, 70, no. 2 (June 1976), 457.
[6]Paperwork Reduction Act and the Regulatory Flexibility Act, 1980.

NINETEEN
THE PRESIDENT AS MANAGER

Dwight A. Ink

Despite the enormous difficulties in the effective management of government, it would seem clear that the present deteriorating state of many government operations, the disenchantment of the citizen with government, and the importance of meeting national needs all require urgently that government begin to be truly managed. Government operations have drifted too long. But where does the president fit in this formidable undertaking?

Much has been written about the many demanding and conflicting roles of the president which make this job an almost impossible task in modern time. In view of these ever-increasing pressures, it is timely, as we celebrate our bicentennial landmark in history, to look at the president's role as manager of the executive branch and consider whether this role has a future.

BACKGROUND

The Constitution does not include such terms as *public administration*, *manager*, *management systems*, or many of the other phrases that compose the basic jargon of our profession.

Although some aspects of administration can be traced back to the beginning of recorded history, it is important to remember that many of our present concepts

Reprinted with permission from *Public Administration Review* (September/October 1976), 508–515. © 1976 by The American Society for Public Administration, 1225 Connecticut Avenue, N.W., Washington, D.C. All rights reserved.

of administration were so little developed after the Revolution that during the proceedings of the Constitutional Convention, fiscally conscious Madison moved to strike "annually" from a proposal to require an account of public expenditures on the basis that it was too stringent (although unbelievably lax by today's standards). He pointed out that the existing semi-annual requirement of the Articles of Confederation often had been found impossible and the practice had ceased altogether. "Require too much and the difficulty will beget a habit of doing nothing," admonished Hamilton as he argued instead for the more flexible wording "shall be published from time to time."[1]

The absence of words which contemplated today's managerial needs should not be interpreted as meaning the founders intended that the president not manage. In fact, one could argue that if this role were not envisaged in some significant fashion, there would have been less attention focused in the convention on checks and balances.

More important, the Constitution states unequivocally that "the executive power shall be vested in a president . . . " who is to "take care that the laws be faithfully executed. . . . " Together with several other references, it seems clear that the Constitution, particularly as the Supreme Court has since developed it into a flexible living document, provides far more legal foundation for the president's role as manager than other competing roles of party head (unforeseen by the convention) or ceremonial leader. Yet these two roles, plus others essential to the nation such as domestic and foreign policy development, leave little time for professional management within the usual context of public administration.

Probably not many voters consciously think of the managerial ability of a candidate when they vote. Congress and the press give presidents very few Brownie points on presidential performance as good managers (though exceedingly alert to credit them with managerial failure). Conventional wisdom states that presidents simply are not elected by records of good management.

Wearing our taxpayer hats, however, we become very indignant about the size of a government which spends hundreds of billions each year, the amount of waste we believe exists, the profusion of governmental activities, and the agonizing red tape we encounter as citizens in seeking governmental actions and explanations. We tell pollsters that government bureaucrats rate very low in our esteem.

It is not surprising that the public perceives government as ineffective. Much of it is. One of the ironies of government is the tremendous amount of dedicated labor that government employees put into their assigned tasks, often with little useful product visible from the standpoint of the public. More than anyone, the president is looked to for solving the "mess in Washington," but we are hesitant to help increase his ability to manage the "mess"; a reluctance fortified by Watergate.

True, efforts have been made since the Brownlow Report and the first Hoover Commission to assist the president in his managerial task. The establishment of the Executive Office of the President, especially the inclusion of the Bureau of the Budget (now the Office of Management and Budget) was particularly important. Unfortunately, the relentless power of the annual budget process and the preoccupation with major policy issues have overshadowed and frequently distorted the managerial efforts of BOB and OMB during most of their history.

Most of us would concede that as the federal government grows more complex, the need for managerial leadership from the very top increases. At the same

---

[1] Debates in the Federal Convention of 1787 as reported by James Madison, *Documents Illustrative of the Formation of the Union of the American States* (Washington, D.C.: U.S. Government Printing Office, 1927), p. 727.

time, modern presidents have discovered that they are less and less able to find time to provide that leadership. There are many who believe it is totally naive to expect a president to manage the executive branch under modern circumstances. Yet they seldom proceed to answer the obvious follow-on question: If not the president, who?

GOVERNMENTAL COMPLEXITY LIMITS THE OPTIONS

There are many dimensions to the complex machinery of our government which have a bearing on whether anyone short of the president can cause the government to be managed so that it can establish meaningful goals and respond to the needs of people quickly and effectively. First, ours is a federal system in which the national government establishes much of the policy on how to attack basic national problems, but in which state and local governments play the principal role in executing most of these policies on the domestic front.

Second, within the national government we find increasing blurring among the three branches concerning the power to make management decisions. For a few examples of how deeply Congress has become involved in management, consider the ability of appropriations subcommittees to determine how a department head organizes his or her immediate office, the ability of these same subcommittees to decide that an effort to improve auditing is unwarranted, or congressional blocking of decentralization of a function within an agency.

Similar illustrations can be given regarding the courts. Based both on recent legislation and the courts' willingness to concern themselves more and more with administrative actions, litigation against federal agencies has skyrocketed. Apart from the merit of individual cases, litigation often exerts a heavy impact on agency management through extended delays, higher costs, and hesitancy to take action.

Third, programs spill badly across agency jurisdictions. Individual river basins tend to be divided somewhat vaguely among the departments of Defense, Agriculture, and Interior, with overlapping and conflicting objectives concerning project justification, sale of water, and sale of energy generated by federal dams. Energy policy is hopelessly fragmented, despite the existence of a Federal Energy Administration and a Federal Energy Council. No single agency head can be held accountable for the national manpower, education, and welfare programs. And think for a moment about the many agencies that play major roles in foreign policy.

Both the overlapping and interdependence of department responsibilities have given rise to hundreds of ineffective interagency coordinating committees and repeated efforts at bilateral agency treaties to minimize the cost and confusion of structural disarray. There is no true accountability in these areas short of the president.

Fourth, a highly dynamic society and a volatile world edging closer to the statistical probability of nuclear war require governmental machinery that can act decisively in time of crisis. The importance of the presidential managerial role in this type of decision making is obvious. Equally clear is the president's managerial role in ensuring that the different agencies gear up adequately, and on an orchestrated basis, for crises we can see approaching.

These points illustrate why well-intentioned but scattered and sporadic efforts among both career and noncareer agency people to make governmental machinery work are so inadequate and generally invisible to the public. The federal government is far too complex to be affected significantly by bandaids applied here and there on a piecemeal basis.

THE PRESIDENT MUST MANAGE

Although management in government is quite obviously a basic responsibility of agency heads and thousands of bureau heads, division directors, and supervisors of smaller units, our government is too complex, the political environment too hostile, and the problems too serious for the federal government to become effective without strong managerial impetus from the president of a type which has credibility within the bureaucracy. Without presidential managerial leadership, the huge and unwieldy executive branch will not be managed.

Even if one were to agree totally with the above assertions that the government urgently needs management, and that the president must among other things be a manager (not one to merely gesture in the general direction of management, but to be an individual who will take on the toughest managerial assignment in the world), is this possible? Management has continuously been overwhelmed by other presidential tasks. Given the best of intentions by a president, where is the time? Can he secure the cooperation of the supposedly uncontrollable bureaucracy?

Despite the unfavorable odds, there are means available to a determined president through which he can fulfill this managerial role, provided he is able to fashion a workable rapport with Congress at the outset.

HOW CAN A PRESIDENT MANAGE?

Our governmental machinery has far too many problems to be solved with a single approach such as reorganization of structure, budget reform, management by objectives, merit system reform, or productivity enhancement. All of these and more are needed. A sustained multipronged attack is essential.

In the hope of stimulating support for the notion that the beginning of our third century represents a good time to advance from rhetoric to action about building an effective government which can respond to the needs of people, the following propositions are advanced in support of the rapid development of a meaningful presidential managerial role.

1. Enlist Cooperation of the Bureaucracy

As many have pointed out, it is very easy for presidents to view themselves as besieged by opposition from all sides, and, in particular, thwarted by a massive bureaucracy actively undermining presidential initiatives. The federal bureaucracy is described frequently as uncontrollable. Its loyalty to the presidency is doubted. Since many careerists have strong ties to Congress and clientele groups, and because there is strong criticism triggered by almost every presidential move, this suspicious perception of the bureaucracy is understandable. However, this perception is wrong and should be changed. The consensus of those who have been in the career service or who have worked extensively with careerists is overwhelmingly at odds with the "can't trust the bureaucrat" myth.

By coming into office proclaiming the need to replace large numbers of employees who are said to owe their loyalty to prior administrations, the incoming president quickly alienates the career service and destroys a normally strong professional incentive to service a new president and his cabinet in facing their new challenges.

One of the best investments the political leadership of a new administration can make is to explain to the career employees the objectives of the new administration, its philosophy, and specifically what it will be asking of the bureaucracy in meeting the challenges as perceived by the new president. Further, the careerists should be recognized as essential participants in these important events and asked to draw upon their knowledge and experience in suggesting ways in which to meet these new challenges.

Hopefully, we have learned by now that although government can usefully adapt a number of business practices to improve the public service, there are fundamental differences between government and business in such key areas as public accountability, relations with Congress, and equity in personnel and contract actions. Political leadership must look to the career ranks, not new recruits from business, for advice on these issues.

As in the case of any large organization, the career service has many different types of men and women, including some who fail to provide the type of professional service to which a president is entitled. There are always those who seem to spend more time complaining than suggesting, and others too preoccupied with an endless series of grievances to produce. And every administration has had to contend with a few careerists who, from a variety of motivations, have worked actively to neutralize or sabotage presidential initiatives. This article proceeds on the assumption that these individuals represent a small minority, and that the large majority take pride in their role of carrying out those presidential objectives in which their agency is involved, provided they understand what these objectives are and what is expected of them in the attainment of these objectives.

Without this information, the top-level bureaucrat finds himself in an impossible position. If he delays actions to wait for the guidance that never comes, he is regarded as the typical lazy bureaucrat without initiative or drive. If he elects to act on the basis of the limited information available to him, such as that which he reads in press releases and general policy statements, he risks missing the mark and his unintended deviations from the plans of the political leadership are regarded as deliberate undermining of the new administration by a disloyal holdover bureaucrat.

A president cannot succeed without the work of our federal employees. Their support and their enthusiasm are essential to effective government. To achieve this support, a president should apply some basic managerial principles of job motivation, rather than the customary negative rhetoric of how to control a supposedly recalcitrant bureaucracy. He sets the tone for the attitude of the White House staff, the cabinet, and the new political leaders who will be working with the bureaucracy. That tone will quickly affect the way in which the bureaucracy responds to the president.

2. Distinguish Between the Bureaucrat and the Bureaucracy

It is difficult for outside critics to distinguish between the "bureaucrat" who typically tries hard to be responsive, and the vast complicated bureaucratic system of which he or she is only a tiny part. We are so engulfed in process, multiple reviews, and demands to explain past actions, as well as in constant changes in program objectives and leadership, that the individual employee is rarely in a position to more than nibble at the bureaucratic ills with which most large organizations are beset.

The careerist is much more the victim than the cause of bureaucratic failure. As a result, broadsides against those in public service tend to obscure the causes of failure and help perpetuate the problems. Both the citizen and the careerist stand to gain from stronger presidential leadership in reforming our unwieldy bureaucratic processes.

Reform cannot result from simply issuing an edict, however. It can result only from accurate fact gathering, careful analysis, development of a comprehensive plan of action, and the development of necessary support from both inside and outside government. In short, it has to be managed under vigorous and sustained direction.

The natural inertia of a large organization, combined with the external forces arrayed against most reform, are factors in addition to those mentioned earlier which require that the initial impetus come from the president.

3. Rapport with Congress

A strong presidential move to manage the executive branch will send out waves of alarm to hundreds of special interest groups, who in turn will move at once to sensitize each of their supporters in Congress to the threat the "dictatorial" presidential plans pose to the favorite programs of that particular congressman. The interest group lobbyist will also then arrange for a reporter to phone the congressman for his reaction. If the congressman has not been first consulted or at least briefed by the executive branch, he will resent having been caught by surprise. He is likely to be genuinely alarmed by the slanted lobbyist report, and will probably be more than willing to signal his displeasure to the administration publicly through the reporter. No amount of reasoning, data presentation, or persuasion is likely to secure that congressman's support or acquiescence after his initial public statement of opposition.

Congressional-executive branch relationships tend to be unnecessarily difficult. Some of the reasons are apparent. Respective leadership from different political parties, rapid turnover of executive branch leadership (by the time an assistant secretary learns almost enough to testify intelligently about his program, he is gone and the committee chairman is again confronted with the all too familiar newcomer who is unable to explain his programs), the fiscal irresponsibility of Congress passing expenditure ceilings lower than the congressionally approved appropriation bills, and the countering abuse of the presidential impoundment power all illustrate a surprising degree of insensitivity of both branches. Watergate further strained relations.

Possibly most significant of all, however, is the paranoid attitude of so many among a typical White House staff against advance consultation with Congress. Last-minute briefings just before the press conference are tolerated, but certainly not substantive consultation which might delay or compromise the president's goals. Yet the right kind of consultation strengthens, rather than weakens, a president. It increases his chances for achieving his principal goals, thereby enhancing his image as a national leader.

In handling reorganization proposals for one president, for example, the author was given successively more severe White House constraints in working with Congress—such as shorter periods for advance congressional consultation—to the point that meaningful dialogue virtually disappeared. Although each of the plans succeeded, the concept of executive-legislative partnership deteriorated to the point that I declined to be further involved. The president's reorganization authority was not renewed because of this White House arrogance, thus blocking further reorganization.

To help strengthen his ties with Congress, after the November election the president should:

- Be prepared to discuss with the House and Senate majority and minority leadership his major management and reorganization goals in relation to the problems they are designed to meet. The flow of programs across agency jurisdiction simply has to be reduced if government is to be made fully manageable, an admittedly very difficult task which runs counter to the established turf of agencies, congressional committees, and scores of powerful special interest groups. The National Academy of Public Administration's proposed Bicentennial Commission on American Government is a good starting point for longer-range change.

- With help from OMB, consult with other congressional leaders—especially the chairpersons and ranking minority members of the Senate and House Government Operations Committee—on how best to meet these goals.
- Propose a newly designed bill authorizing presidential reorganization authority (short of establishing and abolishing departments which should continue to require legislation) that incorporates several of the suggestions for change made in 1971 by Chairman Jack Brooks of the House Government Operations Committee, particularly a requirement for advance consultation and an authorization for the president to modify a reorganization plan with the agreement of the appropriate committees.
- Recognize that despite the parochial views of most special interest groups, no matter how selfish they may appear to one looking at the national interest as a whole, they deserve an explanation of actions which will affect their future. A direct explanation, in contrast to indirect and distorted rumors, generally lessens the intensity of their opposition and may even elicit their support. Whether or not the executive branch talks to these groups, members of Congress will certainly hear their views. Again, early contact is important.

4. White House Staff Role is Critical

The rape of the agencies by the Nixon White House staff should sensitize the next few presidents to the folly of looking to a White House staff as a substitute for agency head leadership and accountability.

Presidential aides rightfully complain that not many agencies fully meet their responsibilities to the president. Their response tends to be either slow or superficial or both. They are turf conscious. They are slow to alert the White House to emerging problems that may affect the president. Generally, they are not well managed, and sometimes are too timid in taking on special interest groups.

Agencies rightfully complain that too often their actions are reported to the president through a White House staff filter which magnifies the positive role of the White House staff and belittles or even falsifies the work of the agency head and the bureaucracy. Further, White House staff dictation of personnel appointments and other interventions in internal agency operations can severely handicap agency heads in meeting presidential goals and legislative requirements.

The president needs to impress upon those in the Executive Office of the President that one of their roles is that of helping to strengthen agency performance, and that they are not to use agency failures as an excuse for attempting to substitute for the agencies in running government.

The "passion for anonymity" befits a White House staff, since it should leave policy pronouncements to the president and agency heads. Such arrangements as the National Security Council and the Domestic Council, each headed by the president with cabinet-level membership, when properly operated can provide useful vehicles for developing policy which spills over agency jurisdictions (a problem which needs to be greatly alleviated, but which cannot be eliminated). Under no circumstances should the staffs of these groups (with very limited public or congressional accountability) be permitted to usurp the policy role of those they serve. To do so obscures accountability and undermines the only entities with the legal authority, expertise, and resources to meet presidential goals—the agencies.

A White House staff can make or break the capacity of departments to manage, and the answer depends primarily on what role a president decides that staff should play.

5. Revitalize the President's Managerial Arms

High priority should be given to the lack of managerial leadership in OMB. Although this article argues for presidential managerial impetus, and stresses the fundamental importance of agency managerial responsibility, the size and complexity of government makes mandatory a presidential staff leadership mechanism which can spend the necessary time in encouraging, assisting and pressing agencies to manage in the manner expected by the president. Although the author strongly supported the OMB objective of giving greater emphasis to management than had been true during much of BOB's history, he also agrees with the critics who maintained the opposite has occurred.

The number of management people in OMB is much greater than existed in BOB, but the pressures of the budget process have again dominated the agency and it has very little managerial credibility. The sporadic managerial leadership BOB managed to exert only in the 1940s and again in the early 1970s (reorganization initiative did last through the years until 1973) suggests strongly that the "M" in OMB must be given an entirely different status within OMB or placed elsewhere in the Executive Office of the President. Otherwise, the president will have no means to translate his management objectives into a governmentwide program of reform.

The General Services Administration should be recognized as a management-oriented agency and utilized as such. Its top staff, including the administrator and deputy, should be selected primarily on the basis of experience and professional qualifications, as Congress originally intended. Often regarded by White House staff as a political dumping ground, GSA's usefulness has been scarcely tapped, although glimpses of its true potential have been evident in recent strong GSA leadership in energy conservation, building design, and crisis management.

OMB and GSA, as well as the Civil Service Commission, must be fully responsive to legal and ethical presidential requirements. However, widespread impressions of political inroads on the professional performance of these agencies have seriously weakened their leadership effectiveness within the executive branch; leadership which is essential to the carrying out of presidential objectives.

6. Agency Management a Presidential Requirement

High priority also should be given to the importance of management in the selection of department and agency heads and their deputies. As soon as most presidential appointments are made at the outset of a term, the president should meet with all of them to outline his goals, and management should be one of the prime items on this agenda and one of the important criteria on which their performance will be judged.

Management is an essential link between presidential goals and their achievement. Too often it is the missing link. The broad term *management* is rather meaningless, however, unless fundamental presidential principles are stated and quickly supplemented with more specific guidelines from OMB and, where appropriate, CSC and GSA. This information must also be forwarded without delay to the field, both through agency channels and by OMB to the Federal Executive Boards and Federal Regional Councils (which need to be strengthened and reconciled organizationally).

Agencies should be required, for example, to modernize accounting systems (most can't even determine overhead), improve procurement (many procurement officers have had no procurement training), develop means of checking program effectiveness (which most agencies are unable to do), and streamline program processes (which are frequently unbelievable in their complexity, to the despair of the local officials or citizens caught up in the maze of federal red tape). Planning and management by objectives, by whatever label, need to be made practical management processes rather than paper-consuming gimmicks.

Agencies also need to go back to some of the fundamentals of management, just as Vince Lombardi went back to the blocking and tackling fundamentals of football to produce his championship teams. Admiral Rickover and others have demonstrated that this approach can produce impressive results. Too often we build highly sophisticated and expensive systems superstructures on a sandy foundation of diffused decision making, archaic (and too often political) personnel selection, rapid turnover of leadership, lack of cost data, and many other violations of basic managerial principles.

Congress and the courts would also do well to listen more carefully to presidential warnings about the suffocating red tape their actions often unintentionally set in motion.

There needs to be a broad attack on agency shortcomings in a way that is perceived by employees as a new type of effort with the focus on reform rather than refinement. Hence, the critical need for early planning which will permit the laying of extensive groundwork with Congress, interest groups, and the bureaucracy as discussed above. Careful thought must also be given to providing the news media with both the philosophical goals and the factual data they need. To secure the support needed for success, wherever possible the problems of our bureaucratic systems have to be graphically portrayed in visual ways which strike home with Congress and the news media. Congress and the public need to see how a proposed reform will help the citizen.

Finally, agencies need to be given credit for good performance. The press will almost never do this, but the OMB and White House staff can arrange presidential recognition.

7. Intergovernmental Considerations Essential

It is essential to recognize that the federal system cannot serve a dynamic society unless the federal, state, and local governments mesh their efforts. It is important to realize that citizens bear the brunt of the total accumulation of overhead and delays which occur at all three levels. They are the victims of all the friction, slippages, and confusion in responsibilities among the levels of government, the totality of which no government official sees.

Ours is a federal system of government, and state and local governments should be regarded as partners in the task of governing the nation, not simply as another crowd of grasping special interest groups. Domestic program planning, execution, and evaluation should be required to include the intergovernmental dimensions.

Three particularly important areas for attention are:

Possible ways in which the federal government can provide nonprescriptive incentives to states to improve their government and to modernize state laws and programs relating to local government,

The role the federal government should or should not play in shaping the role of metropolitan councils of governments (COGs) and other forms of substate and multistate regionalism.

The best way to involve state and local governments in domestic policy formulation and review.

8. Personnel Management

A particularly critical step is the need for a thorough review of the federal merit system. We now have the worst of both worlds—an extremely complex and cumbersome personnel system which has been wracked by abuses the complex systems were designed to prevent. The National Civil Service League and the National Academy of Public Administration should be given support in moving ahead with this important review, which they have been urging for over two years. But there are some steps which cannot await this review.

The next president should make clear well before he takes office that his responsibility to the voters to select highly qualified men and women far outweighs political loyalties and debts. This is essential for setting the proper tone of ethics and professionalism in the next administration. It is also compatible with the political needs of a president. The people of the Midwest are going to be much more impressed with an administration that puts regional administrators in Chicago who have the professional skills to produce visible program results, than with an administration that staffs those regions with political proteges of important Midwest politicians, to whom they owe their primary loyalty (rather than to the president), and who lack the capacity for assuming heavy responsibilities.

Further, it is very important that federal field personnel be perceived by state and local officials and by individual citizens as administering the laws impartially rather than administering them on a political basis. The denial of a grant to a qualified city because the mayor is from the opposite political party, for example, constitutes mass discrimination against all the citizens of that city who would otherwise benefit from the grant.

Since the president holds department heads responsible for the operation of those departments, the White House should permit department heads to select their own noncareer staff, though in consultation with the White House to ensure that these people will support the president's goals. These appointments are a battleground in which both the president and the department head often lose. In judging people, however, the White House staff should not confuse the need for strong independent views within the administration on how best to obtain presidential goals with disloyalty to the president.

9. Limit Drawdown on Presidential Time

No matter how dedicated to the necessity for providing presidential leadership in the improvement of government, a president can nonetheless devote only limited sustained time to this important responsibility. Yet the bureaucracy and others must be persuaded that the president's interest is enduring, rather than merely a typical one-year special drive to be replaced the following year with another highly publicized initiative.

During Lyndon Johnson's presidency, much of Alaska was devastated by an earthquake which wiped out water and sewer systems, knocked out highways and railroads, destroyed thousands of homes and businesses, and rendered essential harbors useless. The economy was in shambles and the short construction season required a combined effort by most federal agencies on a timetable unprecedented in the nation's peacetime history. As executive director of this crash rebuilding, the author knew the depth of the personal concern of the president. I was also dismayed at how quickly the initial nationwide sympathy for the plight of the Alaskans faded as newer problems emerged. Drawing very little on the president's time, Lee White in the White House, Harold Seidman in OMB, and Senator Clinton Anderson nonetheless were able to find many ways in which the continuing strong interest of the president was made known in a convincing fashion to both the bureaucracy and the Alaskans.

In contrast, President Nixon's strong commitment to reorganization was undercut seriously by a White House staff which saw the whole effort as a political liability. This well-known staff attitude, combined with the decline of the stature and effectiveness of the Department of Housing and Urban Development, probably cost the president the proposed Department of Community Development, which had begun to attract considerable bipartisan support.

If a president can convince the White House staff, OMB, and cabinet members that he is serious about making government work, and he is able to lay out a plan of action during his first weeks in office, he need not invest much continuing effort (except in the area of agency consolidation or elimination), provided these presidential groups keep alive within the bureaucracy a recognition of continued presidential interest.

CONCLUSION

To some extent this article is intended as a challenge to those who lament that government is not manageable, that the bureaucracy is disloyal and uncontrollable, and that the presidential role as manager is a naive illusion. It is the thesis here that we can ill afford not to reform our governmental systems. It must be a reform bold enough to produce results the citizens can see as helping them.

The impetus for reform can come only from the president. This impetus is possible, even though the amount of sustained attention a president can give management is admittedly very limited.

It should be stressed, however, that this belief that the management of government can be reformed with strong presidential impetus rests on the propositions that a sustained multipronged attack on our deficiencies must be launched and that congressional consultation is essential.

In short, if we are to meet our increasingly critical domestic and national security problems, management has to be placed much higher on the agenda of the president and the nation. Much of the history of our third century will hinge on this decision.

# TWENTY
PRESIDENTIAL CONTROL OF THE FEDERAL BUREAUCRACY

Howard Ball

THE COMPREHENSIVE REAGAN PLAN FOR REGULATORY REFORM

Reform Efforts Under Presidents Ford and Carter

With the growth of federal regulatory activity during the 1930s, there came the accompanying concern about controlling this federal bureaucratic activity. Early concerns led to the passage, in 1939, of the Budget and Accounting Act which provided the budget office with the power to review the budgets of all executive offices, including the regulatory commissions. Numerous studies (Hoover, Landis, and Ash reports) conducted by presidential commissions and the Congress found flaws in the regulatory system. Efforts were made by various presidents, including John F. Kennedy and Richard M. Nixon, to reorganize the structure of the federal executive bureaucracy by having the White House exert more central control. Given the support in Congress for these federal regulatory agencies, these efforts were constantly challenged by the Congress "as creating a White House czar and establishing a direct chain of political command" over the regulatory agencies.

However, in the mid-1970s there was growing unease in Congress and in the business community, with the activities of the federal regulators. In August 1974,

This selection was originally presented as a paper at the Southern Political Science Association meeting in Memphis, Tennessee (November 1981).

Congress created the Council on Wage and Price Stability (COWPS) to "monitor activities of the private sector of the economy that might add to the rate of inflation. In addition, the Council was directed to 'review the activities and programs of the federal government to discover whether they have any inflationary impact.' From the very beginning, the council interpreted this mandate as requiring benefit-cost analysis of important regulatory actions." For the first time, a government-created agency would determine whether major regulatory rules were inflationary or anti-inflationary using a benefit-cost calculus.

Its role was strengthened when, in November 1974, President Ford issued Executive Order 11821 on "Inflation Impact Statements (IIS)."[1] This order required "that major proposals for legislation, and for the promulgation of regulations and rules by any executive branch agency must be accompanied by a statement which certifies that the inflationary impact of the proposal has been evaluated." The Office of Management and Budget (OMB) was given the task of developing standards for implementing the executive order. The criteria developed by the OMB concerned: cost impact on business, consumers, government; effect on productivity; competition; and impact on important goods and services. Under the Ford plan, the director of the OMB could delegate functions to various units, including the chairperson of the COWPS. "COWPS was given a major role in administering the Inflation Impact Statement program. Under the program, for their major proposed regulations, agencies were required to estimate and analyze the benefits of the proposals, its costs, and the benefits and costs of alternative approaches."

In 1974, due to the congressional action and the executive order, "virtually all regulatory agencies came under purview of COWPS, where a small group of economists reviewed newly proposed regulations and their supporting documents." As a consequence, four products appeared: COWPS written statements became part of the record in formal rule-making process, COWPS publicly testified at the agency hearing; detailed analyses were given to agency staff as part of an internal review; COWPS staff developed studies of significant regulatory issues not related to any proposed rule making. James C. Miller, III, a Reagan administration strategist (presently chairman of the FTC), was the assistant director of the COWPS during the Ford administration. The intent of COWPS, Miller wrote, was to persuade agencies "to avoid the tendency for agencies to serve special constituent interests, often at greater cost to the general public."

The Ford administration strategy was to "get executive department agencies to improve agency decision making by getting them to address the costs and benefits of their proposals." There were problems with the program: (1) lack of a definition of major rules changes, and (2) independent regulatory commissions did not comply, it was argued, because the president did not have the authority to extend the executive order to cover their activities. In addition, (3) agency analyses were done after the head or administrator of the agency had approved the rule or regulation. Since COWPS reviews of these documents were advisory, agencies did not have to comply to delay or halt regulations that agencies wanted enforced. "Agency compliance with the Ford Program depended to a large extent on the power of the president and his staff in OMB and COWPS to persuade through reasoned argument and/or through charm."

President Jimmy Carter, who ran on a platform that called for the streamlining of federal bureaucracy, continued the Ford plan—with three additional improvements. (1) In January 1978, he created the Regulatory Analysis Review

---

[1] On December 31, 1976, EO 11949, the ISS program was extended and renamed the Economic Impact Statement (EIS).

Group (RARG), which consisted of representatives from 17 major executive branch agencies, including the Council of Economic Advisors. (The COWPS provided the economic staff reviewers for the RARG). Its primary task was to review and make recommendations on a small number of proposed rules of the executive branch agencies. (2) In March 1978, President Carter issued Executive Order 12044. Among its provisions, it required each executive branch agency to prepare a regulatory analysis, including the economic consequences of significant new regulations (with agency heads forced to play a prominent role); review old regulations to see if they were still needed; and allow the public more time to get involved in the informal rule making by extending the notice and comment timetables.

The regulatory analysis—both the draft and the final analysis—were to be published in the *Register* for public review and had to include the economic analysis of the consequences of such rules and a perception of alternative ways of reaching the same goal. Significant regulations were those that resulted in an annual economic impact of $100 million or more or major increases in the costs for businesses, consumers, and governments. The key reviewers were the members of RARG—not the OMB. In signing the executive order, Carter said: "I came to Washington to reorganize a federal government which had grown more preoccupied with its own bureaucratic needs than with those of the people. This executive order is an instrument for reversing this trend. It promises to make federal regulations clearer, less burdensome, and more cost-effective." (3) In October 1978 Carter established the Regulatory Council composed of representatives from 36 executive branch and independent regulatory agencies. Chaired by the head of the Council of Economic Advisors, the Council tried to coordinate rule-making activities of the federal agencies by publishing semiannual calendars of agency activities (to avoid duplication) and by encouraging joint, cooperative activities between agencies.

Carter's reforms were somewhat more specific than the Ford programs. However, there were a number of problems that confronted the implementors of the Carter program: (1) an agency could simply ignore the advisory recommendation of the RARG, (2) there was little time for careful analysis of many of the regulations for the RARG analysis had to be accomplished during the public comment period (usually about 60 to 90 days), and (3) politically, it was a horizontal relationship—agency heads dealing with other executives who sat on the RARG. If any agency head wanted to use the technical assistance provided his bureau after being RARGed, he or she could—but he or she was not under any compulsion to do so.

(In addition to these executive actions to exert more control over the federal bureaucracy, the Congress in 1980 passed two pieces of Carter legislation that also attempted to achieve the same goal: the Paperwork Reduction Act and the Regulatory Flexibility Act. The former statute gave OMB the power to review all requests made by governmental agencies for information and reports from businesses and individuals in an effort to reduce the paperwork. The latter public law, written to protect small business from regulations that would be particularly hard on them, required all agency decision makers to analyze a regulation's paperwork and economic impact on small businesses.)

Both the Ford and Carter programs were efforts to exert more executive, White House, pressure and control over the actions of the federal executive board regulatory agencies and the independent regulatory commissions. There were weaknesses in both programs with respect to controlling the outputs of the agencies in the federal government. The Reagan administration's strategy, however, was to build upon the foundation laid by these two administrations but to do so by asserting—clearly and unabashedly—the dominance of the White House in the continuing effort to control federal bureaucratic activity.

THE REAGAN "GAME PLAN" FOR REGULATORY REFORM

(1) The Task Force for Regulatory Relief Formed, January 1981

In President Reagan's first action in his battle against the federal bureaucracy, he announced, on January 22, 1981, the creation of a Presidential Task Force on Regulatory Relief. Through "careful study and close coordination between agencies and bureaus in the federal structure," the task force would "cut away the thicket of irrational and senseless regulations," stated Reagan. There were three essential duties of the task force:

1. review major proposals by executive branch regulatory agencies, especially those proposals that have a major policy significance or where there is overlapping agency jurisdiction;
2. assess executive branch regulations already on the books, especially those that are potentially burdensome to the national economy or to key industrial sectors;
3. oversee the development of legislative proposals in response to congressional timetables and, more importantly, to codify the president's views on the appropriate role and objectives of regulatory agencies.

The guiding principles of the task force reflected Reagan's game plan:

1. regulations approved only when there is a compelling need;
2. regulatory approach taken that imposes the least possible burden on society;
3. regulatory priorities should be governed by an assessment of the benefits and costs of the proposed regulations.

In sum, what the president created was an agency that would review the actions of the federal executive branch agencies and determine which of the new and how many of the old regulations were truly needed as well as cost-effective. It would, working in conjunction with the White House and with the agencies, determine the nature of new legislative proposals in the area of regulatory reform and it would act as a brake on the actions of agencies in general.

The task force is led by Vice-President George Bush. In addition to Chairman Bush, the members of the task force include Donald Regan, Secretary of the Treasury; William French Smith, Attorney General; Malcolm Baldridge, Secretary of Commerce; Raymond Donovan, Secretary of Labor; David Stockman, Director, OMB; Martin Anderson, Assistant to the President for Policy Planning; and Murray Weidenbaum, Chairman, CEA. Until he assumed the chairmanship of the FTC recently, James C. Miller, III, was executive director of the task force (as well as administrator of the Office of Information and Regulatory Affairs, OMB). The two other staffers on the task force group are C. Boyden Grey (who is also counsel for Vice-President Bush) and Rich Williamson (who is assistant to the president, intergovernmental affairs).

"Having the vice-president leading the task force makes a big difference," said Miller (who was on the COWPS staff during the Ford administration). "If it were just OMB [as was the case during the Ford administration when OMB and COWPS attempted to implement the IIS and EIS programs] versus the agencies it would be a loggerhead, it would be horizontal." But with the vice-president rather than the director of the OMB, as the chairman of the task force, there is a vertical centralizing authority. The agency head, or bureau chief, in a dispute regarding a proposed regulation, for example, does not confront another department head; he or she has to confront the vice-president. There was, from the very beginning of the task force's life, a very basic political fact of life quite different from the regulatory control programs developed by Ford and Carter—buck the task force and you are bucking the vice-president and the White House.

Another important characteristic of the task force is the linkage between the task force staff and the White House executive office. There is a fundamental interlocking between the two units: Miller was with OMB, Grey is counsel to the vice-president, and Williamson is a presidential assistant. The creation of the task force to coordinate efforts to curb regulations, in its makeup and in its scope of action, was quite different from Carter's RARG. The task force has political linkages with the White House and does not have the horizontal political characteristics of RARG. It would be very difficult for an agency head to oppose the vice-president when the task force decided that a rule or regulation was cost-inefficient.

(2) The Reagan Executive Order of February 17, 1981

(a) *The parameters of the executive order nr 12291* On February 17, 1981, President Ronald Reagan issued Executive Order 12291 on federal regulation.[2] Written by David Stockman, Miller, Weidenbaum, and Grey, key figures in the Reagan White House, this executive order is the centerpiece of the Reagan effort to centralize regulatory agency management control in the Executive Office of the President. The management tool established by the order centralized review of agency activity by two agencies (OMB and the task force) politically loyal to the president, built upon the Ford and Carter regulatory control executive orders. However, by having Vice-President Bush, the chairman of the task force, as the resolver "of any issues raised under this order," the Reagan order advanced the role of centralized White House management to a much more sophisticated control level than appeared in the earlier programs.

The objectives of the 2/17 order were, in the words of President Reagan:

> to reduce the burdens of existing and future regulations, increase agency accountability for regulatory actions, provide for presidential oversight of the regulatory process, minimize duplication and conflict of regulations, and insure well-reasoned regulations.

Section 2, General Requirements, stated that all regulatory decisions should be based on adequate information and that regulatory actions should not be taken "unless the potential benefits to society outweigh the potential costs to society." Agency policymakers were to "set regulatory priorities with the aim of maximizing net benefits to society." They had to take into account the condition of the particular industry being regulated, the national economy, and contemplated future regulatory actions in the regulated area.

Section 3, Regulatory Impact Analysis and Review, required every executive department agency to prepare a Regulatory Impact Analysis (RIA) for every major

---

[2]On January 29, 1981, President Reagan issued an executive order freezing pending and proposed final rules from publication in the *Federal Register*. The freeze was for 60 days; 172 regulations were effected by the order. After March 30, 1981, 100 of the 172 were actually published; the remainder were either delayed or withdrawn.

rule[3] it is considering. These RIAs of all major rules must be submitted at two stages of the rule-making process: (1) with the notice of proposed rule making and, (2) with the final rule, to the director, OMB—both submittals prior to publication of information in the *Federal Register*. Preliminary RIAs must be submitted to OMB 60 days before the notice of the proposed rule is printed. Final RIAs must be submitted at least 30 days before publication. All other nonmajor rules must be submitted to the OMB at least 10 days before publication.

In this "preclearance" procedure, much like the Section 5 process developed by the Justice Department to implement the 1965 Voting Rights Act, the director of the OMB reviews the PRIA and the final RIA to determine whether or not the agency has developed a cost-benefit analysis which:

1. describes potential benefits and identifies those likely to benefit;
2. describes potential costs and identifies those likely to bear the costs;
3. determines the net benefits of the rule;
4. describes alternative approaches to the problem at lower costs with an explanation of the legal reasons why these are not acceptable to the agency, along with analysis of benefits and costs of each alternative approach;
5. explains, if appropriate, why the proposed rule cannot be reviewed in accordance with the executive order.

The (OMB) director, "subject to the direction of the task force, which shall resolve any issues raised under this order or ensure that they are presented to the president," is authorized to review these analyses and accompanying regulations. Unless he asks for additional information through "consultation" with the agency, the director must conclude the review of a proposed major rule within 60 days of submission, of a final rule within 30 days of submission, and all other nonmajor regulations within 10 days of submission.

If there are problems with a proposed rule, "upon the request of the director, an agency shall consult with the director concerning the review . . . and shall refrain from publishing its RIA . . . until such review is concluded." The director, by requesting such a "consultation," can delay the publication of proposed rule-making and the effective date of final regulations. As soon as the agency head receives word of the delay, the head "shall refrain from publishing . . . until the agency has responded to the director's views, and incorporated these views and the agency's response in the rule-making file."

Section 4, Regulatory Review, requires all agencies covered by the order to make a determination that the regulation they are proposing is "within the authority delegated by law and consistent with congressional intent." The agency must also state that the rule is based on the factual record and that full attention has been paid to public comments.

Section 5, Regulatory Agendas, requires the publication, by every agency, each October and April, of an agenda of proposed regulations that the agency has issued or is expected to issue as well as currently effective rules that are under review by the agency. Agenda are required to contain: a summary of each major rule being

---

[3]A major rule is defined in Section 1 as any regulation that results in an annual effect on the economy of $100 million or more; a major increase in costs or prices for consumers; individual industries; federal, state, or local government agencies; geographic regions; or significant adverse effects on competition, employment, investment, productivity, innovation, or international economic competition. Section 6 empowers the director to designate any proposed or existing rule as a major rule. He also has the power to waive all requirements of the order with respect to other rules.

considered; the name and phone number of an agency contact person working on the proposed rule; a list of existing regulations to be reviewed by the agency and a brief discussion of each one. The director may request additional information from an agency about any of the rules listed on the agenda.

Section 6, The Task Force and the Office of Management and Budget, focuses on the relationship between the two executive branch units and on the powers of the director. The director, "subject to the discretion of the task force," has the power to:

1. designate any proposal or rule as a major one;
2. prepare uniform standards for the identification of major rules;
3. require an agency to obtain and evaluate additional information;
4. waive sections involving RIAs;
5. identify duplication, overlapping, and conflicting rules and require appropriate interagency consultation to minimize or eliminate them;
6. develop procedures for estimating annual benefits and costs of agency regulations for the purpose of establishing a regulatory budget;
7. prepare for the president recommendations for change in organic statutes;
8. monitor agency compliance with the order and advise the president accordingly; and
9. develop and implement procedures for the performance of all OMB functions vested in the director.

Section 7 sets guidelines for Pending Regulations. Agencies are required to suspend or postpone the effective dates of all major rules until the review has been completed. Exemptions are described in Section 8. Any emergency rule that is mandated by statute or judicial decision is exempt from coverage. However, the agency head must explain the exceptional nature to the director—who can ask for consultation and additional information that would delay the effective date of the regulation. In addition, the director may, "under the direction of the task force," exempt any class or category of regulations from any or all of the requirements of the 2/17 order.

(b) Differences between the Reagan and earlier orders There are a number of differences between the 2/17 order and earlier presidential efforts to centralize control of federal regulatory activity. (1) Specific and detailed cost-benefit analyses of all major regulations are required. (2) Whereas earlier plans "depended wholly on hortatory means for achieving compliance," under the Reagan plan the OMB and the task force exert "unprecedented powers" over the development of agency regulations due to the "preclearance" tool found in Section 3 of the 2/17 order. Robert C. Miller, III, who administered the Ford program, is a key economic figure in the Reagan administration who wrote and initially implemented the 2/17 order. He said, noting differences he experienced:

> I'd call up an agency (in 1976) and say, "We just saw this morning in the *Federal Register* a regulation you published. We think it is a major rule which requires an IIS." They'd say no and that was the end of the conversation. Today they say, "Oh yes, we're very sorry, we weren't sure but if you think so, we'll prepare a RIA."

(3) Guidelines are developed by OMB to curb agency actions; consultations and the bargaining and negotiations that occur between OMB and the agency take place in the prepublic stage of the rule-making process.

The 2/17 order is the most detailed comprehensive regulatory agency activity review by White House personnel ever developed and put into place by a president.

It is an effort to get agency policymakers in step with the goals and objectives of the chief executive and his economic advisers. Weidenbaum states that "the first line of defense against overregulation lies with the agencies themselves." Miller has said that "the first line of offense in ferreting out ineffective and excessively burdensome regulations also lies in the agencies." Said Miller,[4] until recently the executive director of the task force:

> Among the people whose behavior we're trying to influence are the GS-13s and -14s who draft the rules. The Executive Order says to them: even if you get a *nonconforming proposal* past your agencyheads, even if you've captured them or just plain fooled them, that proposal is likely to be caught at OMB—and there's not a chance in Hades of your capturing these people. *So if you want to get ahead*, you're going to have to write new rules and review existing rules in conformance with the principles set forth by the President in the Executive Order. I believe that as internal agency procedures and the mechanism for centralized review settle into place, agency personnel will voluntarily comply.

All agencies must now develop systematic cost-benefit analyses of every major rule they would like to promulgate. As Miller suggests, OMB does exert control because it must review all regulations—major and minor. Thomas Hopkins, an economist at OMB stated simply: "We provide the questions, and the agencies must get the answers." And if the answers are not in conformance with administrative objectives, then the regulation will not get by the OMB review.

(i) *Cost Benefit Analysis*. Vice-President Bush, in August 1981, said that the task force and the OMB are not "prejudging whether everything in these regulations is bad. We're trying to find a balance that has not been found in previous rules." Finding the balance is the objective of the cost-benefit analysis. Cost-benefit "is used to improve agency decision making, and this means getting the agencies to address the costs and benefits of their proposals . . . and avoid the tendency for agencies to serve special interests, often at greater cost to the public."

Cost-benefit can be used to evaluate social regulations because "social problems and solutions take on an economic dimension, that is, Is it worth the cost? The old problems of scarcity and necessary trade-offs cannot be avoided." It is somewhat more difficult to measure benefits and costs of clean air and clean water regulations, and so on, "where benefits may be in terms of lives saved or pain and suffering avoided." Such an analysis must take place, however, if the social rule is classified as a major one.

Costs of social regulations have been calculated by some. One study concluded that EPA costs in FY 1981 were: $9 billion for air pollution controls, $4.7 billion for water purification standards, and $0.7 billion for solid waste treatment regulations. Benefits of these kinds of regulations have also been calculated. For example, the MIT Center for Policy Alternatives concluded that $5 to $58 billion in health-medical benefits were not spent because of the control of air pollutants; medical savings of $100 million to $1 billion due to water pollution control regulations (as well as recreational benefits of $9.5 billion). OSHA, the study calculated, prevented 350 work place deaths and about 60,000 work place accidents. The NHTSA, from 1966 to 1974, saved 28,000 lives with its automobile safety regulations.

To determine benefits in terms of lives saved, the agency must often take leaps of faith. Roy Gamse, deputy associate EPA administrator for Policy and Resource

---

[4]Miller recently told *Newsweek*, April 20, 1981: "My friends see me and they say I look like a kid in a toy shop. They're right. I love it. I've been writing about deregulation for so long. Now I have a chance to do it." p. 77.

Management, described the process as applied to a water pollution effluent guideline:

> It you to quantify benefits, you must assign a dollar value to swimming or fishing. You must estimate the number of recreational visits there will be and how much they are worth. You must calculate the number of adverse health effects avoided and assign a dollar value to them. Each step is very uncertain. . . . The range of error is larger and larger. Is it really worth the large expense. . . . Why compound error by building sand castles?

Even though critics might argue the impossibility of assigning values to lives saved or injuries averted, OMB and the 2/17 order insists on quantification of benefits of all major regulations. "Top administration officials seem to be *true believers* in applying strict economic tests to the government's regulatory endeavors." For example, William A. Niskanen, Jr., on the Council of Economic Advisors, called himself "an advocate of more cost-benefit analysis, most importantly in health and safety matters. Though people have backed off from using it here, no special conceptual problems stand in its way."

The 2/17 order institutionalizes cost-benefit analysis for every major rule developed by an executive branch agency. The subsequent delay in rule making does not concern the Reagan administration. With this process settling into a routine pattern, it is made "almost impossible to issue an affirmative regulation, while at the same time making recision of regulations exceedingly easy."

(ii) *Power Linkages between OMB and the Task Force* The Reagan administration has developed the politically astute practice of overlapping assignments in these two agencies for closer coordination in the effort to control the federal regulatory process from the White House. Absent large numbers of staff in OMB (there are only 90 persons to handle the RIAs), a bloody and effective war with the agencies is not probable. Instead, a well-integrated and well-coordinated force, with agreed-upon objectives and definitions, *responds* to agency initiatives.

There is an "ideological" linkage in that the line and staff personnel of the task force and OMB are philosophically committed to the notion of cost-benefit and the presidential view that there have been "irrational and senseless regulations" that must be rolled back and halted. "While previous efforts have failed to manage the proliferation of federal regulations," said Reagan when he issued the 2/17 order, with the linkage of these two White House agencies, there will be the "establishment of central regulatory oversight at the highest level."

This high-level linkage has the consequence of "stiffening the back of an agency head who's been pressured by a constituent," said Murray Weidenbaum. With the cost-benefit requirement and the presidential loyalty of OMB Director David Stockman, it is extremely difficult to imagine a regulation getting approved that was not cost-efficient and in line with presidential objectives in that policy area. Such is the character of White House clout after the announcement of the 2/17 order.

(iii) *OMB Control of the Regulatory Process* There is no doubt that the 2/17 order developed a centralized review mechanism in the White House with the power to "crack the whip" to bring agencies in line with Reagan objectives. The 2/17 order has been characterized by William A. Butler, general counsel to the 430,000 member Audubon Society, as amounting to a "power play that shifts power from the regulatory agencies to the OMB."

Agency heads must now decide how to conform to Reagan's goals and objectives. Executive Order 12291 has made the agency personnel squirm; the mood in the agencies runs from "cautious pessimism to downright gloom." Agency heads must continuously take cues from OMB and the task force. This will lead to delay and withdrawal of final regulations that have not been approved by the OMB. (*See* Figure 20-1, EO 12291: OMB and Agency Rule Making.) Commenting on the *minimum* time period for major regulations, 210 days if there are no consultations or requests for additional information by the director, Miller said: "We think the time is necessary—and well worth it—to make sure that new rules do more good than harm."

Vice-President Bush pointed out in June 1981, that "the Reagan administration has succeeded in *slowing the pace* of regulatory activity and its reviews of agency rules promises to save the private sector several billion dollars." It was estimated by

FIGURE 20-1 EO12291: OMB and Agency Rule Making

```
                    Preliminary RIA &
                 Proposed Regulations to OMB
                      60 Days Prior to
                      NPRM in The FR
                              |
                         60 DAYS
                              |
                        OMB Decision
                        /            \
                OMB Approval      OMB Directs Agency
                       |          to "Consultations"
                       |                /        \
         Publication of Preliminary   Delay    Withdrawal
         Regulations & PRIA in FR              of Regulation
                       |
                   30-90 Days
                 Public Notice and
                    Comment
                       |
         Agency Prepares/Submits
         Final RIA & Final Regula-
         tion to OMB 30 Days Prior
           to Publication in FR
                       |
                    30 DAYS
                       |
                  OMB Decision
                   /         \
            OMB Approval   OMB Directs Agency
                   |       to "Consultations"
                   |           /         \
         Publication of Final Delay    Withdrawal
         Regulations in FR             of Regulation
                   |
           After 30 Days,
         Final Regulation Effective
                   |
              Legislative Veto?
                   |
            Regulation Effective
                   |
            Judicial Review
```

TERMS: NPRM — Notice of Proposed Rulemaking
        FR — Federal Register
        RIA — Regulation Impact Analysis (EO, Feb. 1981)

Presidential Control of the Federal Bureaucracy

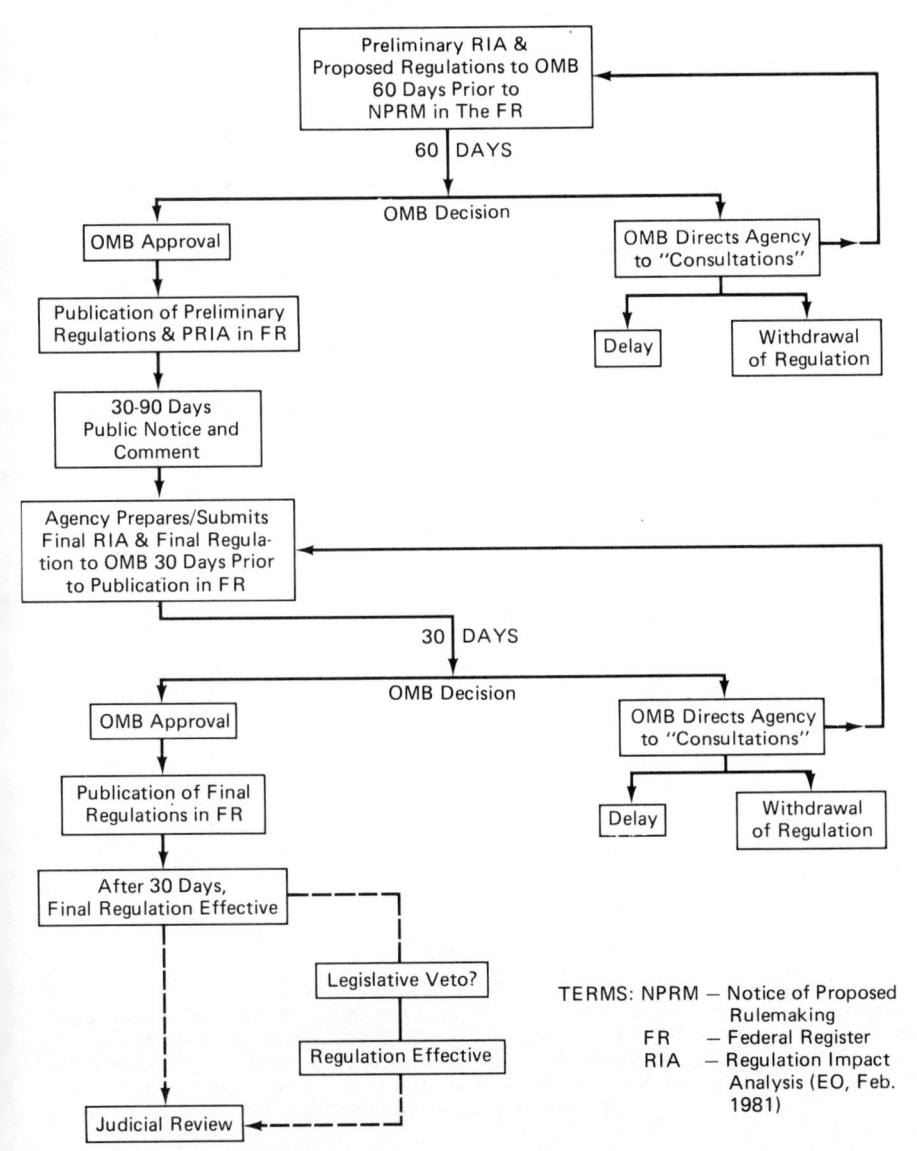

Bush that about 100 major regulations would be reviewed by OMB by the end of 1981. As of June 1981, OMB had received 847 rules for review; all but 56 were approved by the director. (The first federal agency to receive approval of a major rule by the OMB was the U.S. Postal Service. After consultations with OMB, its voluntary nine-digit zip code regulation—"Zip Plus Four"—was determined by the director to provide more benefits to the society than costs.)

Also in June 1981, another form of OMB control over agencies appeared when the agency published its Interim RIA Guidance booklet. Some of the guidelines for developing the cost-benefit analysis follow:

> When costs and benefits cannot be measured in monetary terms, they must be "described in detail and quantified to the maximum extent possible."
>
> Agencies must state the "net benefits" of a major rule by subtracting the "monetary social cost estimate" from the monetary benefit estimate.
>
> A detailed statement must be prepared for each regulation, analyzing the need for each regulation, including alternative approaches—no action or solutions outside the reach of the agency, examining "market-oriented ways of regulating."

Some agency heads voiced their displeasure with the guidelines to OMB, claiming generality, increased amounts of paperwork, and economic jargon[5] of the guidelines. The language has not been modified; it serves to further delay and "slow the pace" of the rule-making process.

---

[5] An example of the Interim RIA Guidance: The monetary social cost should be subtracted from the monetary social benefit to obtain the monetary net benefit estimate (which could be negative). Any remaining nonmonetary but quantifiable benefit and cost information also should be presented, Then, nonquantifiable benefits and costs should be listed, in a way that facilitates making an informed final decision. Where many benefits are not easily quantified, the results should show the cost-effectiveness of the several alternatives.

CHAPTER SIX
JUDICIAL REVIEW OF AGENCY ACTS

INTRODUCTION

Fairness in informal agency rule-making procedures, writes J. Skelly Wright in this chapter, is when there is an open, informal, reasoned, candid dialogue between the agency decision makers and interested publics. Fairness in formal adjudication exists when judgments are made in light of on the record "substantial evidence," that is, that relevant evidence "such that a reasonable mind might accept as adequate and reasonable to support a conclusion."[1] Judicial review of agency actions is the effort to ensure the presence of fairness in regulatory agency decision-making processes.

Judicial review, in addition to legislative and executive efforts to curb regulatory agency abuses of power, is the legal remedy for those who allege that agency policy is arbitrary and denies due process of law. In our constitutional system, courts have had the power to review actions of political decision makers, and determine whether or not the actor exceeded the constitutional grant of power,[2] since *Marbury* v. *Madison*, 1803. Subject only to judicial discretion and political reality, that is, "jurisdiction" and "standing" questions, courts have determined the legitimacy of acts of legislature and of the president ever since 1803. (Judicial review, however, is an ad hoc, passive power in that the judges must respond to cases and controversies that come to them.)

Throughout the nineteenth century and through much of the twentieth century, federal courts did not examine very many decisions of administrative agencies. This doctrine of

[1]*Consolidated Edison* v. *NLRB*, 305 US 197 (1938).
[2]*See* generally Howard Ball, *Constitutional Powers* (St. Paul, MN: West Publishing Company, 1980).

nonreviewability was put to rest when, in 1944, the Supreme Court, in *Stark* v. *Wickard*, stated:

> The responsibility of determining the limits of statutory grants of authority . . . is a judicial function entrusted to the courts by Congress, by the statutes establishing courts and marking their jurisdiction. . . . Under Article 3, Congress established courts to adjudicate cases and controversies as to claims of infringement of individual rights whether by unlawful action of private persons or by the exertions of unauthorized administrative power.[3]

Judicial review of regulatory agency action today, that is, federal court jurisdiction (authority) to hear cases involving agency actions, is largely determined by (1) specific statutes written by Congress or by (2) more general congressional jurisdictional statutes. The former type of review has been called "statutory" judicial review. Agencies such as CAB, EPA, FCC, FERC, NLRB, OSHA, NRC, and the ICC have judicial review written into the specific organic statute. For example, the Hobbs Act, 28 USC 2342–2350, specifically details the circumstances for judicial review of FCC decisions.[4] The more general statutes that provide jurisdiction for courts to hear appeals from agency decisions are called (somewhat erroneously) "nonstatutory" judicial review statutes. For example, 28 USC 1331 ("federal question" jurisdiction) and 1337 ("interstate commerce") enable plaintiffs to come into federal court and challenge agency actions.[5] In sum, a person who believes that he or she has suffered actual injury from agency action (or inaction) and who can find a statutory basis for court jurisdiction, can bring suit against an agency or officials in an agency.

Congress determines, specifically or generally, the extent of judicial review and those circumstances under which judicial review of agency activity is barred. In 1967, the United States Supreme Court stated: "Only upon a showing of 'clear and convincing evidence' of a contrary legislative intent should the courts restrict access to judicial review."[6] Since 1946 the general legislative statement of judicial review of administrative agency action is found in the Administrative Procedure Act (APA). While its provisions do not create an independent basis for court jurisdiction,[7] the APA is very clear as to legislative intent. Section 702 of the APA states that "a person suffering legal wrong because of agency action, or adversely affected or aggrieved by agency action within the meaning of a relevant statute, is entitled to judicial review thereof." Section 704 states that, except for (1) statutes that preclude judicial review, or (2) agency action that is "committed to agency discretion by law" (Section 701), "agency action is made reviewable by statute and final agency action for which there is no other adequate remedy in a court are subject to judicial review."

Given this legislative mandate to the federal courts to conduct judicial review of agency activity, the federal judges examine administrative actions brought to them by plaintiffs who have standing to sue, who have exhausted all administrative remedies, and whose petition is "ripe" for judicial review.[8] Section 706 of the APA describes the scope of judicial review of agency activity: "The reviewing court shall decide all relevant questions of law, interpret constitutional and statutory provisions, and determine the meaning or applicability of the terms of an agency action."

[3]*Stark* v. *Wickard*, 321 US 288 (1944).
[4]Gary J. Edles and Jerome Nelson, *Federal Regulatory Process: Agency Practices and Procedures* (New York: Harcourt Brace Jovanovich, 1981), pp. 180–181.
[5]Ibid., p. 181.
[6]*Abbott Laboratories* v. *Gardner*, 387 US 136 (1967).
[7]Edles and Nelson, *Federal Regulatory Process*, p. 182; see also *Califano* v. *Sanders*, 430 US 99 (1977).
[8]*See* generally Howard Ball, *Courts and Politics* (Englewood Cliffs, NJ: Prentice-Hall, Inc., 1980).

In this review, the federal judge (Section 706) shall be able to:

> hold unlawful and set aside agency action, findings, and conclusions found to be
> (a) arbitrary, capricious, an abuse of discretion, or otherwise not in accordance with the law;
> (b) contrary to constitutional right, power, privilege, or immunity;
> (c) in excess of statutory jurisdiction, authority, or limitations, or short of statutory right;
> (d) without observance of procedure required by law;
> (e) unsupported by substantial evidence in a case subject to sections 556 and 557 of the (APA)....

As the agency's actions subject to judicial review involve either informal rule making or the more formal adjudication, the APA's guidelines in Chapter VII focus on these types of activities. Informal rule making, Section 553 of the APA, are evaluated by the federal courts in light of (a) above. Judges making these evaluations are admonished, by the Supreme Court and others, not to substitute their judgment for that of the agency if the agency action is reasonable. Formal adjudication processes are subject to the "substantial evidence" guideline in (e) above. As the Court said in a 1966 case, *Consolo v. FMC*: "the *possibility of drawing two inconsistent conclusions* from the evidence does not prevent an administrative agency's finding from being supported by 'substantial evidence.'" (As the readings in this chapter will illustrate, the balance between careful review of agency actions and judicial usurpation of the agency's decision-making responsibility to implement legislation, is a very fine one.)

In all agency judicial review litigation there is the presumption of agency validity; the plaintiff challenging an agency action or inaction has the burden of showing capriciousness, lack of due process, lack of "substantial evidence," and so on. (Should the Congress pass and the president sign a Bumpers Amendment-type bill, then, as articles have already pointed out, judicial review will take on a completely different cast with major changes for plaintiff, defendant, and federal judge.)

The plaintiff must try to show the federal court that the agency violated procedural guidelines—developed by the agency or already in existence in legislation—or acted without agency authority, and so forth. The chances of winning on appeal are not too great for the plaintiff; in recent years, the United States Supreme Court's reversal of agency decisions has run between 20–25 percent.[9] Essentially, in judicial review there are two types of questions examined by the federal judges: (1) has the law been applied correctly, (2) whether the decision rests on reasonable grounds or that it reasonably follows from the evidence presented on the record. The possibility of overturning an agency decision is considered good if:

> the agency has violated its own regulations;
> the case raises a significant legal question of first impression and the courts believe it important to intensely examine;
> the decision rests on shaky agency precedent;
> the decision rests on unexplained departure from agency rules or precedent;
> procedural unfairness is present;
> weak agency findings are on the record;
> there is no substantial evidence.[10]

The readings in the chapter reflect on judicial review in the Age of the Administrative State. The Cramton piece is critical of the role the federal judges have been playing in our society. Judge Wright's piece on federal judicial review is an argument for judicial self-restraint. He illustrates the fact that congressional statutes that called for judicial review

---

[9]Edles and Nelson, *Federal Regulatory Process*, p. 169.
[10]Ibid., pp. 170–172.

of agency activity "fastened courts and agencies into an intimate partnership the success of which requires a precarious balance between judicial deference and self-assertion." Finally, the Horowitz essay, paralleling Wright's statement, raises the question of whether the federal judges are capable of substantive policymaking in this complex, technological Age of the Experts. Should federal judges, in an effort to curb agency abuse, substitute their judgment for that of the administrator? He is concerned about the hazards of such judicial guardianship that follows from the granting of judicial review to the federal courts by the legislature.

TWENTY ONE
JUDICIAL LAW MAKING AND ADMINISTRATION

Roger C. Cramton

Seventy years ago in St. Paul, Roscoe Pound gave a famous speech on "The Causes of Popular Dissatisfaction with the Administration of Justice." Recently, a prestigious group of lawyers and judges, assembled by Chief Justice Burger, reconvened in St. Paul to reconsider Pound's theme. A surprising conclusion was that, although the professionals—the lawyers and judges themselves—have many problems with the administration of justice, the tide of popular dissatisfaction is at a relatively low ebb.

In contrast to other agencies of the government, the people have confidence in the fairness and integrity of the courts. True, there is continuing complaint over the law's cost and delay. But, apart from this perennial complaint, popular dissatisfaction appears to stem from two perceptions: first, that decisions in criminal cases turn too often upon procedural technicalities rather than upon the guilt or innocence of the offender; and second, that some judges, and especially the federal judiciary, have been too actively engaged in lawmaking on social and economic issues that are better handled by other institutions of government. The layman, on scanning his newspaper or viewing the television screen, discovers to his surprise that judges are running schools and prison systems, prescribing curricula, formulating budgets, and regulating the environment.

Causation is a tricky matter. A student theme has reported that, since Smokey the Bear posters were displayed in the New York subways, forest fires have disap-

Reprinted with permission from *Public Administration Review* 36 (September/October 1976), 551–55. © 1976 by The American Society for Public Administration, 1225 Connecticut Avenue, N.W., Washington, D.C. All rights reserved. Footnotes omitted.

peared in Manhattan. Despite the risks, I hazard the generalization that several fundamental changes in the nature of our society may have altered the role of the judiciary.

Foremost among those changes is that suggested by the title of this article. The Leviathan is upon us, and it has implications for all branches of government, including the judiciary. Government now attempts so much! Every technical, economic, and social issue seems to end up in the hands of government; and the demand for further government action is combined with charges that existing government is inefficient, heavy-handed, and ineffective. This is one field in which the appetite for nostrums does not fade with the demonstrated failure of prior cures. Each reformer, after criticizing the failure and inefficiency of government, then concludes that the remedy is—more of the same!

But our attitudes about ourselves and about conflict have also changed. The confrontational style of contemporary America assures that social conflict will increase. "Doing your own thing" is the central value of a hedonistic, self-regarding society; and patience is a nearly extinct virtue. Nowadays no one takes "no" for an answer, whether it is a job aspirant or a welfare claimant or a teacher who has been denied tenure. We perceive our society as having grown old; the enthusiastic and venturesome spirit that prompted the uncharted growth of the American past is now suffering from hardening of the arteries. As we experience slower economic development and approach zero population growth, organized groups contend with each other with increasing ferocity for larger shares of a more static pie. There is a declining sense of a common purpose; the prevailing attitude is "what's in it for me?"

These trends give lawyers and judges an even more central role in our society than they have had in the past. The decline of moral consensus and of institutions of less formal control, such as the family and the church, places much more strain on the law as an instrument of conflict resolution and social control. And the increasing contentiousness of groups organized for their own advantage has made conflict resolution a growth industry. If you could buy stock in law firms, I would advise you to do so. Lawyers have a legal monopoly on the conflict resolution industry, and it is the boom industry of today.

To these developments—the increasing reliance on law as an instrument of social control and the rapid growth of group conflict—must be added another factor: the failure of the executive and the legislature to meet the challenge of today's inflated expectations. The public perception that these branches of government have failed—a perception greatly abetted by the debacles of Vietnam and Watergate—has led the people to turn increasingly to the courts for solutions to their problems.

MODELS OF JUDICIAL REVIEW

Consider in the context of the Leviathan State two models of judicial review of administrative action. The traditional model is one of a restrained and sober second look at what government has done that adversely affects a citizen. The controversy is bipolar in character, with two parties opposing each other; the issues are narrow and well-defined; and the relief is limited and obvious. Has a welfare recipient been denied a benefit to which he is entitled by statute? Was fair procedure employed by the agency? Were constitutional rights violated?

Judicial review in this model serves as a window on the outside world, a societal escape valve which tests the self-interest and narrow vision of the specialist and the bureaucrat against the broader premises of the total society. Every bureaucracy develops its own way of looking at things and these belief patterns are enormously resistant to change. In time an agency acquires a tunnel vision in which particular values are advanced and others are ignored. An independent judiciary tests agency outcomes against the statutory framework and the broader legal context.

Judicial review in this form is an absolute essential, especially in a society in which the points of contact between officials and private individuals multiply at every point. The impartial and objective second look adds to the integrity and acceptance of the administrative process rather than undermining it. If the administrator is upheld, as usually is the case, citizen confidence in the fairness and rationality of administration is enhanced. In the relatively small number of cases in which the administrator is reversed, the administrator is forced to readjust his narrower view to the larger perspective of the total society.

During the last 20 years the pace of constitutional change, especially in judicial review of government action, has been astounding. The values implicit in general constitutional provisions such as due process, equal protection, and free speech have been given expanded content and new life. Even more important, constitutional rights have been extended to persons who were formerly neglected by the legal system—blacks, aliens, prisoners, and others. One can disagree with the merits of particular decisions. But the general trends—implementation of fundamental values by the courts and the inclusion of previously excluded groups in the application of these values—constitute a great hour in the long struggle for human freedom.

There is, however, a second model of judicial review that is growing in acceptance and authority. This model of the judicial role has characteristics more of general problem solving than of dispute resolution. Simon Rifkind speaks of a modern tendency to view courts as modern handymen—as jacks of all trades available to furnish the answer to whatever may trouble us. "What is life? When does death begin? How should we operate prisons and hospitals? Shall we build nuclear power plants, and if so, where? Shall the Concorde fly to our shores?"

Thoughtful observers believe that controversies of this character strain the capacities of our courts and may have debilitating effects on the self-reliance of administrators and legislators. At the risk of appearing more reactionary than I am, let me focus not on the achievements of the past but on the possible dangers that arise when the judiciary succumbs to pressures to attempt too much.

THE COURT AS ADMINISTRATOR

The traditional judicial role, earlier described, envisions a lawsuit which is bipolar in character, seeks traditional relief (usually damages), and applies established law to a relatively narrow factual situation. The relief given is backward-looking and does not order government officials to take positive steps in the future.

The traditional model still persists in much private litigation and in many routine cases challenging official action, but in many other constitutional and statutory controversies radical changes have occurred. The changes have led Abram Chayes to argue that the basic character of public litigation has changed. In today's public litigation, a federal judge often is dealing with issues involving numerous parties; indeed, everyone in the community may be affected. Moreover, the issues are complex, interrelated, and multifaceted; and they turn less on proof concerning past misconduct than on complex predictions as to how various social interests should be protected in the future. Since the remedy is not limited to compensating named plaintiffs for a past harm, the judge gets drawn, for example, into coercing school officials to close schools, bus pupils, change curricula, and build new facilities. The federal judge becomes one of the most powerful persons in the community; on the particular issue, he is the one who decides.

Consider the role of one man, Frank Johnson, in the governance of the once sovereign state of Alabama. Johnson, a distinguished United States district judge in Alabama, is supervising the operation of the prisons, mental hospitals, highway patrol, and other institutions of the state. His decrees have directed the state to hire more wardens with better training, rebuild the prisons, and even extend to such details as the length of exercise periods and the installation of partitions in the men's rooms.

What is the authority of a federal judge to take such far-reaching actions? Why isn't the Alabama legislature the proper body to determine what prison or hospital care should be provided, and at what cost, through agencies administered by the state's executive branch? The answer is that all of these actions are designed to remedy violations of the constitutional rights of prisoners, mental patients, and others. And the Alabama legislature and executive have defaulted on their obligation to remedy these violations.

We are caught on the horns of a terrible dilemma. It is unconscionable that a federal court should refuse to entertain claims that state officials have systematically violated the constitutional rights of prisoners, mental patients, or school children. On the other hand, the design of effective relief may draw the court into a continuing role as an administrator of complex bureaucratic institutions. The dangers of the latter choice are worth brief exploration.

First, the judge who assumes an administrative role may gradually lose his neutrality, becoming a partisan who is pursuing his own cause. In one recent class action, a federal judge not only appointed expert witnesses, suggested areas of inquiry, and took over from the parties a substantial degree of the management of the case, but also went so far as to order that $250,000 from an award required of the defendants be paid for social science research on the effectiveness of the decree. That may be good government, but is it judicial justice?

A further problem arises from the tentativeness of our knowledge about such matters as minimum standards in operating a prison or mental hospital. We fervently hope that civilized and humane treatment will be provided to all of those who are confined to public institutions. But is it desirable to take the view of the current generation of experts, especially those self-selected by the plaintiffs or the judge, and to give their views of acceptable standards the status of constitutional requirements, with all that implies concerning their fixed meaning and difficulty of change?

Here as elsewhere, our capacity to anticipate the future or to discern all relevant facets of polycentric problems is limited. Thus, for example, when a federal judge ordered New York City to close the Tombs as a city jail or to rebuild it, the city, faced with an extraordinary financial crisis, opted to close it and prisoners confined to the Tombs were transferred to Riker's Island. The crowded conditions of the Tombs were immediately duplicated on Riker's Island. But a further result was not anticipated: Riker's Island is much less accessible to the families and attorneys of prisoners; and there is reason to believe that the vast majority of prisoners prefer the convenience of the Tombs, despite its problems, to the inaccessibility of Riker's Island.

The underlying truth is that court orders cannot by judicial decree achieve social change in the face of the concerted opposition of elected officials and public opinion. In a representative democracy, the consent of the people is required for lasting change.

The impulse to reform, moreover, is not limited to courts nor to constitutional law. A vigilant press, an informed populace, and the leadership of a committed minority have mobilized forces of change and reform throughout our history. A representative democracy may move slowly, but if we lack patience we may undermine the self-reliance and responsibility of the people and their elected officials.

The danger of confrontation between branches of government is yet another concern. What happens, for example, if Alabama refuses to fund its mental hospitals or prisons at the level required to achieve the standards specified in Judge Johnson's decrees? The next step, Judge Johnson has said, is the sale of Alabama's public lands in order to finance, through court-appointed officers, the necessary changes.

A degree of tension is a necessary concomitant of the checks and balances of a federal system. But in our urge to check we should not forget that balance is involved as well. One of the lessons of the Watergate era is that cooperation, restraint, and patience among the various branches and levels of government is necessary if our system is to survive in the long run. As Ben Franklin said many years ago, we must hang together or we will hang separately.

PRESSURES FOR JUDICIAL ACTION

Why have the courts undertaken these more expansive functions? They have not done so as volunteers desirous of expanding their own powers, but reluctantly and hesitantly in response to public demands for effective implementation of generally held values.

The American people today have little patience or restraint in dealing with social issues. An instant problem requires an instant solution that provides instant gratification. Playing this game under those rules, the executive and legislature have done their best—grinding out thousands of laws and regulations, many of them ineffective and some of them intrusive and harmful. The public, while demanding even more action from legislators and administrators, perceives these bodies as inept, ineffective, and even corrupt. Moreover, issues on which there is a deep social division, such as school busing or abortion, are avoided by elected officials, who view them as involving unacceptable political risks.

Nature abhors a vacuum and the inaction of the executive and lawmaking branches creates pressures for judicial action. A prominent federal judge put it succinctly at the recent St. Paul conference: "If there is a serious problem, and the legislature and executive don't respond, the courts have to act."

And they have done so on one after another burning issue. The mystery is that they have been so successful and that there has been so little popular outcry. The desegregation of Southern schools, of course, is a success story of heroic proportions. Legislative reapportionment is also generally viewed as a success despite the mathematical extreme to which it was carried in its later years. Organs of opinion, especially the TV networks and major newspapers, support the Court's actions in general and especially in such areas as civil rights and criminal procedure. There is no institution in our society that has as good a press as the Supreme Court. Judicial activism, it appears, has the approval of the intellectual elite who have become disillusioned with the effectiveness of social change by other means. It is more doubtful, however, whether the common man concurs either in the elite's support of judicial lawmaking or of its substantive results.

LONG-TERM EFFECTS

Neither popular acclaim nor criticism, of course, can answer the long-term question of the appropriate lawmaking role of the judiciary and the desirable limits on the scope of judicial decrees. More fundamental considerations must be decisive.

First, the practical question of comparative qualifications. Do judges, by training, selection, or experience, have an aptitude for social problem solving that other officials of government lack? And are the techniques of adjudication well designed to perform these broader policymaking functions? Professor Abram Chayes of the Harvard Law School has answered these questions with a confident affirmative. I am inclined to disagree.

Second, what will be the long-term effects of this trend on the credibility of the courts and on the sense of responsibility of administrators and legislators?

After completion of this article, my fears on this score received support from an unlikely source—Anthony Lewis in the *New York Times*. After acknowledging, as I do, that the Boston School Case "presented exceptional difficulties," that "a judge could [not] in conscience remit the complaining black families to their political remedy," and that District Judge Garrity's lonely efforts should be viewed with sympathy, Lewis nevertheless concludes that Garrity's involvement in the day-by-day administration of school affairs "has not worked well" and "is a serious philosophical error."

> American judges have to handle many controversial problems with political implications—redistricting, prisons and the like. Their object should always be to nudge elected officials into performing their responsibility. [Excessive intervention by the judge] tends to take responsibility away from those who ought to be seen to bear it.

And finally, as Simon Rifkind has put it, there is "the ancient question, *quo warranto?* By what authority do judges turn courts into minilegislatures?"

The critical question in a republic is how government by nonelected, lifetime officials can be squared with representative democracy. The magic of the robe, the remnants of the myth that law on these matters is discovered by an elaboration of existing rules (rather than by personal preference), and the prudence of the judiciary in picking issues on which it could command a great deal of popular support—perhaps these factors explain why the judges have been as successful as they have.

I fear, however, that the judiciary has exhausted the areas where broad majoritarian support will sustain new initiatives and that the tolerance of local communities for "government by decree" is fast dissipating. If so, caution is in order lest a depreciation of the esteem in which we hold the courts undermines their performance of the essential tasks that are indisputably theirs and that other institutions cannot perform.

The authority of the courts depends in large part on the public perception that judges are different from other policymakers. Judges (but not elected officials) are impartial rather than willful or partisan; judges utilize special decisional procedures; and they draw on established general principles in deciding individual cases. In short, traditional ideas concerning the nature, form, and functions of adjudication as a decisional technique underlie popular acceptance of judicial outcomes.

While the precise boundaries of the adjudicative technique are flexible rather than fixed, if they are abandoned entirely the judge loses credibility as a judge. He becomes merely another policymaker who, in managing prisons or schools or whatnot, is expressing his personal views and throwing his weight around. When that point is reached, the judge's credibility and authority is no greater than that of Mayor White in Boston or Mayor Rizzo in Philadelphia.

With the credibility of the legislature and executive branches of government in such disrepair, we cannot afford any further depreciation in the judicial currency. General acceptance of the authority of law is a necessary bulwark of our otherwise fragile social order. If it disappears, the resulting collapse of order may put the American people in the mood for that "more effective management" which is likely to characterize any distinctly American brand of authoritarianism.

Opportunities for charismatic and authoritarian leadership, it has been said, derive in considerable measure from the ability to "accentuate [a society's] sense of being in a desperate predicament." If the courts, by overextension and consequent failure, contribute to our growing sense of desperation, our liberties may not long survive. When a people despair of their institutions, force arrives under the masquerade of ideology.

TWENTY TWO
THE COURTS AND THE RULE MAKING PROCESS
The Limits of Judicial Review

J. Skelly Wright

Administrative law has entered an age of rule making. Administrators who once acted on whim and instinct have been judicially constrained to promulgate and adhere to consistent guidelines. Agencies which once generated policy in piecemeal fashion through adjudication are now adopting prospective standards of action valid in a number of different settings and against a wide variety of "parties." And the new agencies established by Congress to deal with contemporary environmental, economic, and energy problems have relied heavily on the promulgation of general regulations. These are healthy and welcome developments. Arguably, some areas of the economy should be deregulated to give fuller play to competitive market forces; and one may doubt that Congress is always wise to delegate to the executive branch and to administrative agencies the responsibility for making fundamental decisions about the economy and the environment. But when Congress *has* adopted a regulatory solution, and when the Delegation Doctrine does not bar that solution, the case for making administrative policy through rules, rather than adjudicatory decisions, is overwhelming.

Trial-like adjudication is extremely costly in time, staff, and money. Before an adjudicatory common law can acquire coherence, conditions typically will have overtaken it. As a consequence, industries subject to adjudicatory regulation are left in a state of perpetual uncertainty, and agencies assume the dangerous power to create new law affecting parties selected at random, or in a discriminatory manner. Orderly innovation is difficult, and emergencies often go unmet. To discern basic

This selection comes from the *Cornell Law Review* 59, 3 (March 1974), 375–97. © Copyright 1974 by Cornell University. All rights reserved. Footnotes omitted.

agency policy, the public must wade through volumes of scarcely relevant testimony and findings. The technicalities of adjudication allow lawyers to minimize the input of experts and to frustrate agency consideration of relevant scientific and economic perspectives. Regulation becomes an advocate's game. Especially in the rapidly expanding realms of economic, environmental, and energy regulation, the policy disputes are too sharp, the technological considerations too complex, the interests affected too numerous, and the missions too urgent for agencies to rely on the ponderous workings of adjudication.

These observations are not novel, and judges have not failed to recognize them. A Supreme Court majority recently suggested that agencies may not use an adjudicatory forum to announce new legal standards which will have only prospective effect. A quarter century ago, the Court advised the agencies that "[t]he function of filling in the interstices of [an act] should be performed, as much as possible, through the quasi-legislative promulgation of rules to be applied in the future." Judge Friendly has persuaded the Second Circuit to take the next logical step, requiring that the National Labor Relations Board promulgate standards of general application only by means of proper rulemaking procedures. The converse claim—that regulated parties have some "right" to an adjudicatory promulgation of general policies merely because these policies affect important interests or preexisting licenses—has been decisively rejected. And when agencies have asserted long dormant rulemaking powers, the courts have been quick to sustain the change of heart.

But a general background of judicial applause is not enough. In rule making, no less than in adjudication, Congress has fastened the courts and agencies into an intimate partnership, the success of which requires a precarious balance between judicial deference and self-assertion. In passing on administrative adjudications, the courts over the years have learned to maintain that balance, but judicial review of rule making is presenting a new and troublesome question. Some courts have recently shown an inclination to force rule makers to adopt triallike procedures—formal hearings, interrogatories, oral argument, cross-examination, and the like—which clearly are not required by the Administrative Procedure Act (APA). Should this tendency become general, rule making will lose most of its peculiar advantages as a tool of administrative policymaking, and the merits of the many rule-making experiments now underway will be denied a fair opportunity to be tested. The trend in agencies toward overproceduralization arose largely because reviewing courts were hostile to regulation and were uncritically fond of adjudicatory methods for resolving social controversies. From the general paralysis of administration which resulted, the agencies are only now emerging. Before throwing history into reverse, we in the judiciary should at least pause for thought.

"FAIRNESS" IN RULE MAKING AND THE APA'S PROCEDURES

While procedures for rule making, like those for adjudication, should no doubt promote "fairness," that slippery term has very different meanings in the two contexts. An adjudication applies a preexisting legal standard to a small set of controverted facts to determine whether a particular individual should receive a benefit or a penalty. An adjudication is fair to the individual only if the facts are accurately found, and Anglo-American jurisprudence assumes that accuracy is best served by traditional adversary procedures. But it makes no sense to speak of a rule as being fair or unfair to an individual in this objective sense of accuracy. A rule allocates benefits and penalties among large classes of individuals according to a specific normative standard, and the fairness of such an allocation is ultimately a political or philosophical question. Thus, in the rule-making context, fairness is not identified with accuracy, and procedures designed to maximize accuracy at the cost of all other values are simply inappropriate.

Nor can adjudicatory procedures be justified on the theory that fairness affords parties some basic right to participate in the formulation of rules which may affect them. Administrative agencies derive their sovereignty from Congress, not from the consent of parties potentially affected by agency rules. Moreover, triallike procedures are a thoroughly illogical vehicle for democratically weighting the views of the interested parties. Such weighting would require instead the election of administrative policymakers or the establishment of some formal system by which interest groups might be represented in the agencies' higher councils.

But there is one sense in which the notion of "fairness" may be applied to administrative rule making. Put simply, the *public* is treated unfairly when a rule maker hides his crucial decisions, or his reasons for them, or when he fails to give good faith attention to all the information and contending views relevant to the issues before him. To this notion of fairness—that rule making must be openly informed, reasoned, and candid—there is a twofold logic. First, if administrators rule in obscurity, Congress cannot intelligently delegate power or police the exercise of power already delegated. Second, although the "public interest" cannot be objectively defined, one can safely conclude that administrators who ignore relevant facts and who take the counsel of blind prejudice will serve the "public interest" only by the operation of chance. Therefore, although a rule maker's decisions cannot be "accurate" in the conventional sense, and although regulated parties have no fundamental "right" to participate in rule making, the administrator owes a duty to the public to give serious consideration to all reasonable contentions and evidence pertinent to the rules he is considering.

The APA provides rule-making procedures which directly enforce this duty. The procedures are uncluttered by inappropriate references to the ways of the courtroom or the world of electoral politics. Section 553 imposes a threefold obligation on a rule maker. First, the rule maker must give public notice of "the legal authority under which the rule is proposed" and of "either the terms of substance of the proposed rule or a description of the subjects and issues involved," at least thirty days before its effective date. Second, he must "give interested persons an opportunity to participate in the ruling making through submission of written data, views, or arguments with or without opportunity for oral presentation." Finally, "[a]fter consideration of the relevant matter presented," the rule maker must "incorporate in the rules adopted a concise and general statement of their basis and purpose."

If accorded a properly expansive reading, Section 553 provides a fully adequate scope for judicial review of rule making. Certainly, the courts have not felt cramped by the section's brevity. Recent cases, for instance, have put useful teeth into the step one notice provision. If an agency's empirical predictions constitute a substantial basis for its rule, the methodology of prediction should be made public so that interested parties have an opportunity to study and criticize it. If a flat rate is to be set for allocating costs between two industry services, the agency should specifically inform the public of this result and not merely report that *some* method of allocation is contemplated. If an agency wishes to base its rulings on facts developed in a corollary adjudication, the agency must say so, and interested parties must be allowed to contest the relevance of the adjudicatory record to the contemplated rulings. It is the common spirit of such decisions that the agency must make continuous disclosure of the facts and assumptions on which it intends to rely in promulgating its rule. Obviously, this philosophy of candor must also characterize the "basis and purpose" statement issued by the agency in step three. It cannot be so "concise" and "general" that the court is faced with merely conclusory assertions; the agency must show that it truly has given serious consideration to possible alternative rulings. Although detailed findings of fact are unnecessary, the reviewing court may demand reasoned explanations for controversial normative and empirical determinations made by the agency. At a minimum, the statement should refer to relevant submissions by interested parties and should rebut or accept these submissions in an orderly fashion.

Section 553 contemplates that rules will be made through a genuine dialogue between agency experts and concerned members of the public. In policing the three-step procedure, the reviewing court must satisfy itself that the requisite dialogue occurred and that it was not a sham.

THE AD HOC APPROACH TO PROCEDURAL REVIEW OF RULE MAKING

There is an important difference between interpreting Section 553 creatively and simply disregarding it. That section mandates a dialogue, not a trial. Nothing in Section 553 says that a rule maker must give individual answers to critical interrogatories, provide oral hearings, allow cross-examination of experts, or develop a testimonial record. Section 553 does not prevent agencies from adopting such procedures if they wish to do so, and in establishing a new rule-making authority or agency, Congress may, of course, carve out exceptions to Section 553 or impose procedures beyond those listed there. Indeed, the APA itself permits Congress to invoke the full panoply of adjudicatory procedures, set out in sections 556 and 557, simply by stating that rule making by a particular agency must be preceded by a "hearing on the record." But if Congress remains silent, the APA clearly contemplates that reviewing courts will insist on neither more nor less than Section 553 requires.

Some recent lower court decisions, however, have urged upon rule-making agencies a variety of procedures not found either in Section 553 or in the particular agency statutes under review. Consider *International Harvester Co. v. Ruckelshaus*, an exceptionally thoughtful decision rendered last term by a panel of our court. There the Environmental Protection Agency (EPA) had decided not to suspend for one year the Clean Air Act's 1975 standards for auto emission control. The act permitted a suspension only if the EPA administrator determined that the technology necessary to meet the 1975 standards was not "available." Because the administrator had determined the availability of such technology by means of a complex "prediction methodology" never revealed to the auto companies, the court remanded the case to the EPA to give "the parties . . . [an] opportunity . . . to address themselves to matters not previously put before them." Arguably, this conclusion followed directly from the notice requirement in Section 553 of the APA, for the methodology itself was an important "issue" which the agency should have publicized for comment and criticism before announcing its final decision.

The court went further, however, stating that

> [i]n the remand proceeding . . . we require reasonable cross-examination as to new lines of testimony, and as to submissions previously made to EPA in the hearing on a proffer that critical questions could not be satisfactorily pursued by procedures previously in effect.

It is true that the opinion permits the EPA to "confine cross-examination to the essentials, avoiding discursive or repetitive questioning." But the fact remains that neither Section 553 nor the Clean Air Act requires *any* cross-examination procedure for rule making. The court rested its order simply on "the interest of providing a reasoned decision."

Similarly, in *Mobil Oil Corp.* v. *FPC*, the court questioned a Federal Power Commission rule under the Natural Gas Act which established flat-rate cost figures for transporting various fuels by pipeline. While acknowledging that the Natural Gas Act did not require a "hearing on the record" and that the adjudicatory procedures of sections 556 and 557 of the APA were not required, the court nevertheless held that the FPC could not "proceed with only the guidance of the . . . standards of Section 553." The court reasoned that "artificial distinctions based upon the language of the APA should be avoided in determining what procedure should be followed." The APA's language was disregarded here because the Natural Gas Act requires "substantial evidence" as support for agency actions. The court did not dictate any particular procedures for use on remand, concluding only that "some sort of adversary, adjudicative-type procedures" would be necessary. Cross-examination and written interrogatories were suggested "by way of illustration."

Although *International Harvester* and *Mobil Oil* depart from the APA with diffidence, dicta in other cases do so rather bluntly. We are told that the APA's distinctions between informal rule-making procedures and full adjudicatory procedures have been "discarded . . . as criteria for determining the type of hearing to which the parties affected by administrative action are entitled." Courts are to devise mandatory procedures according to the "kind" or "importance" of the issues in the proceeding. Hearings, for instance, are deemed necessary whenever "a genuine and substantial issue of fact" has been raised by means of an offer of proof, or at least when "the issue presented is one which possesses a great substantive importance, or one which is unusually complex, or difficult to resolve on the basis of pleadings and argument." The underlying theory of these cases has been accurately conveyed by Professor Claggett:

> In *any* case where a rulemaking proceeding involves a contested issue of fact which has a vital bearing on the reasonableness of the rule and which is readily susceptible to taking of evidence, an agency may well abuse its discretion if it fails to conduct an evidentiary hearing even in an area where no statutory right to an adjudication is involved.

Thus, after an agency has fully completed its consideration and promulgation of a rule, the reviewing court may demand reconsideration under any procedures which, in retrospect, strike the court as being appropriate to the issues raised. This curious "ad hoc" approach to procedural review is not authorized by the APA or by any other statute; nor should it become the law by judicial fiat.

A. CRITIQUE OF THE AD HOC APPROACH TO PROCEDURAL REVIEW

A. Legal Infirmities

The ad hoc approach contravenes recent, authoritative interpretations of the APA. These interpretations make clear that an agency does not "abuse its discretion" by declining to utilize procedures more formal than those set out in Section

553. In *United States* v. *Allegheny-Ludlum Steel Corp.* and *United States* v. *Florida East Coast Ry.*, courts examined Interstate Commerce Commission (ICC) regulations aimed at alleviating the nation's chronic freight car shortage. The commission had formulated these regulations through Section 553 procedures, taking only written submissions on its proposals before issuing final rulings. Noting that the Interstate Commerce Act itself requires a "hearing" prior to commission action, the petitioners in both cases claimed that more formal procedures should have been followed by the ICC. But in *Allegheny-Ludlum*, the Supreme Court held that the term *hearing* in the Interstate Commerce Act is insufficiently close to the APA's term *hearing on the record* to indicate any congressional desire to impose on the ICC the adjudicatory procedures of sections 556 and 557. In *Florida East Coast Ry.*, the Court held that the ICC's receipt of written submissions adequately met the "hearing" provision of the Commerce Act. The message of these cases is clear. Courts are not to impose on agencies the formalities of sections 556 and 557 unless Congress has unmistakably so provided, and courts are not to spin their own procedural requirements from statutory catch phrases of uncertain meaning.

If the APA precludes the ad hoc approach, then that approach can survive only if the Constitution requires it. But there is not even a colorable claim to this effect. Of course, the due process clause often confers triallike procedural rights on an individual who becomes the focus of a government action. However, in the rulemaking context, the constitutional touchstone remains Mr. Justice Holmes's opinion for a unanimous court in *Bi-Metallic Investment Co.* v. *State Board of Equalization*, holding that a hearing was unnecessary before Colorado tax officials could substantially increase the valuation of all property in Denver. *Bi-Metallic* is nearly sixty years old, but just last term, the Supreme Court cited it with approval and reemphasized that the due process clause embodies the "recognized distinction in administrative law between proceedings for the purpose of promulgating policy-type rules or standards, on the one hand, and proceedings designed to adjudicate disputed facts in particular cases on the other." This need not mean that the due process clause has *no* application to rule making. Arguably, all government actions must be surrounded by procedures representing a reasonable balance between fairness and efficiency. For rule making, however, the fairness is owed to the public generally, not to particular individuals, and there is consequently no reason to doubt that the procedures of Section 553 strike other than a reasonable balance.

B. Infirmities of Logic and Policy

Having no foundation in the Constitution or the APA, the ad hoc approach to procedural review of rule making should be rejected as a violation of statutory law. But two general arguments have been advanced in support of the ad hoc approach: (*1*) that it promotes "procedural inventiveness," and (*2*) that it somehow facilitates judicial review of the substance of administrative rules. These arguments sound rather good as slogans, but they do not withstand close scrutiny.

1. "Procedural inventiveness". No one can deny that the ad hoc approach would allow courts to be "procedurally inventive." Judges could custom tailor procedural requirements to each distinct administrative action and could thus discontinue what Professor Claggett calls the "unprofitable exercise" of trying to "draw general and abstract lines separating areas especially appropriate for formal adjudication from those more appropriate for rulemaking." But if judges now have trouble inscribing a clear line between "legislative" and "adjudicatory" actions, how could they reach a consensus on the appropriate procedures to govern the thousands of actions issuing annually from the federal bureaucracy? On occasion, an agency may make a "rule" which applies to only one regulated party, or it may adopt a new legal standard in an adjudication. Such administrative perversions obviously raise problems of fairness with which the courts should deal. But this is no reason to disregard section 553 when reviewing the vast majority of agency actions which are indisputably valid exercises of rule-making power. If reviewing courts ignored the guidance of section 553 and instead operated under a vague injunction to find those procedures "best" suited to *each* agency action presented, judicial review of rule making would become totally unpredictable.

The administrative response would, however, be completely predictable. Fearing reversal of his substantive initiatives, each administrator would clothe his agency's actions in the full wardrobe of adjudicatory procedure. By demanding procedural refinements on an ad hoc basis, reviewing courts would inadvertently induce agencies to adopt maximum procedures in all cases. Seeking administrative variety, we would obtain administrative paralysis. The inherent virtues of rule making—expedition, flexibility to experiment, a sensible balance between expertise and broad public participation—would be forfeited. Like adjudicatory regulation today, rule making would become a lawyer's game.

There is a clear need for procedural innovation in many new areas of administrative rule making. But such innovation can only come, as the APA contemplates, from Congress or from the agencies themselves. To the extent that oral argument and cross-examination are genuinely useful in illuminating the empirical questions that course through some rule making, it is hardly utopian to rely on Congress and the agencies for a proper response. In the past decade, most of the major grants of rule-making authority made by Congress have specified procedures that exceed in one way or another those required by section 553. The excessive fondness of the agencies for adjudicatory methods is a matter of historical record. Therefore, lawyerlike procedures in the rule-making context simply do not need the services of an extrastatutory judicial crusade.

2. Procedural review versus substantive review In this "new era" of environmental, economic, and energy regulation, there would be great attraction to any approach which genuinely facilitated substantive review of agency rules. In the past year, this author has personally received a compulsory education in the intricacies of nuclear breeder reactor development, the difficulties of pipeline construction through the Alaskan tundra, the effect of different gasoline grades on auto engine performance, the economics of air transport between small cities in New England, and the differing methods of producing sulphuric acid. This is a rather rich diet for a "generalist" decision maker who feels more comfortable with a volume from West Publishing Company than with a computer printout. Furthermore, these new rule-making cases raise questions of the utmost political urgency. In the Alaskan pipeline litigation, for instance, the environmental integrity of our largest state was pitted against the immediate economic needs of its citizens, against the huge investments of several oil companies, and against the acute energy and fuel requirements of the entire nation. In the auto emissions case, the court recognized it was dealing with perhaps "the biggest industrial judgment that has been made in the United States in this century."

But how exactly do the difficulties of substantive review justify adopting the ad hoc approach to procedural review? Two suggestions have been advanced. Reasoning that agency use of adjudicatory procedure would guarantee the substantive adequacy of agency rules, Judge Bazelon has argued that the ad hoc approach could—and should—virtually replace substantive review. He fears that in many of the new areas of rule making, the exercise of substantive review dangerously taxes the competence of the courts, converting them into superagencies charged with second guessing the technological, scientific, and economic judgments of rule makers. The other suggestion accepts the need for a wide-ranging substantive review and argues that rule makers must be forced to embrace adjudicatory procedures so that an adequate "record" will be developed for such review.

To both of these suggestions, there is a threshold objection: each tries to facilitate substantive review at the cost of paralyzing agencies with procedures otherwise irrelevant to sound rule making. Surely the court's task can be rendered tolerable without rendering rule making a practical impossibility. Furthermore, both suggestions misconceive the role of substantive review. Since the APA not only disallows the ad hoc approach to procedural review, but also requires substantive review, Judge Bazelon's proposal is doubly doubtful. It is also unnecessary. Substantive review under the APA does not convert the reviewing court into a superagency. The APA standard of review is singularly undemanding, and it allows adequate play to Judge Bazelon's perception that courts can often better assess the way rules are made than the merits of the rules themselves. By the same token, courts do not need an adjudicatory record to undertake the necessary task of substantive review. Rather, they can and should review the legally sanctioned record of rule making which must be generated as a matter of course by section 553 procedures.

a. *The APA Requires Substantive Review.* Under section 706 of the APA, the reviewing court must strike down not only those agency rules which are "in excess of statutory jurisdiction, authority, or limitations, or short of statutory right," but also those actions which are "arbitrary, capricious, an abuse of discretion, or otherwise not in accordance with law." Presumably, the first standard means that an agency rule must conform to the agency's delegated power, just as a statute must conform to the Constitution. However, unless the act's drafters committed a redundancy, the "arbitrary, capricious" standard goes beyond this. It applies to the fact-finding, fact-predicting, and factual reasoning processes which led the agency to adopt the rule. As Judge MacKinnon has pointed out, a contrary interpretation would reduce review under the "arbitrary, capricious" standard to "a relatively futile exercise in formalism," because a "regulation perfectly reasonable and appropriate in the face of a given problem may be highly capricious if that problem does not exist." This is the precise teaching of the Supreme Court's important decision in *Overton Park* v. *Volpe.* There, the secretary of transportation had approved construction of an interstate highway through a public park, even though applicable legislation allowed such approval only if no "feasible and prudent" alternative route existed. Although the secretary's action was not a "rule" in the APA sense, the Court nevertheless applied the "arbitrary, capricious" standard of section 706 and ordered a "searching and careful" review by the district judge of all the facts, studies, and expert views which had provided the basis for the secretary's action. The purpose of review was to determine "whether the decision was based on a consideration of the relevant factors." After *Overton Park*, it is highly doubtful that courts can simply avoid substantive review of rule making, no matter how many "procedures" are imposed on the rule-making agency.

b. *The Standard of Review is Undemanding.* While the converse of arbitrariness and caprice is rationality, the APA authorizes a reviewing court to demand of rule makers only the most basic, minimal sort of rationality. A judge cannot strike down a rule merely because it seems to him "unreasonable," in the sense of being unwise or wrong, any more than he could upset congressional legislation for that reason. Rather, the APA has been interpreted by the Supreme Court to require only that "th[e] inquiry into the facts . . . be searching and careful, [and] the ultimate standard of review [be] a narrow one. The court is not empowered to substitute its judgment for that of the agency." The reviewing court is not even authorized to examine whether a rule maker's empirical conclusions have support in substantial evidence. The APA reserves the substantial evidence test for review of adjudications and of rules which must be made after a "hearing on the record." This exemption of conventional rule making from the substantial evidence test is very important, because that test is not itself terribly demanding. Exercising review under it, a court cannot disturb a fact-finder's weightings of conflicting evidence merely because these seem "clearly erroneous"; only those determinations which are patently unreasonable can be upset. Finding words to formulate a standard of review which is less demanding than substantial evidence is no easy task. It must be conceded that the cases applying the "arbitrary, capricious" test have not approached this problem with great vigor. Simple logic, however, suggests a rough answer. If weightings on conflicting evidence need be only "reasonable" to pass the substantial evidence test, it follows that they can be less than reasonable and still survive the "arbitrary, capricious" test. If this is so, the latter standard subjects a rulemaker to only the most rudimentary command of rationality. In drawing empirical conclusions, he must give actual, good faith consideration to all relevant evidentiary factors. If he has in fact given serious attention to a factor, the weight which he assigns to it in his final judgments is of virtually no concern to the reviewing court.

This is not quite so radical as it sounds. Final empirical conclusions never flow directly or mechanically from the weights assigned to raw items of evidence. In between, there are typically several steps of inferential reasoning and, even under the "arbitrary, capricious" test, these presumably must be something more than exercises in whimsy or free association. Nevertheless, the "arbitrary, capricious" standard seems to require not an evaluation of the rule maker's empirical conclusions, but rather an inquiry into the basic orderliness of the process by which evidence and alternative rulings were considered. Thus, *Overton Park* requires that agency action be "based on a consideration of the relevant factors," and a later case mandates that rule makers conduct "a considered evaluation of the presently available alternatives." These phrases mark out a realistic approach to substantive review. The empirical judgments at stake in rule making necessarily rest on prediction, for a rule has prospective application only, and agency rules typically involve issues of great technical complexity. Reviewing judges can make a valuable contribution to the rationality of rule making by asking questions such as: "Did you take this factor into account?" "What about this possibility?" But once the court is satisfied that the administrator did touch all the bases, absent obvious irrationality, there is little more a court can accomplish. Judges lack the special skills to evaluate sensibly the weightings assigned to technically abstruse evidence; only future historians can assess the merits of a rule maker's predictions.

This analysis of substantive review undermines Judge Bazelon's proposal that substantive review be replaced by the ad hoc approach to procedural review. Substantive review, properly understood, is too modest an enterprise to convert courts into superagencies, and the standard of substantive review itself incorporates Judge Bazelon's underlying, and correct, perception that courts can more competently assess the rationality of the rule-making process than the merits of the resultant rules. The problem with the ad hoc approach to procedural review is that it goes well beyond this sound perception. The ad hoc approach mandates that the courts prescribe precise and formal methods for bureaucratic policymaking. This mandate assumes an expertise in administrative science which duty on the bench simply does not confer. By contrast, the "arbitrary, capricious" standard of substantive review authorizes courts merely to scrutinize the actual making of a rule for signs of blind prejudice or of inattention to crucial evidence—a task of straightforward detective work which is well within the capacities of generalist judges.

Replacing substantive review with the ad hoc approach to procedural review would make sense only if adjudicatory formalities constituted both a necessary and sufficient condition for the rulemaking process to be rational. Neither branch of this proposition is sound. Rule making is adequately rational, under the APA, so long as the administrator is presented with all relevant evidentiary factors, gives serious consideration to those factors, and uses reason rather than whim to progress from initial assumptions to final conclusions. Let us take these requisites in turn.

For purposes of presenting evidence, formalized adjudicatory methods are clearly inessential: The three-step procedure of section 553 is expressly designed to provide the administrator access to all data, criticisms, suggestions, alternatives, and contingencies relevant to his decisions. Adjudicatory methods are in fact insufficient to this task. A rule maker must typically make and coordinate many empirical conclusions dependent on raw material outside the conventional evidentiary categories of "testimony" and "exhibits." For example, the rule maker must often draw upon prior experience, expert advice, the developing technical literature, ongoing experiments, or seasoned predictions.

As for the consideration given to these factors, a rule maker can surely demonstrate his seriousness and good faith without allowing interested parties to cross-examine him or quarrel orally before him. He can, for instance, through the "basis and purpose" statement, detail for the court the actual attention he gave to the factors, and explain his final disposition with respect to each of them. It would indeed be insufficient for him to listen passively to the contentions of the best financed and most skillfully represented formal "parties." An agency is not a judge or a sequestered juror. It cannot "act as an umpire blandly calling balls and strikes for adversaries appearing before it; the right of the public must receive active and affirmative protection at the hands of the Commission." Further, an administrator's attendance at an adjudicatory hearing does not guarantee that he has given good faith attention to all the disparate factors bearing relevantly on his decisions. Indeed, mere attendance does not even ensure attention to factors raised in the hearing itself.

Finally, *no* form of procedure can ensure the minimal rationality of a rule maker's inferences. These after all occur within his head! To see whether he has kept the counsel of reason, the reviewing court must in each instance demand an orderly explanation of the rule maker's inferences. For such an explanation, logic suggests no procedural substitute.

c. *Substantive Review Operates on an "Administrative" Record.* That rule makers should use adjudicatory procedures merely to provide courts with a "record" of those procedures is an argument which may charitably be termed circular. If courts adopt this curious theory, their partnership with the agencies will be transformed into a quaint minuet. Substantive review is an inquiry into the realities of the rulemaking process, not an occasion for pretending that agencies are some species of lower court. Consequently, a proper record must reflect all of the relevant views and evidence considered by the rule maker, from whatever source, and—like a minihistory—it must reveal if and how the rule maker considered each factor throughout the process of policy formation. Such is the "full administrative record" adverted to in *Overton Park* and its progeny. To provide such a record is one of the functions of the three-step procedure in section 553. If that provision receives the broad interpretation and strict enforcement which it merits, the reviewing court will be provided the following record:

Step one of section 553 will yield the agency's initial proposal, its tentative empirical findings, important advice received from experts, and a description of the critical experimental and methodological techniques on which the agency intends to rely. Step two will produce the written or oral replies of interested parties to the agency's proposals and to all the other "step one" materials. And step three will furnish the final rule, accompanied by a statement both justifying the rule and explaining its normative and empirical predicates through reference to those parts of the record developed in steps one and two.

Section 553 thus opens a broad window on the rule-making process, surely broad enough to reveal any unfairness to the public committed by the rule maker. At the same time, the window is not so large as to invite a judicial breaking and entering. By generating a unique sort of "record," the APA's procedures simultaneously facilitate and carefully channel the exercise of substantive review. Upsetting those procedures would almost certainly disturb the appropriate balance between skepticism and deference in substantive review itself.

THE MECHANICS OF RESTRAINT

When based on a proper administrative record, the mechanics of review are quite straightforward. If the subject matter of a rule falls within an agency's delegated authority, there are only two grounds for a court upsetting it. First, the "basis and purpose" statement given by the agency may include no reasons, or merely conclusory reasons, for adopting the rule or for rejecting evidence, criticisms, or alternatives submitted by outsiders. In this instance, the agency has violated the third procedural step of Section 553 and simultaneously has violated the "substantive" standard of review by failing to show good faith consideration to all relevant factors. No matter how the agency's default is labeled, the remedy is of course to remand the rule. But such remand is only to allow the agency, through fuller explanation, to show that the rule-making process was actually animated by reason rather than blind instinct. Since the "basis and purpose" statement is part of the "record," as well as a "procedure," this is in essence a remand "for a fuller record." But there should be no suggestion that the agency need take more submissions from outsiders, and certainly no suggestion that adjudicatory procedures are required.

Second, remand will be proper when the agency has relied on important findings, assumptions, or techniques not made public prior to the rule's promulgation. In this instance, the agency has violated step one of the Section 553 procedures. Since the unfairness here is to the public and not to an individual "party," the remedy is to instruct the agency to return to step one, *not* to order a legally impermissible adjudicatory consideration of issues theretofor unrevealed by the agency.

Compared to this simple routine, the ad hoc approach to procedural review assigns to the judiciary a relentlessly "activist" role. In some other areas of law, this author has not found such a role uncongenial. But the ad hoc approach to administrative review lacks those foundations in law and reason which an activist posture requires. The approach has no statutory underpinnings; indeed, it flies in the face of the APA. It can claim no constitutional mandate, and it certainly protects no minority interests which the political system would otherwise ignore. Furthermore, the approach draws on no talents peculiar to the judiciary. Although we judges may have a professional attachment to cross-examination and oral argument, we have no special expertise in the procedure appropriate to bureaucratic policymaking.

What reviewing courts can realistically do to improve rule making is just what the APA asks them to do—open the agencies to outside information, challenge, and scrutiny. Before dismissing this as a demeaning or trivial task, we should recall how many agencies have become captives of private interests, closed to new methods or regulation and planning, and dedicated to obscuring their policies from the public and Congress. In sections 553 and 706, the APA provides the courts with powerful tools to attack these abuses. We should learn to use these tools and give up playing arcane procedural games authorized by neither statute nor common sense.

TWENTY THREE
THE COURTS AS GUARDIANS OF THE PUBLIC INTEREST

Donald L. Horowitz

Of all the policy processes, the judicial process is the one that is formally most programmed for "rational" decision making. Judicial decisions must rest on evidence. Judicial opinions state results in terms of reasons. Judges and juries are insulated from extraneous influences. They are shielded from the clash of opposing interests and the process of "give and take" that are supposed to constitute integral parts of the other governmental processes. The courts take pride in their ability to work their way through the tangle of "special interests" and to handle issues "on their merits." In the judicial process, no particular virtue is seen in giving everyone something; of far greater importance is reaching the "right result." The assumption of the judicial process is that, where reason resides, the public interest will emerge.

There is a long tradition in the United States of appealing to the courts when efforts in other forums fail. Among other things, the fact that courts operate on avowedly different assumptions from other branches of government makes them attractive as alternative forums in which the play of interests can proceed. The predicate of such appeals is that institutions that are composed differently and proceed on different principles may well reach different results.

Yet the ability of the courts to proceed on different principles rests ultimately on the different burdens they have shouldered. Reason can reign when courts decide cases in which the number of unknowns is limited, in which doctrinal signposts ex-

Reprinted with permission from *Public Administration Review* 37 (March/April 1977), 148–153. © 1977 by The American Society for Public Administration, 1225 Connecticut Avenue, N.W., Washington, D.C. All rights reserved. Footnotes omitted.

ist, in which the relevant facts, though disputed, can be ascertained with a fair degree of reliability for purposes of the litigation, and in which the consequences of a decision one way or the other are limited in scope and generally foreseeable.

Courts still decide many cases of this kind, but their calendars increasingly include suits raising issues that tax their ability to ascertain the relevant facts, gauge the consequences of a decision one way or another, and reason to a conclusion. Most of these cases are challenges to governmental action, action usually taken by an administrative body. Many of them, involving matters such as the registration of pesticides, the regulation of effluent flows, and the approval of drugs and dyes, require complex assessments of risk and choice among alternatives. Some involve experimental social programs, while others deal with investment decisions having potential social costs, such as highway and power plant construction. Wholly new bodies of legal doctrine, such as the law of welfare rights and environmental protection, have grown up. The scope of judicial scrutiny has also enlarged, as the deference that judges formerly paid to administrative decisions has tended to wear thin. Courts today play a more prominent and less interstitial role in defining and protecting the public interest, often against agencies accused of neglecting it.

This article will trace some of the roots of the expanding judicial role in articulating the public interest, evaluate the prospects for resolving such issues through judicial review, and assess some of the consequences of judicial involvement in administrative decisions.

THE ADMINISTRATIVE STATE AND THE JUDICIAL THREAT

When the Administrative Procedure Act was passed in 1946, liberal proponents of the administrative state, eager to protect the New Deal agencies from the predatory attacks of a conservative judiciary and legal profession, were outraged. Among other things, they saw the act's judicial review provisions as granting a license to the courts to thwart the creative work of the administrative process. Three decades later, the same battle is being fought, but the sides have all changed. By and large, the business interests that wanted to use the courts in their crusade against regulation never got to do so. Instead, the liberal reformers now attack the federal agencies their predecessors proudly created. They invoke the aid of the courts against the same interests that earlier fought for access to the courts—and under the same statutory provisions. The courts, far from undoing the work of the federal agencies, have in general required them to do more and better. No one seems to play his or her appointed part.

How have we arrived at this paradoxical turn of events?

The reformers' fears were not wholly ill-founded, but in the short run they proved quite mistaken. The Administrative Procedure Act (APA) was framed against the background of a long campaign to gut the New Deal Agencies. With the American Bar Association in the vanguard, critics charged that the agencies were doing judicial work but without the independence of judges, that they often espoused the case of one of the parties before them or were captives of their staffs. It was argued that agency procedures were haphazard, irregular, and unfair. The ABA in general favored the transfer of much of the work of the agencies to the courts, viewed as more committed to traditional principles of justice.

The Administrative Procedure Act did not do this. Instead, it spelled out basic procedural rules for the agencies to follow. The act made many administrative determinations subject to judicial review, but often within a very narrow compass. This was far short of the hopes of those who saw creeping despotism lurking behind the "fourth branch" of government.

Nevertheless, the result was to regularize and in many ways to formalize administrative procedure. Beyond that, the act allowed judges to sit in judgment on the way in which administrators had conducted themselves. These provisions alone were sufficient to offend those who had fought long and hard for the problem-solving utility of the administrative mechanism. These people wanted "results" rather than rules, and managerial technique rather than what they saw as legal obscurantism. What they most objected to was the sacrifice of flexibility—that most vaunted virtue of the administrative process—on the altar of an abstraction, due process of law. Judges, whose administrative expertise could hardly be acknowledged and whose sympathies were questionable at best, would now have the power to issue orders undoing the work of specialists. Worse still, implementation of administrative decisions might be delayed while the pleasure of the judge was awaited; "vested interests" might use and profit from the lapse of time. This was the ultimate conspiracy of the lawyers against the public interest.

Despite these forebodings, for the first 15 or 20 years of its operation the APA kept the courts out of the work of the federal agencies and departments far more than it let them in. Particularly was this so on the broad policy questions where arguments for administrative expertise and flexibility were most strongly invoked. Resort to the courts was possible in the vast majority of cases only where a showing of procedural irregularity was made. Rarely was it possible to challenge administrative action in court on substantive grounds—that is, by showing that, though the agency had followed the proper procedure, it had nonetheless reached an inappropriate resolution of the problem before it.

The drafters of the APA were only a decade removed from the excesses of the Supreme Court in the 1930s. They were well aware of the Court's flights of fancy into "substantive due process," of the constitutional crisis wrought by judicial immoderation, and the "Court-packing plan" it produced. Out of such concerns came the blanket exception to judicial review for matters "committed to agency discretion." The courts were not to second-guess wholly discretionary judgments. Nor were they to overturn agency action if the agency had followed the appropriate procedure, unless the action was "arbitrary, capricious, an abuse of discretion, or otherwise not in accordance with law" or "unsupported by substantial evidence." The intention was to make the procedures of the agencies predictable, to confine them to decisions that had some demonstrated basis in fact, and to prevent them from acting in disregard of statutory law or fundamental constitutional principles. Courts were not to have a central role in formulating public policy, and for quite some time they did not seek such a role.

These conditions no longer obtain. Over the last decade or more, courts have become a more prominent part of the process of administrative decision making. They have moved beyond protection of the rights of parties aggrieved by administrative action to participation in problem solving and protection of more general public interests against agencies accused of indifference to the public interest. Judicial review has passed from matters of procedure to matters of both procedure and substance. Judicial scrutiny of records of administrative decision making has become far more searching than it once was, and judges have often not liked what they have found. Courts have not merely sat in judgment on administrative action but on inaction as well; they have required agencies to do things the agencies themselves had declined to do.

The signs of this more active role are everywhere—in legal doctrine, in frequency of litigation, in the sweep of decisions, and in judicial pronouncements on and off the bench.

The obstacles to carrying policy problems to the courts have been falling away over the years. The doctrines that barred litigants or certain classes of litigants at the threshold—requirements of standing, jurisdiction, and the like—are now much diluted, and the defenses available to government agencies once suit was begun have also been chipped away.

At the same time, the frequency of litigation challenging governmental action, especially in the federal courts, increased considerably between the early 1960s and the early 1970s, although perfectly accurate figures are difficult to come by. The scope of the challenges raised in such cases seems to have broadened considerably. One indirect measure of this is the steady increase in the percentage of cases brought by nonprofit organizations suing to challenge governmental action. These organizations are more likely than the individual plaintiffs they have proportionately supplanted to challenge not some narrow determination, of interest to only one party, but the policy as a whole and the assumptions on which it is based.

Finally, the scope of the exception to judicial review for matters "committed to agency discretion" has been steadily narrowed. Now even agency determinations of "feasibility" and "prudence"—the kinds of words opponents of judicialization might have made slogans of in 1946—are now immune from judicial scrutiny. Far from eschewing discretionary judgments, some meliorist judges today see themselves as warriors in "the fight to limit discretion" on the part of administrative agencies.

THE BACKWASH OF THE APA

In the long run, then, the anguished prophesies of the reformers have been fulfilled and overfulfilled. Courts have insisted that agencies abide by stringent procedural requirements, and in the main these requirements and the judicial role in enforcing them have been accepted without much question. But what the courts have done goes much beyond administrative procedure. Increasingly, the courts insist on having the last word on the merits of many issues of public importance. It is not anything so modest as the judicialization of the administrative process that is the issue: it is the role of the courts in sharing what was formerly taken to be the agencies' exclusive job.

Needless to say, courts have assumed such functions haltingly, unevenly, incompletely—but far beyond what opponents of the APA imagined they might do. Yet in certain ways these developments were an outgrowth of that act. As the APA and the courts whittled away many of the differences between agency proceedings and court proceedings, so, too, did they obliterate much of the distinctiveness of the administrative process. In some respects, agencies have simply become second-class courts. The new title, "administrative law judge," in lieu of "hearing examiner," is more than just an attempt to share in the prestige of the courts: it also marks the extent to which the trial-type hearing has become a norm of administrative practice. Judicial review of substantive issues is therefore the aftershock of the judicialization of agency proceedings. Why accept the counterfeit administrative version of a just decision when one can have the real currency, robes and all? The more similar the administrative and judicial processes become, the more the same functions will be performed interchangeably.

Furthermore, the APA and similar laws may have demanded of judges exceptional ability to compartmentalize their work. Once a judge has jurisdiction to review for procedural irregularities, how can he be expected uniformly to acquiesce in an "erroneous" decision, even if it is arrived at through impeccable procedure? Jurisdiction to review the one invites review of the other, and it is unrealistic to think that judges will always adhere to a restrictive "arbitrary and capricious" or "abuse of discretion" standard once the subject matter is opened up to them at all.

Broader currents have also shaped the judicial inclination to scrutinize agency action closely. The APA became law at a time of national quiescence, and it is not surprising that it should have been interpreted as it was during such a period. Equally, the courts were affected by the restlessness that affected other institutions in the 1960s, and their eagerness to probe grew apace. The bases of administrative legitimacy came under attack. Claims that once rang true began to ring hollow. "Expertise" can connote narrow-mindedness, and "flexibility" may mask political compromise. The courts have not been especially tolerant of either. Generalists themselves, judges are often disdainful of specialization. They tend to be rationalists, searchers after "solutions," suspicious of the political process and "special interests" as impediments to rationality. As they sensed the growth of clientelism in the federal agencies, of departmental self-aggrandizement and bureaucratic rivalries, and official sloth, inertia, and rigidity, the courts became less and less hospitable to administrative claims to immunity from judicial oversight and more and more disposed to weigh costs and benefits for themselves. What they saw made them, in a word, skeptical.

Those who now invoke the courts against the agencies tend to exalt these qualities of the judicial process: the generalist character of the judges and the distance from the political contest that they seem to possess. Now it is the judges, rather than the managers, who are regarded as the expediters dissolving the sediment that has accumulated on the administrative machine. But do they have the equipment to do this job? In the race to the courthouse, this question has rarely been posed and even more rarely addressed.

HAZARDS OF JUDICIAL GUARDIANSHIP

Judges may be performing new roles in administrative-agency litigation, but they continue to act very much within the framework of an old process, a process that evolved, not to devise new programs or to oversee administration, but to decide controversies. The constraints of that process operate to limit the range of what can reasonably be expected from courts. The principal limitations derive from the way in which cases get to court, the way in which issues are framed and reasons adduced, and the provisions for effectuating court decisions.

Courts are public decision makers, yet they are wholly dependent on private initiative to invoke their powers: they do not self-start. Parties affected by administrative action choose to seek or not to seek judicial redress on the basis of considerations that may bear no relation to the public importance of the issues at stake, to the recurring character of the administrative action in question, or to the competence of courts to judge the action or to change it. This basic feature of judicial review has a number of important consequences.

First of all, the fact that judges do not choose their own menu makes it difficult for them to concentrate in a sustained way on any policy area. Judicial action tends to be spotty and uneven; some agencies may be subject to frequent correction in the courts, others to virtually none at all. The decisions that emerge are ad hoc; they are rarely informed by a comprehensive view of the agency's work, and they cannot aspire to anything approaching the status of a coherent policy. One of the catchwords of the administrative state—and now perhaps one of its biggest disappointments—was "planning." Few agencies do the kind of program planning that was once expected of them. But if this is a deficiency of the administrative process in need of rectification, the courts, whose own process is fundamentally passive and piecemeal, are not the place to sell it.

The fact that courts do not deal with anything resembling a random sample of the work of administrative agencies affects their perspective in another way. They are put in the position of having to prescribe on the basis of very special, indeed often highly atypical, cases—cases that come to decision one at a time. Small wonder that their outlook on the administrative process has tended to become skeptical: they base their inferences on a skewed sample. Courts see the tips of icebergs and the bottoms of barrels. If their perspective is detached, it is not necessarily well informed.

As courts decide only special cases, so do they decide them in a special way. The framing of issues is geared to the litigant and his complaint. The mission of the courts is to set wrongs right. This means that the facts of the single case are highlighted, the facts of all cases slighted. The judicial process has a bias toward the particular and against the recurrent. Judicial standards of relevance are strict. In consequence, everything that can be labeled context or background is relegated to a distant second place in litigation. Elaborate provision is made for proving and weighing the events that give rise to the litigation. Virtually no provision is made for proving anything more general about administrative behavior. Courts are, for example, often ignorant of the scope and nuances of the programs they find themselves judging, and nothing in the rituals of litigation alerts them to this omission. On the contrary, everything pushes them toward a narrow focus on the case before them. It is this feature of adjudication that so often gives outsiders the impression that courts are fascinated by questions that are at best tangential to policy.

The sources of judicial reasoning do, of course, reside in general principles. But those principles are to be found in yet more particular cases—often cases far afield from the administrative action being challenged. The principles tend to cut across the functional divisions along which agencies are organized and policies are formulated. For purposes of decision, reality is organized in terms of categories that seem to make no sense except in court. Thus, perhaps the only thing that social security recipients, produce handlers, and environmentalists have in common is that all must be accorded hearings by the administrators whose actions affect their interests—though the "actions," the "effects," and the "interests" may be completely different in kind. No doubt the propensity of courts to seek their analogies in far-flung places contributes to the development of an integrated jurisprudence, and there is much to be said for it in these terms. But this propensity again detracts from judicial attention to the program being reviewed. It also diminishes the value of the judicial decision as guidance to the administrator as he manages his program.

Judicial decisions thus embrace a limited species of reasoning. Equally important, they are *all reasoning*. The judicial process is tied to reason as the mode of decision and can scarcely be described apart from its resort to reason. Yet there are some questions that lend themselves to other modes of decision—particularly to negotiation and compromise. Sometimes that is the only way to satisfy conflicting interests and keep them from turning against the political system. Sometimes reason provides no clues to an appropriate answer. There may be a shortage of knowledge sufficient to provide answers or a shortage of resources to find the answers at the time that they are needed, at a cost that makes sense. The administrative process has at least its fair share of such problems. Courts are not the place to look for their solution.

Perhaps the ultimate hazard of relying on courts to guard the public interest is that their decisions stand a good chance of being ineffective or effective in ways not intended. Some administrators have been known to act on the view that courts decide only individual cases. A succession of cases repudiating the lawfulness of agency policy brings a series of concessions to individual litigants but no change in policy. Those with the resources, initiative, and foresight to bring suit may force a "policy change" applicable only to their cases.

Even more generous views of the authority of courts to lay down policy can raise problems of uniformity. Decisions of the federal courts, short of the Supreme Court, are binding only in the circuit or district in which the court sits. Although this principle is a useful safeguard against settling difficult policy questions prematurely, it also permits recalcitrant bureaucrats to wait until at least several courts have spoken before bringing general policies into line with court decisions. Typically, this time is measured in years, and there are some agencies that do not feel obliged to alter their course until the Supreme Court itself has spoken. Given the multitude of issues competing for Supreme Court consideration, this may be never. The fact that courts decide one case at a time, against agencies with varying degrees of responsiveness to judicial decisions, makes it hard for courts to force policy change all by themselves.

There is, however, a problem of impact beyond this. It lies in the propensity of all policies to have unanticipated consequences. In this respect, policies enunciated by courts are no different from the policies that emanate from other decision makers. But the courts are unusually short of machinery to detect and correct unintended consequences after they have occurred. They have no monitoring mechanisms, no inspectors, no grapevines. Quite the opposite: judicial prosperities foster isolation of the decision maker from the environment in which his or her decisions must operate. Unless a litigant provides the courts with feedback about the consequences of their decisions, there is every likelihood that they will pass unnoticed—and unaltered. Here, again, private initiative seems inadequate to protect public interests.

CONCLUSION

Different institutions tend to perform well at different kinds of tasks. Each has its own characteristic modes of operating, and these leave an indelible stamp on the matters they touch. In the case of the courts, I have argued, their procedures remain attuned to the disposition of individual controversies. This means that they function on a basis that is too intermittent, too spotty, too partial, too ill-informed for them to have a major constructive impact on administrative performance. They can stop action in progress, they can slow it down, and they can make it public (their exposing function has been too little noted). Perhaps most important, they can bring moral judgment to bear, for moral evaluation is a traditional judicial strength. But courts cannot build alternate structures, for the customary modes of judicial reasoning are not adequate for this. When it comes to framing and modifying programs, administrators are far better situated to see things whole, to obtain, process, and interpret complex or specialized data, to secure expert advice, to sense the need to change course, and to monitor performance after decision. Courts can limit the discretion of others, but they find it harder to exercise their own discretion where that involves choosing among multiple, competing alternatives.

Although the tendency to resort to the courts for the vindication of broad public interests continues unabated, the impact of judicial intervention on administrative behavior remains uncertain. There has surely been no rush in the federal agencies to embrace judicially enunciated standards of performance beyond what is minimally required by individual decrees. Even then, many government lawyers and program managers have been inclined to read judicial opinions as narrowly as the words would warrant, secure in the knowledge that many things escape the attention of the courts, that judicial correction comes, not every budget session, but every so often and, at that, frequently in a different court and usually in a fresh factual setting.

But it is wrong to reckon the benefits and costs only by the effects of judicial action inside the departments and agencies. The growing judicial role has implications for the courts, too. They have so far been remarkably slow to enhance their ability to meet the new burdens they face. It is, as I have suggested, the fact that they continue to face new challenges with the old machinery very much intact that limits their ability to handle complex data, to monitor the consequences of their decrees, or to do the other things that might make them more effective partners in the process of defining the public interest.

Yet even in this failing there is something to be celebrated. The outstanding characteristic of the judicial process remains the way in which it generalizes from the particular instance. So committed are the courts to the individual case that all their machinery is tuned to resolving it. From the standpoint of policymaking, this is a weakness. Retooling the judicial process means essentially giving it the capacity to function more systematically in terms of general categories, to draw probabilistic inferences, to forecast effects. Should retooling proceed beyond marginal improvements, it seems highly likely that it will occur at the expense of the commendable attention currently given to the individual case and that courts, in trying to improve other institutions, will become much more like them. The distinctiveness of the judicial process—that which unfits it for much of the important work of government—lies in its willingness to expend social resources on individual complaints one at a time. That distinctiveness is worth preserving.

CHAPTER SEVEN
TORT LIABILITY OF PUBLIC OFFICIALS

INTRODUCTION

If regulatory agency action by nonelected policymakers causes injury which is remediable by civil action for damages, then another method to control for regulatory abuses of power (a reflection of the problem of accountability in a constitutional democracy) is the tort liability action by the injured party. Nonelected federal (and state/local) administrators can be kept accountable, if all other controls are ineffective, by having aggrieved persons bring suit in court for damages caused by overzealous administrators.

Unfortunately, however, for centuries (in England and in America) there has existed, in common, statutory, and constitutional law, a basic doctrinal protection against such civil suits: the concept of immunity—sovereign and official. Sovereign immunity is the doctrine, developed in England,[1] that prohibits citizens from bringing suits against a sovereign state unless it gives its permission. It is "a personal privilege which it may waive at pleasure."[2] (In 1974 amendments to the APA, Congress did create a limited waiver of sovereign immunity—see Section 702, Right of Review.) The doctrine became established in America with the passage of the Eleventh Amendment, although it was "never discussed nor reasons given" for its existence.[3]

[1]Lawrence Tribe noted that sovereign immunity in England was "an historical accident caused by the pyramidal structure of feudal courts, and not a basic idea implicit in any concept of sovereignty." *American Constitutional Law* (Mineola, NY: Foundation Press, 1978), p. 130, fn 5.
[2]*Clark* v. *Barrard*, 108 *US* 447 (1883).
[3]Rosenbloom essay, this chapter.

Official immunity "renders government officials immune from liability for their actions even though their conduct, if performed in other contexts, would in itself be unconstitutional or otherwise contrary to criminal, or civil statute."[4] Absolute official immunity now extends to judges, prosecutors, public defenders, and legislators; some form of limited immunity extends to all other public administrators.

The doctrine of immunity creates the dilemma for a constitutional democracy. Those who govern must act responsibly; the persistence of the immunity doctrine has the effect of negating civil actions against public officials. If tortious actions are committed by agency officials and there is no means of assisting the plaintiff and deterring future instances of wrongdoing, then maintaining a sense of responsibility becomes a matter of individual self-restraint and self-discipline. If civil liability suits are not possible, or very difficult to win, then a very basic external check on the agency is eliminated. If there are no well-defined rules of legal responsibility that agency personnel must adhere to or face the possibility of civil damages or loss of job, then the administrative system must fall back on the notion of professionalism or internal checks that enhance the value and importance of official responsibility.[5]

However, men are not angels, as Madison and others throughout history have noted. The force of internal checks is not, in itself, sufficient to curtail irresponsible, tortious maladministration. For this, and other reasons, the immunity doctrine has come under heavy attack as being, in the Age of the Administrative State, "inequitable, outmoded, unduly harsh, and antithetical to concepts of American justice."[6]

In the past decade, this concern about the seeming unfairness of the immunity concept has led Congress and the federal courts to modify this ancient doctrine.

> Possibly the most significant development occurred during the 1970's when the congress, with approval of the courts, took from public officials many of the official immunity protections which for so long had made it virtually impossible for citizens to sue public agencies and their officials for grossly irresponsible and malicious conduct.[7]

In addition to the Federal Tort Claims Act, written by Congress in 1946 and substantively modified in the 1970s by the legislature, the Supreme Court's decisions in the past decade (as discussed in the Rosenbloom essay) have modified the official immunity doctrines somewhat for federal (see the Rabin essay) and for state and local officials and municipalities (see the Colella article).

Tort liability actions against federal and state agencies and their personnel should optimally have an external deterrent effect. Justice William J. Brennan, in the U.S. Supreme Court's *Owen* opinion suggested some form of strict liability would curb future abuses of rights by agency officials:

> The knowledge that a municipality will be liable for all of its injurious conduct, whether committed in good faith or not, should create an incentive for officials who may harbor doubts about the lawfulness of their intended actions to err on the side of protecting citizens' constitutional rights. Furthermore, the threat that damages might be levied against the city may encourage those in a policy making position to institute internal rules and programs designed to minimize the likelihood of unintentional infringements on constitutional rights.[8]

[4] Ibid.

[5] Phillip Cooper, "Government, Law, and Responsibility: The Supreme Court on Sovereign and Official Immunity," paper presented at the National American Society for Public Administration Meeting, April 1981.

[6] William Olson, "Government Immunity From Tort Liability: Two Decades of Decline, 1959-1979," *Baylor Law Review* 487 (Winter 1979).

[7] Kenneth F. Warren, *Administrative Law in the American Political System* (St. Paul, MN: West Publishing Company, 1982), p. 411.

[8] *Owen v. City of Indianapolis*, 455 US 622 (1980), at 694

Given recent judicial decisions, "there is and . . . there ought to be some anxiety on the part of [both federal and local] public officials concerning their vulnerability to suits."[9]

The readings in this chapter focus on the recent Supreme Court opinions in the area of tort liability and on their impact on federal and local agency personnel. Rosenbloom's essay examines tort liability litigation using, as his framework for analysis, the basic postulate that the citizen is sovereign and that federal regulatory agencies (and local bureaucracies) are the servants of the soverign people. Rabin, Miller, and Hildreth examine the impact of recent Supreme Court decisions on federal managers while Coletta examines the impact of these recent tort liability opinions on local officials.

---

[9]Cooper, *Government, Law, and Responsibility*, p. 63.

TWENTY-FOUR
PUBLIC ADMINISTRATORS' OFFICIAL IMMUNITY AND THE SUPREME COURT:
Developments During the 1970s

David H. Rosenbloom

The decade of the 1970s witnessed many changes in public administration in the United States. At the forefront of these have been the Civil Service Reform Act of 1978, the emergence of "Proposition 13" style taxpayer protests in the wake of public sector labor strife and depleted governmental resources, the rise of "affirmative action," and the decline of the citizen participation movement. Consistent with the past, the core values of representatives, executive leadership, and neutral competence continued to play a major role in American public administration. Toward the end of the decade, the latter two values and their accompanying concerns with accountability, responsibility, efficiency, and economy were particularly central to public administrative debate. Although less well-known, the 1970s also witnessed a number of Supreme Court decisions of fundamental importance to public administration in the United States. Some of these, including decisions dealing with the rights of public employees and federalism, have been analyzed elsewhere, but others of equal or even greater potential importance, such as those involving the immunity of administrative officials have been largely ignored. Broadly stated, the doctrine of official immunity renders government officials ". . . immune from liability for their actions . . . even though their conduct, if performed in other . . . contexts, would in itself be unconstitutional or otherwise contrary to criminal or civil statute." This article will analyze the content of Supreme Court decisions affecting public adminis-

Reprinted with permission from *Public Administration Review* 40 (March/April 1980), 166–171. © 1980 by The American Society for Public Administration, 1225 Connecticut Avenue, N.W., Washington, D.C. All rights reserved. Footnotes omitted.

trators' immunity and explain their importance for the contemporary administrative state.

THE CITIZEN IN THE ADMINISTRATIVE STATE

The rise of the administrative state has had profound consequences for citizenship in democratic nations. As Frederick Mosher notes, "The accretion of specialization and of technological and social complexity seems to be an irreversible trend, one that leads to increasing dependence upon the protected, appointive public service, thrice removed from direct democracy." By placing increasing political power in the hands of nonelected, nonpolitically appointed career administrators, the administrative state has reduced the relative importance of elected and politically appointed officials. Wallace Sayre captured this development in a passage that is worth quoting at length:

> The staffs of executive branch agencies have come to exercise an important share of the initiative, the formulation, the bargaining, and the deciding in the process by which governmental decisions are taken. They are widely acknowledged to be leading "experts" as to the facts upon which issues are to be settled; they are often permitted to identify authoritatively the broad alternatives available as solutions; and they frequently are allowed to fix the vocabulary of the formal decision. These powers are shared and used by the career staffs in an environment of struggle and competition for influence, but the relatively new fact to be noted with emphasis is that others who share the powers of decision—the President, Congress, the political executives, the congressional committees and staffs, the interest groups, the communications media—now rarely question the legitimacy of the career staff spokesmen as major participants in the competition.
>
> Great power also belongs naturally to those who carry out decisions of public policy. In this stage, the career staffs have a paramount role. The choice of means, the pace and tone of governmental performance, reside largely in the hands of the federal service. Constraints are present, and most of these uses of discretion by the career staffs are subject to bargaining with other participants, but the civil servants have a position of distinct advantage in determining how public policies are executed.

To a considerable extent the growth of administrative power has been the result of an increase in the governmental penetration of the economic and social life of the nation. However, as Mosher and Sayre suggest, there has also been a shift in power from elective to appointive officials. Indeed, so pronounced has this change been that in 1973, 65 per cent of the public and 57 per cent of elected officials agreed that: "The trouble with government is that elected officials have lost control over the bureaucrats, who really run the country." Moreover, only 17 per cent of the public and 29 per cent of the elected officials disagreed with this statement.

One of the complexities of the administrative state is that the shift in power from elective to administrative officials results in a loss of citizens' influence over government. The importance of the franchise declines; indeed, it has been argued that today the citizen's best hope for political change lies in "abstentionism," which has the effect of withholding legitimacy from the administrative state. Many of the efforts made in the 1970s to insure the accountability of administrators to elective officials may help mitigate this situation. However, it it clear that neither "sunshine," "sunset," new budgetary techniques, nor the civil service reforms of 1978 will do much to affect directly the relationship between citizen and administrator, or as Erich Strauss puts it, between citizen and "ruling servant." Consequently, administrative accountability to the public at large will remain tenuous at best, and the connection between the citizen and the direction of the administrative state will be attenuated. It is for this reason that the lack of major success with citizen participation in the poverty and model cities programs was so important; had it worked better, a new and effective link between citizen and administrator might have been forged.

Yet, while the shift in power from elective to administrative officials was becoming more evident and as citizen participation was declining in promise, the Supreme Court was altering traditional doctrines concerning administrators' official immunity and consequently was developing some *new* protections for citizens vis-à-vis public administration. Although the steps taken thus far are modest, they are not without important consequence: They contain within them the concept that the public administrator can be held personally accountable to the citizen under certain circumstances.

SOVEREIGN IMMUNITY AND OFFICIAL LIABILITY

The doctrine of sovereign immunity holds that the government cannot be sued for civil damages in the absence of its own consent. The doctrine's origin is bound up in the position of the English monarch; its consequences for life in the modern administrative state are perplexing. As Kenneth Culp Davis writes:

> . . . the unaltered common law seems clearly contrary to what is deemed common sense during the 1970's. For instance, if two truck drivers are negligent in the same way, and each runs over a pedestrian, but one truck belongs to a state or local government and the other belongs to a private corporation, the pedestrian has a cause of action against the owner of the second truck but not against the owner of the first one. If any modern reason justifies that result, it has not been brought out in the literature on the subject.

Why the doctrine of soverign immunity was adapted to American law in the first place is puzzling. In *United States* v. *Lee* (1882), the Supreme Court rather startlingly acknowledged that "while the exemption of the United States and of the several states from being subjected as defendants to ordinary actions in the courts has . . . repeatedly been asserted here, the principle has never been discussed or the reasons for it given, but it has always been treated as an established doctrine."

Given the peculiar nature of the doctrine of sovereign immunity, it is not surprising that as the state and federal governments expanded their services and became more involved in the everyday life of the citizenry, they waived large portions of their immunity. For example, as early as 1855, the federal government established the United States Court of Claims and waived its immunity where contracts were at issue. Under the Federal Tort Claims Act of 1946, the federal government sacrificed even more of its immunity. The importance of sovereign immunity has consequently been receding over time—indeed, it has been substantially diminished. Thus, a citizen who is harmed by negligent governmental activity or governmental breach of contract may now have some recourse in court.

What is the situation, however, if the citizen seeks to sue a public official, as an individual, for wrongs done in connection with the official's employment, rather than attempting to sue the government itself? According to Davis, "The old common law, broadly viewed, was that an agent was liable to a third party for his torts, whether or not within the scope of employment, and that as between principal and agent, the ultimate liability rested upon the agent, whether the tort was deliberate or involved nothing more than negligence. . . ." Under this approach, the citizen might sue the public official and recover damages for the public administrator's torts. However, it contained two inherent problems, both of which have been the subject of litigation and important doctrinal development in recent years. One deals with the question of when and why administrative officials are immune from suits for civil damages, and the other concerns the issue of whether an individual can bring a suit against a federal official for monetary damages for breach of the individual's constitutional rights.

ADMINISTRATORS' IMMUNITY: THE TRADITIONAL APPROACH

Allowing aggrieved citizens to sue governmental officials affords some measure of protection against the wrongful action of administrators and provides the citizen with a kind of "last ditch" defense against the administrative state. However, it has long been recognized that such suits could be used in a frivolous or harassing fashion so as to constrain or control the behavior of public officials. Indeed, the Constitution provides federal legislators with "privileged speech" by making them absolutely immune from suits for damages caused by their remarks in "any speech or debate in either House," and the Supreme Court has afforded similar protections to judges and public prosecutors. As the administrative state emerged, the question arose whether the discretionary actions of high-ranking *administrative* officials ought not to be similarly protected.

In 1896, the Supreme Court addressed this issue in the case of *Spaulding* v. *Vilas*. United States Postmaster General Vilas had sent a communication to several postmasters who were seeking a salary increase and who were represented by Spalding. It allegedly placed Spalding ". . . before the country as a common swindler," and brought ". . . him into public scandal, infamy, and disgrace . . . and . . . injure[d] his business. . . ." The communication also made it clear that Spalding's clients were under no legal obligation to pay him. Consequently, Spalding sought damages in court. In its decision, the Supreme Court established the constitutional principle that:

> In exercising the functions of his office the head of an Executive Department, keeping within the limits of his authority, should not be under an apprehension that the motives that control his official conduct may, at any time, become the subject of inquiry in a civil suit for damages. It would seriously cripple the proper and effective administration of public affairs as entrusted to the executive branch of the government, if he were subject to any such restraint.

Thus, federal department heads were provided with an *absolute* immunity from civil suits arising out of their actions connected with their official functions, regardless of the motives that may have controlled their behavior.

The Spaulding decision may have comported well with the realities of power in the federal executive branch in 1896, but as the administrative state emerged in its modern form, the logic of the case became equivocal. On the one hand, absolute immunity underestimates the harm that might be done by administrative officials in a day and age when the penetration by government of the life of the society is so intense. Certainly, at the very least, the citizen needs some protection against a public official such as a department head who is acting in *bad* faith. On the other hand, restricting immunity to department heads ignores the nature of power in the administrative state. While not without authority and influence, political executives do not ordinarily control public bureaucracies in any simple sense. Indeed, most observers would undoubtedly agree that "accountability gets lost in the shuffle somewhere in the middle ranges of the bureaucracy." This is partly the case, as Max Weber explained, because "the 'political master' finds himself in the position of the 'dilettante' who stands opposite the 'expert,' facing the trained official who stands within the management of administration." In the United States, however, the tendency for upper-level career bureaucrats to possess considerable authority and influence is compounded by the relatively short tenure of political executives and the absence of a "shadow government," which would enable them to begin their jobs with intimate knowledge of the organizations they are assigned to head. Consequently, if one is concerned that civil suits "would seriously cripple the proper and effective administration of public affairs as entrusted to the executive branch," then some provision for immunity for lower ranking administrators would be necessary.

The Supreme Court addressed the latter question in *Barr* v. *Matteo* (1959). Barr, the acting director of the Federal Office of Rent Stabilization, announced his intention to suspend two employees for their part in a plan for utilizing agency funds which would have allowed employees to take terminal leave payments in cash and then be rehired on a temporary, though indefinite, basis. The plan was criticized in Congress as "an unjustifiable raid on the Federal Treasury," "a new racket," and as involving "criminal action." The employees sought damages for defamation. So perplexing did the Court find the issues presented by this set of events that it could not formulate a majority opinion. Four justices subscribed to an opinion by Justice Harlan, whose grandfather had written the Court's opinion in Spalding. He framed the question in the following fashion:

> We are called upon in this case to weigh in a particular context two considerations which now and again come into sharp conflict—on the one hand, the protection of the individual citizen against pecuniary damage caused by oppressive or malicious action on the part of officials of the Federal Government, and on the other, protection of the public interest by shielding responsible governmental officers against the harassment and inevitable hazards of vindictive or ill-founded damage suits brought on account of action taken in the exercise of their official responsibilities.

Harlan went on to argue:

> It has been thought important that officials of the government should be free to exercise their duties unembarrassed by the fear of damage suits in respect of acts done in the course of those duties—suits which would consume time and energies which would otherwise be devoted to governmental service and the threat of which might appreciably inhibit the . . . administration of policies of government.
>
> To be sure, the occasions upon which the acts of the head of a department will be protected by the privilege are doubtless far greater than in the case of an officer with less sweeping functions. But it is because the higher the post, the broader the range of responsibilities and duties, and the wider the scope of discretion it entails. It is not the title of his office but the duties with which the particular officer sought to be made to respond in damages is entrusted—the relation of the act complained of to "matters committed by law to his control or supervision" . . . which must provide the guide in

delineating the scope of the rule which clothes the official acts of the executive officer with immunity from civil defamation suits.

Harland concluded that the action involved was within the line of duty and therefore entitled to "absolute privilege."

Justice Black concurred on the ground that if restraints were to be placed on federal employees' speech concerning how the government service might be improved ("whistleblowing"), these should be imposed by congressional legislation rather than the general libel laws of the states or the District of Columbia. On the other hand, Chief Justice Warren, joined in dissent by Justice Douglas, was less worried about governmental performance than about the rights of individuals. He felt that the extension of immunity in this area could lead to the destruction of "the opportunity to criticize the administration of our Government and the action of its officials without being subjected to unfair—and absolutely privileged—retorts." Subsequently, the *Barr* holding was extended to a host of public administrators, including a deputy U.S. marshal, a district director and collection officer of the IRS, a claims representative of HEW, and a secret service agent.

Under the *Spalding-Barr* line of reasoning, then, many of the actions of the agents of the administrative state are cloaked in immunity. The citizen who suffers wrongful action has no recourse in court; there is no effort made to render the administrator directly accountable to the citizen even in extreme instances of negligent or purposeful harm. The needs of the administrative state for smooth operation are placed above protections for the citizenry. Although some categories of public officials such as police were generally exempt from immunity of this sort, abuses were inevitable and it was only a matter of time before the Supreme Court would have to readdress the concept of *absolute* immunity.

DEVELOPMENTS IN THE 1970s

An occasion for reassessing the *Spalding* and *Barr* precedents was presented to the Supreme Court in *Bivens* v. *Six Unknown Named Federal Narcotics Agents* (1971). Bivens was seeking $15,000 from each of the agents for humiliation, embarrassment, and mental suffering caused when they broke into his apartment, handcuffed him in the presence of his family, threatened the entire family with arrest, searched the apartment, used excessive force, and subjected Bivens to a "visual strip search" after taking him to a federal court house. This action was accomplished in the absence of a warrant or probable cause.

Traditionally, Bivens' standard recourse would have been to bring an action in tort in the state court, under prevailing state law, rather than to seek asssignment of damages for the violation of his constitutional rights in the federal forum. However, the Supreme Court, per Justice Brennan, rejected this approach on the grounds that it failed to recognize the power realities of the administrative state:

> Respondents seek to treat the relationship between a citizen and a federal agent unconstitutionally exercising his authority as no different from the relationship between two private citizens. In so doing, they ignore the fact that power, once granted, does not disappear like a magic gift when it is wrongfully used. An agent acting—albeit unconstitutionally—in the name of the United States possesses far greater capacity for harm than an individual trespasser exercising no authority other than his own.

Consequently, the Court held that Bivens' only realistic remedy was the kind of suit he brought. In theory, the right to sue for monetary damages resulting from unconstitutional treatment by public officials would not be confined to Fourth Amendment cases.

It is important to note that while establishing the above principle in *Bivens*, the Court did not examine the issue of whether the narcotics agents possessed immunity under the logic of the *Spalding-Barr* approach. Instead, it remanded the case to the Court of Appeals for a consideration of this question. Subsequently, that court held that the agents lacked immunity ". . . because we do not agree that the Agents were alleged to be engaged in the performance of the sort of 'discretionary' acts that require the protection of immunity" and "it would be a sorry state of affairs if an officer had the 'discretion' to enter a dwelling at 6:30 A.M., without a warrant or probable cause, and make an arrest by employing unreasonable force." The Appeals Court, however, left the door open for a "good faith" defense based on the reasonableness of the officials' actions at the time that they occurred.

The significance of the *Bivens* holding lies primarily in the Supreme Court's willingness to strike a different balance between the desire to protect citizens from ill-used administrative power and the functional requirements of the administrative state. In several cases following Bivens, the Court substantially refined the nature of administrators' immunity.

Scheuer v. Rhodes (1974) grew out of a decade of tragedy and confrontation. Representatives of the estates of three students, fatally shot by the Ohio National Guard during demonstrations at Kent State University against the United States invasion of Cambodia in 1970, sought damages against the governor of Ohio and other officials. The officials, it was alleged, had "acted either outside the scope of their respective office or, if within the scope, acted in an arbitrary manner, grossly abusing the lawful powers of office."

The primary legal vehicle for the suit was 42 U.S. Code 1983. Originally enacted as part of the Civil Rights Act of 1871, and largely dormant after the close of Reconstruction until 1961, it reads:

> Every person who, under color of any statute, ordinance, regulation, custom, usage, or any State or Territory, subjects, or causes to be subjected, any citizen of the United States or other person within the jurisdiction thereof to the deprivation of any rights, privileges, or immunities secured by the Constitution and laws, shall be liable to the party injured in an action at law, suit in equity, or other proper proceeding for redress.

However, despite the potential sweep of this provision, previous judicial interpretation left open the possibility that officials such as those involved in the Scheuer case would be considered immune from its application.

In addressing the immunity question, a unanimous Supreme Court held that:

> . . . in varying scope, a qualified immunity is available to officers of the executive branch of government, the variation being dependent upon the scope of discretion and responsibilities of the office and all the circumstances as they reasonably appeared at the time of the action on which liability is sought to be based. It is the existence of reasonable grounds for the belief formed at the time and in light of all the circumstances, coupled with good-faith belief, that affords a basis for qualified immunity of executive officers for acts performed in the course of official conduct.

Thus, the Court rejected the concept of "absolute" administrative immunity, which had prevailed since 1896, in favor of the notion of "qualified" immunity. Whether such an immunity existed depended on the judiciary's view of the reasonableness of the official's judgment and the extent to which the action was taken in good faith. Again, however, the Supreme Court remanded the case, which was eventually resolved out of court, to the court of appeals for a further exploration of the application of this approach to the specific set of facts at hand.

Whereas the Scheuer case grew out of tragedy, *Wood* v. *Strickland* (1975), in which the Supreme Court adopted a new standard for judging the scope of administrators' immunity, arose from a high school prank. Three tenth-grade public high school students in Mena, Arkansas "spiked" the punch at a school gathering. Although, as Justice White put it, "the punch was served at the meeting without apparent effect," the students were subsequently expelled for their misdeed. They turned to the federal courts for damages, injunctive and declaratory relief on the grounds that their expulsions, in the absence of a full-fledged hearing, violated their constitutional right to due process of law. In examining the immunity issue, the majority of the Supreme Court held, per Justice White, that both an "objective" and a "subjective" standard must be applied in assessing the extent of official immunity:

> The official himself must be acting sincerely and with a belief that he is doing right, but an act violating a student's constitutional rights can be no more justified by ignorance or disregard of settled, indisputable law on the part of one entrusted with supervision of students' daily lives than by the presence of actual malice.

The Court went on to hold that:

> ... a school board member is not immune from liability for damages ... *if he knew or reasonably should have known* that the action he took within his sphere of official responsibility would violate the constitutional rights of the students affected, or if he took the action with the malicious intention to cause a deprivation of constitutional rights or other injury to the student.

Justice Powell, joined by Justices Blackmun and Rehnquist as well as Chief Justice Burger, dissented on the Court's creation of a new standard for immunity, arguing that it was unreasonable for the judiciary to have to assess what school board members "reasonably should have known." Nevertheless, the importance of this new standard for administrator's immunity would be hard to overstate. It establishes a sound balance between the needs of the individual and those of the administrative state by requiring public administrators to be cognizant of the constitutional and legal rights of private individuals before acting upon them. Should public administrators act without adequate knowledge of the rights of others, they can be taken to federal court and successfully sued for monetary damages. Consequently, the *Wood* standard goes a long way toward guaranteeing that public administrators will have a sufficient *personal* stake in their actions to force them to avoid engaging in arbitrary unconstitutional actions vis-à-vis members of the general public. At the same time, however, the standard is not so general or ill-defined as to invite a rash of unfounded lawsuits against public officials.

In short, the *Wood* approach affords the injured individual a constitutional vehicle for assuring administrative competence and a form of direct accountability without rendering the administrative state impotent. In *Barr*, Justice Brennan asked, "Where does healthy administrative frankness and boldness shade into bureaucratic tyranny?" In *Wood*, the majority answered, where administrative officials act with malice or in the absence of knowledge they should have; that is, where their inadequate knowledge directly infringes upon the well-established rights of private individuals. It would be difficult to conceive of a more satisfactory compromise, or one that would impel public administrators to be more fully aware of the constitutional rights of others.

The *Wood* decision left open the possibility that the standard for the application of immunity it set forth might be confined to school board members, rather than applied to administrative officials generally. In subsequent cases, the same standard was applied to the superintendent of a state hospital and to prison administrators. However, in *Butz* v. *Economou* (1978), while leaving no doubt that only "a qualified immunity from damages liability should be the general rule for executive officials charged with constitutional violations," the Supreme Court established an "absolute" immunity for administrative officials exercising adjudicatory roles, including hearing examiners, administrative law judges, and agency attorneys exercising "prosecutorial" functions. The Court's logic in so doing was that judges and public prosecutors; who are "functionally comparable" to such executive branch officials have long enjoyed such an immunity, which is considered to be essential to the proper performance of their jobs. In the Court's view, the chief criteria in determining which administrative officials had such adjudicatory roles were: (1) The duty to decide cases involving the pecuniary interests, character, or liberty of specific individuals or organizations, (2) the discretion to decide whether a proceeding should be sought and, if so, to recommend various sanctions, and (3) the extent of the administrator's independence and presumptive impartiality. Given the Court's division in *Wood*, it is important to note that it reiterated and accepted as established doctrine the standard developed there in its discussion of the issues presented in the *Butz* case. Consequently, the latter decision cannot be construed as a movement away from the former standard.

CONCLUSION: THE SUPREME COURT AND PUBLIC ADMINISTRATION

The rise of the administrative state has placed strains on the constitutional system of checks and balances. Congress, the president, and the judiciary have all made substantial adjustments in the face of bureaucratic power. To a large extent, these changes have been problematic. The role of congressman now entails a heavy dose of ombudsmanship, which may detract from that of legislator and appears to enhance the advantages of incumbents at the polls. Congress itself has added so many staff whose influence is such that one can seriously ask, "Who's in charge here?" The presidential response has relied heavily on the Executive Office of the President, which has emerged as a sizable, powerful, and somewhat independent facet of the federal government, and one that has altered the traditional relationship between president and political executive within the bureaucracy. Yet, "the swelling of the presidency" has not been without serious shortcomings. The Supreme Court's response to the rise of the administrative state has been more limited, but it has fared somewhat better.

Toward the end of the 1960s, Martin Shapiro concluded in *The Supreme Court and Administrative Agencies* that "Judicial review of administrative decisionmaking is . . . marginal in the sense that, at least in the current Washington situation, policy differences are unlikely to arise in most of the instances in which review is theoretically possible." Yet, while this observation remains substantially true, the Supreme Court has generally responded to the rise of the administrative state by affording the individual greater defenses against bureaucratic power. This approach became pronounced first with regard to public employees, who have been afforded a considerable set of new substantive and procedural rights vis-à-vis their governmental employers during the past quarter century. The rights of those especially dependent upon bureaucratic decisions and activities, such as welfare recipients, were also afforded greater protection. In the early part of the 1970s, the Supreme Court moved to make it somewhat easier for citizens opposed to administrative action to gain standing in court. Toward the middle of the 1970s, however, the Court showed considerable reluctance to render decisions requiring widespread administrative change or placing administrative agencies under continuing judicial supervision. Instead of confronting administrative power systemically, the Court turned its attention to the traditional law regarding the immunity of administrative officials and altered it so as to enhance the opportunity for unconstitutionally injured persons to recover damages from the *individual* agents of the administrative state under certain conditions. Thus, the Supreme Court has moved to confront bureaucratic power, not by overturning the decisions or procedures of administrative agencies, but rather by affording individuals a greater potential to oppose successfully administrators in court. While the price of this approach has been paid in the coin of increased case loads on the already crowded dockets and, sometimes, in ambiguity that makes administrative action difficult, in the area of immunity the Court has contributed to the premise that "the sovereign of this Nation is the people, not the bureaucracy," by protecting the former without crippling the latter. Hence, the 1980s might well witness practical efforts to facilitate effective implementation of the new judicial approach to the official immunity of public administrators by reducing some of the barriers and expenses involved in individual suits against administrative officials and by insuring that the citizen's victories are not rendered hollow by minimal judgments or administrators' inability to pay.

TWENTY-FIVE
SUING FEDERAL EXECUTIVES FOR DAMAGES

Jack Rabin, Gerald J. Miller, and W. Bartley Hildreth

The U.S. Supreme Court's decision in *Butz* v. *Economou* removes the absolute immunity federal officials have enjoyed when *personally sued* for allegedly depriving a person of civil rights. The decision, moreover, foreshadows an increasing number of suits initiated against federal executives by persons who want to prove that injuries resulted from federal executives' decisions. The purpose of this brief essay is twofold: (1) to examine the *Butz* decision, and (2) to outline some of the implications the decision holds for federal executives in their dealings with the public.

THE HISTORY OF BUTZ V. ECONOMOU

The U.S. Supreme Court's decision came from action involving Arthur N. Economou, a commodities futures trader, and Earl Butz, the Secretary of Agriculture. A Department of Agriculture (DOA) audit indicated that Economou had not maintained the minimum financial reserves prescribed by the department. As a result, DOA initiated an administrative complaint to "suspend or revoke" Economou's registration. A DOA hearing examiner sustained the department's complaint. DOA's chief legal officer later affirmed the hearing examiner's decision and suspended Economou's registration for 90 days.

Economou asked for review, and the U.S. Court of Appeals for the District of

This selection comes from *The Bureaucrat* 7, 1 (Spring 1978), 54–56. Copyright 1978, The Bureaucrat, Inc. Reprinted by permission. Footnotes omitted.

Columbia set aside the department's enforcement order. The Court's decision was based upon the lack of a customary warning letter which might have led Economou to correct the financial reserves problem.

Economou then sued Butz, the hearing examiner, the department's chief legal officer, and others *personally* for depriving him of constitutional rights. Essentially, Economou charged that officials took property from him—his right to trade—without a warning letter. In addition, he contended that officials issued press releases which hurt his business reputation. Moreover, Economou claimed that the DOA officials initiated the trading suspension to "chill" his First Amendment, free expression rights since he had been a vocal critic of DOA commodity policymakers.

In reply to Economou's suit, Butz and the other defendants claimed official immunity. Action against Economou, they argued, was within their discretionary authority as top departmental officials. The DOA officials relied on what they felt was settled law and invoked the doctrine of "discretionary" duties, which they claimed satisfied the prerequisite for gaining a shield against personal suit. Defendants claimed that only when executives have "ministerial" duties, or tightly defined duties which grant no leeway in making decisions, could they lose the protective immunity.

LOWER COURT ACTION

The U.S. District Court, which heard the suit first, dismissed Economou's claim. Federal officials, according to the court, enjoy absolute immunity for all discretionary acts carried out within the scope of their authority.

Upon appeal, the U.S. Court of Appeals held that executive officials do not have absolute immunity. The court based its decision on the Civil Rights Act of 1871. That act (42 U.S.C.A. 1983) holds that:

> Every person who, under color of any statute, ordinance, regulation, custom, or usage, of any *State or Territory,* subjects, or causes to be subjected, any citizen of the United States or other person within the jurisdiction thereof to the deprivation of any rights, privileges, or immunities secured by the Constitution and laws, shall be liable to the party injured in an action at law, suit in equity, or other proper proceeding for redress [emphasis added].

Previous U.S. Supreme Court decisions under this act had allowed state and local government executives only a qualified immunity from suit. Although the act applies to state and local government officials, the Court of Appeals reasoned that officials of the federal executive branch should have the same immunity and no more. Therefore, the court granted Butz and other DOA officials only a qualified immunity from suits filed against them personally.

SUPREME COURT ACTION

In their appeal to the U.S. Supreme Court, department officials argued again that they "were absolutely immune from any liability for damages even if in the course of enforcing the relevant statutes they infringed [Economou's] constitutional rights and even if the violation was knowing and deliberate." This broad immunity was settled federal law, they again contended.

The U.S. Supreme Court dismissed the officials' claim as "unsound." In addition, the Court pointed out that the general rule has been that "a federal official may not with impunity ignore the limitation which the controlling law has placed on his powers."

The Supreme Court then removed the protection from personal suit and money damages which federal executives had enjoyed, saying that federal officials and employees are not absolutely immune from liability for injuries if they deprive others of their constitutionally protected rights.

THE BUTZ DECISION IN PERSPECTIVE

The Court made distinctions between *Butz* and earlier cases which at the time seemed to place federal officials and employees under the immunity umbrella. Prior to *Butz*, federal employees seemed to have broad protection in damage actions, as the DOA officials argued.

The U.S. Supreme Court, in *Barr* v. *Mateo* (1959), a case involving a District of Columbia agency director, applied the traditional rule that discretionary authority provides absolute immunity to suit for torts. The *Barr* Court held that federal executives were not held personally liable for actions taken in performance of their duties even if the actions violated an individual's constitutional rights.

Nevertheless, absolute immunity got trimmed later in the case *Bivens* v. *Six Unknown Named Agents of the Federal Bureau of Narcotics* (1971). The U.S. Supreme Court in *Bivens* found that federal narcotics agents made a warrantless search of an apartment without probable cause. The Court held the agents *personally* liable for damages and said that the Fourth Amendment acted as an implied remedy for the victims of the narcotics agents. Based upon this reading, the Court could then allow personal damage suits against federal officials.

In *Bivens* the Court allowed money damages to be levied against federal officials. The Court added two conditions besides the discretionary authority specified in *Barr* which the officials must have met to avoid damages: good faith and reasonable action. In failing to show probable cause, the Court believed the agents injured the apartment dwellers' constitutional rights. As a result, the Court held that federal officials acted unreasonably and in bad faith.

The *Bivens* case was important for two reasons. First, the immunity of federal officials became based on an entirely new dimension. Rather than the *Barr* method of determining whether officials had discretionary authority, the Court used the circumstances as a guide to determine whether the action the official took was reasonable or whether it was taken in good faith belief that probable cause existed. Second, the Court implied that each right in the Constitution contains a remedy for its violation, including the personal damage suit against the official.

The recent Supreme Court action in *Butz* explains and spells out the *Bivens* criteria and then applies them to a larger class of federal officials. First, the Court placed federal executive personal liability suits squarely within the long line of precedents surrounding the Civil Rights Act of 1871 and state/local officials. Thus, liability arises if a federal official knew, or reasonably should have known, that action would deprive another of civil rights unless by the circumstances in the case, the federal official can show reasonable action and good faith. These 1983 precedents provide greater detail for identifying a constitutional rights deprivation and for applying Court-mandated principles in determining good faith and reasonable action in a given set of circumstances.

Second, the *Butz* decision seems to imply that not only will federal law enforcement agents face liability for their acts (*Bivens*), but many other federal officials having discretionary authority will also. This expansion may open the door to suits against federal inspectors, grant providers, and a plethora of other administrators.

IMPLICATION OF THE BUTZ DECISION

From the U.S. Supreme Court's decision in the *Butz* case, three major implications can be drawn. First, the *Butz* decision places the law of immunity for federal officials alongside that of state and local officials, and the experiences of these latter officials may tell something of the impact of *Butz* for federal officials. State and local officials have faced a growing number of suits, questioning all aspects of administrative decision making. The growing number of suits has prompted a resort to personal liability insurance among these officials, a type of insurance increasingly hard to find and expensive to maintain. Even with insurance, state and local officials, some claim, are more reluctant to make decisions which involve the risk of a suit. Finally, officials confronting the potential for personal suits and money damages often reject holding public executive positions because the risks exceed their willingness to serve.

Second, *Butz* implies the Court's greater regard for the rights of citizens than for broad executive discretion. The *Barr* case (which *Butz* overruled) held that the public interest lies in the ability of federal executives to use their decision without fear of reprisal.

In *Butz*, the Court espoused qualified immunity as a deterrent to wrongdoing, a method of preventing federal executives from discharging their duties with impunity or "in a manner which they should know transgresses a clearly established constitutional rule."

Although the Court made allowances for mistakes in judgment by federal officials, the emphasis on protection of citizens' rights remains clear. Federal officials have to consider the possibility that if they discriminate in their decisions, they may pay for it later—personally. Likewise, decisions of federal officials get questioned through a damage suit if an injured client believes he or she can prove a constitutional violation.

Third, *Butz* implies changes in management procedures within federal agencies. These changes include recognizing questionable or clearly unconstitutional practices, training personnel in correct procedures, and continually watching the courts for other changes which executives must follow. Executives must add the area of personal liability to the ever-increasing list of subjects requiring their personal attention and training.

SUMMARY

The U.S. Supreme Court's decision in *Butz* v. *Economou* changed the approach to determining whether federal officials should be held liable in damages for deprivation of constitutional rights. Where a federal official had absolute immunity from suit before *Butz*, the official has only a qualified immunity from suit today.

Furthermore, the decision shows the Court's shift in emphasis from protecting the federal official's discretion to curbing discretion when decisions can be shown to violate constitutional rights.

The major implication of *Butz*, however, is clearly that the courts will look with more scrutiny at executives' actions and assess damages against them personally, if they have been found not to act in good faith and reasonably under the circumstances.

TWENTY-SIX
THE MANDATE, THE MAYOR, AND THE MENACE OF LIABILITY

Cynthia Cates Colella

While the virtue of self-assurance is by no means limited to the heartland, one can hardly imagine the officialdom of New York, Chicago, or Los Angeles voting to throw in the municipal towel. Yet, the furor which has resulted from recent Supreme Court decisions based on Section 1983—in many instances, nothing short of apocalyptic—suggests that just such a scenario is possible, if not probable. At the very least, critics claim that the law, as presently interpreted, could result in serious inertia at the state and local levels. And, like a haunting, if such dire predictions materialize, they will be the legacy of a single sentence passed into law over a century ago.

SECTION 1983: REVENGE OF THE RADICAL REPUBLICANS

Like biblical lineage, the Civil Rights Act of 1866 begat the Fourteenth Amendment, the Fourteenth Amendment begat the Civil Rights Act of 1871, the Act of 1871 begat an amendment in 1875, and the amendment begat Section 1983, a seemingly simple sentence which, in its old age, has been doing a lot of begatting itself—begatting some condemnation, some commendation, and a great deal of consternation.

Passed in the waning days of Radical Reconstruction—a period not particu-

This selection comes from the *ACIR Intergovernmental Perspective* (Fall 1981). It is in the public domain. Footnotes omitted.

larly "conducive to the enactment of carefully considered and coherent legislation"—Section 1983 was designed to implement the first section of the Fourteenth Amendment by providing a direct remedy through the federal courts. Hence, the law, as codified, reads:

> Every person who, under color of any statute, ordinance, regulation, custom, or usage, of any state or territory, subjects, or causes to be subjected, any citizen of the United States or other person within the jurisdiction thereof to the deprivation of any rights, privileges, or immunities secured by the Constitution and laws, shall be liable to the party injured in an action at law, suit in equity, or other proper proceeding for redress.

No doubt, the congressional authors of the legislation were concerned primarily with securing equal protection of the laws and guarantees of due process for the recently freed black population. Indeed, over the next few decades, court interpretation supported that concern—if not adequately, then, at least almost exclusively. Thereafter, however, the Fourteenth Amendment "took off"—giving rise, through ingenious interpretation, to one "constitutional revolution" after another. Yet, despite the fact that the amendment rather quickly (and continuously) came to be seen as the most significant of constitutional provisions—"not even second in significance to the original document itself"—its remedial counterpart, Section 1983, lay practically dormant for nearly a century—cited by the Supreme Court a mere 36 times in the first 90 years of its existence. Obviously, then, the Court, though experiencing often radical changes in leadership and ideological bent, chose to view the statute solely as a remedy for gross constitutional violations—a "loosely and blindly drafted" remedy to be broached only with a great deal of trepidation.

Even had the Court been willing to interpret broadly what constituted deprivation under color of state law, long-standing common law immunity shielding state and local officials and municipalities on the basis of their "good faith" and the Eleventh Amendment offering absolute immunity to the states would have rendered the bringing of Section 1983 suits virtually meaningless for the purposes of collecting damages. Jurisdictions and their officials, therefore, had little to fear due, on the one hand, to narrow statutory construction and, on the other, to broad common law construction and constitutional prohibition.

If, as many now suggest, current interpretation of Section 1983 has left municipalities and their strained treasuries vulnerable to every manner of attack, interpretation, prior to the 1960s, was clearly in the other direction—often making it exceedingly difficult for even heinously wronged individuals to receive just remedies. Such relative freedom from the need to consider individual rights when making or implementing policy could not but help, in some cases, to lead to insensitivity to, if not outright violation of, constitutional protections. And, protection of individual rights is of equal if not greater consequence to the continued viability of American Constitutionalism as adherence to the principles of federalism. Thus, the underutilization or disregard of Section 1983—and civil rights statutes generally—often led to badly unbalanced policy, for "[w]hatever other concerns should shape a particular official's actions, certainly one of them should be the constitutional rights of individuals who will be affected by his actions. . . ."

THE INITIAL UNSHACKLING

In 1961, 13 Chicago police officers, in a flagrant misuse of authority, entered a home without warning and forced its occupants to stand naked while the premises were virtually torn apart in a search effort. The subsequent court action, brought against both the city and the police officers under Section 1983, culminated in the Supreme Court case of *Monroe* v. *Pape*. The resulting landmark opinion had three major effects:

> it significantly expanded the scope of the phrase "under color of state [law]," for the officers involved clearly had not acted according to any state policy;
>
> in ruling that municipalities were not "persons" under Section 1983, it directed potential litigants to file suits against individual officials; and
>
> rather predictably, it produced a rush of that most cherished of American pastimes—going to court.

While *Monroe* marked the initial unshackling of Section 1983's vast potential, it still effectively precluded many suits "because of the difficulties presented by having to identify individual officials responsible for a violation, finding responsible officials with financial means to pay substantial judgments, a jury's natural sympathy for 'an official who is perceived to be under attack for doing what he thought to be his job,' and the good faith defense of officials to a Section 1983 action."

MUNICIPALITIES AS "PERSONS"

Seldom do legal concepts remain static and "personhood" is no exception. Thus, 17 years following *Monroe*, the Court had reason to reevaluate application of that concept and thereby nudge local governments somewhat further into the " 'Wonderland' of Section 1983 liability." In a significant reversal of previous policy, the Court declared that municipalities could indeed be characterized as Section 1983 "persons." And, though it would not have been impossible prior to 1978 to assert a direct cause of action againste a locality, *Monell* v. *Department of Social Services* promised to make the bringing of municipal liability suits easier and, consequently, more attractive.

In effect, the *Monell* decision established a number of "touchstones" that would trigger a Section 1983 cause of action—in other words, the right to bring suit. First, a municipality was liable for its "constitutional tort" if that wrong resulted from "a policy statement, ordinance, regulation, or decision officially adopted or promulgated by that body's officers." Moreover, the Court acknowledged that "official policy" under Section 1983 could also include custom and usage, not formally adopted, but pervasive enough to have the force of law.

Despite this rather stunning reversal of *Monroe* and of traditional local tort law, the Court indicated in *Monell* that it was not completely willing to open municipalities to an all out assault by damage seekers. The Court rejected the notion that a city might be liable for damages simply because it employed an official who, acting contrary to policy, had committed a constitutional wrong. And, although the Court had stripped municipalities of the sort of absolute immunity which states enjoy under the Eleventh Amendment, it left open—and by implication, seemed to approve of—the application of qualified, good faith immunity to local governments.

DEMISE OF THE "GOOD FAITH" DEFENSE

> [W]e can discern no "tradition so well grounded in history or reason" that would warrant the conclusion that in enacting Section 1 of the Civil Rights Act, the Forty-second

Congress *sub silentio* extended to municipalities a qualified immunity based on the good faith of their officers. Absent any clearer indication that Congress intended to so limit the reach of a statute expressly designed to provide a "broad remedy for violations of federally protected civil rights . . ." we are unwilling to suppose that injuries occasioned by a municipality's unconstitutional conduct were not also meant to be fully redressable through its sweep.

From slow beginnings, the accumulated force of judicial opinions may build to fast-paced finales. Thus, while it took nearly two decades for the Supreme Court to bestow "personhood" upon municipalities, a mere two years stood between pre-*Monell* immunity and post-*Owen* liability. In *Owen* v. *City of Independence,* the Supreme Court determined that the dismissal of the chief of police without formal written reason or hearing violated his constitutional rights to procedural and substantive due process—a violation to be remedied by the ward of declaratory and injunctive relief, including back pay. The violator—the city of Independence through the official acts of its city manager and city council members—was deemed liable for those damages and could not assert the "good faith" of its officials to avoid liability. Though the majority justices went to great lengths to establish continuity between *Owen* and previous Section 1983 decisions, most commentators viewed the opinion as a dramatic departure from the past—a departure with serious and costly implications for cities across the nation.

Indeed, the decision added three new elements—one stated, one implied, and one in practical effect—to the increasingly crowded Section 1983 milieu. First, by virtue of denying cities a good faith defense, it imposed upon them strict liability for damages. This is particularly burdensome in the realm of constitutional violation since the fluidity of constitutional interpretation, the constant expansion of constitutional rights, and the often arcane points of constitutional law combine to make it nearly impossible for city officials to know when and if they have committed a minor violation. For instance, in the *Owen* case, city officials had no way of knowing they had acted unconstitutionally since "Supreme Court decisions declaring a right to . . . a hearing were issued weeks after Chief Owen had been fired." Although court expansions in the scope of rights protected by the Constitution are to be applauded and though no one would suggest that blatantly or obviously unconstitutional acts such as racial or sexual discrimination or denial of religious freedom should go uncorrected, the *Owen* holding appears to ascribe to the average municipal agent an above average ability to anticipate future refinements in constitutional law.

Second, by implication, the decision appears to extend municipal liability for "official policy" to liability for "official conduct." Owen's constitutional deprivation resulted from the actions and inactions of the city manager and city council and the arguable indiscreet statements of a council member. Those circumstances and the resulting decision caused a mystified Court minority to respond sarcastically that "[t]he statements of a single councilman scarcely rise to the level of municipal policy."

Finally, in practical effect, the Court's decision to make cities liable for damages imparts to Section 1983 judgments three of the more onerous characteristics of federal mandates: intrusiveness, excessive costs, and the potential displacement of preferred local activities.

One of the major effects of the *Owen* decision is certain to be in increase in Section 1983 litigation. Americans, as our preeminent observer, Tocqueville, noted nearly 150 years ago, love to go to court. And, it is no mean incentive to go even more frequently if telling it to the judge brings financial reward. While Section 1983 actions may be initiated, and even settled, in state courts, the measure is, in fact, a federal law, generally litigated in federal courts and settled by federal judges. Hence, an increase in such litigation ultimately will mean an increase in federal intervention into local affairs, a point of which *Owen's* dissenters were keenly aware:

> The Court's decision also impinges seriously on the prerogatives of municipal entities created and regulated primarily by the states. At the very least, this Court should not initiate a federal intrusion of this magnitude in the absence of explicit Congressional action.

In addition, in setting localities up as "convenient targets for capricious and expensive damage suits," *Owen* is likely to generate a further drain on already troubled municipal treasuries. In fact, the potential for such suits is astounding. Thus, discretionary municipal hiring and firing aside, local decisions in the areas of land use, zoning, licensing, permits, servicing, tax assessments, health and building codes, and environmental regulations may give (and in some cases have already given) rise to Section 1983 actions. The potential of the cost aspect of Section 1983 "mandates" is nothing less than staggering—if damages were collected for all current civil rights claims pending against municipalities, the dollar cost to local treasuries would be an estimated $4.1 billion.

Finally, the *Owen* decision may work, both directly and circuitously, to displace preferred local activities and functions. In a direct sense, of course, the payment of damages distorts budgetary preferences. Pothole repair is far easier to put off than is payment of a court-ordered damage claim. Moreover, hedging one's bets against potential suits may in itself be enormously expensive.

It is indirectly, however, that the *Owen* decision stands most seriously to distort local policymaking:

> Because [the Court's] decision will inject constant consideration of Section 1983 liability into local decisionmaking, it may restrict the independence of local governments and their ability to respond to the needs of their communities. . . . If officials must look over their shoulders at strict municipal liability for unknowable Constitutional deprivations, the resulting degree of governmental paralysis will be little different from that caused by personal liability.

ENTER "PANDORA'S MANDATE"

A mere two months and nine days following the announcement of its *Owen* decision, the Supreme Court chose, in what has been dubbed "Pandora's Mandate," to extend the scope of Section 1983 even further. In *Maine* v. *Thiboutot*, a majority of six justices declared that Section 1983 actions would no longer be limited to constitutional deprivations:

> The question before us is whether the phrase "and laws" as used in Section 1983, means what it says, or whether it should be limited to some subset of laws. Given that Congress attached no modifiers to the phrase, the plain language of the statute undoubtedly embraces respondents' claim that petitioners violated the Social Security Act.

The opinion thus treated as simple and obvious, an issue over which both judicial and scholarly opinion had been sharply divided—with many contending that despite the phrase "and laws" Section 1983 referred only to constitutional rights and derivative federal equal rights legislation. The Court's decision to explicitly add statutory mal-, mis-, and nonfeasance to the increasingly catchall character of Section 1983—the opening of a legal can of worms, almost unprecedented in potential magnitude—was attended by a rash of adverse commentary, some of which came quite close to forecasting the ultimate demise of American federalism. . . . (T)he ruling could affect the administration of a very wide range of federal programs.

"And laws" aside, the Court appeared to beg no end of business for itself, lower federal, and state courts by applying the Civil Rights Attorney's Fees Award Act to statutory Section 1983 claims. That law allows the prevailing party in, among others, Section 1983 cases, to collect "a reasonable attorney's fee as part of the costs." Moreover, the probable increase in case filings will be attended by an even greater financial burden on losing jurisdictions, for attorney's fees may be a large—even the largest—part of the cost of a case. In fact, a recent case, involving $33,000 in back pay, resulted in an attorney's fee of $130,000. And, in civil rights cases, the fees awarded have been getting increasingly more substantial.

In no small way, then *Thiboutot* may be viewed as a mandate aiding in the enforcement of other mandates or, a "mandate's mandate." Certainly, prior to the decision, it was not always easy for potential litigants to enforce conditions of aid:

> Plaintiffs in these actions frequently encounter[ed] serious "threshhold" difficulties, including the question of whether they [had] a "cause of action" if the underlying grant statute does not provide for such suits. (Such provisions are rare.)

However, these difficulties may now be greatly diminished:

> If the grantee whose actions are challenged is a unit of state or local government *Thiboutot* may sweep away cause of action obstacles previously facing such plaintiffs.

Ironically, though *Thiboutot* was fought over a state action, its impact will, in all likelihood, be felt most keenly at the local level. State governments are protected, by the terms of the Eleventh Amendment, from suits originating in the federal courts seeking retroactive monetary damages. So too, officials at both the state and local levels can, at least, assert their own "good faith" in defense of their actions or inactions. That, of course, leaves only one suable entity, unprotected by either the Constitution or its good faith—the municipality as "person."

SECTION 1983: THE SEARCH FOR EQUILIBRIUM

"Refusal to recklessly extend the reach of a Section 1983 damages action is not a denial of the worth of a plaintiff's interests, as much as it is a recognition that the term *constitutional tort* should not mean all things to all people; Section 1983 does not require compensation for all deprivations of constitutional [and statutory] rights through open-ended municipal liability which would treat city treasuries as a fund for mutual insurance."

While the above sentiment was voiced by the attorney for the city of Independence—obviously, a less than impartial critic—is being echoed with increasing frequency throughout the nation. Indeed, it is sentiment borne of genuine and well-founded state and local alarm, as well as a growing "fear in the civil rights community that the too-ready availability of civil rights claims, and the attendant attorneys' fees, will influence the courts' delineation of the civil rights themselves." Yet, the alteration or reinterpretation of a law so vital to the safekeeping of fundamental civil rights and enforcement of the Fourteenth Amendment requires an exceptionally delicate hand—certainly one which would preserve and protect the essential equal rights aspects of the law. While no constitutional or statutory modification should be undertaken with a meat ax, the special significance of Section 1983 requires more than extraordinary sensitivity and no little amount of trepidation.

Three basic approaches have been suggested as means to restoring some balance to Section 1983 litigation. Of the three, the most obvious and, at the same time, the most complex, involves judicial reinterpretation of several Section 1983 issues. The second and most direct approach, involves congressional amendment. Finally, the third and most novel response to the increase in the scope and frequency of Section 1983 claims involves the creation of state and local legal defense funds.

JUDICIAL REINTERPRETATION

In deciding future cases, the courts may seek to limit Section 1983 in at least three major ways: by restricting the ability of potential litigants to bring suit under the statute; by reappraising the meaning of "and laws"; and by placing some limits on the extent of liability and damages. In fact, the 1980–81 Supreme Court term resulted in a few limited steps in these directions.

Restricting Access to the Courts In his dissent to the *Thiboutot* decision, Justice Powell suggested that a Section 1983 cause of action would not be available where the "governing statute provides an exclusive remedy for violations of the act." In 1981, a different majority—this time including Powell—expressed some sympathy for this means of limiting third party statutory litigation via Section 1983. Hence, in *Pennhurst State School and Hospital* v. *Halderman*, the Supreme Court, though remanding the issue to the Court of Appeals, hinted that the lower court

TABLE 26-1 The Judicial Development of Section 1983: Selected Major Cases

1961	Monroe v. Pape	Expanded the scope of the phrase "under color of state [law]" and ruled that municipalities were not "persons."
1978	Monell v. Department of Social Services	Declared that municipalities may be characterized as "persons" for purposes of Section 1983 litigation.
1980	Owen v. City of Independence	Held that a municipality could not assert the "good faith" of its officials in order to avoid liability.
1980	Maine v. Thiboutot	Asserted that individuals may bring suit under Section 1983 for violations of federal statutory law as well as constitutional law and upheld application of the Civil Rights Attorney's Fees Award Act to statutory Section 1983 claims.
1981	Pennhurst State School and Hospital vs. Halderman Middlesex County Sewerage Authority v. National Sea Clammers Association	Suggested that when federal statutes provide their own exclusive remedies for violations, "they may suffice to demonstrate congressional intent to preclude the remedy of suits under Section 1983."
1981	Newport v. Fact Concerts, Inc.	Held that municipalities are "immune from punitive damages under Section 1983."

The Mandate, the Mayor, and the Menace of Liability

might look favorably upon Powell's suggestion. The law in question, the Developmentally Disabled Assistance and Bill of Rights Act, does indeed provide an exclusive remedy—enjoining the federal government ot terminate federal assistance. Under this law, then, third parties would, effectively, be precluded from seeking or receiving damages. Moreover, several weeks later in *Middlesex County Sewerage Authority* v. *National Sea Clammers Association*, the Court once again found that "[w]hen the remedial devices provided in a particular act are sufficiently comprehensive, they may suffice to demonstrate Congressional intent to preclude the remedy of suits under Section 1983."

Reexamining "And Laws." In his *Thiboutot* opinion, the Court grappled with the meaning of the phrase "and laws" and decided that since Congress had "attached no modifiers," it could not be assumed that Section 1983's "plain language" was "limited to some subset of laws" such as those dealing with equal rights. This interpretation, of course, has been widely challenged. And, indeed, some of the strongest criticism has come from the federal judiciary itself, finding encouragement in echoes of the past.

Thus, in 1939, Justice Harlan Stone sought to limit the application of Section 1983 to deprivations of personal liberty, as opposed to property rights questions. In 1972, the Court rejected that limitation. Recently, however, there has been some support for returning to the Stone definition as a method for restoring balance and meaning to Section 1983.

Judge Henry J. Friendly, senior judge of the U.S. Court of Appeals for the Second Circuit, has asserted that a return to the Stone doctrine would come "closer to capturing the spirit of the Civil Rights statute," which, as he notes, was originally drafted to protect the rights of Southern blacks. Moreover, Judge Ruggero J. Aldisert of the U.S. Court of Appeals for the Third Circuit has alleged, with more than a little acrimony, that recent decisions of the Supreme Court have "made the federal court a nickel and dime court. A litigant now has a passport to federal court if he has a 5-dollar property claim and can find some state action."

The Court, in fact, had the opportunity in the 1980-81 term to consider at least a small portion of the Section 1983 property claim issue, but chose not to address that particular question. At issue in *Parratt vs. Taylor* was a Nebraska state prisoner's claim that the negligent loss by prison officials of his $23 hobby kit violated his civil rights and therefore triggered a Section 1983 cause of action. State officials asked the Court to "bar 1983 claims based on simple negligence," to estop 1983 relief when a state remedy is available, and to declare "that certain property is so 'de minimis' in value that it is undeserving of the due process protection afforded by the civil rights statutes."

The Court, with Justice Marshall dissenting only in part, ruled against the prisoner, holding that he had "not stated a claim for relief under 42 U.S.C. Section 1983," due, on the one hand, to his failure to prove that a deprivation of due process had occurred and, on the other hand, to his failure to seek initial remedy through the state tort claims procedure. Thus, the Court saw no need to address the value of the property under contention.

Limitations on Liability and Damages. Finally, the Court can choose to reconsider the extent of municipal liability and damages awarded. And, while thus far it has not overturned or modified *Owen*, in its 1980-81 session it saw fit to hold the line.

Indeed, the Court's 6-3 decision in *Newport* v. *Fact Concerts, Inc.* must have evoked an enormous sigh of municipal relief. In that case, musical promoters Fact Concerts felt that their Section 1983 civil rights had been violated when city officials of Newport, RI, refused to allow a performance by rock group Blood, Sweat, and Tears on grounds that the group was likely to "attract a rowdy and undesirable audience to Newport." The district court agreed with promoters and awarded Fact Concerts $72,000 in compensatory damages. Had it stopped at that award, the decision would have constituted little more than a business-as-usual approach to municipal liability cases. However, Fact Concerts also asked for and was granted punitive damages of $200,000 against the city and an additional $75,000 against city officials—a precedent which, according to some, would "impact on the states' balance sheets [in a way which] may be close to devastating." Despite the city's failure to object to the punitive damages at the trial level, the Supreme Court decided to consider the issue, ruling, on June 26 of this year, that "[a] municipality is immune from punitive damages under Section 1983." Although, according to preliminary estimates, 169 local jurisdictions across the nation remain liable, under pending cases, for approximately $4.2 billion in Section 1983 damages claims, the Court's decision offered considerable relief for 38 localities previously facing over $1 billion in punitive damages.

CONGRESSIONAL REVISION

To those who would question his judgment in *Thiboutot,* Justice Brennan responded:

> Petitioners' arguments amount to the claim that had Congress been more careful, and had it fully thought out the relationships among the various sections, it might have acted differently. That argument, however, can best be addressed to Congress, which, it is important to note, has remained silent in the face of our many pronouncements of the scope of Section 1983.

Indeed, it is to the direct heirs of the authors of Section 1983, that one, logically, would look for relief from its more onerous aspects. Two current companion bills, S.584 and S.585, sponsored by Senator Orrin Hatch (UT), would seek to do just that by addressing the major issues in *Thiboutot* and *Owen.*

S.584 would qualify "and laws" to mean those laws "providing for equal rights of citizens or of all persons within the United States," thus, effectively overruling the *Thiboutot* decision. S.585, the anti *Owen* companion bill, would bar actions against municipalities which have "acted in good faith with a reasonable belief that the actions of the political subdivision were not in violation of any rights, privileges, or immunities secured by the Constitution or by laws providing for equal rights of citizens or persons." Such attempts to congressionally circumscribe Section 1983 have been supported by Supreme Court Judge Sandra Day O'Connor, commenting recently that, "Congressional action might be taken to limit the use of Section 1983."

Additional measures have been proposed. For example, the National Institute of Municipal Law Officers (NIMLO) suggests that Congress could discourage "the impulse to file frivolous Section 1983 actions" by amending the Civil Rights Attorney's Fews Award Act of 1976" to limit the discretionary award of fees to awards against the United States in enforcement of actions under Title VI of the Civil Rights Act of 1964."

STATE AND LOCAL RESPONSE

In the past, it has often been difficult for individual municipalities and states to muster the necessary resources and information with which to defend themselves adequately against damage claims. Thus, a final means for restoring balance to Section 1983 litigation, as well as other legal action both initiated by and against states and localities, may rest in the creation of pooled defense funds and/or legal talent, such as the establishment of a joint state-local legal defense organization of the type recently recommended by ACIR.

Other groups and individuals have advocated similar defense strategies. For instance, NIMLO has proposed the creation of a National Municipal Legal Defense Fund. The NIMLO fund would "direct litigation activities to cases of obvious nationwide importance, aid all fund members with information," and carry on a variety of additional activities such as assisting members in strike management. Speaking to the National Governors' Association (NGA), Professor A.E. Dick Howard of the University of Virginia has recommended that the states create a legal advocacy committee following the lines of the NIMLO model. Still others favor joint state-local endeavors. For example, Washington lawyer Stewart A. Baker, arguing that "of all the institutional litigants appearing regularly before the Supreme Court, state and local governments consistently present the weakest legal defenses," urges the creation of a "Federalism Legal Defense and Education Fund" which would develop the type of skills and expertise now available to the federal government through the Solicitor General's Office.

CONCLUSION

Unlike William Ernest Henley's unsung hero in *Invictus*, state and local officials are not masters of their fate. They do not know what clutch of circumstances will bring them before the courts in a 42 U.S.C. 1983 lawsuit as the Supreme Court wrestles over the meaning and application of the rights, privileges, and immunities secured by the Constitution and other laws of the United States. If past history is any guide, there will evolve newly defined rights for individuals with a commensurate loss of traditional prerogatives and immunities for state and local government.

> At little expected cost, the *Thiboutot* holding offers the promise that all state and local officials will be both held accountable for past deprivations and deterred from committing future errors. These ends will best be served if *Thiboutot* plaintiffs are able to recover damages. Only then will effective compensations and deterrence take place.

As the two quotations noted above make clear, the recent history of Section 1983 brings into conflict two cherished American values: a strong federalism and the constant extension of rights. Indeed, as one commentator has noted, "the relationship between the themes of federalism and individual rights is one that runs deep in American intellectual and social history." While this article has focused primarily on the dangers inherent in the increasingly broad application of Section 1983 for independent state and local decisionmaking, it would be an equally dangerous business to seriously undermine individual rights in the name of state and local autonomy. An imbalance in favor of "states' rights," as all too much of our history has shown us, can undermine not only the equal rights and privileges of which we are justifiably proud, but the validity of federal principles as well. Thus, any change in the scope of Section 1983—whether judicial or congressional—must be handled with the type of kid glove approach generally reserved to constitutional questions. Resolving whatever problems currently exist in the application of Section 1983 requires a delicate policy balance rather than a drastic swing of the pendulum.

CHAPTER EIGHT
OPENING FEDERAL AGENCIES UP TO THE PUBLIC

INTRODUCTION

Public access and awareness of federal agency operations and activities is yet another strategy developed to counter agency secrecy and to hold agencies accountable to the citizenry and to the elected officials. The Freedom of Information Act (1966, 1974, 1976—*see* Section 552, APA) and the Government in the Sunshine Act (1977—*see* Section 552b, APA) passed by Congress, "whistleblowing" by federal officials concerned about perceived abuses of power by other officials in their agencies, and an "ombudsman" acting as official "watchdog" on behalf of the public are a few of the responses to the query "How do you open up government operations to public review and monitoring?"

The essential direction of these activities is openness and full disclosure. Public access to governmental information about agency operations and policy is at the heart of the federal legislation. The landmark Freedom of Information Act (FOI), passed in 1966 and amended in 1974, calls for all federal agencies (except Congress, the federal courts, and persons whose sole function is to serve as presidential advisers) to quickly respond to reasonable requests from persons for information contained in agency records. Prior to passage of the FOI, it was very difficult for persons dealing with a government agency to get badly needed data. Since its passage, FOI has become the "single most important discovery tool"[1] for persons dealing with the federal bureaucracy.

[1] Glen O. Robinson, Ernest Gellhorn, and Harold H. Bruff, *The Administrative Process* (St. Paul, MN: West Publishing Company, 1980), p. 521.

While quite controversial (the federal bureaucracy was very hostile to FOI and both presidents Lyndon Johnson and Gerald Ford tried to scuttle it), the Freedom of Information Act has become the

> legislative realization of a principle, fundamental to the welfare of a functioning democracy. The timely provision of information to the American people, upon their own petition, is a requisite and proper duty of government.[2]

Agency secrecy to a large extent (there are nine basic exemptions, listed in FOI, from the imperative that agencies turn over information to the requestors) has been replaced by disclosure through FOI actions.

A companion piece of federal legislation, with the same goal of disclosure, is the Government in the Sunshine Act (passed in 1977). As reflected in the public law written by Congress, the policy of the federal government is that the public is "Entitled to the fullest practicable information regarding the decision-making processes of the federal government." All federal agencies (over fifty in number) headed by collegial bodies of presidential appointees who were confirmed by the Senate, must open all their meetings to the public and announce times and places of meeting in advance of the actual session.

Both FOI and Sunshine statutes enable persons to acquire data, for whatever their reasons, from federal agencies. This legislation has given persons unique opportunities to examine the character of the federal executive and regulatory agencies; it has also "led to more litigation and increased cost of government more than any single regulatory program adopted in the past decade."[3]

Still another way that governmental operations have been opened up, albeit haphazardly, is through the operations of the conscientious public official who "blows the whistle" on governmental corruption in the person's agency in front of governmental operations committees in the Congress. This public official, the "whistleblower" who offers insights into the mechanics of governmental operations to the public, has always faced personal ostracism and professional penalties for his or her actions. However, there continues the practice of whistleblowing and efforts have been made to formally protect these persons from penalties.

One additional way to confine public management to constitutional parameters without crippling agency initiative is the development of the official "ombudsman" to serve as a mediator between the government official and the public. The ombudsman, serving as a professional critic of administration, would provide an independent "protective mechanism against official mistake, malice, or stupidity."[4] Functioning as a general complaint bureau to which people can turn to complain about administrative abuse, the ombudsman's attributes are as follows:

1. All are instruments of the legislature but function independently of it, with no links to the executive branch and with only the most general answerability to the legislature itself.
2. All have practically unlimited access to official papers bearing upon matters under investigation, so that they can themselves review what prompted administrative judgment.
3. All can express an ex officio expert's opinion about almost anything that governors do and that the governed do not like.
4. All take great pains to explain their conclusions, so that both administrators and complaining citizens well understand the results reached.[5]

[2]Harold C. Relyea, "Freedom of Information Act a Decade Later," *Public Administration Review*, (July/August 1979), 310.

[3]Robinson, Gellhorn, and Bruff, *Administrative Process*, p. 520.

[4]Walter Gellhorn, *When Americans Complain: Governmental Grievance Procedures* (Cambridge, MA: Harvard University Press, 1966), p. 6.

[5]Ibid., pp. 9–10.

The readings in this chapter examine these types of efforts to open government up to the public and to ensure that agency activities are within constitutional boundaries. The Schick essay examines the FOI a few years after its legislative birth. He sees the public interest group benefitting immensely from the FOI; the right to know was broadened considerably by the federal legislation. Archibald examines the FOI after a decade of full disclosure activity under the legislation. The Vaughn and Kaufman pieces examine the role and the status of the federal "whistleblower" and the Meyer piece focuses on the effects an ombudsman can have on the relationship between the public and the government.

TWENTY-SEVEN
LET THE SUN SHINE IN

Allen Schick

Information is one of the perennial battlegrounds of American politics. The issue cannot be settled by words or sentiments, for divergent interests and values are at stake. The same revolutionary generation which gave America the First Amendment closed the doors of its Constitutional Convention. The same president who on July 4, 1966, told us "a democracy works best when the people have all the information that the security of the nation permits," made "credibility gap" a household phrase. It is now five years since the Freedom of Information Act (FOI) took effect, yet the Pentagon Papers, the Anderson columns, and hundreds of lesser-known episodes attest to the closure of vital public acts from public view.

THE FREEDOM OF INFORMATION ACT

Under the act which went into effect in 1967, all persons are entitled to access to the records of federal agencies. Exempting nine categories of information to protect national security, confidentiality personnel files, and certain other specified interests, the act strives for a "formula which encompasses, balances, and protects all interests, yet places emphasis on the fullest possible disclosure." The act also requires each federal agency to publish regulations governing access to its records, and pro-

> This selection comes from *The Bureaucrat* 1, 2 (Summer 1972) 156–160. Copyright 1972, The Bureaucrat, Inc. Reprinted by permission.

vides judicial remedies in case a request for information is turned down. But the act is not self-enforcing; it takes an attempt to obtain information to activate the law, and willingness to go through a costly and time-consuming litigative process to make use of the judicial remedies. Thus, the actual effects of FOI depend on how it is used by the public and how it is interpreted by administrators and the courts. Because many of its provisions—in particular the nine exemptions—are worded ambiguously, FOI furnishes ample room for political controversy, administrative maneuvering, and judicial activity.

Most requests for information have been granted routinely, even before FOI, and most have been handled on an informal basis. Each day, thousands of exchanges are processed over the phone, through office visits, and so on. What is important about FOI is the fraction of instances in which access is denied, for these are likely to be the cases in which public policies are contested; there is a need to balance conflicting rights and interests, and agencies are unwilling to open themselves to public scrutiny.

The difference between routine and difficult explains one of the anomalies of the FOI field. For years there has been controversy over the openness of government operations, and this has not been abated by passage of the legislation. One organization that spends full time tracking FOI conditions has written of the law's first years: "It has been hailed as a triumph for freedom of information and condemned as a poor substitute for a viable open records law." Generally, those who argue that FOI is ineffective point to difficult cases in which access was refused. The Freedom of Information Act has operated under political conditions and with effects that were not foreseen by its sponsors, who waged a decade-long campaign to establish the "right to know" as federal information policy in place of the "need to know" test that had been promulgated under the Administrative Procedure Act of 1946. The political climate of the late 1960s and early 1970s has been quite different from what it was in the years preceding the enactment of FOI. In particular, the rise and activism of public interest groups dealing with consumer and environmental protection have turned FOI from a declaration of the public's right to be informed into a potent and much-used instrument of political pressure. Moreover, the implementation of FOI has coincided with growing concern over the right to privacy and the confidentiality of government-held data.

INFORMATION AS A POLITICAL RIGHT

The coalition which led the protracted campaign for FOI was drawn primarily from the news media (especially newspapers) and certain congressional committees. Both groups were irked by the proclivity of federal agencies to conceal their actions and records from public view—the media, because secrecy interferes with their newsgathering functions; congressmen, because it bars effective legislative oversight of administrative agencies. The "people's right to know" (the title of an influential book by an early FOI crusader) was the guiding principle of the movement, and it dominated the many congressional hearings and investigations that preceded enactment of the law. The original FOIers wanted "to establish a general philosophy of full agency disclosure" that would make impossible attainment of important democratic values: an informed and responsible electorate; a government accountable to the public; an independent and vigilant press; and an executive branch that is responsive to the people's representatives in Congress. Thus they conceived of FOI in terms of the political processes of democracy (informed voters, free competition of ideas, and separation of powers) and personal liberty (freedom of expression and communication).

But in the several years since FOI was passed, a new political force with a substantially different conception of the political use of information has moved to the forefront, while the original FOI sponsors have been relatively quiescent. The media have made little discernible use of FOI; very few of the more than 100 lawsuits challenging agency refusal to grant access have been brought by newspeople.

Yet, the significance of FOI has grown, for it has been activated by public interest groups for whom the right to know is not an end in itself but an instrument of antibureaucratic political action. As one of Ralph Nader's associates has explained:

> Some who urged the adoption of new legislation simply believed that unclassified information should be available to private persons. Others . . . also sought an instrument to expose some of the internal workings of government agencies . . . the ultimate goal was substantial administrative reform, achieved in part through heightened public awareness of administrative deficiencies.

By prying information loose from recalcitrant administrators and by focusing public attention on controversial administrative policies, the public interest crusaders aim to challenge both the ways government agencies decide and the decisions themselves, and in addition to break what they regard as the unwarranted bonds between government agencies and their regulated clients. To accomplish this, the convergence of FOI and public interest law has been very crucial. Before FOI, public records were available to "persons properly and directly concerned," a standard which could easily be satisfied by business firms and trade associations, but not by consumers or environmentalists. The emergence of public interest law has brought political organization and resources to these previously underrepresented areas; FOI has given these groups administrative and judicial standing which they previously lacked. Many of the FOI suits, and some of the most far-reaching ones, have been brought by public interest groups, and many have involved consumer and environmental interests.

FOI AS A POLITICAL PROBLEM

FOI has become enmeshed with the separable but often conjoined issues of privacy and confidentiality. Through FOI, government can become the vehicle for informing citizens of the activities of others. This danger has been heightened by the role of government as the leading collector of private data, by the prospect of what the Ervin Subcommittee on Constitutional Protection recently termed *dossier dictatorship*, and by the pressures to open government records to public scrutiny. Although several of the exemptions in FOI pertain to confidential or private matters, the fact is that agencies are buffeted by powerful pressures to disclose and, as Alan Westin has pointed out in *Privacy and Freedom*, "the difficulty with the Freedom of Information Act . . . is that it seems to appoint the government the necessary champion of the citizen's right to privacy." The person whose private affairs are to be unveiled is not a party to the FOI process.

PUBLIC AND PRIVATE
INFORMATION

As the growth of government has turned information from a political right into a political resource, the struggle for access has entered new ground. No longer is it a matter of an informed citizenry alone, information is now sought to bolster the private roles of consumers, investors, and all partners in the ecological drama of our times. This broadened concept has its antecedents in the first consumer protection laws enacted early in this century which cast the federal government as the agent of private citizens. Through governmental intervention, foods and drugs had to be accurately labeled and stock underwriters were required to disclose basic financial data. The case for full disclosure of private information was put in a Nicholas Von Hoffmann column of May 12, 1972:

> From every standpoint, the public's need to know how immense corporations like RCA are run is as important as its need to know how the government is run. All sorts of laws and public policies in everything from foreign trade to tax allowances are predicated on the assumption of optimally efficient managers chosen by merit and not by their taste in tailors. If management productivity is slacking off, we needs must know it.

The struggle thus boils down to the issue of whether there exists any longer a meaningful and clear distinction between public and private. At the present time, a unit of the American Institute of Certified Public Accountants is at work trying to redefine the principles of the profession. It must decide between those who demand that social impacts should be incorporated into corporate financial statements (led by Ralph Nader's Corporation Accountability Research Group) and those who believe that corporate reporting should concern itself primarily with the interests of shareholders and creditors.

The issue carries one step further because the federal government accumulates vast amounts of information by virtue of being a buyer and seller in private markets. What about the test data gathered by federal agencies when they evaluate products offered by private vendors? One of the early freedom of information suits was brought by the Consumers Union to obtain VA data on hearing aids. Following a partial defeat in the courts, the Veterans' Administration (along with other federal agencies such as GSA) reversed its policies and decided to make public much product information.

Those who insist on full disclosure are fearful that any breach in their access to governmental files would enable the government to withhold information which is of incontestable public value. They do not trust government with the role of arbiter of the conflicting interests which must be balanced. Under the Freedom of Information Act this task now is within the jurisdiction of the courts which, in effect, weigh the equities in much the manner that bureaucracies once did. The advantage of a judicial remedy is not only that it affords a view of agency actions, but also that it breaks the bonds between regulating agencies and their regulated clients.

This does not mean, however, that private data always will be stripped of confidential protection. Coexisting on the books with the Freedom of Information Act are dozens of statutes which authorize or require confidentiality, including the blanket provision of 18 USC 1905, which puts under lock and key all information pertaining "to the trade secrets, processes, operations, style of work" of any firm. Exemption three of the FOI preserves these statutory prohibitions. Nevertheless, there is a broad grey area covering instances where confidentiality is not tendered but expected, and where the public is denied access even when no specific statute can be cited. Concerning these, the President's Commission on Federal Statistics recommended in September 1971 that ''a promise to hold data in confidence should not be made unless the agency has authority to uphold such a promise.''

CONFIDENTIALITY VERSUS PRIVACY

The Freedom of Information Act recognizes that a difference must be made between business confidentiality and personal privacy. Thus, one of the exemptions covers trade secrets and financial information, while another deals with personnel and medical files. In practice, however, it is not always easy to maintain the distinction. An interesting case arose out of a newsperson's request to the Internal Revenue Service to inspect the lists of persons and firms registered under the Gun Control Act of 1968. Insisting that confidentiality and privacy must be treated differently, IRS granted access to lists of gun dealers, but refused permission for the lists of gun collectors.

A claim of privacy has dubious validity when it is used to withhold information from the person whose privacy presumably is being protected. From time to time the House Subcommittee on Foreign Operations and Government Information (now chaired by Representative William Moorhead), which acts as an unofficial ombudsman on informational policies, receives complaints from federal employees that they were denied access to their own personnel files. Proposals are pending in Congress to establish a new writ of *habeas data*, under which a citizen would have the right to inspect private credit files. No less a right ought to be available to citizens in their dealing with government.

When privacy involves someone else's desire to inspect the files, consideration might be given to a reinstatement of the discredited "need to know" test that was operative under the administrative Procedure Act of 1946. In fact, the U.S. Court of Appeals recently applied a version of that test in allowing university professors to examine certain NLRB records. The Court felt assured that the data drawn by academic researchers would not be misused, but it suggested that a different outcome might be appropriate if the same data were requested for a different use or by a different user. In deciding on the basis of the quality of the user, the Court cast aside the FOI standard which entitles all persons to equality of access, but it was weighing the conflicting equities as courts have done for many centuries.

THE CONTINUING STRUGGLE

Public versus private is only one version of the never-ending battle over freedom of information. Over the past year, attention has been fixed on the issue of national security classification, a problem which will not now disappear because President Nixon issued Executive Order 11652 on March 8, 1972. That order tightened the rules for classification, cut in half the number of agencies authorized to classify and by two-thirds the number of classifiers, and established a timetable for the automatic declassification of most documents. In addition, a committee has been appointed to monitor the classification system. Yet, these moves, desirable as they are, will not keep the Pentagon from overclassifying, for the incentives built into the national security apparatus of the United States are overwhelmingly on the side of secrecy and hidden files.

Nor will the warring end between those interdependent adversaries—the news media and government agencies. Nothing less than full disclosure will satisfy the media, except perhaps when truly national security matters such as troop movements are involved. For its part, government will want to maneuver news reporting to ensure favorable coverage, and news leaks will coexist with secrecy as two of the main ploys. A 1972 survey by the American Society of Newspaper Editors asked 28 top Washington correspondents whether, in their opinion, governmental secrecy has increased or decreased. Only one replied that more information is available today, while 19 said that secrecy has increased, and 8 detect no substantial change in governmental practices.

Another battleground will be the relationship between Congress and the president. While Congress has been ambivalent about the openness of its own operations, it has no doubt that it is entitled to just about everything in the possession of federal agencies, including files developed by the White House bureaucracy. In his article for this forum, Professor Arther Miller suggests that the issue be given to the courts for resolution. However laudable and effective the recourse to judiciary, I suspect that the matter cannot be put to rest in a courtroom. The Constitution and American political processes cast the president and Congress in adversary roles, and they will continue to battle over scraps of paper whenever their divergent political interests are involved.

If the informational wars ever end, it will not be because government is an open book, but because the public and its agents no longer care or fight. In urging a continuing struggle, it is worth bearing in mind what Mr. Justice Brandeis wrote nearly 60 years ago: "Sunlight is said to be the best of disinfectants; electric light the most efficient policeman." Let the battle go on and let the sun shine in.

TWENTY-EIGHT
THE FREEDOM OF INFORMATION ACT REVISITED

Samuel J. Archibald

THE LAW IN OPERATION

The Freedom of Information Act, which became effective on July 4, 1967, was a difficult law to use, but it would have been an effective law if properly administered. It was the result of an eleven-year public relations program educating most of the press and the Congress and much of the public on the dangers of government secrecy. It was a result of the legislative process and, as such, it was a compromise.

The Freedom of Information Act was used primarily by private interests to get public reports for personal gain. Perhaps this was to be expected. The democratic system permits the clash of private interests, and the system permits the balancing of those interests in the hope that the greatest general good will prevail. Minimal press use of the new FOI Act also was understandable, even though it had become law with the support of the more articulate members of the information industry who really believed in their First Amendment duties to inform the public. To sell its information product, the press has to get information fast and must disseminate it before a competitor does. There were three problems which the press had with the Freedom of Information Act.

First, it was not an information law. It did not provide information from the federal government. It did not require an agency to develop facts or answer questions; it merely required the agency to give the press and the public records of its of-

Reprinted with permission from *Public Administration Review* 39 (July/August 1979), 315–317. © 1979 by The American Society for Public Administration, 1225 Connecticut Avenue, N.W., Washington, D.C. All rights reserved. Footnotes omitted.

ficial actions. The great majority of the daily news stories are based on what some official says has happened or will happen, not upon a careful searching of government records. Second, it did not require federal officials to meet press deadlines. Even if a reporter wanted to use public records for a story, the law did not require federal agencies to provide records in a timely manner. Third, reporters who pushed, demanded, and, finally, got access to public records might be given those materials only after they had been provided to the competition. The law was for the public's right to know, not the right of the press to get exclusive stories. Federal officials could rationalize retaliation against demanding reporters by claiming they had to make the records available to all members of the public; it was not their fault that the records happened to be distributed on the competition's time schedule.

The public also had problems with the original FOI law. Although it did not require federal agencies to set up internal systems requiring high level officials to act on appeals after a subordinate initially had refused to give out a public record, nearly all agencies did establish an administrative appeals system. In only 16 percent of the cases studied in the first four years of the Freedom of Information Act's operation were the initial refusals appealed. When a citizen did insist on the right to know and appealed the initial refusal to the head of the agency, all or part of the public records were made available nearly 26 percent of the time. A few final agency appeals were appealed to the courts. The court enforcement provision may well have been the most important part of the original Freedom of Information Act, for it required government agencies to prove that secrecy was necessary. The effectiveness of this sanction is indicated by the fact that, when there was a court decision on an FOI case, the petitioners got all or part of what they wanted from the government in 58 percent of the cases.

In spite of legislative compromise and executive branch foot-dragging, the progression from 16 percent to 26 percent to 58 percent indicated the original Freedom of Information Act was becoming a valuable tool to dig out the facts of government. So the federal agencies adopted their own administrative amendments.

They developed secrecy by delay, taking many weeks to answer an initial request for access to a public record. They developed secrecy by dollars, charging far in excess of costs for copying public records. They used the investigatory files exemption as a major shield of secrecy. The original FOI Act included nine categories of public records which might be exempt from public disclosure. One category was investigatory files compiled for law enforcement purposes. Federal agencies often claimed their public records were investigatory files even though the investigation had been completed long ago. When all else failed, federal agencies forced insistent applicants for public records to go to court. It was easy to get a case into court, for the law required federal district courts to give FOI cases expeditious handling. However, litigation was expensive, and agencies knew public records applicants would be likely to back away from their demands for documents rather than to go to court.

AMENDING THE ACT

By the time the Freedom of Information Act had been in operation long enough to determine how well—or how poorly—it was working, Congressman John E. Moss no longer was chairman of the congressional subcommittee which had made the freedom of information concept a federal law. He headed another major congressional investigating unit, and the Moss panel was taken over by William S. Moorhead, a Pittsburgh Democrat who had many political and social interests.

Moorhead followed the Moss lead, moving toward amendment of the Freedom of Information Act with a careful staff study of the administration of the law. By 1972, when the study was completed by a special Library of Congress task force, the Missouri senators who had been the titular freedom of information leaders in the upper legislative chamber were replaced by Senator Edward Kennedy (D.-Mass.), who also took a strong interest in FOI problems. The House and Senate subcommittees held hearings based on the Library of Congress study and developed amendments to make the Freedom of Information Act more effective.

The amendments abolished the federal agencies' secrecy-by-delay tactics, requiring them to answer all initial requests for public records within ten days, to answer all administrative appeals within twenty days, and to take an extra ten days only in extreme cases. The amendments abolished the federal agencies' system of secrecy by dollars, permitting them to charge only the actual cost for searching and copying public records and requiring the agencies to provide copies free of charge if the general public would benefit. The amendments limited to six specific types the investigatory files which could be withheld, and the amendments made it potentially less costly to go to court to enforce the right to know by permitting the assessment of court costs and attorneys' fees against the government agency which lost its FOI case.

However, most important among more than a dozen other amendments designed to improve the Freedom of Information Act was one proposed by Ralph Nader and championed by Senator Kennedy. For the first time since the housekeeping laws were adopted by the First Congress in 1789, statutory provision made it possible to punish federal employees who hid government records from the public. Nevertheless, the antisecrecy sanction finally adopted by the Congress was much weaker than the original Nader-Kennedy proposal. It permitted a court to direct the U.S. Civil Service Commission to order disciplinary action against any federal employee who arbitrarily and capriciously withheld executive branch records.

The sometimes conflicting amendments to the Freedom of Information Act developed by the Moorhead and Kennedy subcommittees were being reconciled in a conference committee when President Richard M. Nixon resigned from office and Gerald R. Ford became president. Ford asked his former congressional colleagues for time to think over the FOI amendments they planned to send him and, as a result of his suggestions, they made a few changes in the proposals. However, when the Congress passed the amendments, the new chief executive vetoed them. Once more the press and the Congress cooperated on the same sort of public relations program which had pushed through the first Freedom of Information Act. The Congress overwhelmingly rejected Ford's veto, and the amended Freedom of Information Act became law.

FOIA TODAY

Is the amended FOI Act working any better? It will take another major congressional study to find out, but there are some indications that, after eleven years of initial development of the freedom of information idea, after eight and one-half years of experience with the original law, and after nearly five years of experience under the amended law, information may not be completely free but it is much more reasonably accessible.

One indication of success is the massive publicity program the Federal Bureau of Investigation has mounted to complain that the agency must spend valuable time resurrecting files of past peccadillos. Another indication of positive effect may be drawn from a comparison of the Library of Congress study, which prompted the Freedom of Information Act amendments, to the administration of the law after the amendments. One amendment required each federal agency to file with Congress an annual report on its stewardship of the act. Comparison of the 1976 report with the Library of Congress study covering July 1967 through July 1971 indicates how false were President Ford's fears that the republic would crumble because of the FOIA amendments.

A major reason for his veto, Ford said, was his fear that the amendments to the law placed an unreasonable limit on the amount of time an agency could take in replying to a Freedom of Information Act request. The Library of Congress study indicates it took federal agencies, under the original law, an average of seventy days to answer requests for public records. The amendments cut that time to ten days for an initial request, twenty days for an appeal and an additional ten days under special circumstances. In 1976, in spite of the fears of Ford and the fulminations of the FBI, the average time to answer the hard Freedom of Information demands—those requests appealed to the head of the agency after an initial denial—was ten and one-half days.

The Library of Congress study indicates that all or part of a public record was made available under the original Freedom of Information Act 25 percent of the time. In 1976, reports indicate the agencies made all or part of the documents available 59 percent of the time. The Library of Congress study shows that, of the nine categories of public records which could be withheld, the federal agencies relied most upon category number four, permitting the withholding of so-called trade secrets, and category number five, permitting the withholding of internal memoranda. Moreover, the study showed, the government lost more of the court cases testing these exemptions than it won. The 1976 report indicates that federal agencies back away from trade secrets and internal memoranda exemptions. Instead, the most-used exemption was number seven—the investigatory files category which the Congress had amended to make application more specific. Finally, a comparison between the 1976 agency reports and the Library of Congress study shows that only 5 percent of the refusals of access were appealed in 1976 compared to 16 percent appealed in the early years.

What—in addition to the need for another full congressional study—does it all mean? It means that the freedom of information public relations program which began in 1955 to educate the Congress, the press, and the public was very successful as far as the Congress is concerned. Nevertheless, the press and the public—the supposed beneficiaries of the legislation—are not making much use of the law. The number of requests for access to public records probably has increased, but effective use of the Freedom of Information Act certainly has not progressed, since 16 percent of the initial refusals were appealed in 1967-1971, but only 5 percent were appealed after it was amended.

The partial comparison of preamendment to postamendment administration of the law also means that many agency complaints about the difficulties of honoring the people's right to know are largely the manifestation of traditional bureaucratic "bitching." The strict time limits mandated by the amendments apparently have been met with ease. If the average time taken to answer demands for records is ten and one-half days when a case could take a maximum of forty days, federal agencies do not seem harassed by the need for speed. Finally, the analysis shows what observers of the Washington bureaucracy have known for a long time. Somewhere, deep within the memory bank of each federal agency, is some sort of mechanism that tells the bureaucrats how to keep ahead of the lawmakers. The agencies were losing court cases based on the trade secrets and internal memorandum exemptions of the Freedom of Information Act. They did not admit the use of those exemptions was wrong, but, nevertheless, they stopped using them.

Today the agencies raise new barriers against the slings and arrows of freedom of information. Possibly a complete congressional study of the effectiveness of the amended Freedom of Information Act will show ways to breach the new barriers. Vigorous congressional oversight of the statute will not only identify problems of administrative policy and practice, but can do much to discourage even the contemplation of less than faithful execution of this or any federal law.

TWENTY-NINE
WHISTLEBLOWING AND THE CHARACTER OF PUBLIC EMPLOYMENT

Robert G. Vaughn

As government becomes more pervasive and intrusive, it becomes all the more essential to control the exercise of government power. But how can we encourage our public servants to make sure that government power won't be abused? How do we create a public service that more effectively serves the interests of the public? In other words, how can we insure democratic control of our institutions? These are the underlying issues of this conference on federal whistleblowing.

Many Americans seem to believe that civil service reform is far removed from the general question of the legal control over government conduct. Too often the term *civil service* conjures up long compilations of esoteric regulations. Yet the crucial and important variable in how government performs is how public employees behave.

Among the most chilling revelations of the Senate Select Committee on Presidential Campaign Activities were those which exposed how the Nixon administration abused the personnel system. The hearings of that committee demonstrate how easily the structure of democracy can be threatened by those who control the civil service and can coerce illegal or improper conduct. In fact, the hearings of the select committee remain a blueprint for executive tyranny, waiting only to be dusted off by some future president with Nixonian inclinations.

Those who called for civil service reform at the end of the nineteenth century believed that such measures were required in order to preserve democratic government. Supporters of the Pendleton Act of 1883 asserted that civil service reform was

This selection comes from *The Bureaucrat* 6, 4 (Winter 1977), 29-34. Copyright 1977, The Bureaucrat, Inc. Reprinted by permission.

crucial to the impartial enforcement of the laws and essential for effective and efficient government. Although the reforms of the Pendleton Act may appear somewhat narrow today, at the time they were perceived as fundamental and were motivated by the same contemporary concerns which underlie the conference. When the Pendleton Act became law, Senator Hoar wrote that its passage had been "necessary for free government . . . I am now better convinced than ever that our form of government is safe for another century."

As we near that centennial, we must now consider what further changes in our public service may be required to protect our democratic institutions for the next hundred years. In an age when we rely so heavily on complex technologies, remote computers, and legions of public employees, I believe the concept of personal responsibility must now become the touchstone for restructuring the public service. Whistleblowing and two related issues—the right to disobey illegal or unconstitutional orders, and the personal accountability of government officials—all illustrate the importance of this fundamental concept.

At the very heart of the legal, professional, and ethical justifications which have been advanced for blowing the whistle, is the notion that public employees who know of impropriety and wrongdoing have a personal responsibility to speak out on behalf of the government and the citizenry. However, in the civil service as it exists today, public officials who consider taking such action run a very substantial risk of damaging or even ending their careers. That we do not expect employees to blow the whistle speaks of our realism; that we do not protect those who do, reveals our cynicism. Numerous mechanisms are available to punish outspoken or troublesome employees. The hearings of the Senate Select Committee on Presidential Campaign Activities and of the Subcommittee on Administrative Procedure and Practice of the Senate Judiciary Committee on S. 1210 document the extensive use made of disciplinary actions, personal actions, and informal harassment during the Nixon years. But these techniques are as old as bureaucracy itself.

Limited protections are available to whistleblowers. The only significant judicial protection rests upon the constitutional right of free speech embodied in the First Amendment. The U.S. Supreme Court in *Pickering* v. *Board of Education*, 391 U.S. 563 (1968), held that public employees could not be denied the right of free speech, but did allow the government to limit that right if an employee's comments would so adversely affect his relationship with his immediate superiors as to impair the efficiency of the government. *Pickering* sets out a very practical rationale for protecting employees' speech, namely that the unique understanding of an agency's operations and practices gives such employees a special ability to inform and to alert the public in cases of illegality and impropriety.

However, even if an employee's speech is clearly protected by the First Amendment, and even if the employee's exercise of First Amendment rights plays a substantial role in an agency's disciplinary action, an employee may still be unable to vindicate his rights before the courts. In *Mount Healthy School District* v. *Doyle*, 97 S. Ct. 568 (1977), the U.S. Supreme Court held that even when a public employee's exercise of First Amendment rights is a substantial or motivating factor in a dismissal, a court should allow the public employer to show by a preponderance of the evidence that it would have reached the same decision even in the absence of the protected speech.

Outside the area of free speech, the courts offer little protection to whistleblowers. *Parrish* v. *Civil Service Commission of Alameda*, 425 P. 2d 223 (1967), is the most significant case to date which discusses the right of public employees to disobey illegal or unconstitutional orders. In this case, the Supreme Court of California reversed the dismissal of a young social worker who refused to participate in midnight welfare searches that he believed unconstitutional. The court did find that the searches were illegal. However, it failed to decide whether an employee would be protected if he acted with reasonable and good faith but had been *mistaken* in believing that the act was illegal.

The courts are particularly reluctant to respond to the nondisciplinary and informal sanctions to which most whistleblowers are subjected. At present, administrative remedies are also inadequate to protect whistleblowing employees. The administrative process provides few avenues for redress for actions not strictly defined as disciplinary, and the orientation of the U.S. Civil Service Commission has been consistently biased in favor of federal executive agencies. Significant protection for whistleblowers must rely on restructuring of administrative practices and remedies.

The interests of public employees, of public employers, and of the general public would all be strengthened by a clear recognition that public employees are entitled to disobey orders reasonably believed in good faith to be illegal or unconstitutional.

An *employee* has an interest in not having to obey orders which violate his sense of self or sense of integrity, or which might jeopardize his reputation within the community. Moreover, an employee may be subject to criminal, civil, and administrative liability for following an order that he reasonably believes in good faith to be illegal or unconstitutional. Under regular torts standards and under Section 1983 of the Civil Rights Act of 1871, an employee is subject to personal damages and even criminal liability for participating in an illegal or unconstitutional act which deprives a third party of his constitutional rights. That a government employee has acted under orders is not by itself a legally acceptable defense against criminal liability. (Conceivably, professionals such as doctors and lawyers, too, could be subject to professional disciplinary action for following orders they believe to be illegal or unconstitutional.)

Public employers have a particular interest in insuring that the action and conduct of public officials are limited and controlled by law. While agency managers may seek to discourage subordinates from independently judging the legality of acts they are asked to perform, the ultimate interest of the public employer is to insure that governmental power is exercised within appropriate restraints. From this longer range perspective, a clear right to disobey may increase efficiency, because employees who exercise that right are likely to raise questions which encourage a more thorough and searching evaluation of policy by an agency's principal decision makers.

Citizens, of course, have an exceptionally strong interest in insuring that government operates within the law and that governmental power is not abused. As government involvement in private activity increases, so does the need of a democratic society to subject its government to law. This overall goal gives citizens a particular reason for insisting on a standard that will incline employees to resist unlawful and unconstitutional orders.

Significant changes should be made in administrative procedures in order to protect employees who disobey orders which they reasonably believe to be illegal or unconstitutional. For example, the Swedish Freedom of Press Act has a provision requiring consultation with higher authority regarding the legality of orders. The final guarantee of democratic and civilized government are the words of the single individual who says, "This I will not do."

Theoretically, the present civil service embodies, if not rests upon, the concept of personal responsibility. The basic premise of the civil service is that individual conduct is to be judged by external standards, and that disciplinary action is to be used to insure that government operates fairly and efficiently. At present, however, because the system operates as a monopoly for those who yield power within individual agencies, the civil service system has failed to implement the concept of personal responsibility and has become instead a vehicle for forcing conformity, a means of coercing or encouraging illegal or improper conduct.

Two simple procedural reforms could make the concept of personal responsibility more meaningful. First, there must be a mechanism by which a "victim" of government actions can initiate an evaluation of those actions. Second, this evaluation or review must be conducted in some structure other than the agency where the employee works.

These procedural principles are simple. Their implementation is more difficult. However, there are some existing bases on which we can build. First, under the sanctions provision of the Freedom of Information Act Amendments of 1974, citizens who have been denied information by the arbitrary or capricious conduct of a public employee, may initiate a rather lengthy process to discipline the employee who has withheld the information. The efficacy of the provision is unclear, both because it is cumbersome and because the U.S. Civil Service Commission (which has enforcement authority under the provision) is apparently unwilling to carry out both the spirit and the letter of congressional intent. However, the provision is crucially important. It is Congress's first clear statement that government employees should be personally subject to sanction through a process initiated by individuals who are affected by that conduct. It also clearly establishes a forum outside the employing agency for making the final decision. Second, in at least 18 states, conflict-of-interest provisions now allow citizens or employees to initiate complaints regarding conflicts of interest by government officers or employees.

It is clear that we have a long way to go. A great deal of thinking remains to be done regarding the kind of protections that we want. But we are already past the time when a beginning should have been made.

Any reform involves risk. We can never know all the effects of changes in our civil service. However, considering what we have witnessed in this country over the past decade, at the very least we should be willing to take some risks in an attempt to limit and control the abuses of government power. Perhaps the best way we can judge our efforts in this endeavor is by asking ourselves whether we have a system which accepts and welcomes acts of conscience by individual employees.

THIRTY
WHISTLEBLOWING AND FULL DISCLOSURE

Richard F. Kaufman

The struggle over the people's right to know what their government is doing is as old as government itself. Peter Zenger's freedom of the press case arose because Zenger published the exorbitant salary being paid to the colonial governor of New York. Zenger is perhaps our most preeminent whistleblowing forefather. Years later, a modern whistleblower and a modern newspaper came up against a modern government—still trying to suppress information the people have a right to know—when the Pentagon Papers were given to the *New York Times*.

We will always have a few public officials courageous enough to blow the whistle on waste and corruption in government. However, there will also be those in government anxious to silence the whistleblower and conceal the truth.

The tactics and opportunities for punishing whistleblowers are infinite in their variety. In the Soviet Union, whistleblowers are sent directly to criminal psychiatric wards. In this country, we drive our whistleblowers to the borders of insanity and sometimes over the edge by humiliating them, taking their jobs, demoting them, or forcing them to do nonwork; slander and character assassination are frequently used. Two specific tactics of suppression have been used to particularly great effect. Both should be seen as clear and present dangers to all persons who are committed to the principles of full disclosure and a free and open society.

The first tactic is simply to reorganize. Government reorganization is always undertaken with the avowed aim of making government function better. A major reorganization is being developed now by the Carter administration and I do not at-

This selection comes from *The Bureaucrat* 6, 4 (Winter 1977), 35-40. Copyright 1977, The Bureaucrat, Inc. Reprinted by permission.

tribute any ulterior motives to this effort. The president and the people involved in the current reorganization plans seem genuinely bent on improving the effectiveness while reducing the costs of government.

But in the past, however, government reorganizations undertaken in the name of efficiency have been excuses to purge employees and emasculate programs legislated by Congress. We need only to think back to the death by reorganization which Richard Nixon decreed for the Office of Economic Opportunity and the war against poverty; the purge of the arms controllers in the Arms Control Agency was also carved out under Nixon. Reorganization was also the method chosen for ousting Ernie Fitzgerald following his testimony before the Joint Economic Committee. Officially, Fitzgerald's job was eliminated through a reduction in force allegedly required for reasons of economy.

One looks with a certain amount of anxiety, therefore, at the coming reorganization. While it may have originated with the best of intentions and been planned for the most noble of purposes, it will be implemented outside the White House, down in the departments and agencies. Inevitably, choices will have to be made. There will be winners and losers.

Government reorganizations have often been a time for upper management to solve the problems of obstreperous employees who insist upon carrying out the policies of Congress, rather than those of their bosses. Such reorganizations present opportunities for vindictive supervisors to even up old scores with subordinates who have refused to close their eyes while laws were being subverted or intentionally violated. Reorganizations provide a chance to economize by getting rid of economizers—in short, a chance to silence the whistleblowers.

The anxieties with which some people view reorganization may not be fully appreciated within the administration. Understandably, the president is looking at the big picture. But who is looking out for those whose truthfulness has marked them for bureaucratic reprisals? I predict that unless active steps are taken immediately to protect such individuals, we may not have enough whistleblowers left to hold a seminar, much less a conference, a year after the Carter reorganization goes into effect. We could hold our meeting in Ralph Stavins's office or in my cubbyhole in the Dirksen Building.

Among the many other forms of retaliation against those who commit the sin of telling the truth, there is one that I did not understand until recently. A whistleblower can be stifled, without going after him individually, by going after his agency. The final solution for an unreconstructed whistleblower who is named to the head of the agency that previously tried to gag him is to liquidate his agency.

An alternative approach is to defeat his nomination. Something like this took place (although other factors were also involved) when Theodore Sorenson was named to head the CIA. One of the most serious charges against him was that he leaked information from Kennedy's White House. The accusation was not that the information was false nor that its release was harmful to the nation—merely that it was made public.

The frontal attack to abolish an entire agency can also be effective, especially if the agency is small and without a strong constituency. Such an attempt is going forward today against the Renegotiation Board. This is an interesting case because it illustrates the influence that corporations can exert in government when whistleblowers threaten private economic interests.

The Renegotiation Board was created in 1951 to recapture excess profits on defense contracts. During the Korean War and immediately afterward it was a strong agency which recovered hundreds of millions of dollars in excess profits. Steadily, through the years, the law against excess profits has been laced with loopholes, while more recent appointees to the board typically have had few qualifications and less enthusiasm for their work.

In 1973 Goodwin Chase, a former banker, was named to the board, and soon became convinced that the other board members were lax, inefficient, or worse. Chase dissented from many board decisions—made by majority vote—on grounds that tens of millions of dollars in excess defense profits were being allowed to escape renegotiation. When word of these dissents reached Congress and he was called upon to testify to the improprieties of his colleagues, Chase lost his bonafides as a team player. He became a whistleblower.

In 1977, President Carter dismissed the remaining members of the board and named Chase as chairman of a new board. In addition, bills were introduced in the House and Senate, strongly endorsed by the president, to plug the loopholes and strengthen the board. Until this time, the defense contractors and the Renegotiation Board had coexisted for years. The board was considered a nuisance but not a great one. Suddenly, however, a board headed by someone determined to enforce the law loomed as a serious threat to those who enjoy exorbitant profits on defense contracts. It became time for the defense contractors to spring into action, and they have sprung.

In the most concerted lobbying effort I have witnessed in 14 years on the Hill, the defense industries, the steel industry, the tool die makers, the computer industry, the auto industry, and others have decided that the board must be crippled or killed. They argue that the Renegotiation Board—with 180 employees and a budget of $5.5 million—is not cost-effective and, further, that this is the place where President Carter should make good his promise to reduce red tape and streamline the bureaucracy. (It is, Senator Proxmire has said, as if Nixon had suggested abolishing the special prosecutor on the grounds that it would save the taxpayers money.) As a result of effective lobbying the bills have now been stalled while the Renegotiation Act has technically expired. Whether the board and Goodwin Chase can survive remains to be seen.

My first point, then, is that we need to be on guard against two variations on a very old government theme: how to get rid of the whistleblower. One of the tried and true methods is to reorganize him out of a job or at least out of the way. If the whistleblower has risen too high in the bureaucracy to be "riffed," an alternate tactic is to abolish his agency.

The other side of the coin is that we must be equally diligent in protecting employees who tell the truth, who refuse to become involved in cover-ups of wrongdoing, and who disclose improprieties, illegalities, and taxpayer rip-offs.

First, it should be recognized that when we speak of the rights of employees to be truthful, honest, and law-abiding we are also speaking of the American public's right to know about lies, dishonesty, and illegal actions inside our government. Whistleblowing is an important, indispensable instrument of full disclosure. It is for this reason that all citizens share an interest in safeguarding the rights of government employees. A continuing public information program is necessary to dramatize the policy issues which have motivated whistleblowers to risk their jobs and careers in the first place. Public awareness may be the only way to offset private pressures for shutting down programs or agencies who remain loyal to the public interest.

Second, if whistleblowers are to survive, their jobs must be protected. The Civil Service Commission does protect jobs up to a point, but the commission also serves as a management tool which enables other agencies to function smoothly. Many view it as a personnel service for management throughout government, with a built-in bias against employees who create waves. One way to insulate whistleblowers from reprisals within their own agencies would be to provide a statutory hiring preference for employees wrongfully fired or acted against. The hiring preference would enable an employee to find another job at equal rank and pay elsewhere within his agency or in another agency. If such a preference is to have any meaning, the individual should be able to enforce it through the courts rather than have to depend upon action by the Civil Service Commission.

Third, punishment for wrongdoers is as important as protection for rightdoers. The existing system of rewards and punishments is upside down because agency heads normally back their supervisors in disputes with employees—while themselves, as top-ranking officials, remaining effectively beyond the reach of the law (except in extreme circumstances like Watergate). Criminal laws against intimidating witnesses or giving false information to Congress are not likely to be enforced in cases where the Attorney General might be forced to prosecute the secretary of defense, to choose an arbitrary example. Nor would any president be enthusiastic about exposing illegal behavior to his official family.

A solution to this dilemma was proposed by Senator Proxmire in 1975 in testimony before the Kennedy subcommittee on administrative practices. Proxmire outlined a three-step procedure by which any citizen, whether or not employed by the government, could complain about official wrongdoing and receive more than the kind of pro forma response such complaints usually evoke. Under this proposal the Justice Department would be required to investigate any complaint alleging official wrongdoing, and to decide within six months whether or not a criminal prosecution was warranted.

If Justice decided not to seek prosecution, it would have to prepare a written report explaining its decision and supply a copy to the citizen who filed the complaint. If Justice refused to prosecute, the citizen would be entitled to petition a federal district court for an order to compel prosecution. The court would have discretion to act one way or another, but it could hold a hearing on the matter. If it found sufficient evidence to warrant prosecution, the court could then refer the case to a grand jury.

This procedure would give citizens an opportunity to obtain reviews of their complaints by a body outside the executive branch, in cases where the Justice Department failed to satisfactorily explain its inaction. The repeated failure of Justice and the individual agencies to take action against official wrongdoing amply documents the need for such a law.

Finally, it should go without saying that whistleblowers need protection against catastrophic legal fees when incurred to defend themselves against wrongful actions by their superiors. Such protection can be easily provided by a law requiring reimbursement for attorney fees in cases which are decided in an employee's favor.

THIRTY-ONE
THE EFFECT OF AN OMBUDSMAN

Paul R. Meyer

The question to be examined in this article is: Does the existence of an ombudsman improve the image of the public service?

It is an accepted fact that all government has come to be viewed with suspicion by the general public. There was a time when general services, specialization of work, the application of uniform rules and procedures, the establishment of an official hierarchy, and graded levels of authority were looked upon in a positive way to describe a mature organization. These methods of organization now seem to be barriers. Getting an answer out of an agency which has "matured" can be frustrating.

A PART OF THE PROCESS

The time has come when people will not accept just words; citizens want to "feel" their government. They want to be a part of the process and to have a chance to talk to somebody when something is not right. Each person carries a perceptual road map in his or her mind. That road map increasingly does not jibe with the spoken words, especially from a "helpful" public servant. Other means are therefore necessary to have good communication. The tone of voice, angle of head, and other body language tell a far greater story. If we want to get closer to the truth, eye contact is essential. But underneath this desire to have all levels of communication is a much

This selection comes from *The Bureaucrat* 8, 4 (Winter 1979), 19–24. Copyright 1979, The Bureaucrat, Inc. Reprinted by permission.

stronger desire to hear and feel the warmth of another person who can express empathy.

The general concern about the increasing control and influence of government in our lives has prompted a quest for protective devices to insure that the citizen receives fair treatment from administrative authorities. The origins of the ombudsman concept go back to 1809 in Sweden. The first such program in the United States was established in Hawaii in 1967; two years later King County, Washington, a metropolitan government with over one million residents with Seattle as the central city, established the second such program in this country.

Since 1969, 135 offices which handle citizen complaints have been established in the United States. Not all are ombudsmen in the classical form, but the term has been broadened to mean an impartial government officer who reviews complaints from citizens against administrative decisions. With access to departmental files, the ombudsman aids in the communication with citizens where there are problems. The powers to criticize and make recommendations are outgrowths of investigations into misconduct of government activities.

VIEWS OF THE SERVICES

The services provided by an ombudsman are viewed by many as outside the normal channels for appeals which serve as alternatives to the judicial process rather than the political process. When you consider the substantial number of governmental entities providing services—states, counties, cities, school districts, and special-purpose districts—the number of ombudsmen and other complaint-handling programs is relatively small. Many public officials approve and support the concept but view it as an iceberg, and are fearful of what lurks below. Some legislators are apprehensive about the ombudsman undermining their own casework function that provides a vital link to their constituencies. Still others may see the ombudsman's role as threatening because of the information which may eventually be surfaced publicly. Some government employees may see the ombudsman as another critic who must be answered and thus detrimental to staff efficiency. Whatever these fears have been, there is a growing acceptance of the process and the concept of an additional advocate looking at government from a different perspective.

Added to this is general apprehension about another layer of bureaucracy in governments which are already overburdened by what some critics think is excessive bureaucracy. It must be acknowledged that ombudsmen have their own problems of establishing public acceptance. Any criticism that is made in this article about the bureaucracy must also imply that ombudsmen are not free of criticism. Programs which have been abandoned, such as Buffalo, New York, and Atlanta, Georgia, must be examined from the standpoint of adequate performance and sensitivity to criticism. In short, the blade cuts both ways.

TYPES OF PROBLEMS

Before offering any solutions to the ills of bureaucracy and the threat of a tarnished public image, I would like to focus for a moment on the types of problems which most frequently cause alienation. They are: clerical errors, failure to carry out legislative intent, unreasonable delay, administrative error, abuse of discretion, lack of courtesy, oversight, negligence, inadequate investigation, unfair policy, partiality, failure to communicate, rudeness, unreasonableness, arbitrariness, arrogance, inefficiency, physical and mental abuse, and denial of services.

These are the types of problems which cause conflict between the citizen and government. Because of the nature of bureaucracies, there may be failures in communication, inadequate resources, and poor use of people. Even with the best of intentions of administrators, services may be inadequate to meet the needs of the citizen. It is most often the process which gets an agency into trouble. The pace does not allow enough time to explain things. The simple issuing of death certificates by health authorities is a case in point. Family members are often stunned by the death of a loved one. Sometimes the death has been connected with violence. There needs to be an explanation by someone with access to the records to help soften the trauma and to hear out the grief. Service organizations like medical examining agencies get criticized because of the high volume of work with not enough staff to follow up each concern adequately to insure that sensitive information like a death is properly presented to the next of kin.

BIGNESS IS HERE TO STAY

Whether we like it or not, bigness is here to stay. Citizens must learn to live with structure. Whatever the arrangement of affairs, all complex societies must be governed by a corps of professional administrators. There is tension between the demands for efficiency on the one hand and accountability and responsiveness on the other side. A normal gulf will always be there.

Anytime we criticize our government agencies and employees we must look at ourselves and the value we place on the service. Cartoonist Walt Kelly through his character Pogo has expressed it very aptly: "I has met the enemy and they is us." In the political sense we are the government. The finger points right back to ourselves. Through our elected and appointed leaders, we, the taxpayers, create the systems, rules, and regulations and help to set the priorities. We have not gotten everything we have wanted.

To express it another way, we sometimes get more government than we bargained for. For example, the use of speed traps to catch speeders is something most people have mixed feelings about. Sometimes we seem to resent government taking aggressive action. It seems like the mark comes too close to home. There are, of course, exceptions, but the image of government is affected both by what it does and what it chooses not to do. The availability of service seems to be perceived much like a water tap; it gets turned on when you want service, but stays shut most of the time. But the attitude seems to be "Don't give us too much at once."

ENTER THE OMBUDSMAN

The ombudsman usually enters the picture when the situation gets so bad that nobody wants anything more to do with the problem. The ombudsman then provides a telescope through which a citizen can look first at governmental services and then focus on the area which he or she thinks needs attention. In many instances the ombudsman provides an oasis in the middle of a governmental desert for a person who is frustrated and weary of getting referred from one office to another.

The ultimate solution, however, must come from the department itself. With the help of the ombudsman, the citizen begins to view the government as more approachable. This attitude is especially true in dealing with the police. Many people who think they have a complaint will want to "warm up" to the problem by finding out just how much information they have to give about themselves before going forward with a complaint. Quite often an individual who has a complaint about the police has a criminal record and feels in greater jeopardy if he or she deals directly with the police.

The ombudsman therefore becomes a safe haven for such an inquiry. There are ethical problems the ombudsman faces, particularly when he or she finds that there is criminal activity. Confidentiality is important in order to gain and maintain trust from the complainant. People who come to the ombudsman with questionable backgrounds and involvement in any kind of criminal activity must feel that they can speak candidly. In a 1976 case, the Seattle-King County office learned about a planned prison break. Without revealing the identity of the individual who had reported the plot, the administration was informed of the plan, which resulted in a section of the jail given particularly strong security. Confidentiality was maintained as far as identity, but a potential criminal action which could have endangered the lives of many people was averted.

THE GREATEST ASSET

The greatest asset of an ombudsman is helping to establish government as more humane, a counter against dehumanization. Thousands of cases reported in Seattle-King County responded to allegations of insensitivity, inefficiency, and strict adherence to rules—all of which gets translated to "red tape." Because the ombudsman process is outside the normal channels and not mandatory as an appeal process, it does not provide an unhurried look at the problem and ample time to deal with an individual's anger. I compare this aspect of ombudsman work to the "Willie Loman Syndrome." Loman, a principal character in Arthur Miller's *Death of a Salesman*, did not have anybody to talk to. Nobody, not even his son or wife, would listen to him. Out of desperation he ended up taking his own life. If ombudsman offices would serve no other purpose than to listen, in my opinion they would be worth the expenditure of public funds.

The ombudsman is not a panacea for the ills of government. It should not be viewed as a substitute for other normal appeal processes. The literature, written mostly by lawyers and political scientists, which supports the creation of an ombudsman, carries high ideals of what can and should be expected from this office. However, there must be some harmony between the ideal and what can reasonably be accomplished. Basically, the ombudsman is a service which protects human rights of the citizen with respect to complaints against government. The ombudsman should be viewed as a supplement to existing institutions and not a replacement of them. In other words, an ombudsman is not an end in itself.

ENLIGHTENED GOVERNMENT

The process of a citizen submitting a complaint and the existence of a formal complaint program, whether it is known as an ombudsman or by some other designation, is not necessarily an indication of fault. Quite the contrary, the existence of an ombudsman is indication of an enlightened government. The creation of such a program is a strong indication that such a government is willing to take risks, innovate, delegate, and seek solutions that don't have clear answers within the existing frame of government. In fact, the relinquishment of power by a legislative body (in the case of a classical model) or an elected or appointed executive (in the case of an executive ombudsman) is in reality the most powerful action that such a person or group can take. A government can simply gain greater support from the public and the press by creating an ombudsman office.

Funding has been a problem for most ombudsman offices. Most offices receive appropriated public funds. There are a few offices which receive partial funding from either foundations or private sources. Thus ombudsman offices often must rely on the government they criticize for funding. To a certain extent the independence of an ombudsman is an illusion. The uniqueness of the ombudsman in the United States may tend to overglamorize the concept. The bottom line is funding. Those who control the funds have the greatest impact on the general direction the office will take. A broad funding base is necessary for a certain amount of independence.

THERE ARE SOME RISKS

There are some risks in having an ombudsman. Such a program provides at a minimum a quick redress to problems where, in certain instances, the normal appeal process can be bypassed through an ombudsman. To do this often can create an alternative system of appeals and thus weaken the main process, especially if people are encouraged frequently to bypass it.

If the ombudsman gives the impression that government is open and through this process a citizen can get redress, when in fact this does not occur, then the existence of such an office only stalls the day when major reform or changes in leadership are needed.

Every ombudsman runs a high risk of being "co-opted" by the administration he or she is investigating. Most problems build very slowly over a long period of time. They require looking back at patterns and comparing what has happened against some reasonable standard. When is a prisoner's medical right violated? If a general practitioner examines a patient for possible cancer, but does not call in a specialist who can run a series of tests, that prisoner's medical rights are violated. An ombudsman, when confronted with a double standard, must push for more thorough, and sometimes more expensive, treatment to insure that the same standard for the general community is applied to those being served by governmental institutions and programs. The old expression "It is close enough for government standards" may evoke laughs, but not if you are a prisoner and suffering because of a poorly trained medical staff or cut-rate medications.

SERVICES AND RESULTS

There are four major components which make up the services of an ombudsman: (1) listening, (2) educating and interpreting, (3) evaluating, and (4) recommending. The first two components emphasize the citizen; the latter two focus on government. If the system is working as it is intended, an ombudsman will be employing all phases of power granted to the office. The result is a more open government, a reduction of cost (including lawsuits and claims), and a strengthening of the due process system.

I have frequently been asked about an agency with a high number of complaints, if this was an indication of poor administration. The answer is both yes and no. Yes, if the complaints are repeated and no action is taken to correct the problem; no, if the nature of the agency is regulatory and would be expected to receive a great number of complaints. In fact, for some agencies, complaints are a positive indication that they are doing their jobs properly. At the local level, an agency responsible for licensing animals or finding building code violations can be faced with a strong public backlash if too many citations are given or if a hunt and search operation is established to find every last violator in the community.

The targets or issues must be carefully selected. An ombudsman must work through the existing channels of government and thereby strengthen them. The ombudsman does not create new channels as much as building on those which already exist. A good ombudsman program will force administrators to deal with issues that do not normally bubble up to the top.

In the state of Washington, for many years local police agencies worked with an outdated territorial law regarding the disposal of lost, found, and abandoned property. A very cumbersome statute forced a finder to wait an entire year and then pay for half of the value of any property found and turned over to the police. The ombudsman's office prepared legislation and sought sponsors to change the law. After two legislative sessions the proposal was adopted. It was the impetus of the ombudsman which brought about the needed change.

EXPECTATIONS

We do expect a lot of our public servants. Some citizens provoke public officials in ways that cause angry outbursts. Police, for example, may respond to name-calling by getting tougher and making more arrests. When we call for investigations of police brutality, for example, we need to look at the actions which began the chain reaction to insure that our demands for "justice" are fair for both sides. We can expect such high standards that a reasonable person could never meet them. Most of the work carried out by an ombudsman is helpful in pointing the direction for improving service, but the public must determine how much money will be spent to "enrich" the programs.

The ombudsman is certainly not a platform upon which major reforms should be launched. Most of the activities and issues involve very small and human need problems. Charter reform and task forces are better vehicles for those who want government given a major facelifting.

The ombudsman serves as a balance wheel, so to speak. There are really no petty complaints. Even the smallest matter can fit into a pattern which will allow the policymaking body to make a better determination about what kind of priorities best reflect the community. A complaint of cold food or a dirty towel given to a prisoner may signal that some essential equipment is breaking down or that supplies are running short and someone needs to be alerted to restock.

GUMMING TO DEATH

Herman S. Doi, ombudsman for the state of Hawaii, in one of his annual reports, refers to an ombudsman "gumming the bureaucracy to death." It is this tenacity which gives ombudsmen around the world the reputation of getting things done after all others have failed. The problem is not an overt act directed to injure a citizen; rather, it is the absence of any action, a delay or ignoring that there is a problem which gives rise to citizen complaints.

The notion of tenacity and patience have an interesting relationship with the ombudsman process. Many problems get resolved simply because someone sticks with an issue until it is adequately resolved. The idea that the "squeaky wheel gets the grease" has behind it that someone is willing to hang in and keep pressure on an agency until something gets done. So it is with the ombudsmen.

The best illustration of this principle is found in a cartoon by Bill Mauldin, drawn during World War II, depicting a forward artillery observer in a foxhole over which a German tank has stopped. The observer radios his base: "I got a target, but ya gotta be patient." Waiting for the right opportunity and moving on a recommendation when the time is ripe is the mark of an astute ombudsman!

A QUALIFIED YES

In answering the question of whether an ombudsman enhances the image of the public service, the answer is a qualified yes. If the ombudsman is nothing more than a shill, acting on behalf of the bureaucracy, then the problem remains the same. But, generally, the ombudsmen and the administrators are both seeking the same end—to improve services to the public. My experience has taught me that the vast majority of public officials are interested in improving their operations and are willing to consider the most effective and fairest means of resolving disputes between citizens and the public agencies.

The increase in government powers has given rise to an extremely complex administration which is built upon extensive rules and regulations. Add to this mix considerable discretionary powers given to public officials and a balancing of interests is absolutely necessary. Arthur Maloney, former ombudsman to the Ontario government in Canada, states in his resignation letter of August 15, 1978: "Considering the millions of dollars that the government of Ontario must spend annually to investigate the citizen, this is a small fraction to set aside to enable the citizen to investigate the agencies of government that he feels, rightly or wrongly, have been unfair to him. The people are surely entitled to no less."

The government more than anything else needs men and women of good will and ability. A positive attitude toward the citizen is vital. The right relationship between citizen and bureaucrat can best be described by the dialogue between Professor Henry Higgins and Eliza Doolittle in George Bernard Shaw's *Pygmalion:*

HIGGINS: The great secret, Eliza, is not having bad manners or good manners or any other particular sort of manners, but having the same manner for all human souls: in short, behaving as if you were in heaven, where there are no third-class carriages, and one soul is as good as another.
ELIZA: Amen, you are a born preacher.
HIGGINS: The question is not whether I treat you rudely, but whether you ever heard me treat anyone else better.

In the final analysis, government is built on relationships. The ombudsman's office helps to keep the relationship healthy and provide additional insurance that all "human souls" are treated one as good as another.

APPENDIX
ADMINISTRATIVE PROCEDURE ACT*

TABLE OF SECTIONS

551. Definitions.
552. Public Information; Agency Rules, Opinions, Orders, Records, and Proceedings.
552a. Records Maintained on Individuals.
552b. Open Meetings.
553. Rule Making.
554. Adjudications.
555. Ancillary Matters
556. Hearings; Presiding Employees; Powers and Duties; Burden of Proof; Evidence; Record as Basis of Decision.
557. Initial Decisions; Conclusiveness; Review by Agency; Submissions by Parties; Contents of Decisions; Record.
558. Imposition of Sanctions; Determination of Applications for Licenses; Suspension, Revocation, and Expiration of Licenses.
559. Effect on Other Laws; Effect of Subsequent Statute.

§ 551. DEFINITIONS

For the purpose of this subchapter—

*P.L. 404, 60 Stat. 237 (1946) as amended through Ninety-sixth Congress, First Session (1979). 5 U.S.C.A. §§ 551–559, 701–706, 1305, 3105, 3344, 5372, 7521.

(1) *agency* means each authority of the government of the United States, whether or not it is within or subject to review by another agency, but does not include—

(A) the Congress;
(B) the courts of the United States;
(C) the governments of the territories or possessions of the United States;
(D) the government of the District of Columbia;

or except as to the requirements of Section 552 of this title—

(E) agencies composed of representatives of the parties or of representatives of organizations of the parties to the disputes determined by them;
(F) courts martial and military commissions;
(G) military authority exercised in the field in time of war or in occupied territory; or
(H) functions conferred by sections 1738, 1739, 1743, and 1744 of title 12; chapter 2 of title 41; or sections 1622, 1884, 1891–1902, and former Section 1641(b)(2), of title 50, appendix;

(2) *person* includes an individual, partnership, corporation, association, or public or private organization other than an agency;

(3) *party* includes a person or agency named or admitted as a party, or properly seeking and entitled as of right to be admitted as a party, in an agency proceeding, and a person or agency admitted by an agency as a party for limited purposes;

(4) *rule* means the whole or a part of an agency statement of general or particular applicability and future effect designed to implement, interpret, or prescribe law or policy or describing the organization, procedure, or practice requirements of an agency and includes the approval or prescription for the future of rates, wages, corporate or financial structures or reorganizations thereof, prices, facilities, appliances, services or allowances therefor or of valuations, costs, or accounting, or practices bearing on any of the foregoing;

(5) *rule making* means agency process for formulating, amending, or repealing a rule;

(6) *order* means the whole or a part of a final disposition, whether affirmative, negative, injunctive, or declaratory in form, of an agency in a matter other than rule making but including licensing;

(7) *adjudication* means agency process for the formulation of an order;

(8) *license* includes the whole or a part of an agency permit, certificate, approval, registration, charter, membership, statutory exemption or other form of permission;

(9) *licensing* includes agency process respecting the grant, renewal, denial, revocation, suspension, annulment, withdrawal, limitation, amendment, modification, or conditioning of a license;

(10) *sanction* includes the whole or a part of an agency—

(A) prohibition, requirement, limitation, or other condition affecting the freedom of a person;
(B) withholding of relief;
(C) imposition of penalty or fine;
(D) destruction, taking, seizure, or withholding of property;
(E) assessment of damages, reimbursement, restitution, compensation, costs, charges, or fees;
(F) requirement, revocation, or suspension of a license; or
(G) taking other compulsory or restrictive action;

(11) *relief* includes the whole or a part of an agency—

(A) grant of money, assistance, license, authority, exemption, exception, privilege, or remedy;
(B) recognition of a claim, right, immunity, privilege, exemption, or exception; or

(C) taking of other action on the application or petition of, and beneficial to, a person;

(12) *agency proceeding* means an agency process as defined by paragraphs (5),(7), and (9) of this section;

(13) *agency action* includes the whole or a part of an agency rule, order, license, sanction, relief, or the equivalent or denial thereof, or failure to act; and

(14) *ex parte communication* means an oral or written communication not on the public record with respect to which reasonable prior notice to all parties is not given, but it shall not include requests for status reports on any matter or proceeding covered by this subchapter.

§ 552. PUBLIC INFORMATION; AGENCY RULES, OPINIONS, ORDERS, RECORDS, AND PROCEEDINGS

(a) Each agency shall make available to the public information as follows:

(1) Each agency shall separately state and currently publish in the *Federal Register* for the guidance of the public—

(A) descriptions of its central and field organization and the established places at which, the employees (and in the case of a uniformed service, the members) from whom, and the methods whereby, the public may obtain information, make submittals or requests, or obtain decisions;

(B) statements of the general course and method by which its functions are channeled and determined, including the nature and requirements of all formal and informal procedures available;

(C) rules of procedure, descriptions of forms available or the places at which forms may be obtained, and instructions as to the scope and contents of all papers, reports, or examinations;

(D) substantive rules of general applicability adopted as authorized by law, and statements of general policy or interpretations of general applicability formulated and adopted by the agency; and

(E) each amendment, revision, or repeal of the foregoing.

Except to the extent that a person has actual and timely notice of the terms thereof, a person may not in any manner be required to resort to, or be adversely affected by, a matter required to be published in the *Federal Register* and not so published. For the purpose of this paragraph, matter reasonably available to the class of persons affected thereby is deemed published in the *Federal Register* when incorporated by reference therein with the approval of the director of the *Federal Register*.

(2) Each agency, in accordance with published rules, shall make available for public inspection and copying—

(A) final opinions, including concurring and dissenting opinions, as well as orders, made in the adjudication of cases;

(B) those statements of policy and interpretations which have been adopted by the agency and are not published in the *Federal Register*; and

(C) administrative staff manuals and instructions to staff that affect a member of the public;

> unless the materials are promptly published and copies offered for sale. To the extent required to prevent a clearly unwarranted invasion of personal privacy, an agency may delete identifying details when it makes available or publishes an opinion, statement of policy, interpretation, or staff manual or instruction. However, in each case the justification for the deletion shall be explained fully in writing. Each agency shall also maintain and make available for public inspection and copying current indexes providing identifying information for the public as to any matter issued, adopted, or promulgated after July 4, 1967, and required by this paragraph to be made available or pub-

lished. Each agency shall promptly publish, quarterly or more frequently, and distribute (by sale or otherwise) copies of each index or supplements thereto unless it determines by order published in the *Federal Register* that the publication would be unnecessary and impracticable, in which case the agency shall nonetheless provide copies of such index on request at a cost not to exceed the direct cost of duplication. A final order, opinion, statement of policy, interpretation, or staff manual or instruction that affects a member of the public may be relied on, used, or cited as precedent by an agency against a party other than an agency only if—

(i) it has been indexed and either made available or published as provided by this paragraph; or

(ii) the party has actual and timely notice of the terms thereof.

(3) Except with respect to the records made available under paragraphs (1) and (2) of this subsection, each agency, upon any request for records which (A) reasonably describes such records and (B) is made in accordance with published rules stating the time, place, fees (if any), and procedures to be followed, shall make the records promptly available to any person.

(4)(A) In order to carry out the provisions of this section, each agency shall promulgate regulations, pursuant to notice and receipt of public comment, specifying a uniform schedule of fees applicable to all constituent units of such agency. Such fees shall be limited to reasonable standard charges for document search and duplication and provide for recovery of only the direct costs of such search and duplication. Documents shall be furnished without charge or at a reduced charge where the agency determines that waiver or reduction of the fee is in the public interest because furnishing the information can be considered as primarily benefiting the general public.

(B) On complaint, the district court of the United States in the district in which the complainant resides, or has his principal place of business, or in which the agency records are situated, or in the District of Columbia, has jurisdiction to enjoin the agency from withholding agency records and to order the production of any agency records improperly withheld from the complainant. In such a case the court shall determine the matter de novo, and may examine the contents of such agency records in camera to determine whether such records or any part thereof shall be withheld under any of the exemptions set forth in subsection (b) of this section, and the burden is on the agency to sustain its action.

(C) Notwithstanding any other provision of law, the defendant shall serve an answer or otherwise plead to any complaint made under this subsection within thirty days after service upon the defendant of the pleading in which such complaint is made, unless the court otherwise directs for good cause shown.

(D) Except as to cases the court considers of greater importance, preceedings before the district court, as authorized by this subsection, and appeals therefrom, take precedence on the docket over all cases and shall be assigned for hearing and trial or for argument at the earliest practicable date and expedited in every way.

(E) The court may assess against the United States reasonable attorney fees and other litigation costs reasonably incurred in any case under this section in which the complainant has substantially prevailed.

(F) Whenever the court orders the production of any agency records improperly withheld from the complainant and assesses against the United States reasonable attorney fees and other litigation costs, and the court additionally issues a written finding that the circumstances surrounding the withholding raise questions whether agency personnel acted arbitrarily or capriciously with respect to the withholding, the Special Counsel shall promptly initiate a proceeding to determine whether disciplinary action is warranted against the officer or employee who was primarily responsible for the withholding. The Special Counsel, after investigation and consideration of the evidence submitted, shall submit his findings and recommendations to the administrative authority of the agency concerned and shall send copies of the findings and recommendations to the office or employee or his representative. The administrative authority shall take the corrective action that the Special Counsel recommends.

(G) In the event of noncompliance with the order of the court, the district court may punish for contempt the responsible employee, and in the case of a uniformed service, the responsible member.

(5) Each agency having more than one member shall maintain and make available for public inspection a record of the final votes of each member in every agency proceeding.

(6)(A) Each agency, upon any request for records made under paragraph (1),(2), or (3) of this subsection shall—

(i) determine within ten days (excepting Saturdays, Sundays, and legal public holidays) after the receipt of any such request whether to comply with such request and shall immediately notify the person making such request of such determination and the reasons therefor, and of the right of such person to appeal to the head of the agency any adverse determination; and

(ii) make determination with respect to any appeal within twenty days (excepting Saturdays, Sundays, and legal public holidays) after the receipt of such appeal. If on appeal the denial of the request for records is in whole or in part upheld, the agency shall notify the person making such request of the provisions for judicial review of that determination under paragraph (4) of this subsection.

(B) In unusual circumstances as specified in this subparagraph, the time limits prescribed in either clause (i) or clause (ii) of subparagraph (A) may be extended by written notice to the person making such request setting forth the reasons for such extension and the date on which a determination is expected to be dispatched. No such notice shall specify a date that would result in an extension for more than ten working days. As used in this subparagraph, "unusual circumstances" means, but only to the extent reasonably necessary to the proper processing of the particular request—

(i) the need to search for and collect the requested records from field facilities or other establishments that are separate from the office processing the request;

(ii) the need to search for, collect, and appropriately examine a voluminous amount of separate and distinct records which are demanded in a single request; or

(iii) the need for consultation, which shall be conducted with all practicable speed, with another agency having a substantial interest in the determination of the request or among two or more components of the agency having substantial subject-matter interest therein.

(C) Any person making a request to any agency for records under paragraph (1), (2), or (3) of this subsection shall be deemed to have exhausted his administrative remedies with respect to such request if the agency fails to comply with the applicable time limit provisions of this paragraph. If the government can show exceptional circumstances exist and that the agency is exercising due diligence in responding to the request, the court may retain jurisdiction and allow the agency additional time to complete its review of the records. Upon any determination by an agency to comply with a request for records, the records shall be made promptly available to such person making such request. Any notification of denial of any request for records under this subsection shall set forth the names and titles or positions of each person responsible for the denial of such request.

(b) This section does not apply to matters that are—

(1)(A) specifically authorized under criteria established by an executive order to be kept secret in the interest of national defense or foreign policy and (B) are in fact properly classified pursuant to such executive order;

(2) related solely to the internal personnel rules and practices of an agency;

(3) specifically exempted from disclosure by statute (other than Section 552b of this title), provided that such statute (A) requires that the matters be withheld from the public in such a manner as to leave no discretion on the issue, or (B) establishes particular criteria for withholding or refers to particular types of matters to be withheld;

(4) trade secrets and commercial or financial information obtained from a person and privileged or confidential;

(5) interagency or intra-agency memorandums or letters which would not be available by law to a party other than an agency in litigation with the agency;

(6) personnel and medical files and similar files the disclosure of which would constitute a clearly unwarranted invasion of personal privacy;

(7) investigatory records compiled for law enforcement purposes, but only to the extent that the production of such records would (A) interfere with enforcement proceedings, (B) deprive a person of a right to a fair trial or an impartial adjudication, (C) constitute an unwarranted invasion of personal privacy, (D) disclose the identity of a confidential source and, in the case of a record compiled by a criminal law enforcement authority in the course of a criminal investigation, or by an agency conducting a lawful national security intelligence investigation, confidential information furnished only by the confidential source, (E) disclose investigative techniques and procedures, or (F) endanger the life or physical safety of law enforcement personnel;

(8) contained in or related to examination, operating, or condition reports prepared by, on behalf of, or for the use of an agency responsible for the regulation or supervision of financial institutions; or

(9) geological and geophysical information and data, including maps, concerning wells.

Any reasonably segregable portion of a record shall be provided to any person requesting such record after deletion of the portions which are exempt under this subsection.

(c) This section does not authorize withholding of information or limit the availability of records to the public, except as specifically stated in this section. This section is not authority to withhold information from Congress.

(d) On or before March 1 of each calendar year, each agency shall submit a report covering the preceding calendar year to the Speaker of the House of Representatives and President of the Senate for referral to the appropriate committees of the Congress. The report shall include—

(1) the number of determinations made by such agency not to comply with requests for records made to such agency under subsection (a) and the reasons for each such determination;

(2) the number of appeals made by persons under subsection (a)(6), the result of such appeals, and the reason for the action upon each appeal that results in a denial of information;

(3) the names and titles or positions of each person responsible for the denial of records requested under this section, and the number of instances of participation for each;

(4) the results of each proceeding conducted pursuant to subsection (a)(4)(F), including a report of the disciplinary action taken against the officer or employee who was primarily responsible for improperly withholding records or an explanation of why disciplinary action was not taken;

(5) a copy of every rule made by such agency regarding this section; and

(6) a copy of the fee schedule and the total amount of fees collected by the agency for making records available under this section; and

(7) such other information as indicates efforts to administer fully this section.

The Attorney General shall submit an annual report on or before March 1 of each calendar year which shall include for the prior calendar year a listing of the number of cases arising under this section, the exemption involved in each case, the disposition of such case, and the cost, fees, and penalties assessed under subsections (a)(4)(E), (F), and (G). Such report shall also include a description of the efforts undertaken by the Department of Justice to encourage agency compliance with this section.

(e) For the purposes of this section, the term *agency* as defined in Section 551(1) of this title includes any executive department, military department, government corporation, government-controlled corporation, or other establishment in the executive branch of the government (including the Executive Office of the President), or any independent regulatory agency.

§ 552a. RECORDS MAINTAINED ON INDIVIDUALS

(a) **Definitions.** For purposes of this section—

(1) the term *agency* means agency as defined in Section 552(e) of this title;

(2) the term *individual* means a citizen of the United States or an alien lawfully admitted for permanent residence;

(3) the term *maintain* includes maintain, collect, use, or disseminate;

(4) the term *record* means any item, collection, or grouping of information about an individual that is maintained by an agency, including, but not limited to, his education, financial transactions, medical history, and criminal or employment history and that contains his name, or the identifying number, symbol, or other identifying particular assigned to the individual, such as a finger or voice print or a photograph;

(5) the term *system of records* means a group of any records under the control of any agency from which information is retrieved by the name of the individual or by some identifying number, symbol, or other identifying particular assigned to the individual;

(6) the term *statistical record* means a record in a system of records maintained for statistical research or reporting purposes only and not used in whole or in part in making any determination about an identifiable individual, except as provided by Section 8 of title 13; and

(7) the term *routine use* means, with respect to the disclosure of a record, the use of such record for a purpose which is compatible with the purpose for which it was collected.

(b) **Conditions of disclosure.** No agency shall disclose any record which is contained in a system of records by any means of communication to any person, or to another agency, except pursuant to a written request by, or with the prior written consent of, the individual to whom the record pertains, unless disclosure of the record would be—

(1) to those officers and employees of the agency which maintains the record who have a need for the record in the performance of their duties;

(2) required under Section 552 of this title;

(3) for a routine use as defined in subsection (a)(7) of this section and described under subsection (e)(4)(D) of this section;

(4) to the Bureau of the Census for purposes of planning or carrying out a census or survey or related activity pursuant to the provisions of title 13;

(5) to a recipient who has provided the agency with advance adequate written assurance that the record will be used solely as a statistical research or reporting record, and the record is to be transferred in a form that is not individually identifiable;

(6) to the National Archives of the United States as a record which has sufficient historical or other value to warrant its continued preservation by the United States government, or for evaluation by the administrator of General Services or his designee to determine whether the record has such value;

(7) to another agency or to an instrumentality of any governmental jurisdiction within or under the control of the United States for a civil or criminal law enforcement activity if the activity is authorized by law, and if the head of the agency or instrumentality has made a written request to the agency which maintains the record specifying the particular portion desired and the law-enforcement activity for which the record is sought;

(8) to a person pursuant to a showing of compelling circumstances affecting the health or safety of an individual if upon such disclosure notification is transmitted to the last known address of such individual;

(9) to either house of Congress, or, to the extent of matter within its jurisdiction, any committee or subcommittee thereof, any joint committee of Congress or subcommittee of any such joint committee;

(10) to the comptroller general, or any of his authorized representatives, in the course of the performance of the duties of the General Accounting Office; or

(11) pursuant to the order of a court of competent jurisdiction.

(c) **Accounting of certain disclosures.** Each agency, with respect to each system of records under its control, shall—

(1) except for disclosures made under subsections (b)(1) or (b)(2) of this section, keep an accurate accounting of—

(A) the date, nature, and purpose of each disclosure of a record to any person or to another agency made under subsection (b) of this section; and

(B) the name and address of the person or agency to whom the disclosure is made;

(2) retain the accounting made under paragraph (1) of this subsection for at least five years or the life of the record, whichever is longer, after the disclosure for which the accounting is made;

(3) except for disclosures made under subsection (b)(7) of this section, make the accounting made under paragraph (1) of this subsection available to the individual named in the record at his request; and

(4) inform any person or other agency about any correction or notation of dispute made by the agency in accordance with subsection (d) of this section of any record that has been disclosed to the person or agency if an accounting of the disclosure was made.

(d) **Access to records.** Each agency that maintains a system of records shall—

(1) upon request by any individual to gain access to his record or to any information pertaining to him which is contained in the system, permit him and upon his request, a person of his own choosing to accompany him, to review the record and have a copy made of all or any portion thereof in a form comprehensible to him, except that the agency may require the individual to furnish a written statement authorizing discussion of that individual's record in the accompanying person's presence;

(2) permit the individual to request amendment of a record pertaining to him and—

(A) not later than 10 days (excluding Saturdays, Sundays, and legal public holidays) after the date of receipt of such request, acknowledge in writing such receipt; and

(B) promptly, either—

(i) make any correction of any portion thereof which the individual believes is not accurate, relevant, timely, or complete; or

(ii) inform the individual of its refusal to amend the record in accordance with his request, the reason for the refusal, the procedures established by the agency for the individual to request a review of that refusal by the head of the agency or an officer designated by the head of the agency, and the name and business address of that official;

(3) permit the individual who disagrees with the refusal of the agency to amend his record to request a review of such refusal, and not later than 30 days (excluding Saturdays, Sundays, and legal public holidays) from the date on which the individual requests such review, complete such review and make a final determination unless, for good cause shown, the head of the agency extends such 30-day period; and if, after his review, the reviewing official also refuses to amend the record in accordance with the request, permit the individual to file with the agency a concise statement setting forth the reasons for his disagreement with the refusal

of the agency, and notify the individual of the provisions for judicial review of the reviewing official's determination under subsection (g)(1)(A) of this section;

(4) in any disclosure, containing information about which the individual has filed a statement of disagreement, occurring after the filing of the statement under paragraph (3) of this subsection, clearly note any portion of the record which is disputed and provide copies of the statement and, if the agency deems it appropriate, copies of a concise statement of the reasons of the agency for not making the amendments requested, to persons or other agencies to whom the disputed record has been disclosed; and

(5) nothing in this section shall allow an individual access to any information compiled in reasonable anticipation of a civil action or proceeding.

(e) **Agency requirements.** Each agency that maintains a system of records shall—

(1) maintain in its records only such information about an individual as is relevant and necessary to accomplish a purpose of the agency required to be accomplished by statute or by executive order of the president;

(2) collect information to the greatest extent practicable directly from the subject individual when the information may result in adverse determinations about an individual's rights, benefits, and privileges under federal programs;

(3) inform each individual whom it asks to supply information, on the form which it uses to collect the information or on a separate form that can be retained by the individual—

(A) the authority (whether granted by statute, or by executive order of the president) which authorizes the solicitation of the information and whether disclosure of such information is mandatory or voluntary;

(B) the principal purpose or purposes for which the information is intended to be used;

(C) the routine uses which may be made of the information, as published pursuant to paragraph (4)(D) of this subsection; and

(D) the effects on him, if any, of not providing all or any part of the requested information;

(4) subject to the provisions of paragraph (11) of this subsection, publish in the *Federal Register* at least annually a notice of the existence and character of the system of records, which notice shall include—

(A) the name and location of the system;

(B) the categories of individuals on whom records are maintained in the system;

(C) the categories of records maintained in the system;

(D) each routine use of the records contained in the system, including the categories of users and the purpose of such use;

(E) the policies and practices of the agency regarding storage, retrievability, access controls, retention, and disposal of the records;

(F) the title and business address of the agency official who is responsible for the system of records;

(G) the agency procedures whereby an individual can be notified at his request if the system of records contains a record pertaining to him;

(H) the agency procedures whereby an individual can be notified at his request how he can gain access to any record pertaining to him contained in the system of records, and how he can contest its content; and

(I) the categories of sources of records in the system;

(5) maintain all records which are used by the agency in making any determination about any individual with such accuracy, relevance, timeliness, and completeness as is reasonably necessary to assure fairness to the individual in the determination;

(6) prior to disseminating any record about an individual to any person other than an agency, unless the dissemination is made pursuant to subsection (b)(2) of this section, make

reasonable efforts to assure that such records are accurate, complete, timely, and relevant for agency purposes;

(7) maintain no record describing how any individual exercises rights guaranteed by the First Amendment unless expressly authorized by statute or by the individual about whom the record is maintained or unless pertinent to and within the scope of an authorized law enforcement activity;

(8) make reasonable efforts to serve notice on an individual when any record on such individual is made available to any person under compulsory legal process when such process becomes a matter of public record;

(9) establish rules of conduct for persons involved in the design, development, operation, or maintenance of any system of records, or in maintaining any record, and instruct each such person with respect to such rules and the requirements of this section, including any other rules and procedures adopted pursuant to this section and the penalties for noncompliance;

(10) establish appropriate administrative, technical, and physical safeguards to insure the security and confidentiality of records and to protect against any anticipated threats or hazards to their security or integrity which could result in substantial harm, embarrassment, inconvenience, or unfairness to any individual on whom information is maintained; and

(11) at least 30 days prior to publication of information under paragraph (4)(D) of this subsection, publish in the *Federal Register* notice of any new use or intended use of the information in the system, and provide an opportunity for interested persons to submit written data, views, or arguments to the agency.

(f) **Agency rules.** In order to carry out the provisions of this section, each agency that maintains a system of records shall promulgate rules, in accordance with the requirements (including general notice) of Section 553 of this title, which shall—

(1) establish procedures whereby an individual can be notified in response to his request if any system of records named by the individual contains a record pertaining to him;

(2) define reasonable times, places, and requirements for identifying an individual who requests his record or information pertaining to him before the agency shall make the record or information available to the individual;

(3) establish procedures for the disclosure to an individual upon his request of his record or information pertaining to him, including special procedure, if deemed necessary, for the disclosure to an individual of medical records, including psychological records, pertaining to him;

(4) establish procedures for reviewing a request from an individual concerning the amendment of any record or information pertaining to the individual, for making a determination on the request, for an appeal within the agency of an initial adverse agency determination, and for whatever additional means may be necessary for each individual to be able to exercise fully his rights under this section; and

(5) establish fees to be charged, if any, to any individual for making copies of his record, excluding the cost of any search for and review of the record.

The office of the *Federal Register* shall annually compile and publish the rules promulgated under this subsection and agency notices published under subsection (e)(4) of this section in a form available to the public at low cost.

(g)(1) **Civil remedies.** Whenever an agency

(A) makes a determination under subsection (d)(3) of this section not to amend an individual's record in accordance with his request, or fails to make such review in conformity with that subsection;

(B) refuses to comply with an individual request under subsection (d)(1) of this section;

(C) fails to maintain any record concerning any individual with such accuracy, relevance, timeliness, and completeness as is necessary to assure fairness in any determination relating to the qualifications, character, rights, or opportunities of, or benefits to the individual that may be made on the basis of such record, and consequently a determination is made which is adverse to the individual; or

(D) fails to comply with any other provision of this section, or any rule promulgated thereunder, in such a way as to have an adverse effect on an individual,

the individual may bring a civil action against the agency, and the district courts of the United States shall have jurisdiction in the matters under the provisions of this subsection.

(2)(A) In any suit brought under the provisions of subsection (g)(1)(A) of this section, the court may order the agency to amend the individual's record in accordance with his request or in such other way as the court may direct. In such a case the court shall determine the matter de novo.

(B) The court may assess against the United States reasonable attorney fees and other litigation costs reasonably incurred in any case under this paragraph in which the complainant has substantially prevailed.

(3)(A) In any suit brought under the provisions of subsection (g)(1)(B) of this section, the court may enjoin the agency from withholding the records and order the production to the complainant of any agency records improperly withheld from him. In such a case the court shall determine the matter de novo, and may examine the contents of any agency records in camera to determine whether the records or any portion thereof may be withheld under any of the exemptions set forth in subsection (k) of this section, and the burden is on the agency to sustain its action.

(B) The court may assess against the United States reasonable attorney fees and other litigation costs reasonably incurred in any case under this paragraph in which the complainant has substantially prevailed.

(4) In any suit brought under the provisions of subsection (g)(1)(C) or (D) of this section in which the court determines that the agency acted in a manner which was intentional or willful, the United States shall be liable to the individual in an amount equal to the sum of—

(A) actual damages sustained by the individual as a result of the refusal or failure, but in no case shall a person entitled to recovery receive less than the sum of $1,000; and

(B) the costs of the action together with reasonable attorney fees as determined by the court.

(5) An action to enforce any liability created under this section may be brought in the district court of the United States in the district in which the complainant resides, or has his principal place of business, or in which the agency records are situated, or in the District of Columbia, without regard to the amount in controversy, within two years from the date on which the cause of action arises, except that where an agency has materially and willfully misrepresented any information required under this section to be disclosed to an individual and the information so misrepresented is material to establishment of the liability of the agency to the individual under this section, the action may be brought at any time within two years after discovery by the individual of the misrepresentation. Nothing in this section shall be construed to authorize any civil action by reason of any injury sustained as the result of a disclosure of a record prior to September 27, 1975.

(h) **Rights of legal guardians.** For the purposes of this section, the parent of any minor, or the legal guardian of any individual who has been declared to be incompetent due to physical or mental incapacity or age by a court of competent jurisdiction, may act on behalf of the individual.

(i)(1) **Criminal penalties.** Any officer or employee of an agency, who by virtue of his employment or official position, has possession of, or access to, agency records which contain individually identifiable information the disclosure of which is prohibited by this section or by rules or regulations established thereunder, and who knowing that disclosure of the specific material is so prohibited, willfully discloses the material in any manner to any person or agency not entitled to receive it, shall be guilty of a misdemeanor and fined not more than $5,000.

(2) Any officer or employee of any agency who willfully maintains a system of records without meeting the notice requirements of subsection (e)(4) of this section shall be guilty of a misdemeanor and fined not more than $5,000.

(3) Any person who knowingly and willfully requests or obtains any record concerning an individual from an agency under false pretenses shall be guilty of a misdemeanor and fined not more than $5,000.

(j) **General exemptions.** The head of any agency may promulgate rules, in accordance with the requirements (including general notice) of sections 553(b)(1), (2), and (3), (c), and (e) of this title, to exempt any system of records within the agency from any part of this section except subsections (b), (c)(1) and (2), (e)(4)(A) through (F), (e)(6), (7), (9), (10), and (11), and (i) if the system of record is—

(1) maintained by the Central Intelligence Agency; or

(2) maintained by an agency or component thereof which performs as its principal function any activity pertaining to the enforcement of criminal laws, including police efforts to prevent, control, or reduce crime or to apprehend criminals, and the activities of prosecutors, courts, correctional, probation, pardon, or parole authorities, and which consists of (A) information compiled for the purposes of identifying individual criminal offenders and alleged offenders and consisting only of identifying data and notations of arrests, the nature and disposition of criminal charges, sentencing, confinement, release, and parole and probation status; (B) information compiled for the purpose of a criminal investigation, including reports of informants and investigators, and associated with an identifiable individual; or (C) reports identifiable to an individual compiled at any stage of the process of enforcement of the criminal laws from arrest or indictment through release from supervision.

At the time rules are adopted under this subsection, the agency shall include in the statement required under Section 553(c) of this title, the reasons why the system of records is to be exempted from a provision of this section.

(k) **Specific exemptions.** The head of any agency may promulgate rules, in accordance with the requirements (including general notice) of sections 553(b)(1),(2), and (3),(c), and (e) of this title, to exempt any system of records within the agency from subsections (c)(3), (d), (e)(1), (e)(4)(G), (H), and (I) and (f) of this section if the system of records is—

(1) subject to the provisions of Section 552(b)(1) of this title;

(2) investigatory material compiled for law enforcement purposes, other than material within the scope of subsection (j)(2) of this section: *provided, however,* that if any individual is denied any right, privilege, or benefit that he would otherwise be entitled by federal law, or for which he would otherwise be eligible, as a result of the maintenance of such material, such material shall be provided to such individual, except to the extent that the disclosure of such material would reveal the identity of a source who furnished information to the government under an express promise that the identity of the source would be held in confidence, or, prior to the effective date of this section, under an implied promise that the identity of the source would be held in confidence;

(3) maintained in connection with providing protective services to the president of the United States or other individuals pursuant to Section 3056 of title 18;

(4) required by statute to be maintained and used solely as statistical records;

(5) investigatory material compiled solely for the purpose of determining suitability, eligibility, or qualifications for federal civilian employment, military service, federal contracts, or access to classified information, but only to the extent that the disclosure of such material

would reveal the identity of a source who furnished information to the government under an express promise that the identity of the source would be held in confidence, or, prior to the effective date of this section, under an implied promise that the identity of the source would be held in confidence;

(6) testing or examination material used solely to determine individual qualifications for appointment or promotion in the federal service the disclosure of which would compromise the objectivity or fairness of the testing or examination process; or

(7) evaluation material used to determine potential for promotion in the armed services, but only to the extent that the disclosure of such material would reveal the identity of a source who furnished information to the government under an express promise that the identity of the source would be held in confidence, or, prior to the effective date of this section, under an implied promise that the identity of the source would be held in confidence.

At the time rules are adopted under this subsection, the agency shall include in the statement required under Section 553(c) of this title, the reasons why the system of records is to be exempted from a provision of this section.

(l) **Archival records.**

(1) Each agency record which is accepted by the administrator of General Services for storage, processing, and servicing in accordance with Section 3103 of title 44 shall, for the purposes of this section, be considered to be maintained by the agency which deposited the record and shall be subject to the provisions of this section. The administrator of General Services shall not disclose the record except to the agency which maintains the record, or under rules established by that agency which are not inconsistent with the provisions of this section.

(2) Each agency record pertaining to an identifiable individual which was transferred to the National Archives of the United States as a record which has sufficient historical or other value to warrant its continued preservation by the United States Government, prior to the effective date of this section, shall, for the purposes of this section, be considered to be maintained by the National Archives and shall not be subject to the provisions of this section, except that a statement generally describing such records (modeled after the requirements relating to records subject to subsections (e)(4)(A) through (G) of this section) shall be published in the *Federal Register*.

(3) Each agency record pertaining to an identifiable individual which is transferred to the National Archives of the United States as a record which has sufficient historical or other value to warrant its continued preservation by the United States Government, on or after the effective date of this section, shall, for the purposes of this section, be considered to be maintained by the National Archives and shall be exempt from the requirements of this section except subsections (e)(4)(A) through (G) and (e)(9) of this section.

(m) **Government contractors.** When an agency provides by a contract for the operation by or on behalf of the agency of a system of records to accomplish an agency function, the agency shall, consistent with its authority, cause the requirements of this section to be applied to such system. For purposes of subsection (i) of this section any such contractor and any employee of such contractor, if such contract is agreed to on or after the effective date of this section, shall be considered to be an employee of an agency.

(n) **Mailing lists.** An individual's name and address may not be sold or rented by an agency unless such action is specifically authorized by law. This provision shall not be construed to require the withholding of names and addresses otherwise permitted to be made public.

(o) **Report on new systems.** Each agency shall provide adequate advance notice to Congress and the Office of Management and Budget of any proposal to establish or alter any system of records in order to permit an evaluation of the probable or potential effect of such proposal on the privacy and other personal or property rights of individuals or the disclosure of information relating to such individuals, and its effect on the preservation of the constitutional principles of federalism and separation of powers.

(p) **Annual report.** The president shall submit to the Speaker of the House and the President of the Senate, by June 30 of each calendar year, a consolidated report, separately listing for each federal agency the number of records contained in any system of records which were exempted from the application of this section under the provisions of subsections (j) and (k) of this section during the preceding calendar year, and the reasons for the exemptions, and such other information as indicates efforts to administer fully this section.

(q) **Effect of other laws.** No agency shall rely on any exemption contained in Section 552 of this title to withhold from an individual any record which is otherwise accessible to such individual under the provisions of this section.

§ 552b. OPEN MEETINGS

(a) For purposes of this section—

(1) the term *agency* means any agency, as defined in Section 552(e) of this title, headed by a collegial body composed of two or more individual members, a majority of whom are appointed to such position by the president with the advice and consent of the Senate, and any subdivision thereof authorized to act on behalf of the agency;

(2) the term *meeting* means the deliberations of at least the number of individual agency members required to take action on behalf of the agency where such deliberations determine or result in the joint conduct or disposition of official agency business, but does not include deliberations required or permitted by subsection (d) or (e); and

(3) the term *member* means an individual who belongs to a collegial body heading an agency.

(b) Members shall not jointly conduct or dispose of agency business other than in accordance with this section. Except as provided in subsection (c), every portion of every meeting of an agency shall be open to public observation.

(c) Except in a case where the agency finds that the public interest requires otherwise, the second sentence of subsection (b) shall not apply to any portion of an agency meeting, and the requirements of subsections (d) and (e) shall not apply to any information pertaining to such meeting otherwise required by this section to be disclosed to the public, where the agency properly determines that such portion or portions of its meeting or the disclosure of such information is likely to—

(1) disclose matters that are (A) specifically authorized under criteria established by an executive order to be kept secret in the interests of national defense or foreign policy and (B) in fact properly classified pursuant to such executive order;

(2) relate solely to the internal personnel rules and practices of an agency;

(3) disclose matters specifically exempted from disclosure by statute (other than Section 552 of this title), provided that such statute (A) requires that the matters be withheld from the public in such a manner as to leave no discretion on the issue, or (B) establishes particular criteria for withholding or refers to particular types of matters to be withheld;

(4) disclose trade secrets and commercial or financial information obtained from a person and privileged or confidential;

(5) involve accusing any person of a crime, or formally censuring any person;

(6) disclose information of a personal nature where disclosure would constitute a clearly unwarranted invasion of person privacy;

(7) disclose investigatory records compiled for law enforcement purposes, or information which if written would be contained in such records, but only to the extent that the production of such records or information would (A) interfere with enforcement proceedings, (B) deprive a person of a right to a fair trial or an impartial adjudication, (C) constitute an unwarranted invasion of personal privacy, (D) disclose the identity of a confidential source and, in the case of a record compiled by a criminal law enforcement authority in the course of a criminal investigation, or by an agency conducting a lawful national security intelligence investigation, confidential information furnished only by the confidential source, (E) disclose investigative techniques and procedures, or (F) endanger the life or physical safety of law enforcement personnel;

(8) disclose information contained in or related to examination, operating, or condition reports prepared by, on behalf of, or for the use of an agency responsible for the regulation or supervision of financial institutions;

(9) disclose information the premature disclosure of which would—

(A) in the case of an agency which regulates currencies, securities, commodities, or financial institutions, be likely to (i) lead to significant financial speculation in currencies, securities, or commodities, or (ii) significantly endanger the stability of any financial institution; or

(B) in the case of any agency, be likely to significantly frustrate implementation of a proposed agency action.

except that subparagraph (B) shall not apply in any instance where the agency has already disclosed to the public the content or nature of its proposed action, or where the agency is required by law to make such disclosure on its own initiative prior to taking final agency action on such proposal; or

(10) specifically concern the agency's issuance of a subpena, or the agency's participation in a civil action or proceeding, an action in a foreign court or international tribunal, or an arbitration, or the initiation, conduct, or disposition by the agency of a particular case of formal agency adjudication pursuant to the procedures in Section 554 of this title or otherwise involving a determination on the record after opportunity for a hearing.

(d)—

(1) Action under subsection (c) shall be taken only when a majority of the entire membership of the agency (as defined in subsection (a)(1)) votes to take such action. A separate vote of the agency members shall be taken with respect to each agency meeting a portion or portions of which are proposed to be closed to the public pursuant to subsection (c), or with respect to any information which is proposed to be withheld under subsection (c). A single vote may be taken with respect to a series of meetings, a portion or portions of which are proposed to be closed to the public, or with respect to any information concerning such series of meetings, so long as each meeting in such series involves the same particular matters and is scheduled to be held no more than thirty days after the initial meeting in such series. The vote of each agency member participating in such vote shall be recorded and no proxies shall be allowed.

(2) Whenever any person whose interests may be directly affected by a portion of a meeting requests that the agency close such portion to the public for any of the reasons referred to in paragraph (5), (6), or (7) of subsection (c), the agency, upon request of any one of its members, shall vote by recorded vote whether to close such meeting.

(3) Within one day of any vote taken pursuant to paragraph (1) or (2), the agency shall make publicly available a written copy of such vote reflecting the vote of each member on the question. If a portion of a meeting is to be closed to the public, the agency shall, within one day of the vote taken pursuant to paragraph (1) or (2) of this subsection, make publicly available a full written explanation of its action closing the portion together with a list of all persons expected to attend the meeting and their affiliation.

(4) Any agency, a majority of whose meetings may properly be closed to the public pursuant to paragraph (4), (8), (9)(A), or (10) of subsection (c), or any combination thereof, may provide by regulation for the closing of such meetings or portions thereof in the event that a majority of the members of the agency votes by recorded vote at the beginning of such meeting, or portion thereof, to close the exempt portion or portions of the meeting, and a copy of such vote, reflecting the vote of each member on the question, is made available to the public. The provisions of paragraphs (1), (2), and (3) of this subsection and subsection (e) shall not apply to any portion of a meeting to which such regulations apply: *provided,* that the agency shall, except to the extent that such information is exempt from disclosure under the provisions of subsection (c), provide the public with public announcement of the time, place, and subject matter of the meeting and of each portion thereof at the earliest practicable time.

(e)—

(1) In the case of each meeting, the agency shall make public announcement, at least one week before the meeting, of the time, place, and subject matter of the meeting, whether it is to be open or closed to the public, and the name and phone number of the official designated by the agency to respond to requests for information about the meeting. Such announcement shall be made unless a majority of the members of the agency determines by a recorded vote that agency business requires that such meeting be called at an earlier date, in which case the agency shall make public announcement of the time, place, and subject matter of such meeting, and whether open or closed to the public, at the earliest practicable time.

(2) The time or place of a meeting may be changed following the public announcement required by paragraph (1) only if the agency publicly announces such change at the earliest practicable time. The subject matter of a meeting, or the determination of the agency to open or close a meeting, or portion of a meeting, to the public, may be changed following the public announcement required by this subsection only if (A) a majority of the entire membership of the agency determines by a recorded vote that agency business so requires and that no earlier announcement of the change was possible, and (B) the agency publicly announces such change and the vote of each member upon such change at the earliest practicable time.

(3) Immediately following each public announcement required by this subsection, notice of the time, place, and subject matter of a meeting, whether the meeting is open or closed, any change in one of the preceding, and the name and phone number of the official designated by the agency to respond to requests for information about the meeting, shall also be submitted for publication in the *Federal Register.*

(f)—

(1) For every meeting closed pursuant to paragraphs (1) through (10) of subsection (c), the general counsel or chief legal officer of the agency shall publicly certify that, in his or her opinion, the meeting may be closed to the public and shall state each relevant exemptive provision. A copy of such certification, together with a statement from the presiding office of the meeting setting forth the time and place of the meeting, and the persons present, shall be retained by the agency. The agency shall maintain a complete transcript or electronic recording adequate to record fully the proceedings of each meeting, or portion of a meeting, closed to the public, except that in the case of a meeting, or portion of a meeting, closed to the public pursuant to paragraph (8), (9)(A), or (10) of subsection (c), the agency shall maintain either such a transcript or recording, or a set of minutes. Such minutes shall fully and clearly describe all matters discussed and shall provide a full and accurate summary of any actions taken, and the reasons therefor, including a description of each of the views expressed on any item and the record of any roll call vote (reflecting the vote of each member on the question). All documents considered in connection with any action shall be identified in such minutes.

(2) The agency shall make promptly available to the public, in a place easily accessible to the public, the transcript, electronic recording, or minutes (as required by paragraph (1)) of the discussion of any item on the agenda, or of any item of the testimony of any witness received at the meeting, except for such item or items of such discussion or testimony as the agency determines to contain information which may be withheld under subsection (c). Cop-

ies of such transcript, or minutes, or a transcription of such recording disclosing the identity of each speaker, shall be furnished to any person at the actual cost of duplication or transcription. The agency shall maintain a complete verbatim copy of the transcript, a complete copy of the minutes, or a complete electronic recording of each meeting, or portion of a meeting, closed to the public, for a period of at least two years after such meeting, or until one year after the conclusion of any agency proceeding with respect to which the meeting or portion was held, whichever occurs later.

(g) Each agency subject to the requirements of this section shall, within 180 days after the date of enactment of this section, following consultation with the office of the chairman of the Administrative Conference of the United States and published notice in the *Federal Register* of at least thirty days and opportunity for written comment by any person, promulgate regulations to implement the requirements of subsections (b) through (f) of this section. Any person may bring a proceeding in the United States District Court for the District of Columbia to require an agency to promulgate such regulations if such agency has not promulgated such regulations within the time period specified herein. Subject to any limitations of time provided by law, any person may bring a proceeding in the United States Court of Appeals for the District of Columbia to set aside agency regulations issued pursuant to this subsection that are not in accord with the requirements of subsections (b) through (f) of this section and to require the promulgation of regulations that are in accord with subsections.

(h)—

(1) The district courts of the United States shall have jurisdiction to enforce the requirements of subsections (b) through (f) of this section by declaratory judgment, injunctive relief, or other relief as may be appropriate. Such actions may be brought by any person against an agency prior to, or within sixty days after, the meeting out of which the violation of this section arises, except that if public announcement of such meeting is not initially provided by the agency in accordance with the requirements of this section, such action may be instituted pursuant to this section at any time prior to sixty days after any public announcement of such meeting. Such actions may be brought in the district court of the United States for the district in which the agency meeting is held or in which the agency in question has its headquarters, or in the district court for the District of Columbia. In such actions a defendant shall serve his answer within thirty days after the service of the complaint. The burden is on the defendant to sustain his action. In deciding such cases the court may examine in camera any portion of the transcript, electronic recording, or minutes of a meeting closed to the public, and may take such additional evidence as it deems necessary. The court, having due regard for orderly administration and the public interest, as well as the interests of the parties, may grant such equitable relief as it deems appropriate, including granting an injunction against future violations of this section or ordering the agency to make available to the public such portion of the transcript, recording, or minutes of a meeting as is not authorized to be withheld under subsection (c) of this section.

(2) Any federal court otherwise authorized by law to review agency action may, at the application of any person properly participating in the proceeding pursuant to other applicable law, inquire into violations by the agency of the requirements of this section and afford such relief as it deems appropriate. Nothing in this section authorizes any federal court having jurisdiction solely on the basis of paragraph (1) to set aside, enjoin, or invalidate any agency action (other than an action to close a meeting or to withhold information under this section) taken or discussed at any agency meeting out of which the violation of this section arose.

(i) The court may assess against any party reasonable attorney fees and other litigation costs reasonably incurred by any other party who substantially prevails in any action brought in accordance with the provisions of subsection (g) or (h) of this section, except that costs may be assessed against the plaintiff only where the court finds that the suit was initiated by the plaintiff primarily for frivolous or dilatory purposes. In the case of assessment of costs against an agency, the costs may be assessed by the court against the United States.

(j) Each agency subject to the requirements of this section shall annually report to Congress regarding its compliance with such requirements, including a tabulation of the total number of agency meetings open to the public, the total number of meetings closed to the public, the reasons for closing such meetings, and a description of any litigation brought against the agency under this section, including any costs assessed against the agency in such litigation (whether or not paid by the agency).

(k) Nothing herein expands or limits the present rights of any person under Section 552 of this title, except that the exemptions set forth in subsection (c) of this section shall govern in the case of any request made pursuant to Section 552 to copy or inspect the transcripts, recordings, or minutes described in subsection (f) of this section. The requirements of chapter 33 of title 44, United States Code, shall not apply to the transcripts, recordings, and minutes described in subsection (f) of this section.

(l) This section does not constitute authority to withhold any information from Congress, and does not authorize the closing of any agency meeting or portion thereof required by any other provision of law to be open.

(m) Nothing in this section authorizes any agency to withhold from any individual any record, including transcripts, recordings, or minutes required by this section, which is otherwise accessible to such individual under Section 552a of this title.

§ 553. RULE MAKING

(a) This section applies, according to the provisions thereof, except to the extent that there is involved—

(1)   a military or foreign affairs function of the United States; or
(2)   a matter relating to agency management or personnel or to public property, loans, grants, benefits, or contracts.

(b) General notice of proposed rule making shall be published in the *Federal Register*, unless persons subject thereto are named and either personally served or otherwise have actual notice thereof in accordance with law. The notice shall include—

(1)   a statement of the time, place, and nature of public rule-making proceedings;
(2)   reference to the legal authority under which the rule is proposed; and
(3)   either the terms or substance of the proposed rule or a description of the subjects and issues involved.

Except when notice or hearing is required by statute, this subsection does not apply—

(A)   to interpretative rules, general statements of policy, or rules of agency organization, procedure, or practice; or

(B) when the agency for good cause finds (and incorporates the finding and a brief statement of reasons therefor in the rules issued) that notice and public procedure thereon are impracticable, unnecessary, or contrary to the public interest.

(c) After notice required by this section, the agency shall give interested persons an opportunity to participate in the rule making through submission of written data, views, or arguments with or without opportunity for oral presentation. After consideration of the relevant matter presented, the agency shall incorporate in the rules adopted a concise general statement of their basis and purpose. When rules are required by statute to be made on the record after opportunity for an agency hearing, sections 556 and 557 of this title apply instead of this subsection.

(d) The required publication or service of a substantive rule shall be made not less than 30 days before its effective date, except—

(1) a substantive rule which grants or recognizes an exemption or relieves a restriction;
(2) interpretative rules and statements of policy; or
(3) as otherwise provided by the agency for good cause found and published with the rule.

(e) Each agency shall give an interested person the right to petition for the issuance, amendment, or repeal of a rule.

§ 554. ADJUDICATIONS

(a) This section applies, according to the provisions thereof, in every case of adjudication required by statute to be determined on the record after opportunity for an agency hearing, except to the extent that there is involved—

(1) a matter subject to a subsequent trial of the law and the facts de novo in a court;
(2) the selection or tenure of an employee, except an administrative law judge appointed under Section 3105 of this title;
(3) proceedings in which decisions rest solely on inspections, tests, or elections;
(4) the conduct of military or foreign affairs functions;
(5) cases in which an agency is acting as an agent for a court; or
(6) the certification of worker representatives.

(b) Persons entitled to notice of an agency hearing shall be timely informed of—

(1) the time, place, and nature of the hearing;
(2) the legal authority and jurisdiction under which the hearing is to be held; and
(3) the matters of fact and law asserted.

When private persons are the moving parties, other parties to the proceeding shall give prompt notice of issues controverted in fact or law; and in other instances agencies may by rule require responsive pleading. In fixing the time and place for hearings, due regard shall be had for the convenience and necessity of the parties or their representatives.

(c) The agency shall give all interested parties opportunity for—

(1) the submission and consideration of facts, arguments, offers of settlement, or proposals of adjustment when time, the nature of the proceeding, and the public interest permit; and

(2) to the extent that the parties are unable so to determine a controversy by consent, hearing and decision on notice and in accordance with sections 556 and 557 of this title.

(d) The employee who presides at the reception of evidence pursuant to Section 556 of this title shall make the recommended decision or initial decision required by Section 557 of this title, unless he becomes unavailable to the agency. Except to the extent required for the disposition of ex parte matters as authorized by law, such an employee may not—

(1) consult a person or party on a fact in issue, unless on notice and opportunity for all parties to participate; or

(2) be responsible to or subject to the supervision or direction of an employee or agent engaged in the performance of investigative or prosecuting functions for an agency.

An employee or agent engaged in the performance of investigative or prosecuting functions for an agency in a case may not, in that or a factually related case, participate or advise in the decision, recommended decision, or agency review pursuant to Section 557 of this title, except as witness or counsel in public proceedings. This subsection does not apply—

(A) in determining applications for initial licenses;

(B) to proceedings involving the validity or application of rates, facilities, or practices of public utilities or carriers; or

(C) to the agency or a member or members of the body comprising the agency.

(e) The agency, with like effect as in the case of other orders, and in its sound discretion, may issue a declaratory order to terminate a controversy or remove uncertainty.

§ 555. ANCILLARY MATTERS

(a) This section applies, according to the provisions thereof, except as otherwise provided by this subchapter.

(b) A person compelled to appear in person before an agency or representative thereof is entitled to be accompanied, represented, and advised by counsel or, if permitted by the agency, by other qualified representative. A party is entitled to appear in person or by or with counsel or other duly qualified representative in an agency proceeding. So far as the orderly conduct of public business permits, an interested person may appear before an agency or its responsible employees for the presentation, adjustment, or determination of an issue, request, or controversy in a proceeding, whether interlocutory, summary, or otherwise, or in connection with an agency function. With due regard for the convenience and necessity of the parties or their representatives and within a reasonable time, each agency shall proceed to conclude a matter presented to it. This subsection does not grant or deny a person who is not a lawyer the right to appear for or represent others before an agency or in an agency proceeding.

(c) Process, requirement of a report, inspection, or other investigative act or demand may not be issued, made, or enforced except as authorized by law. A person compelled to submit data or evidence is entitled to retain or, on payment of lawfully prescribed costs, procure a copy or transcript thereof, except that in a nonpublic investigatory proceeding the witness may for good cause be limited to inspection of the official transcript of his testimony.

(d) Agency subpenas authorized by law shall be issued to a party on request and, when required by rules of procedure, on a statement or showing of general relevance and reasonable scope of the evidence sought. On contest, the court shall sustain the subpena or similar process or demand to the extent that it is found to be in accordance with law. In a proceeding for enforcement, the court shall issue an order requiring the appearance of the witness or the production of the evidence or data within a reasonable time under penalty of punishment for contempt in case of contumacious failure to comply.

(e) Prompt notice shall be given of the denial in whole or in part of a written application, petition, or other request of an interested person made in connection with any agency proceeding. Except in affirming a prior denial or when the denial is self-explanatory, the notice shall be accompanied by a brief statement of the grounds for denial.

§ 556. HEARINGS; PRESIDING EMPLOYEES; POWERS AND DUTIES; BURDEN OF PROOF; EVIDENCE; RECORD AS BASIS OF DECISION

(a) This section applies, according the provisions thereof, to hearings required by Section 553 or 554 of this title to be conducted in accordance with this section.

(b) There shall preside at the taking of evidence—

(1) the agency;
(2) one or more members of the body which comprises the agency; or
(3) one or more administrative law judges appointed under Section 3105 of this title.

This subchapter does not supersede the conduct of specified classes of proceedings, in whole or in part, by or before boards or other employees specially provided for by or designated under statute. The functions of presiding employees and of employees participating in decisions in accordance with Section 557 of this title shall be conducted in an impartial manner. A presiding or participating employee may at any time disqualify himself. On the filing in good faith of a timely and sufficient affadavit of personal bias or other disqualification of a presiding or participating employee, the agency shall determine the matter as a part of the record and decision in the case.

(c) Subject to published rules of the agency and within its powers, employees presiding at hearings may—

(1) administer oaths and affirmations;
(2) issue subpenas authorized by law;
(3) rule on offers of proof and receive relevant evidence;
(4) take depositions or have depositions taken when the ends of justice would be served;
(5) regulate the course of the hearing;
(6) hold conferences for the settlement or simplification of the issues by consent of the parties;
(7) dispose of procedural requests or similar matters;
(8) make or recommend decisions in accordance with Section 557 of this title; and
(9) take other action authorized by agency rule consistent with this subchapter.

(d) Except as otherwise provided by statute, the proponent of a rule or order has the burden of proof. Any oral or documentary evidence may be received, but the agency as a matter of policy shall provide for the exclusion of irrelevant, immaterial, or unduly repetitious evidence. A sanction may not be imposed or rule or order issued except on consideration of the whole record or those parts thereof cited by a party and supported by and in accordance with the reliable, probative, and substantial evidence. The agency may, to the extent consistent with the interests of justice and the policy of the underlying statutes administered by the agency, consider a violation of Section 557(d) of this title sufficient grounds for a decision adverse to a party who has knowingly committed such violation or knowingly caused such violation to occur. A party is entitled to present his case or defense by oral or documentary evidence, to submit rebuttal evidence, and to conduct such cross-examination as may be required for a full and true disclosure of the facts. In rule making or determining claims for money or benefits or applications for initial licenses an agency may, when a party will not be prejudiced thereby, adopt procedures for the submission of all or part of the evidence in written form.

(e) The transcript of testimony and exhibits, together with all papers and requests filed in the proceeding, constitutes the exclusive record for decision in accordance with Section 557 of this title and, on payment of lawfully prescribed costs, shall be made available to the parties. When an agency decision rests on official notice of a material fact not appearing in the evidence in the record, a party is entitled, on timely request, to an opportunity to show the contrary.

§ 557. INITIAL DECISIONS; CONCLUSIVENESS; REVIEW BY AGENCY; SUBMISSIONS BY PARTIES; CONTENTS OF DECISIONS; RECORD

(a) This section applies, according to the provisions thereof, when a hearing is required to be conducted in accordance with Section 556 of this title.

(b) When the agency did not preside at the reception of the evidence, the presiding employee or, in cases not subject to Section 554(d) of this title, an employee qualified to preside at hearings pursuant to Section 556 of this title, shall initially decide the case unless the agency requires, either in specific cases or by general rule, the entire record to be certified to it for decision. When the presiding employee makes an initial decision, that decision then becomes the decision of the agency without further proceedings unless there is an appeal to, or review on motion of, the agency within time provided by rule. On appeal from or review of the initial decision, the agency has all the powers which it would have in making the initial decision except as it may limit the issues on notice or by rule. When the agency makes the decision without having presided at the reception of the evidence, the presiding employee or an employee qualified to preside at hearings pursuant to Section 556 of this title shall first recommend a decision, except that in rule making or determining applications for initial licenses—

(1) instead thereof the agency may issue a tentative decision or one of its responsible employees may recommend a decision; or

(2) this procedure may be omitted in a case in which the agency finds on the record that due and timely execution of its functions imperatively and unavoidably so requires.

(c) Before a recommended, initial, or tentative decision, or a decision on agency review of the decision of subordinate employees, the parties are entitled to a reasonable opportunity to submit for the consideration of the employees participating in the decisions—

(1) proposed findings and conclusions; or

(2) exceptions to the decisions or recommended decisions of subordinate employees or to tentative agency decisions; and

(3) supporting reasons for the exceptions or proposed findings or conclusions.

The record shall show the ruling on each finding, conclusion, or exception presented. All decisions, including initial, recommended, and tentative decisions, are a part of the record and shall include a statement of—

(A) findings and conclusions, and the reasons or basis therefor, on all the material issues of fact, law, or discretion presented on the record; and

(B) the appropriate rule, order, sanction, relief, or denial thereof.

(d)—

(1) In any agency proceeding which is subject to subsection (a) of this section, except to the extent required for the disposition of ex parte matters as authorized by law—

(A) no interested person outside the agency shall make or knowingly cause to be made to any member of the body comprising the agency, administrative law judge, or other employee who is or may reasonably be expected to be involved in the decisional process of the proceeding, an ex parte communication relevant to the merits of the proceeding;

(B) no member of the body comprising the agency, administrative law judge, or other employee who is or may reasonably be expected to be involved in the decisional process of the proceeding, shall make or knowingly cause to be made to any interested person outside the agency an ex parte communication relevant to the merits of the proceeding;

(C) a member of the body comprising the agency, administrative law judge, or other employee who is or may reasonably be expected to be involved in the decisional process of such proceeding who receives, or who makes or knowingly causes to be made, a communication prohibited by this subsection shall place on the public record of the proceeding:

(i) all such written communications;

(ii) memoranda stating the substance of all such oral communications; and

(iii) all written responses, and memoranda stating the substance of all oral responses, to the materials described in clauses (i) and (ii) of this subparagraph;

(D) upon receipt of a communication knowingly made or knowingly caused to be made by a party in violation of this subsection, the agency, administrative law judge, or other employee presiding at the hearing may, to the extent consistent with the interests of justice and the policy of the underlying statutes, require the party to show cause why his claim or interest in the proceeding should not be dismissed, denied, disregarded, or otherwise adversely affected on account of such violation; and

(E) the prohibitions of this subsection shall apply beginning at such time as the agency may designate, but in no case shall they begin to apply later than the time at which a proceeding is noticed for hearing unless the person responsible for the communication has knowledge that it will be noticed, in which case the prohibitions shall apply beginning at the time of his acquisition of such knowledge.

(2) This subsection does not constitute authority to withhold information from Congress.

§558. IMPOSITION OF SANCTIONS; DETERMINATION OF APPLICATIONS FOR LICENSES; SUSPENSION, REVOCATION, AND EXPIRATION OF LICENSES

(a) This section applies, according to the provisions thereof, to the exercise of a power or authority.

(b) A sanction may not be imposed or a substantive rule or order issued except within jurisdiction delegated to the agency and as authorized by law.

(c) When application is made for a license required by law, the agency, with due regard for the rights and privileges of all the interested parties or adversely affected persons and within a reasonable time, shall set and complete proceedings required to be conducted in accordance with sections 556 and 557 of this title or other proceedings required by law and shall make its decision. Except in cases of willfulness or those in which public health, interest, or safety requires otherwise, the withdrawal, suspension, revocation, or annulment of a license is lawful only if, before the institution of agency proceedings therefor, the licensee has been given—

(1) notice by the agency in writing of the facts or conduct which may warrant the action; and

(2) opportunity to demonstrate or achieve compliance with all lawful requirements.

When the licensee has made timely and sufficient application for a renewal or a new license in accordance with agency rules, a license with reference to an activity of a continuing nature does not expire until the application has been finally determined by the agency.

§ 559. EFFECT ON OTHER LAWS; EFFECT OF SUBSEQUENT STATUTE

This subchapter, chapter 7, and sections 1305, 3105, 3344, 4301(2)(E), 5372, and 7521 of this title, and the provisions of Section 5335(a)(B) of this title that relate to administrative law judges, do not limit or repeal additional requirements imposed by statute or otherwise recognized by law. Except as otherwise required by law, requirements or privileges relating to evidence or procedure apply equally to agencies and persons. Each agency is granted the authority necessary to comply with the requirements of this subchapter through the issuance of rules or otherwise. Subsequent statute may not be held to supersede or modify this subchapter, chapter 7, sections 1305, 3105, 3344, 4301(2)(E), 5372, or 7521 of this title, or the provisions of Section 5335(a)(B) of this title that relate to administrative law judges, except to the extent that it does so expressly.

Chapter 7—Judicial Review

TABLE OF SECTIONS

701. Application; Definitions.
702. Right of Review.
703. Form and Venue of Proceeding.
704. Actions Reviewable.
705. Relief Pending Review.
706. Scope of Review.

§ 701. APPLICATION; DEFINITIONS

(a) This chapter applies, according to the provisions thereof, except to the extent that—

(1) statutes preclude judicial review; or
(2) agency action is committed to agency discretion by law.

(b) For the purpose of this chapter—

(1) *agency* means each authority of the Government of the United States, whether or not it is within or subject to review by another agency, but does not include—

(A) the Congress;
(B) the courts of the United States;
(C) the governments of the territories or possessions of the United States;
(D) the government of the District of Columbia;
(E) agencies composed of representatives of the parties or of representatives of organizations of the parties to the disputes determined by them;
(F) courts martial and military commissions;
(G) military authority exercised in the field in time of war or in occupied territory; or
(H) functions conferred by sections 1738, 1739, 1743, and 1744 of title 12; chapter 2 of title 41; or sections 1622, 1884, 1891–1902, and former Section 1641(b)(2), of title 50, appendix; and

(2) *person, rule, order, license, sanction, relief,* and *agency action* have the meanings given them by Section 551 of this title.

§ 702. RIGHT OF REVIEW

A person suffering legal wrong because of agency action, or adversely affected or aggrieved by agency action within the meaning of a relevant statute, is entitled to judicial review thereof. An action in a court of the United States seeking relief other than money damages and stating a claim that an agency or an officer or employee thereof acted or failed to act in an official capacity or under color of legal authority shall not be dismissed nor relief therein be denied on the ground that it is against the United States or that the United States is an indispensable party. The United States may be named as a defendant in any such action, and a judgment or decree may be entered against the United States: *provided*, that any mandatory or injunctive decree shall specify the federal officer or officers (by name or by title), and their successors in office, personally responsible for compliance. Nothing herein (1) affects other limitations on judicial review or the power or duty of the court to dismiss any action or deny relief on any other appropriate legal or equitable ground; or (2) confers authority to grant relief if any other statute that grants consent to suit expressly or impliedly forbids the relief which is sought.

§ 703. FORM AND VENUE OF PROCEEDING

The form of proceeding for judicial review is the special statutory review proceeding relevant to the subject matter in a court specified by statute or, in the absence or inadequacy thereof, any applicable form of legal action, including actions for declaratory judgments or writs of prohibitory or mandatory injunction or habeas corpus, in a court of competent jurisdiction. If no special statutory review proceeding is applicable, the action for judicial review may be brought against the United States, the agency by its official title, or the appropriate officer. Except to the extent that prior, adequate, and exclusive opportunity for judicial review is provided by law, agency action is subject to judicial review in civil or criminal proceedings for judicial enforcement.

§ 704. ACTIONS REVIEWABLE

Agency action made reviewable by statute and final agency action for which there is no other adequate remedy in a court are subject to judicial review. A preliminary, procedural, or intermediate agency action or ruling not directly reviewable is subject to review on the review of the final agency action. Except as otherwise expressly required by statute, agency action otherwise final is final for the purposes of this section whether or not there has been presented or determined an application for a declaratory order, for any form of reconsideration, or, unless the agency otherwise requires by rule and provides that the action meanwhile is inoperative, for an appeal to superior agency authority.

§ 705. RELIEF PENDING REVIEW

When an agency finds that justice so requires, it may postpone the effective date of action taken by it, pending judicial review. On such conditions as may be required and to the extent necessary to prevent irreparable injury, the reviewing court, including the court to which a case may be taken on appeal from or on application for certiorari or other writ to a reviewing court, may issue all necessary and appropriate process to postpone the effective date of an agency action or to preserve status or rights pending conclusion of the review proceedings.

§ 706. SCOPE OF REVIEW

To the extent necessary to decision and when presented, the reviewing court shall decide all relevant questions of law, interpret constitutional and statutory provisions, and determine the meaning or applicability of the terms of an agency action. The reviewing court shall—

(1) compel agency action unlawfully withheld or unreasonably delayed; and

(2) hold unlawful and set aside agency action, findings, and conclusions found to be—

(A) arbitrary, capricious, an abuse of discretion, or otherwise not in accordance with law;
(B) contrary to constitutional right, power, privilege, or immunity;
(C) in excess of statutory jurisdiction, authority, or limitations, or short of statutory right;
(D) without observance of procedure required by law;
(E) unsupported by substantial evidence in a case subject to sections 556 and 557 of this title or otherwise reviewed on the record of an agency hearing provided by statute; or
(F) unwarranted by the facts to the extent that the facts are subject to trial de novo by the reviewing court.

In making the foregoing determinations, the court shall review the whole record or those parts of it cited by a party, and due account shall be taken of the rule of prejudicial error.

PART II—THE UNITED STATES CIVIL SERVICE COMMISSION

Chapter 13—Special Authority

§ 1305. ADMINISTRATIVE LAW JUDGES

For the purpose of sections 3105, 3344, 4301(2)(D), and 5372 of this title and the provisions of Section 5335(a)(B) of this title that relate to administrative law judges, the Office of Personnel Management may, and for the purpose of Section 7521 of this title, the Merit System Protection Board may investigate, require reports by agencies, issue reports, including an annual report to Congress, prescribe regulations, appoint advisory committees as necessary, recommend legislation, sub-ena witnesses and records, and pay witness fees as established for the courts of the United States.

PART III—EMPLOYEES
SUBPART B—EMPLOYMENT AND RETENTION

Chapter 31—Authority for Employment

§ 3105. APPOINTMENT OF ADMINISTRATIVE LAW JUDGES

Each agency shall appoint as many administrative law judges as are necessary for proceedings required to be conducted in accordance with sections 556 and 557 of this title. Administrative law judges shall be assigned to cases in rotation so far as practicable, and may not perform duties inconsistent with their duties and responsibilities as administrative law judges.

Chapter 33—Examination, Selection, and Placement

§ 3344. DETAILS; ADMINISTRATIVE LAW JUDGES

An agency as defined by Section 551 of this title which occasionally or temporarily is insufficiently staffed with administrative law judges appointed under Section 3105 of this title may use administrative law judges selected by the Office of Personnel Management from and with the consent of other agencies.

SUBPART D—PAY AND ALLOWANCES

Chapter 53—Pay Rates and Systems

§ 5372. ADMINISTRATIVE LAW JUDGES

Administrative law judges appointed under Section 3105 of this title are entitled to pay prescribed by the Office of Personnel Management independently of agency recommendations or ratings and in accordance with subchapter III of this chapter and chapter 51 of this title.

SUBPART F—EMPLOYEE RELATIONS

Chapter 75—Adverse Actions

§ 7521. ACTIONS AGAINST ADMINISTRATIVE LAW JUDGES

(a) An action may be taken against an administrative law judge appointed under Section 3105 of this title by the agency in which the administrative law judge is employed only for good cause established and determined by the Merit Systems Protection Board on the record after opportunity for hearing before the board.

(b) The actions covered by this section are—

(1) a removal;
(2) a suspension;
(3) a reduction in grade;
(4) a reduction in pay; and
(5) a furlough of 30 days or less;

but do not include—

(A) a suspension or removal under Section 7532 of this title;
(B) a reduction-in-force action under Section 3502 of this title; or
(C) any action initiated under Section 1206 of this title, [that is, by the special counsel of the board].